Library of
Davidson College

VIEWS FROM A MANY-WINDOWED TOWER

Studies of imagination in the works of Gregory of Tours

Giselle de Nie

VIEWS FROM A MANY-WINDOWED TOWER

STUDIES IN CLASSICAL ANTIQUITY - Band 7

Cover photograph: Merovingian reliquary, ca. 700.
    copyright Rijksmuseum Het Catharijnenconvent,
        Ruben de Heer

cover calligraphy: sixth-seventh century uncial and semi-uncial script
    by J.H. Moesman

VIEWS FROM A MANY-WINDOWED TOWER
studies of imagination in the works of Gregory of Tours

Waarnemingen vanuit een toren met vele vensters
Studiën over verbeelding in de werken van Gregorius van Tours
(met een samenvatting in het Nederlands)

door

Giselle de Nie

AMSTERDAM 1987

CIP-GEGEVENS KONINKLIJKE BIBLIOTHEEK, DEN HAAG

Nie, Giselle de

Views from a many-windowed tower : studies of imagination
in the works of Gregory of Tours / Giselle de Nie. —
Amsterdam : Rodopi. — (Studies in classical antiquity,
ISSN 0167-6679 ; vol. 7)
Ook verschenen als proefschrift Utrecht.
ISBN 90-6203-719-4
SISO 901.2 UDC 929 Gregorius van Tours
Trefw.: Gregorius van Tours.
©Editions Rodopi B.V., Amsterdam 1987
Printed in The Netherlands

For
my daughter
    Lideweij Schipper

my parents
    W.L.J. de Nie and A. de Nie-van Rijnbach

my teachers and my friends
    H.A. Oberman and G.R. Oberman-Reesink

Le merveilleux est à la fois vécu comme théophanie et utilisée par l'homme comme un langage apte à exprimer l'indicible.
(M. Meslin)

... the world we perceive is a dream we learn to have from a script we have not written.
(S. Tomkins)

FOREWORD

It is with great pleasure that I take this occasion to thank those who have helped to make this book possible.

It was Professor Dr. F.W.N. Hugenholtz who suggested Gregory of Tours as a possible subject. The encouragement he gave me to choose my own angle and approach meant that I had the opportunity to discover and formulate a question which no one had thought of asking before — and to find my own way of answering it. It has taken a long time. Also because, meanwhile, I chose to spend at least an equal amount of time raising my daughter myself in a single-parent household. If my obscure gropings have now taken on a more or less recognizable form, this is due in no small measure to the encouragement and support of others. First of all, my daughter Lideweij Schipper, who managed to be understanding about a mother who got up at five and not infrequently went to bed before she did. During many years, Professor Dr. A.P. Orbán has always been ready to help with textual problems and, even more important, to give encouragement. In a number of stimulating and thoroughly enjoyable discussions, especially about light and darkness, I learned a great deal from Professor Dr. W.P. Gerritsen's sympathetic and penetrating comments on a large part of the semi-final version of the text. Ms Lidy van Roosmalen not only transformed my manuscript into a readable text and made this, for me, a highly pleasurable experience, but also continued to give valuable advice on and assistance in the practical and aesthetic problems that arose. Dr. A.R.W. Baxter was so kind as to give conscientious and extremely helpful comments on the English style as well as sometimes on the content of the text (before its final revision). My colleagues Ms Drs. Louise van Tongerloo and Ms Drs. Geke Wassink, Ms Annelies Kruijshoop and my 'paranymphs' Ms Drs. Monic Slingerland and Ms Drs. Jeannette Nieuwland gave generously of their time and energy to help get the book through its final stages. Finally, I wish to thank the members of *Nil volentibus arduum*, those active in Medieval Studies, and those of my friends, colleagues and students who, by their enthusiasm and their critical questions through the years, have helped me to discover and develop the insights that have now taken the form of this book. Long before the subject of this book was even thought of, however, there were two people who encouraged me to engage — and, later, to persist — in creative research. Without them this book would probably not have been written: Professor Dr. H.A. Oberman, in whose friendship I have been privileged to delight and learn now for more than 25 years; and from even earlier, of course, my father Dr. W.L.J. de Nie, whose steady perseverance and humane, as well as scientific, interest in the world around him are still inspiring me.

CONTENTS

Introduction: 'in a mixed and muddled manner'?   1
   Gregory's life and world   2
   His writings   8
      Composition   9
      Presentation of individual events   14
   Approach and themes of the essays   22

I. *Roses in January:*
   discontinuity and coherence in the 'Histories'   27
   Introduction. A landslide, a comet and a plague   27
   Books 1-4. The development of a viewpoint:
      prodigies as indications of divine anger   29
   Books 5 and 6. 'Figures' and events:
      announcements of ravages and the deaths of kings   36
   Books 7-10. Uncertainty and false prophets:
      signs of the approaching end of the world   46
   The prefaces. Gregory's view of his own time:
      a balance attempted and lost   57
   Conclusion. Synchronic symbolical patterning as historical
      coherence   68

II. *The wonders of nature:*
   models of sudden transformation   71
   Introduction. 'The works of men...have fallen into ruins'   71
   A. Water   76
      The tide as 'the first wonder': an original poetic image?   76
      'The living spring': a symbol of divine, eternal life   77
      'The turbulent waves and rocky crags of this worldly life':
         society or the human mind?   88
      'Suddenly a most hideous rain-cloud': the diabolical menace   102
      Water: destruction and regeneration   107

   B. Plant life   108
      'The sprouting of seeds': an image of rebirth   108
      'Nature', 'mystery' and the Virgin Birth: the patterns of
         miracle   111

  'The tree of life' or its 'pleasant shade': symbol or object of
    aesthetic pleasure?   116
  'It flourished as though it were painted': the transience of
    earthly gardens   119
  'Roses and lilies': the inexpressible as fragrance   121
  Plant life: Paradise lost and sometimes regained   128

  Conclusion. 'Image-logic', the miracle of renewal and society   128

III. *Light and fire in a 'dark world': metaphors and reality*   133
  Introduction. 'This dark place, the worldly habitation'   133
  A. Fire as burning heat   139
    'Treacheries of Satan'?: natural fire as visible violence   140
    'Fire from heaven': an instrument of justice   144
    'Flaming hell': a fear-inspiring image   146
    'Bedewed in the midst of fire': spirituality and materiality   151
    'Divine fire': punishment or purification?   157

  B. Light, and fire as luminosity   161
    Light and darkness: metaphors and sensory phenomena   161
    Metaphors   165
     'A large flame': metaphors of interior illumination   165
     'Stars' and 'a new sun': more than metaphors?   168
    Perceptions of spontaneous effulgence   176
     'The brilliance of a new light': the desire for illumination   176
     'Suddenly a terrifying blaze': visible 'virtus'   183

  C. Light as purificatory power   193
    'The contemplation of the flame': from metaphor to reality   193
    'Heavenly purification': life, light and holy power   200

  Conclusion: Gregory's chiaroscuro world   207

IV. *Dreams of a venerable person: the power of an ideal*   213
  Introduction. Armentaria: dream, waking vision or sensory
  reality?   213
  A. Dream-visions instituting new cults   217
    'Virgins whiter than snow': the desire for the visible presence
     of the holy   217

  B. The saint in visionary experience during cures   227
    'A filthy and deadly shade': the exorcism of negative emotions   230

'He spoke in a tender and loving manner': the ideal of the spiritual bridegroom 237
'Chained by the devil': images of immobilization and release 239
'As though someone': the doctor 243
'A healing touch': exorcism or the transmission of vital energy? 247
The smiling, white-haired man as a symbol: the transforming power of a human ideal 250

C. Visions of advice and aid 251
'A venerable old man in clerical habit': an image of reassurance and stability 253
'Someone who looked like a bishop': the solution of practical problems 255
'I am Martin...your liberator': the release of prisoners 257
'A luminous man': prophecy 260
'The pleading of the bishop': heavenly diplomacy 265
The heavenly patron: the image of the ideal governor 267

D. Visionary warning and punishment 268
'A frightening person': criticism, warning and intimidation 272
'A threatening face': curses and instant vengeance 276
Dead bishops as rulers of the kingdom?: the personalization of immanent divine justice 287

Conclusion. Gregory: the dream element in perception, transformation and society 287

General conclusion: views from a many-windowed tower 295

Bibliography 301

Samenvatting 331

Indices 337

INTRODUCTION
'in a mixed and muddled manner'?

In the sixth century Gregory, bishop of Tours from 573 to 594, wrote *Ten books of histories*, eight of miracles and saints' lives, a (largely lost) *Commentary on the Psalms* and a liturgical calendar, *On the course of the stars*.[1] He is the only historian of sixth-century Gaul whose writings have survived, and during the first half of the Middle Ages he was one of the most-read.

Nineteenth and twentieth-century historians, however, have found a great deal to criticize in his lively histories. Besides tending to ridicule Gregory's almost unlimited belief in miracles and questioning the historical veracity of the facts he relates, they have been surprised or exasperated by his — by the standards of Classical Latin — awkward manner of expression and by what seems to be the lack of orderly arrangement of the material. The latter they have ascribed not only to his own incompetence but often also to the influence of the chaotic, half-barbaric society in which he found himself. M.J.-J. Ampère's opinion in 1839 that Gregory 'présente la barbarie naivement telle qu'il la voit', 'sans lien, sans transition, avec toute l'incohérence de la société contemporaine'[2] was the beginning of something like a tradition. More than a hundred years later, however, the philologist E. Auerbach, in his well-known and sensitive *Mimesis* (1946), gave a positive value to Gregory's visual, dramatic presentation of individual, unconnected and unordered events, regarding it, however, as a successful imitation (i.e. mimesis) of 'concrete reality'. But he too said about the *Histories* that '... the pattern of events Gregory has to report meets his style halfway': the small-scale, primitive and 'brutal' life under the Frankish kings '... becomes a sensible object; to him who would describe it, it presents itself as devoid of order and difficult to order, but tangible, earthy, alive'.[3]

1. Many scholars add *The miracles of the apostle Andrew* and *The history of the seven sleepers*; see Bonnet 1890: 8-9 and Vollmann 1983: 896-7. Since these are, respectively, an adaptation and a translation of another author's work, and since — also because Gregory did not include them in the list of his works in *Hist.* 10.31 — there has been some doubt about their ascription to him, I have not utilized them.
2. Ampère 1839: 294, 298.
3. Auerbach 1946: 91, 93; translated in Auerbach 1957: 77, 79.

These judgments raise fundamental questions. Is the relation between society and the perception of one's world really this simple? And does what we know of Gregory's life and deeds accord with a view of his thinking as purely passive, unordered, incoherent? Is his evident preoccupation with the visual, sensory aspects of events a sufficient explanation for his avoiding organizing abstractions? Finally, does not the possibility need to be considered, and investigated, that there may be a coherence in a manner not immediately evident for modern readers?

The studies or essays in this book are the result of following a hunch — at first indistinct but nevertheless very persistent — that Gregory's writings should be read and understood in a non-discursive way. Accordingly, I have attempted to reach through his awkward and obscure formulations, his apparent contradictions and the gaps and crevices in the continuity of his presentation to find any connections and meanings that might be concealed under the surface narrative. As will become evident, what I found was indeed a coherence of a different kind, consisting of the integration of images rather than the organization of concepts and imagined in a non-discursive manner rather than systematically thought out. Modern psychological research has shown that this kind of non-verbal thinking in images, also known as 'primary thought processes', goes on at an unconscious level also in modern individuals, and not only in dreams. We may, after all, be closer to Gregory's seemingly strange experience of reality than we had thought.

For up to now there has been more or less unanimous agreement among scholars on the fact that Gregory is difficult if not impossible to understand. In this Introduction I will review the most important opinions about Gregory's arrangement of the stories as units (i.e. his composition) on the one hand, and about his presentation of individual events on the other, with the reasons that are given for their specific character and the views expressed on their relation to his environment. For the reader to be able to assess the latter — but also to do justice to Gregory as a human being who was not only, or perhaps not even primarily, a writer — it is necessary, but also pleasant, to begin with a sketch of his life and world. All we know about the former, however, is what he himself has told us.

GREGORY'S LIFE AND WORLD

In 1926 S. Dill's sympathetic judgment of Gregory as an eminent administrator, astute diplomat, as well as an independent and saintly bishop who also found time to be a forceful and original writer, was at that time, as he says, highly unusual:

> Gregory, from his limited culture, is seldom recognized by pedantic scholars as the commanding figure that he was... He saw more of the Merovingian world than any man of that time. He held the greatest and most sacred spot in Gaul, full of great memories, the scene of continued miracles, thronged with princes and nobles, flying from wrong or from justice, continually visited by great envoys or curious travellers who claimed the hospitality of the bishop. He was constantly engaged in diplomatic business at the courts of rival and warring kings, privy to all their plots and faithless designs, and striving to soften their enmities. He was himself the mark for deadly plots for his ruin [...] He lived in an atmosphere of miracle at home and on the journey. And his works show that he was continually collecting tales of miracles and recording [...] them with every minute and picturesque detail which, with his rude but deliberate art, he wished to transmit to posterity.[4]

In 1983 L. Pietri, in her ample and readable chapters on Gregory as bishop of Tours (the fullest biography of Gregory that has yet appeared and the most recent one) corrected and supplemented the information contained in Dill's delightful pages. She stressed Gregory's 'prodigious activity' and 'remarkable efficacity' in making Tours 'a symbol... of Christian hope, in an epoch of violence and misery'.[5]

Georgius Florentius, better known as Gregorius, the name he assumed when he became bishop of Tours, was born in 539 in what is now Clermont-Ferrand into a pious and wealthy Gallo-Roman family with a proud tradition of public leadership and Christian service. In the course of his works he tells us that, in various generations, six of his older relatives living in the sixth century were bishops. He was brought up in an atmosphere of devotion to saints and firm belief in the efficacy of relics. At this time the Auvergne had been under Frankish domination, like the rest of Gaul, for about a generation. Since most of the newcomers had settled in the north, this meant that life went on much as before except for the presence of Frankish officials and occasional violent clashes with the reigning king, which were punished with devastation of the territory.[6] In contrast to most of the other barbarians who had overrun the western part of the Roman Empire in the fifth century however, the Franks, led by their conqueror-king, the Merovingian Clovis, had been converted to Catholic Christianity. This had won them acceptance by their Gallo-Roman subjects and the support of the relatively powerful Christian bishops in the towns. In the course of the sixth century a slow fusion between Franks and Gallo-Romans took place through intermarriage

4. Dill 1926: 349-50.
5. Pietri 1983: 334. Unless otherwise indicated, the main facts about Gregory have been taken from Pietri's description of Gregory's life: Pietri 1983: 246-334. An equally recent but shorter survey of Gregory's life and works in Vollmann 1983.
6. Pietri 1983: 249 n. 13.

and common service to the kings. The official profession of Christianity did not mean, however, that the Franks' old customs and thinking habits were at once replaced by new, Christian ones. Among the Franks, but also among the Gallo-Roman lower strata, a great deal of superstition and magical practices remained, sometimes turning up even among the servants of an aristocratic household such as Gregory's.[7]

The manner of Merovingian government was that of a primitive Germanic monarchy, often divided between several warring kings, who could not prevent arbitrary justice or violence in their officials, much less keep any powerful man in check if he had a mind to add to his property at his neighbour's expense or to oppress the poor; a number of Gregory's stories show this happening.[8] At least since the fifth century the cities were losing their vitality, communications became more dangerous and difficult, commerce slowed down, people tended to move to the countryside where they could find work and protection on or near the great landed estates of the Gallo-Roman aristocracy in the fertile river valleys. New small village-communities also colonized the hilly plateaux.[9] In addition to the physical insecurity due to inadequate government and civil wars, the primitive and insanitary conditions and chronic malnutrition of large parts of the population must have been a factor in the recurrence of epidemics of bubonic plague, dysentery, and cholera from 546 onwards. Gregory's descriptions also give the distinct impression that all this insecurity and misery led to many instances of nervous ailments, and psychic disorders. Whoever wished to survive in such a society had to be able to protect himself and to use some kind of influence or power to gain his ends. It cannot be an accident that many of Gregory's stories in one way or another concern power, either physical or spiritual.

After his father died when he was about ten, he remained for a time with his mother Armentaria, a strong personality, of whom he was very fond and whose influence upon him may have been decisive in more ways than we are told.[10] In any case, he later lets her appear to him in a dream as though she were somehow a supernatural figure (notwithstanding the fact that she was at that moment still alive) and urge him in no uncertain terms to begin recording St Martin's miracles at Tours: not only his professional acitivity but also his heart was more deeply involved with

---

7. *Virt. Jul.* 46a.
8. For instance *Virt. Jul.* 14, 15, 16.
9. J. Boussard, [Essai sur] le peuplement [de la Touraine du Ier au VIIIe siècle], *Moyen Age* 60 (1954): 278-91, cited in Stancliffe 1979: 46.
10. Pietri 1983: 256. Gregory mentions her in: *Hist.* 5.5, *Glor. mart.* 50, 85; *Virt. Mart.* 1. prol.; 3.10, 60; *Glor. conf.* 3, 40, 84; *Vit. patr.* 7.2.

this saint than with any other.[11] When she moved thereafter to the vicinity of Châlon-sur-Saône to manage the family estates there, she entrusted the education of her sons to bishops who were members of the family: the elder son Peter to her uncle Tetricus of Langres (539-72), and Gregory to her late husband's brother, Gallus of Clermont (525-51), a man for whom Gregory had a life-long veneration. From him, the young aristocrat must have heard many tales about the events in that region in the period before, during and after the Frankish conquest. The daily supervision of Gregory's studies was entrusted to the archdeacon Avitus, thirty years older than he, who later became bishop of the city (571-after 592). Apart from what may have been compendia with selections from ancient authors such as Virgil (but Gregory may also have read some classical works independently, later), he gave Gregory exclusively Christian literature to read: the Bible, saints' lives, works of Gallic authors such as Bishop Hilary of Arles, perhaps Hilary of Poitiers, and of poets such as Prudentius, Sedulius, Paulinus of Nola and Paulinus of Périgueux.[12] For one reason or another, possibly through the influence of the negative attitudes toward classical culture then current among clerical circles in Gaul, inadequate attention was given to grammatical training in classical (as opposed to spoken) Latin, the consequences of which Gregory later deeply regretted. This did not however prevent Avitus from also encouraging his pupil's ambitions as a writer. Gregory's religious sensibility was developed by being taken on trips to visit shrines and saintly hermits living in the wilds of Auvergne. From the beginning of his life, then, Gregory was imbued with miraculous lore. In this formative period of his life he once fell seriously ill and, despairing of a natural recovery, let himself be carried to the tomb of St Illidius, promising there to take clerical orders if the saint should heal him. He probably carried out the promise soon after his cure and thereby started upon his ecclesiastical career. His stories show, however, that his health was not strong and that throughout his life he sought such cures from time to time.

What Gregory did between 551, when his uncle Gallus died, and his consecration as bishop of Tours in 573 is not entirely clear. He may have left Clermont when the disreputable Cautinus became the new bishop there, and seems to have spent some time at the shrine of St Julian in Brioude, to whose feast Gregory's family had taken him annually. His journeys — he apparently had a certain liberty of movement — took him

---

11. *Virt. Mart.* 1. prol.
12. On Gregory's knowledge of earlier authors see Bonnet 1890: 63-5 and Kurth 1919: 1-29.

in any case to Châlon-sur-Saône and Tours. It is clear, however, that he settled for a time in Lyon to serve among the clergy of his maternal great-uncle Bishop Nicetius (552-73). There he probably spent a considerable part of his time studying; his reading knowledge of Christian historians is unique for his time. Perhaps it was in this period that he read (parts of) Virgil's *Aeneid* and *Eclogues*, and it is likely that it was at that time that he also began collecting information for his *Histories* and hagiographical works.

In this period another cure, this time at the shrine of St Martin in Tours in 563, changed his life once more. Nicetius may have suggested a pilgrimage there. During the journey Gregory, who was by now a deacon, became so ill that his companions urged him to go home rather than die in a strange unfamiliar countryside. He told them however that he had made up his mind to go to St Martin, dead or alive. There he was miraculously cured and stayed in the city — for how long we do not know — with his great-uncle Euphronius who was bishop there (561-73). It was almost certainly during this stay that Gregory became extremely impressed by St Martin, whose miracles he may have witnessed himself and heard about from his uncle. The latter had an opportunity to become acquainted with the qualities of his nephew (once-removed) and it is not unlikely that he later suggested to King Sigebert that Gregory would be a worthy successor to his see. It must have been in this period too that Gregory gained the friendship of the saintly Queen Radegunde in her convent in Poitiers. Gregory's friend, the poet Venantius Fortunatus, whom Gregory may then also have met, seems to suggest that she, as well as Sigebert's Queen Brunhilde, used her influence with the king to procure him the nomination.[13] This means that Gregory must also have had contacts with the court, doubtless through his uncles.

He says that all but five of Tours' bishops up to then had belonged to his family. Nevertheless, perhaps because of the intrigues of the priest Riculf, who had marked out this prize for himself, Gregory's access to the episcopate in 573 was decidedly irregular. Instead of a canonical election by the clergy and people of the city, followed by the king's approval, and consecration in his diocese, he seems to have been designated by King Sigebert and hurriedly consecrated elsewhere by Bishop Aegidius of Reims. This is probably because the city of Tours was a key point in the realm and it was being coveted and threatened by the king's brother Chilperic: Sigebert needed a strong bishop there whom he could trust to be loyal. In fact, Gregory had been installed for only a few weeks at

---

13. Fortunatus, *Carm.* 5.3.14-5.

Tours when Chilperic allowed his eldest son Theodebert to occupy the city. During Gregory's entire episcopate, which was to last something more than 21 years (he probably died in 594), rival kings quarrelled about and successively occupied Tours and the surrounding region, often devastating it in the process of doing so. Gregory had to try to spare the city and accommodate himself to these changes of power and at the same time stay on peaceful terms with all the kings. He did this by exhibiting tact as well as a firm independence, no mean achievement in this brutal time and one which earned him the respect of all.

Besides his frequent journeys to court, to confer about church matters or taxes, to complain of a count's intolerable conduct or to defend himself against dangerous accusations by those ambitious for power, to plead for what were often violent men who had sought refuge from royal punishment in St Martin's church or to negotiate peace and understanding between the quarrelsome kings, Gregory made Tours the most important city and centre of pilgrimage in the Frankish kingdom. He tried to see to it that the royal officials administered justice and he often intervened to mitigate punishments or, when he could interpret some event such as the falling off of prisoners' chains as a miracle by the saint, to avoid punishment altogether. In this time, those who did not have the economic and family position to exert power needed a powerful patron to defend them against injustice. Gregory, in all his works, continually presents St Martin, and all other saints, as possible patrons for rich and poor alike. In actual practice, it can only have been episcopal diplomacy that made this saintly 'patronage' effective. In his diplomacy at court too, Gregory often tended to speak as the mouthpiece of St Martin — and, on a number of crucial occasions, got his way. His hagiographical writings, which he caused to be circulated as they were completed, were intended not only for posterity. They were at the same time propaganda, on the one hand to effect the moral conversions of those who were only superficial Christians, and on the other, as is often explicitly said, to impress upon those in power the notion that God and his saints were in fact constantly intervening in human events to reward the just and punish the wicked. The threat of supernatural punishment was a professionally unarmed bishop's only weapon in this society in which arms tended to decide everything.

As bishop, Gregory supervised the rites and the discipline of the churches of his city and diocese. He also concerned himself with church building or restoration in the city and consecrated a not inconsiderable number of churches and chapels in the countryside. The ample landed wealth of the church of Tours, which Gregory was careful to protect and enlarge, was also used for many charitable purposes: to provide food for prisoners languishing in dreadful, insanitary conditions, to arrange the release of the debtors from prison by paying their debts, as well as of hostages by paying their compensations; and to establish hostels with meals for the destitute. Those sick pilgrims who were not quickly cured and needed care which they could not afford, seem to have been lodged in the various monasteries. The cures which Gregory describes in his books on miracles and which, in my opinion, need not be substantially doubted, can only be ascribed to a kind of integrative experience that still occurs in religious contexts today. Gregory's writings show that the cult of the saints, the late antique discovery of a new human ideal that the church handed on to the Middle Ages, tended to be experienced first in forms that were already familiar to the uneducated people of the country regions. What they had formerly expected from pagan soothsayers and wizards, they now sought from the saint: in several stories Gregory reports a soothsayer's failure followed by the success of a saint. Not surprisingly, one of his favourite maxims seems to have been 'Let the facts decide the matter'. For him, cures were facts, and miracle stories were the best kind of preaching.[14] He was, as should be clear by now, a man who knew what he wanted and went after it, a man firmly grounded in practical reality.

HIS WRITINGS

This clear-headed leader, practical administrator in the best Roman tradition and for his time relatively learned man has left writings that appear to modern readers as superstitious and uncritical as well as unclear and unorganized. The last 150 years of discussion about these writings is marked by agreement on certain general points and continuing, sharp dissension on others. While everyone more or less agrees on Gregory's liveliness notwithstanding his often awkward formulation, an important point of disagreement has been the relation — if any — of his stories to 'historical facts' (whatever these may be). Other disagreements have been about the evaluation of his general arrangement of the stories and of his almost unbounded belief in miracles. If real progress has been made it is, in my opinion, in the slowly increasing specific recognition and the positive appreciation of the non-rational element in Gregory's writings. At first this appreciation was found primarily, but not exclusively, among historians of literature. Although Dill pointed the way already in 1926, it is only since about 1950 that some non-literary historians began to devote serious and sympathetic attention

---

14. As also Stancliffe 1979: 56.

to it. In general, one can say that whereas earlier scholars tended to emphasize Gregory's exclusive preoccupation with concrete, sensory facts, more recent studies have stressed his not so immediately apparent symbolical thinking. As will be seen, my own analysis of his writings includes both elements and sees the explanation for his lack of interest in rationally-ordered writing in a specific kind of imaginative thought process.

Because of the somewhat different principles involved, it seems best in what follows to separate the review of the opinions on the general arrangement of the material — which I shall refer to as 'composition' — from that of Gregory's descriptions of individual events, which I shall here call 'presentation'.

COMPOSITION

There has been substantial agreement on the fact that, so far as his choice of subjects is concerned, Gregory had a decided preference for the Church and the Franks: his *Ten books of histories* were long taken to be 'The history of the Franks'. The arrangement of the material in the first two books shows deliberate choice. Book 1 begins with Adam and ends with the death of St Martin of Tours; book 2 begins with his successor at Tours and ends with the death of King Clovis. The next two books each end with the death of a Frankish king, but thereafter the division is less clear. However, within these books and also in what he writes about contemporary events, preserving the chronological order appears to be more important than anything else. The result is a variegated assemblage of different kinds of apparently unconnected stories. It is this jumbled mosaic that has puzzled and exasperated historians.

Auerbach's nuanced and appreciative approach to Gregory's composition and presentation as such appeared in 1946. Even though, as I will indicate later, it is incomplete, it broke through established attitudes and made a new understanding of his writings possible. I therefore propose to divide my review of scholarly opinions into those which appeared before and those which appeared after 1946. Mentioning first those writers who saw in Gregory's histories no more than a 'naive' presentation of unconnected events, I shall then consider those who insisted that, under the guise of simple, direct reporting, he actually carried out a certain amount of conscious rearrangement of his material to suit his religious and political views. Subsequently, I shall look at any explanations that have been offered for what, on the whole, still appeared to be an inability to connect events into larger wholes.

In 1735 the Benedictine scholars of St Maur had simply noted that

Gregory did not select or arrange the stories he related.[15] Ampère's opinion in 1839 has been given above. In the introduction to his translation of the *Histories* (1851), W. Giesebrecht attributed their jumbled appearance partly to later additions and the lack of opportunity for a complete revision, and partly to Gregory's lack of interest in placing his stories in a recognizable whole: Gregory simply reports that which interests him from what he knows from reading or from hearsay.[16] R. Köpke (1852) was less charitable and put it down to incapacity: 'Er hat so viel zu sagen. Eines durchkreuzt und verdrängt das Andere, kaum weiss er es zu bewältigen und übersichtlich zusammenzustellen'.[17] In 1872, however, G. Monod although admitting that 'il est impossible que la barbarie de son langage n'ait pas jété quelque trouble dans sa pensée', saw practical circumstances as the cause of his lack of clear composition: scarcity of documents, writing material and time; all of Gregory's writing had to be done in brief stints, with insufficient opportunity to revise the work as a whole.[18] Two years later A. Ebert stressed chronological order as Gregory's conscious organizing principle but added again that he was not able to connect the individual stories he relates.[19] What these scholars looked for and did not find was a coherent system of intrahistorical connections. They seem to ascribe this absence to simple lack of ability, except perhaps Giesebrecht and certainly Monod, who explicitly credits Gregory with remarkable intelligence, lucidity, firmness and good sense.[20] He does not, however, go into the problem of how such an intelligent individual could be content with unclear thinking. For those who recognized Gregory's intelligence and artistic qualities, his lack of clarity remained a puzzle. It is this puzzle that was the point of departure for the present investigation.

As we saw, Ampère was the only one who, already in 1839, stressed the connection with what he regarded as Gregory's 'naive' presentation 'just as he saw it', with 'the incoherence of contemporary society'. He describes it as

> ... un récit pour ainsi dire passif qui, sans intention de rapprocher les faits, sans art, sans calcul, par cela seul qu'il les présente avec le désordre et le pêle-mêle qui leur est naturel, exprime merveilleusement la physionomie de ces faits et du temps qui les produit à son image.[21]

15. *Hist. lit.* 1735:391.
16. Giesebrecht 1851: xxx, xxiv, xxviii-ix.
17. Köpke 1852 in Köpke 1872: 301.
18. Monod 1872: 111, 118.
19. Ebert 1874: 543-4.
20. Monod 1872: 114, 142.
21. Ampère 1839: 304.

Here an assumption is made which, though it may have been at the back of others' minds, is nowhere else made explicit: Gregory, without any intermediate mental activity worth speaking of, simply translates the disorder around him into words. Did Ampère ever ask himself how Gregory managed to hold his job as one of most prominent bishops in Gaul with a perception as incoherent as the literary historian seems to think?

J.L. Löbell, finally, seems to be repeating Ampère's view when he says (in 1869): 'Man kann daher Gregor's Werk fast eine in die Uratome der Ereignisse aufgelöste Geschichte nennen'. He says too that Gregory reported events just as he experienced them, directly, and without looking for connections between them or trying to fit them into a larger whole. What makes his view different and more profound, however, is that he adds that Gregory presupposed the coherence of all events in the divine government of the world, although he was not able to recognize this government in more than incidental ways such as the temporal rewards of the righteous and punishments of the wicked.[22]

After World War II some historians began to stress the legitimacy of the chronological order in the *Histories* as a principle of composition.[23] W. Wattenbach and W. Levison (1952) saw Gregory's mood as dominated by the imminent end of the world, and F.W.N. Hugenholtz (1960) showed that the latter was an excellent reason for writing in chronological order: to be able to reckon the years until that Last Day.[24] Wattenbach and Levison, G. Misch (1955), and H. Grundmann (1965), however, regarded Gregory's *Histories* more as a kind of memoirs than as straightforward annals, and accordingly justified their rambling character.[25] As for those who saw another kind of coherence in the *Histories*, J.M. Wallace-Hadrill (1951) again stressed Gregory's aim of writing for the pilgrims who came to Tours, and thought that this aim constituted the unity of Gregory's work — a general coherence, therefore, on another, non-historical level.[26] F.L. Ganshof (1966) pointed once more to the internal coherence inherent in the choice of his subjects: history in general as divine government, and the history of the Frankish kingdom.[27] In 1974 F. Thürlemann showed that Gregory, within his consciously chosen organizational principle of chronological order, often

---

22. Löbell 1869: 349, 344.
23. For instance R. Latouche 1963, R. Buchner 1967 and M. Oldoni 1977.
24. Wattenbach and Levison 1952: 102; Hugenholtz 1960: 116-7, 121.
25. Wattenbach and Levison 1952: 105; Misch 1955: 367; Grundmann 1965: 13.
26. Wallace-Hadrill 1951: 27-8.
27. Ganshof 1966: 13-14.

creates meaning indirectly, for instance by comparing contemporary events with those in the Bible or in early Roman history. The latter practice, known as historical typology, creates a coherence between events that is atemporal and based on analogy.[28]

Typological or 'figural' thinking was, as far as I know, first consistently described by Auerbach in 1938 — but neither then nor later ascribed by him to Gregory. For him, Gregory's inadequately connected stories lacked coherence on any plane because they were the faithful reflection of the discrete, visual perceptions that in Auerbach's view constitute the basis of all human experience. The disintegration of larger wholes in political society as well as the decay of Latin as an organizing language was to have 'liberated' Gregory's immediate sensibility for what Auerbach calls 'concrete reality'.[29] I think there is a great deal of truth in this view, but Auerbach does not seem to realize that it is not large enough to fit the whole man, who was also a passionate believer in miracles as well as an astute bishop. Had Auerbach analysed one of Gregory's miracle stories alongside that of the blood feud of Sicharius and Chramnesindus, he would have seen the applicability too of what he himself had said so well about figural thinking: 'the horizontal, that is the temporal and causal, connection of occurrences is dissolved; the here and now is no longer a mere link in an earthly chain of events, it is simultaneously something which has always been, and which will be fulfilled in the future'. But this probably did not seem reconcilable with his — perhaps too passionately held — view that Gregory's writings were the purest form of *mimesis*, the representation of raw reality as it is perceived (or so he thought) before any reflective thinking about it takes place.[30]

In 1954 the literary historian P. Zumthor remarked that all more or less learned early medieval works exhibit an absence of composition as we understand it. Attention centers on small units. He calls it a kind of 'literary impressionism', but does not suggest an explanation.[31] H.L. Mikoletzky (1970), and S. Boesch Gajano (1977) similarly note a lack of perspective: all events seem to take place on the same level.[32] Ms Boesch Gajano explicitly agrees with Auerbach's characterization of Gregory's writings but includes the miracles in her consideration; the hagiographic chapters in the *Histories* are not digressions but an essential part of

28. Thürlemann 1974: 86-94.
29. Auerbach 1938; Auerbach 1946: 96, 91; translated in Auerbach 1957: 82, 77.
30. Auerbach 1946: 91-2; translated in Auerbach 1957: 77-8. Compare the criticism of Auerbach's use of the term 'mimesis' and of his characterization of Gregory's style in Chatillon 1968.
31. Zumthor 1954:37.
32. Mikoletzky 1970: 20; Boesch Gajano 1977: 40.

Gregory's view of historical reality, which includes miracles as well as massacres.[33] The literary historian F. Brunhölzl (1975) also observes that the atomized, 'flächenhaft' presentation of events runs from late antique literature through the whole early Middle Ages: the background is not visible and connections are not stated. But this need not mean, he says, that they are not there; the place to look for the underlying assumptions and coherence is in the prefaces.[34] Already in 1952, however, B. Smalley in her book *The study of the Bible in the Middle Ages* had suggested another explanation for the disorganized appearance of early medieval works. She connects the preference for small, limited subjects and the lack of interest in connecting them with each other in any obvious way with the late antique habit of interpreting Scripture by allegorical digressions. Individual words and events are interpreted as 'figures' or 'types' of certain points of doctrine, whose place in the whole of Christian belief is taken to be self-evident.[35] This is, of course, similar to the 'figural' thinking which Auerbach had noticed in early Christian literature, seen this time as a philological-theological working habit. Ms. Smalley hereby seems to suggest that the unexpressed religious coherence is probably taken to be, in a more or less vague manner, self-evident.

A number of historians, too, indicated that the coherence in Gregory's works was in fact to be sought in the religious sphere. In 1955 G. Misch stated that for Gregory and his contemporaries the unity of events lay not in their earthly connections but in their transcendent religious meaning. Every individual event as well as the whole of history was (potentially) explicable in terms of God's will. Gregory was dominated by a 'religiöse Ordnungsgedanke'.[36] The view which D. Bianchi expressed in 1961 in a more general way — that religion was central for all Gregory's choices and thoughts in his *Histories* — was amply demonstrated, qualified and nuanced in 1970 by I. Blume.[37] As we saw, Thürlemann showed in 1974 that Gregory's stories in the *Histories* are shot through with religious typology. These, although he does not explicitly say so, give it, at these moments in any case, a certain inner coherence, that is more convincing than previous generalizing remarks by others on Gregory's having written the history of the Frankish kings in Old Testament style.

To summarize the present state of research on Gregory's composition in the *Histories*: there still is agreement only about the conscious choice of

---

33. Boesch Gajano 1977: 52-3.
34. Brunhölzl 1975: 137.
35. Smalley (1952) 1964: 2, 32.
36. Misch 1955: 370-1.
37. Bianchi 1961: 150; Blume 1970: 63 and passim.

chronological order, about the preoccupation with the church and with the Frankish kings and about the lack of explicitly stated connections between most of the events reported. Whereas some scholars regard the conscious choice of chronological order and an inability to see larger wholes as a sufficient explanation, others stress religion or the purpose of edification as an incompletely stated, extra-historical coherence. Through these groups, however, runs the divided opinion on the degree of Gregory's 'naivety': was he presenting 'disconnected' reality just as he saw it or was he consciously altering the picture here and there? Those of the former opinion tend to assume some kind of more or less passive connection between his presentation and his environment, whereas those of the latter opinion insist on his attempt to influence this environment in the direction of his prejudices and aims. The relation of Gregory's writing to his environment is more easily discernible, however, in his presentation of individual events, and it is the views on this topic which will be considered next.

PRESENTATION OF INDIVIDUAL EVENTS
From the above survey, we can see that, for scholars, Gregory's composition, which at first had seemed so simple, in fact turned out to be a far from uncomplicated phenomenon. Their discussion of his presentation of individual events is also marked on the one hand by a substantial agreement on the qualities of 'naivety' or 'artifice', 'obscurity', 'originality' and 'visuality' and on the other by a more or less violent disagreement about what exactly is meant by these terms and whether they should be positively or negatively valued. On the whole, historians of literature were readier to appreciate Gregory's writings than historians of society and politics, who kept stumbling over his obscurities and checking him against 'what actually happened'. Their conclusion was almost invariably that Gregory cannot be regarded as an historian in the modern sense of the word. In the course of time, however, his writings came to be increasingly examined less for his 'facts' than for his views, insights into the mental world of his time. This means that, instead of being annoying obstacles, Gregory's quirks and obscurities eventually came to be objects of interest in and for themselves.

Whereas in 1869 the historian Löbell noticed Old Testament influence on Gregory's style,[38] in 1852 Köpke had described Gregory's presentation as simply inadequate. According to Köpke, where Gregory reported something as an eyewitness his style was 'simple' and 'artless', but when reflection became necessary he became

38. Löbell 1869: 348.

unklar, dunkel und geschraubt, seine Ausdrücke werden vieldeutig und beginnen zu verschwimmen. Augenblicklichen Ideenverbindungen folgend, verknüpft er Ungehöriges, schachtelt er Satz in Satz, bis er am Ende seinen eigenen Gedanken verloren hat.[39]

In 1872, as we saw, Monod published a study of Gregory's *Histories* (which he then like everyone else called 'The history of the Franks') in which he praised his lucidity, firmness and good sense, and attributed his incidental obscurities of thought to faulty grammar. What Ebert (1874) did not hesitate to call Gregory's 'crass superstition', Monod elegantly spoke of as his 'imagination toujours surexcitée'.[40]

In 1890 the philologist M. Bonnet published what is still the standard reference work on Gregory's language. Since I am concerned not with philology but rather with Gregory's thinking and perception I will here note only a few things that seem directly and generally relevant to these topics in Bonnet's wealth of material. Gregory's language, he says, was deeply formed by the Psalms. Metaphors between physical and moral phenomena, as Gregory uses them, were common in late Antiquity, and often an image in fact covers an abstract idea. (Bonnet does not develop the latter insight; as will become evident, I found it to be a central characteristic of Gregory's thinking.) Equally interesting is what Bonnet says about Gregory's pattern of presentation: when he is not trying to be ornate, the order of his sentence is analytical, principal subject first, then secondary ones, etc.; when he wants to embellish his presentation however, the order becomes synthetic, resembling oratorical forms. He has a rich vocabulary and loves word-play, especially on proper names. Besides a fresh, rude originality, Bonnet ascribes to Gregory a predilection for poetic ornament, not always successfully carried out.[41] Other scholars, too, have credited Gregory with definite literary qualities. G. Kurth (1893, 1919) said that Gregory writes as a poet, not as a chronicler, and called his stories great, if perhaps unconscious, art. M. Manitius (1896) noticed a metrical or rhythmic form and a smattering of what he called 'poëtischen Floskeln' as well as the strong influence of the older Latin translation of the Bible, the Itala, especially in its use of imagery. A. Molinier (1901), after listing Gregory's stylistic shortcomings, concluded that he was nevertheless 'perhaps... a great writer' and Dill (1926) too valued him as 'a literary and historical artist' especially 'in the

---

39. Köpke 1852 in Köpke 1872: 303.
40. Monod 1872: 142, 111, 123; Ebert 1874: 546.
41. Bonnet 1890: 53, 705, 724, 731, 734, 737, 752,

arrangement and proper placing of events' so as to get his point across without explicitly stating it.[42]

Similarly, historians were busy showing that a number of Gregory's stories were more imagination than history: S. Hellmann (1911) showed that Gregory's apparently naive, direct presentation of the facts as they happened was an illusion; L. Halphen (1925) concluded that the conversations Gregory reports must be inventions and that he achieves his liveliness by the conscious use of visual detail. B. Krusch also pointed out that Gregory was more a novelist than an historian — but he obviously intended this as a negative judgment. At the end of an article on the *Unzuverlässigkeit* of Gregory's historical information (1931) he waxed so acrid on the subject of Gregory's inaccuracies and inventions that he said there was not one true statement in Gregory's description of Clovis' baptism except the one that this king was actually baptized.[43] As evidence of political as well as literary shaping began to be recognized in Gregory's stories, that which had seemed to some to be his 'child-like simplicity' and 'naive honesty' began to come under suspicion.

In addition, alongside the problem of Gregory's no-longer-classical-and-not-yet-Romance language (interesting to Romanists and exasperating to classicists and historians), there remained something like a fundamentally unclear quality about his writings, also in their content. Neither admirer nor critic really knew what to do with it. In 1926 S. Dill stated what, in my opinion, was the real problem and suggested a way to its solution:

> The dim religious life of the early Middle Ages is severed from the modern mind by so wide a gulf, by such a revolution of beliefs, that the most cultivated sympathy can only hope to revive it in faint imagination. Its hard, firm, realistic faith in the wonders and terrors of an unseen world seems to evade the utmost effort to make it real to us... we think the nearest approach to that far-gone age might be made by a sympathetic study of Gregory's tales of miracle, so rich in human interest, so boundless in faith in Unseen Powers ... [44]

Nevertheless, in 1942 J.W. Thompson described Gregory's *Histories* as 'the supreme example of vigorous, barbaric, Christo-German historiography', repeating (once more) that he had 'the naiveté of a child, the simplicity and charity of a saint and the loyalty of a hero to his rights and ideals. He is the first really medieval man, together with Pope Gregory

---

42. Kurth 1893: 70-1 and 1919: 176; Manitius 1896: 550-1; Molinier 1901: 60; Dill 1926: 348.
43. Hellmann 1911: 76-99; Halphen 1925: 241-3; Krusch 1931: 490.
44. Dill 1926: 324, 351.

and Isidore. He was credulous but otherwise honest and sincere'.[45] The word 'otherwise', expressing an opposition between credulity and honesty, probably reflects this historian's concern for facts and not views.

In 1946 the literary historian Auerbach, as we saw, did look for a view, a 'representation of reality' rather than facts. Continuing the tradition of Gregory's 'naivety', he pointed to the latter's 'direct' representation — along the trellis (as it were) of a 'decaying language' and 'monstrous' sentences — of 'concrete, visual reality' in separate, unconnected units, just as he experienced it in a brutal, chaotic environment. 'In all his works', Auerbach says, 'he writes for general, immediate, sensory-concrete comprehension'. The only influence of the Bible that Auerbach would admit was its use of direct discourse — and not its paratactic style and emphasis on the meaning of events rather than their sensory aspect, which he had described earlier in his book.[46] Unfortunately, Auerbach also neglected to look in Gregory's writings for 'figural' thinking, about which he says earlier that it 'annihilated' the mentality of late Antiquity down to 'the very structure of... its literary language', resulting in 'a fragmentary, discrete presentation, constantly seeking interpretation from above'.[47] Nevertheless, it looks as though Auerbach's sensitive and sympathetic analysis of Gregory's perception had a definite impact on at least a number of historians who now began to give Gregory's views as such serious attention. This does not mean, however, that they came to the same conclusions. B. Friedrich (1951), alongside her description of Gregory's conscious literary and rhetorical devices in the cataloguing of persons, nevertheless characterizes his whole attitude as unconscious, unreflective. She speaks of 'die mangelnde Fähigkeit, Dinge ins Bewusstsein zu heben, bzw. über sie klar zu werden' as the reason for his creviced presentation — a significant insight which she unfortunately does not develop. Describing at length the nature and consequences of Gregory's constant sense of the divine presence (as 'eine mehr gefühlsmässig erfassbare Schicht, die über dem Erzählten liegt') she

---

45. Thompson 1942: 148, 149-50.
46. Auerbach 1946: 91-2, 96, 29, 79, 54-5; translated in Auerbach 1957: 77-8, 81-2, 19, 66, 42-3. In a later work (Auerbach 1958: 78-83) he says 'damals war mir aber noch nicht ganz klar geworden, wie energisch er seinen Ausdruckswillen betont' and calls his talent for expression and originality unique for his time; he persists, however, in seeing this manifested in 'brühwarm' descriptions of concrete, sensory reality and does not consider the possibility of typological or symbolical content. H.F. Muller's interesting attempt, in 1945, to link social and linguistic history is unconvincing: see Mohrmann 1947. Compare on this combination also: Sas 1955 and Ropert 1976.
47. Auerbach 1946: 495-6, 77-9; translated in Auerbach 1957: 490, 64-5.

connects this with his absence of doubt in religious matters but not with his unreflective attitude in general.[48] Her view of Gregory is very different from that of Auerbach, and penetrates to a certain extent into what is felt rather than said.

In his review of Krusch and Levison's new edition of Gregory's *Histories* in 1951, H. Löwe attacked Krusch's premise that, since the Latinity of many texts was 'corrected' in the Carolingian period, the most incorrect text must represent Gregory's original one. Citing E.R. Curtius (1948), he says that Gregory was, for his time, a learned man who deliberately used the vernacular language in order to be understood by his public, but who also used rhetorical devices, and that his orthography was probably less corrupt than that of the seventh-century manuscript upon which the edition is based.[49] In 1977 K. Zelzer expressed adherence to this view and noted that the orthography of the text of the miracle books was more correct.[50] Although the orthography of the text is, strictly speaking, not relevant to Gregory's thought and perception it does help to clear him somewhat of the charge of 'barbarism'.

In the introduction to his translation of the *Histories* in 1963 R. Latouche speaks of Gregory's 'stammering style', his 'puerile, unconnected ideas' and his inability to handle abstract ideas. Nevertheless, he credits Gregory with a 'simple and direct', anecdotal and original style. He is 'un visuel'. What Latouche is in fact saying is that Gregory provides visual units without connections (which had also been the view of Auerbach) but as an historian Latouche is somewhat less appreciative of this fact.[51] Where F. Ganshof (1966) describes Gregory's writing as 'without style ... with an inborn feeling for the picturesque' (thereby perhaps demonstrating the lack of communication between literary and other historians), M. Oldoni (1977) calls his presentation 'at times disorganized, at times connected but then always imprecise'. Was Gregory's imprecision 'puerile' or was it perhaps something else? More than a hundred years after Monod, the problem itself had not yet been formulated. Nevertheless, Oldoni regards Gregory as a forceful and original writer.[52] As we have seen, S. Boesch Gajano (1977) explicitly expresses adherence to Auerbach's interpretation of Gregory's presentation. Although she does integrate Gregory's miracle stories into it, this does not result in an expanded view of Gregory's perception. Her

---

48. Friedrich 1951: 39, 19.
49.* Löwe 1951: 341-2.
50. Zelzer 1977: 235-9.
51. Latouche 1963: 82, 90, 20, 18.
52. Ganshof 1966: 18; Oldoni 1977: 254.

suggestive statements that Gregory was a witness to a 'new reality' and to 'a religiosity in which the primordial needs of security are expressed'[53] are unfortunately not developed.

J.T. Roberts' philological article in 1980 on Gregory's paratactic style continues where Auerbach left off. Gregory's language, she says, is a reversion to an earlier, archaic form of Latin that had not yet attained rational, ordering capacities with the attendant replacement of immediacy with formality. Gregory's formulation is sloppy and the pattern of his presentation as a whole is 'unthinking, alogical': antecedents are not obvious, connectives are inadequate, absent, exclusively temporal or vague. She concludes, 'He was not thinking at all. For his orientation was not fundamentally intellectual. In his work we do not find ... the human mind interposing itself between the subject matter and the reader. Gregory perceives his matter directly'. This had also been Auerbach's view. In the paratactic style verbs follow each other quickly, 'as in poetry, in which the reader must do much of the intellectual work himself'. On the nature of his perception she says that it was more the response of a poet than of an historian: 'he associates freely and creatively rather than strategically'. Large and small things are presented as perceived in the same way: the awareness of God and of urinating horses are not distinguished. The lack of subordinate syntax in the paratactic sentence also points to a lack of perspective. There are 'no barriers between himself and his writing' just as there are no barriers between him and his audience: 'they are supposed to understand'. The latter attitude is said to resemble that of children.[54] Although Ms. Roberts' sensitive treatment identifies the linguistic style of Gregory's presentation and points to its poetic rather than rational quality, she unfortunately still does not take into account the religious dimension — which could equally well be a very adult kind of 'what-everyone-is-supposed-to-understand'. Even more regrettably, Gregory's intelligence and complexity is still under-rated: non-rational language is regarded as necessarily childish and undeveloped.

Ms Roberts also says nothing about the reason for Gregory's using the paratactic style. M. Du Plessis (1968) however noted — as Manitius had already done in 1911 — that the older Latin translation of the Bible, which had followed the archaic forms perpetuated in the spoken language, was probably Gregory's example.[55] A number of other scholars too in one way or another were inclined to stress Biblical influence on

---

53. Boesch Gajano 1977: 91.
54. Roberts 1980: 179-85.
55. Du Plessis 1968: 60.

Gregory's style. F. Lehmann (1962) cited Bonnet and Manitius on the influence of the poetic imagery of the Psalms and says that even where there is no recognizable Biblical quotation, there are reminiscences of tone. D. Bianchi (1961) had also noted Gregory's poetic quality, as well as his sincerity and passionate convictions. P. Antin (1967) thinks he uses Scriptural expressions and reminiscences to describe everything because they were the only way he knew of to describe life in the presence of God. F. Brunhölzl (1975) however, believes he detects the influence of the Old Testament style in the treatment of Frankish history, and E.H. Walter (1966) as well as M. Oldoni (1977) indicate a strong hagiographical influence on Gregory's style in general.[56] The assumption implicit in most of these opinions seems to be that this Biblical imitation was largely unconscious.

Other scholars, however, continued to assert that Gregory himself was not 'naive' and must also be credited with, or criticized for, deliberate strivings for effect. P. Courcelle (1951) says he combines 'candour with all the tricks of a not untalented novelist', and B. Friedrich (1951) analyzes his use of indirect characterization of persons. H. Beumann (1964) regards him, as Curtius had done, as a conscious innovator in writing in the rustic style.[57] Thürlemann (1974) also exposes as such the illusion of Gregory's 'objectivity' or 'naivety' by showing how he manages to slip in his own interpretation of the facts he relates by the use of suggestive dialogue, significant detail and unmistakable analogy. All this shows that Gregory was 'thinking' some of the time, at least. Thürlemann also shows, however, that where Gregory retells stories from others' writings, for instance from Prudentius, and intends to tell only 'the facts', he gives his own view of the event in a context very different from that in which the original author presented it; Gregory, according to Thürlemann, is not able to perceive the difference. Thürlemann also thinks the language that Gregory uses in his writing about miracles is more formalized than that he uses for other matters and suggests that the world of religion was at that time not one of primarily individual experience but of holy rules to be observed by the community. Surprisingly he does not connect this with another one of his observations about Gregory's descriptions: that word and act together sometimes have the character of a liturgical rite.[58] Like Walter (1966), he also points to the 'miracle-structure' of stories in which there is no explicit reference to divine influence. He sees in this a

---

56. Lehmann 1963 in La Bibbia 1963a: 131-2; Bianchi 1961: 151-2, 162; Antin 1967: 781; Brunhölzl 1975: 139; Walter 1966; Oldoni 1977: 610.
57. Courcelle 1951: 311; Friedrich 1951: 112-47; Beumann 1964 in Beumann 1972.
58. Thürlemann 1974: 25-6, 47-8, 100, 105, 82-3.

'secularization' of this structure,[59] evidently taking for granted that where divine influence is not explicitly mentioned or otherwise noticeably indicated it is absent. Thürlemann's analysis indicates where Gregory was consciously shaping his text and where he unconsciously did so. He does not, however, relate these insights to what others had persistently called Gregory's preoccupation with concrete, sensory reality. Neither does he go under the patchy surface structure of the presentation to search out the unstated assumptions in its discontinuities. As for Gregory's style, J.-B. Jungblut (1977) shows that his prose in the first three books of the *Histories* is 'metrical', following the Roman rhetorical tradition, and that it resembles that of Augustine's sermons as well as that of the latter's pupil Quodvultdeus in his *Liber de promissionibus*.[60] In 1978 M. Banniard points to what he considers to be Gregory's conscious 'aménagement de l'histoire' in the account of the Hunnic invasion of 451 to make it accord with his own priorities.[61]

In 1966 Walter was the first to attempt to solve the apparent contradiction between the 'naive realism' of Gregory's apparently empirical interest in visual detail and his equally unmistakeable and 'uncritical' belief in miracles at every turn. Citing Kurth's well-known dictum that Gregory 'ne connaît rien de plus naturel que le surnaturel', Walter says that for Gregory there is almost no tension between miracle and everyday reality: sacred meaning can and even should be looked for in the visible world. His predilection for sensory reality plays an important role in his attempt to present the manifestations of God as concretely and visually as possible. Belief in miracles, empiricism and pleasure in concrete reality (*Weltfreudigkeit*), Walter says, are for Gregory one and the same thing. Accordingly, Gregory's descriptions of certain secular persons in Biblical or hagiographical style are regarded as the result of an unconscious habit[62] and not as a 'secularization'. As I hope to show, Walter is right as far as he goes but fails to discern and 'integrate' into his view the symbolic character of Gregory's thinking. The latter was vigorously put forward in 1982 by P. Gautier Dalché who turned all Gregory-research upside-down with his analysis of Gregory's treatment of space in the miracle books. Setting out to analyze what everyone had designated as Gregory's 'concrete, visual perception of

---

59. Walter 1966: 304-5; Thürlemann 1974: 79-80.
60. Jungblut 1977: 338, 342-3, 345, 349. As will be seen below (p. 89-90), I have, also, found some similarity of formulation between Quodvultdeus' and Gregory's writing.
61. Banniard 1978: 37.
62. Kurth 1919: 122; Walter 1966: 304-5.

reality' in his treatment of space in the miracle books, Gautier Dalché came to the conclusion that the space (localities) in which miracles occur is not treated as a concrete situation. It is an abstract framework for miracles as symbolic manifestations: spiritual truth is exemplified by spatial illustrations. Real space — geography — is irrelevant; Gregory, Gautier Dalché says provocatively, contradicting everyone and especially Auerbach, refuses the sensory for its own sake.[63] This may be substantially true for the treatment of space in miracle books, but it certainly cannot stand without qualification for the *Histories*; there, for instance, Gregory now and then takes pleasure in concrete descriptions and measurements of churches and cities. Furthermore, space is far from constituting the whole of palpable, visible reality: it is events, gestures, words and small objects that Gregory often describes so visually. Nevertheless, Gautier Dalché has convincingly pointed to the central importance, so long overlooked, of symbolical thinking in Gregory's writings.

No more than on his composition, then, is there a consensus on Gregory's presentation: 'naivety' and 'artifice', both shown to be present, seem to be irreconcilable. Unconnected visual impressions in an 'unthinking' archaic Latin do not seem to accord well with passionately held prejudices, conscious strivings for effect and typological shaping. Gregory's preoccupation with 'concrete sensory reality', on the one hand, and his belief in miracles and the abstract, symbolic treatment of (at least part of) sensory reality on the other, looks like an inescapable contradiction. And finally, the relation of Gregory's composition and presentation to the circumstances in which he lived is regarded either as one of more or less passive 'reflection' or as its opposite, one of deliberate manipulation for purposes of propaganda. On all these issues there seems to be evidence on both sides. What could lie behind these paradoxes?

APPROACH AND THEMES OF THE ESSAYS
The following studies or essays — arranged and designated as 'chapters' — are an exploration into the persistent puzzle of Gregory's discontinuities and imprecision and their relations (if any) to the society in which he lived. Taking cognizance of his literary be described, in one way or another, as his 'naivety'. Especially, however, I have tried to discover what he did *not* say: what he was thinking, and especially imagining, in and around the discontinuities and ambiguities in some of his otherwise so visually described 'concrete' as well as 'miraculous' events. In my opinion, Gregory's lack of time, interest and

63. Gautier Dalché 1982: 412-3.

training on the one hand, and his conscious preference for chronological order and typology on the other still do not fully explain the discontinuities in overall composition or his imprecision in the presentation of individual events. I have looked for an inexplicit kind of coherence as well as for his view of how events happen. Throughout, I have also tried to feel my way into what has seemed to be his 'credulousness', 'bias', 'lack of perspective', 'unreflectiveness' and 'simplicity', and have attempted to connect these with his position and possibilities in the society in which he found himself. After a great deal of trial and error, I noticed that this kind of indirect evidence is best discovered, analyzed and understood as it appears around specific groups of phenomena or themes that frequently appear in Gregory's writings. From the various possibilities, I have selected ones that had not received serious attention before: ordinary and extraordinary natural phenomena and prodigies, light imagery and perceptions of luminosity, and the dreams, visions and apparitions connected with the saints.

These themes were not preconceived as a plan. They presented themselves in the course of reading and re-reading Gregory's writings with the suspicion that he had been writing, thinking and perceiving as an unconscious poet even more than has up to now been recognized, and that this could be the most fundamental reason for his discontinuities and imprecision. Another thing that had struck me in Gregory's writing is that it exhibits many of the same characteristics as the world-view of oral cultures in the present and recent past — which anthropologists at first also described as 'naive' and 'childlike'. In this century there have been many attempts to demonstrate the complexity and sophistication, in its own way, of what has nevertheless usually continued to be called 'primitive' thought. I have looked primarily at two, opposing, views. L. Lévy-Bruhl, in the first quarter of this century, described 'la mentalité primitive' as functioning essentially in an affective manner: 'pre-logically'. In 1962, C. Lévi-Strauss published his *La pensée sauvage* in which he stated, as the title indicates, that this thinking is in its own way every bit as rational and as dialectical as our own. Accordingly, instead of concentrating on the 'surface' texture of Gregory's events and their interrelations, I have tried to detect connections, associations and meanings at other levels. As we have seen, Dill (1926)[64] recommended a detailed study of Gregory's miracle stories as the gateway to understanding his thinking. Setting as much as possible my own thought-models aside, I attempted to expand my imaginative range by acquainting myself, in a general way, with a number of relevant insights from other

---

64. Dill 1926: 324, 351; Vollrath 1981: 592.

fields of knowledge on the subject of thought and perception as related to the social environment.[65] Then, without attempting anything like an interdisciplinary study, I have tried to discover empirically what Gregory did not put into words — either because he took it to be self-evident or because he could not (adequately) verbalize it, or both. This has meant an exploration-in-depth of the specific, the detail. The discovery of more general patterns in Gregory's thinking becomes possible only after such a solid groundwork has been laid.

These essays bear the mark of this searching without (at first) knowing exactly what one is looking for: a 'growing into' Gregory's thought and perception that is something like a dialogue between intuition and feeling on the one hand, and clear, conceptual thinking on the other. Along the way, all manner of discoveries, both more and less expected, are made: indeed, right up to the end, one is not quite sure what the total configuration will finally look like. And even then, one suspects there is still more, just out of reach. I am aware that following this process demands sustained interest and patience from the reader and that it does not make for easy reading. But I have, substantially, let the 'growing process' stand because I believe it is the only way to *enter into* this, for us so unfamiliar, mode of thinking and perception. At the end of each section and of each essay, however, I have summarized and synthesized the most important findings in a conceptual manner. Some readers may find it a help to look at these first. In the general conclusion at the end of the book I have tried to present the essence of my findings in such a way as to be clear also for those who are interested in the conceptualized results only.

Extraordinary natural phenomena and prodigies, the subject of the first essay, suggested themselves as an object for examination in the context of my general aim when it became increasingly clear that Gregory tended to see temporal correspondences between these phenomena and certain types of human events. Although Orosius, one of Gregory's models, had followed the pagan historiographical tradition by including prodigies in his version of the history of pagan Rome and mentioning a few in its Christian period, Gregory is the first Christian historian to

65. As an historian I do not, of course, claim any competence whatsoever in these disciplines. I am especially indebted to the works of Eliade 1952, 1957, 1958, 1959 and 1967, and those of Van der Leeuw 1961, Durkheim 1960, Lévy-Bruhl 1922a, 1922b and 1963; Evans-Pritchard 1937, Müller 1957, Douglas 1966; Kirk 1970; Meslin 1973, 1974, 1975, Huxley 1959, Jung 1949, 1952 and 1971, Koestler 1972, Singer 1974, Leuner 1980, Langer 1980 and 1953, Bachelard 1960, Lévi-Strauss 1962, Ricoeur 1975; Wheelwright 1959 and 1968, Lewis 1961. Complete list and full bibliographical information in the bibliography on p.305 ff.

integrate large numbers of them into a description of more recent and contemporary events. I found that his view of prodigies changed in the course of writing the *Histories* and reflected his changing view of the contemporary situation. In the course of the investigation, the manner in which he makes implicit connections between events and thus creates meaning without explicitly saying so also began to emerge: these connections revealed an additional, hitherto unsuspected, symbolical kind of coherence in the *Histories*. After this, an exploration into his thinking about and perception of natural phenomena in general — also as they figured in miracles — seemed an obvious complement, and subject for the second essay, especially since virtually no research had been done on this topic with respect to the early Middle Ages. What I found is that ordinary and miraculous natural phenomena too, in all their immediacy and sensory concreteness, tend to be experienced simultaneously as symbols or symbolic agents of sudden transformations, according to a number of definite models.

While musing over Gregory's stories, my attention was increasingly arrested by the frequent occurrence and ambiguous presentation of light imagery and luminous phenomena, and it is to these that the third essay is devoted. Late antique inscriptions, liturgy, hymns, and pagan as well as Christian mystical writings also show a marked preoccupation with the qualities of light and darkness as metaphors for metaphysical and religious values. Until the end of the sixth century, however, Gregory is the only historian-hagiographer who not only uses light imagery with conspicuous frequency but also reports numerous perceptions of luminous phenomena in the context of everyday religious life, i.e. outside of explicitly so designated mystical or ecstatical conditions (although he does also describe a few of these). The analysis of the context and meaning in his stories of light — and also of fire, which was in practice inseparable from light — showed that Gregory's attention centered not only on the notion of regeneration but also on those of purification and power. Perhaps even more important, it revealed an 'archaic' and truly poetic view of reality, structured more by images and dreams than by concepts and logic. Accordingly, Gregory tends to see metaphors as independent realities.

The last essay is an attempt to discover more about what Gregory reports about dreams, visions and apparitions recognized as such. I found that most of the recorded visionary experiences, almost always of an ideal, venerable person, were either pivotal in a personal regenerative process or tended to be closely related to the perception of social reality as well as to its manipulation.

All this revealed that the problem of Gregory's thinking itself and of its relation to his environment is a great deal more complicated than was supposed by those who spoke of 'simplicity', 'confusion' and (passive) 'reflection' of the society in which he lived. Contradicting Auerbach's unstated assumption, the psychologist S. Tomkins has said that the information that comes to us through the senses 'is not directly transformed into a conscious report. What is consciously perceived is *imagery* which is created by the organism itself. [...] The world we perceive is a dream we learn to have from a script we have not written. It is neither our capricious construction nor a gift we inherit with our work'.[66] To make Gregory's thought recognizable for twentieth-century Europeans, I have tried, among other things, to isolate models, so different from ours, through which he perceived and thought about reality, and to discover their possible relations with his social environment. As we shall see, much of his thinking continues in patterns that had persisted through centuries of social change and that are only in a secondary way related to his social reality. As for this last, without greatly increasing the volume of this book I can do no more than indicate the relations to its main characteristics briefly, referring the reader to other works which have this society as their main subject.

The fact that Gregory himself called his arrangement of historical events 'mixed and muddled'[67] can only mean that he was capable of imagining a more obvious order, but did not use it. As I hope to show, his 'naivety' and 'simplicity', too, turn out to be an intellectualistic illusion of modern historians. I have tried to realize empirically, in my own way, something of what (as I later found) M. Meslin has said so well: 'Pour comprendre tant soit peu de l'essence du fait religieux, il nous faut aller sans cesse de l'historique et du social vers les structures profondes de la pensée, du langage parlé et de l'inconscient humain.'[68]

---

66. Tomkins 1962: 13.
67. *Hist.* 2. *praef.*: 'As we continue to follow the order of the succession of the times, we record in a mixed and muddled manner (*mixte confusequae* [sic]) the miracles of the saints as well as the slaughterings of peoples'.
68. Meslin 1973: 260.

I

ROSES IN JANUARY
discontinuity and coherence in the *Histories**

INTRODUCTION. A LANDSLIDE, A COMET AND A PLAGUE

A great prodigy appeared in Gaul at the fortress of Tauredunum, which was situated on high ground above the River Rhône. Here a curious bellowing sound was heard for more than sixty days: then the whole hillside was split open and separated from the mountain adjoining it, and fell into the river, carrying with it men, churches, property and houses. The banks of the river were blocked and the water backed up. This place was shut in by mountains on both sides, for the stream flows there through narrow gorges. The water then flooded the higher reaches and submerged and carried away everything which was on its banks. A second time the inhabitants were taken unawares, and as the accumulated water forced its way through, it again drowned those who lived there, just as it had done higher up, destroying their houses, killing their cattle, and carrying away and overwhelming with its violent and unexpected inundation everything which stood on its banks as far as the city of Geneva. Many people said that the volume of the water was so great that it flowed right over the walls of Geneva: and this is doubtless possible, for, as I have told you, at this spot the Rhône runs through mountainous gorges and, once its course was blocked, there was nowhere for it to turn on either side. It burst through the mountain which had fallen into it and washed everything away. [...]

Before the plague which ravaged Clermont[-Ferrand], great prodigies terrified the people of that region in the same way. On a number of occasions three or four large shining lights appeared round the sun, and these the country folk also called suns. 'Look!' they shouted, 'There are three or four suns in the sky!' Once, on the first day of October, the sun was in eclipse, so that less than a quarter of it continued to shine, and the rest was so dark and discoloured that one would have said it was made of sackcloth. Then a star, with a tail like a sword, which some call a comet, appeared over the region for a whole year, and the whole sky seemed to burn, and many other signs appeared. [For instance,] in the main church of Clermont[-Ferrand], while early morning matins were being celebrated on a certain feast-day, a bird called a crested lark flew in, spread its wings over all the lamps

---

*This essay appeared as an article under the title 'Roses in January: a neglected dimension in Gregory of Tours' *Historiae*' in the *Journal of Medieval History* 5 (1979): 259-89 and is reprinted with the permission of Elsevier's Science Publishers B.V. (North-Holland), Amsterdam. I have made a number of alterations and additions.

which were shining and put them out so quickly that one would have thought that someone had seized hold of them all at once and dropped them into a pool of water. It then flew into the sacristy, under the curtain, and tried to extinguish the candle there, but the vergers managed to catch it and they killed it. In the same way another bird put out the lamps lighted in St. Andrew's church.

When the plague finally began to rage, so many people were killed throughout the whole region and the dead bodies were so numerous that it was not possible to count them...[1]

What, in fact, was Gregory of Tours talking about in this passage from his *Histories*? At first sight it seems to be exactly what modern historians have long been accusing him of: a collection of unconnected events. The first story is that of a (for us, more or less recognizable) landslide; the second appears to be an assemblage of unrelated facts. For the author, the stories are alike in that they are both, as he explicitly says, about 'great prodigies'. In the first case it is a landslide which — though it is presented as a 'great prodigy that appeared (*magnum prodigium... apparuit*)' rather than as an event that 'happened' — he is capable of describing in physical, causal terms:[2] the water rose high because it was contained by the narrow chasms. What makes it a prodigy? Perhaps its extraordinariness, its 'violent and unexpected (*violenta atque subita*)' quality. This is a prodigy that stands by itself. The phenomena observed in Clermont, on the other hand, are explicitly presented as in some way announcing the coming of the plague. They too are all extraordinary, too much light, too much darkness. The eclipsed, dark sun 'in sackcloth' suggests mourning (*sol obscuratus... teter atque decolor... quasi saccus videbatur*), but also reminds one of the opening of the sixth seal in Revelation 6:12: 'the sun became black as sackcloth'. The comet's sword-tail (*radium tamquam gladium habens*) suggests slaughter. In another work he describes this same comet as a bloody sword, spreading 'hairs' around it in the darkness, that indicated the devastation of one's country (*gladium ferens, rutilans, cum nigrore sparserit comas, patriae monstrat excidium*).[3] Except for the birds extinguishing the lamps in church, we are not told what the 'many other signs' were that 'appeared'. This terminology (*signa, apparuerunt*), as also 'sudden (*subita*)', is that which is also used for miracles.[4]

There are no causal connections between the various phenomena themselves and they in turn are not described as causing the plague. However, they appeared beforehand as a 'sign' of it. Correspondence or

1. *Hist.* 4.31: translation based on Thorpe 1974: 224-6 and Buchner 1967a: 237-9.
2. As also Friedrich 1951: 44-5.
3. *De cursu stell.* 34.
4. See Thürlemann 1974: 79-80.

congruence of form is the link between all these otherwise unconnected events. Elsewhere Gregory reveals the 'cause' of the plague: *ingruentibus peccatis populi*, which may be translated as '(because) the sins of the people had increased'.[5] This kind of reasoning leads in another direction.

Many questions at once arise. What kind of phenomena does Gregory include in the category of signs, prodigies and portents (*signa, prodigia, portenta*)?[6] What kind of human events could be 'indicated' by prodigies? Is there any discernible regular connection of specific prodigies with specific human events? If he does not label certain irregular events as prodigies nor connect them with human events, are they prodigies or not? When prodigies seem to stand alone, what can they mean? When these questions are answered, another set, this time of a more fundamental nature must be asked. By what agency do prodigies and their corresponding human events, if any, 'appear' and occur? If there is 'natural' as well as 'more-than-natural' causation, how are they related? And lastly, how does Gregory, in the case of prodigies, use and combine causative thinking — of which he is evidently capable — and what has been called 'figurative' thinking, that is, relating phenomena and events by their similar forms or 'figures'?[7] To find answers to these questions, we shall examine Gregory's prodigies and the related material in the order of their occurrence in the *Histories*.

BOOKS 1-4. THE DEVELOPMENT OF A VIEWPOINT: PRODIGIES AS INDICATIONS OF DIVINE ANGER

These books constitute the first phase of the work; Gregory later added six more. To understand the placing of the prodigies, it is necessary recall the overall periodizations. Book 1 begins with the Creation and fifteen short chapters touch upon a number of essential moments in biblical history before Christ is born. Gregory quickly shifts the center of attention to his own country and Book 1 ends with the death in 396 of his patron and hero, St Martin, bishop of Tours and apostle of Gaul. In Book 2 Gregory relates the rise to power of the Franks under the leadership of King Clovis and this book ends with the death of Clovis, his other hero, in 511. Books 3 and 4 take the history of Gaul, in ever increasing detail, up to the death of King Sigebert, who held Tours, in 575. Gregory completed these books in or soon after that year.[8] From the

5. *Virt. Jul.* 45.
6. Compare on these terms Blaise 1954: 635, 667, 759; Moule 1966: 235-8; Hofius 1971. Vetere 1979: 174-7 gives a brief description of Gregory's use of prodigies.
7. Thürlemann 1974: 98. On *figura* see Auerbach 1938; on typology: Ohly in *Simboli* 1976b: 429-73.
8. Buchner 1967a: xxi.

latter part of Book 3 onward, then, it is the history of sixth-century Gaul that is being treated. Books 5-10 give more or less contemporaneous history after 575, arranged year by year. These are the facts to be kept in mind when we consider his treatment of signs and prodigies.

Gregory, of course, was not the first to see and record signs and prodigies. Their observance was a tradition in the ancient world and in late antique Rome. There they might indicate either the anger or the favour of the gods or point to an imminent or important event,[9] and were included in historical writing. In the Bible, which it is clear influenced Gregory profoundly, extraordinary natural phenomena abound. The emphasis there, however, is on these as manifestations or messages of a personal divine power and not as impersonal presages of coming events. The latter are associated with the Chaldean tradition of divination, which is explicitly rejected.[10] In Jewish and Christian apocalyptic literature, however, Hellenistic influence had led to an ambiguity in the meaning of divine 'signs': instead of only *accompanying* the events in the times just before the end of the world, they could also indicate merely their imminence. As will be seen below, there is some evidence in the Gospels too of the Hellenistic tradition of signs and prodigies as an indication of the favour of the gods toward a great man.[11]

Of the historians Gregory says he has read — they are exclusively Christian ones[12] — Eusebius and Jerome mention a few prodigies, Sulpicius Severus does not mention any, and Orosius, since it is his purpose to stress the misery of the pre-Christian era, mentions a fair number, most of which however occurred in pagan times.[13] Gregory, though he does not say so, may also have looked at two Christian chronicles (i.e. short notices of events listed by year) written in Gaul in the fifth century. Whereas Prosper Tiro's *Short Chronicle* speaks of 'signs of the demons (*daemonum significationes*)' when he means omens acquired through divination and does not mention any prodigies, the anonymous *Gallic Chronicle* mentions several, mostly in the sky: pillars (of light, presumably), eclipses, and unspecified *signa*; none of which are

---

9. Bloch 1963: 229. A general description of portents and prodigies in Wallis 1918; for pagan antiquity: Bloch 1963; pagan, Jewish and early Christian traditions in: Berger 1980; on divination in ancient cultures: Caquot 1968; in the Middle Ages: Harmening 1979: 76-216. See also Meslin 1974.
10. Moule 1966: 235-8; Hofius 1971: 1447-52.
11. Berger 1980 in Haase 1980: 1438, 1447-51.
12. *Hist.* 1. *praef.*; 2. *praef.* In *Vit. patr.* 2. *prol.* Gregory explicitly says that his education did not include the reading of pagan authors.
13. *Hist. adv. pag.* 1. *prol.* 1.

explicitly brought into relation with any events.[14] In his *Divine Institutes*, the Church Father Lactantius (c. 260-c. 325) lists a number of extraordinary phenomena and 'prodigies', however, which almost exactly coincide with the ones Gregory tends to observe and record. On earth, he mentions the destruction of states by armies or by fire, earthquakes, floods, unnavigable seas, illness, famine, pestilence, drought, unseasonable cold or heat, trees and grapevines that flower but do not yield fruit, springs drying up, water turning into blood or becoming undrinkable. In the sky, Lactantius describes 'prodigies' such as 'hairy comets', eclipses, coloured moons, falling stars, new stars, and finally the sound of a trumpet. Only the latter Gregory does not record as actually having been heard. Lactantius' context is apocalyptic, and the phenomena are clearly culled from the Gospels and the Book of Revelation as well as from the Sibylline writings, which he mentions as his source. He sees all these things as happening in his time and as indicating that the end of the world is near. It is impossible to say whether Gregory ever saw Lactantius' passage. He also makes no allusion to the *Chronicle* (covering the years 455-581) of his older contemporary Marius, bishop of Avenches. The latter mentions a lunar eclipse in 560 (which is omitted by Gregory) and the landslide of Tauredunum in 563, both without apposite events, as well as 'a sign in the sky for 70 days' and a severe winter (both omitted by Gregory) in the year that Emperor Justinian died (566).[16] Marius does not explicitly connect these events with each other, however.

Orosius, who wrote around 419, is closest to Gregory in time and approach. They share the view of the world as a stage for the battle of good against evil,[17] and there are similarities too between their view of prodigies. Gregory, however, though he used what he found, probably developed his own view of prodigies, as will be seen below.

The first extraordinary natural event (the word sign or prodigy is not used) mentioned in the *Histories* is the solar eclipse after Jesus' death (*his igitur actis, tenebrae super universum mundum factae sunt*).[18] It effected many conversions, probably through its interpretation as a confirmation of his divinity. Gregory does not say this; he expects it to be understood.

14. Prosper, *Epit. Chron.* a. 1335 (a. 440) in Mommsen 1892: 476; *Chron. Gal.* in Mommsen 1892: 648, 652, 656, 662.
15. Lactantius, *Div. inst.* 7.16.6-11. The relevant passages in the Bible and in the Sibylline literature are cited in Berger 1980: 1455-9 and passim.
16. Marius Avent., *Chron.* a. 560.1; 563; 566.1-3 respectively.
17. Oldoni 1972: 689.
18. *Hist.* 1.20. Compare Orosius, *Hist. adv. pag.* 7.4.13-4. The Gospels however (for instance Matth. 27:45) place the eclipse before Jesus' actual death. See Berger 1980: 1445 on this prodigy as a Hellenistic tradition.

The second extraordinary natural event is another earthquake after the Arian Vandal King Huneric's persecution of Catholic Christian martyrs. Gregory connects the eclipse with these crimes and the shedding of innocent blood: *Tunc et sol teter apparuit ...; credo pro tantis sceleribus et effusione sanguinis innocentes* [sic].[19] *Pro* can mean 'as retribution for' as well as 'in conformity with': the eclipse then is a suitable requital for such deeds.

An epidemic (*lues*) and an earthquake (*terra tremuit*)[20] in the time of the Roman general Aegidius (mid-fifth century) are mentioned along with other miscellaneous facts which are not discernibly brought into relation with these phenomena or with each other. In the very next chapter the death of the Arian Visigothic King Euric, who had held southern Gaul including Clermont and had also persecuted Catholic Christians there, is recorded.[21] Gregory adds that then, too, (*etiam et tunc*) there was a great earthquake. It is not clear whether this occurred before or afterwards, but the direct juxtaposition of the two events does seem to indicate that Gregory saw or suspected a significant connection.

Later, the people of the city of Vienne were terrified by many prodigies (*multis terreretur prodigiis*): frequent earthquakes and deer and savage wolves roaming about fearlessly inside the city walls.[22] An earthquake is certainly violent and unexpected; while the presence of wild animals in the city is an anomaly, and potentially dangerous as well. The frightened reaction of the people — the only time a reaction is mentioned in the first four books, except for that of the many conversions through the solar eclipse after Christ's crucifixion — reveals how such phenomena were regarded in this time, and thus the tradition upon which Gregory drew. Avitus of Vienne's *Homily on the Rogations* may be the source for this story.[23] When these prodigies had lasted for a whole year and Easter was approaching 'the people devoutly hoped for divine mercy' so that these great solemn feast-days would mean the end of the terrors (*huic terrori terminum darent*). The fact that God's mercy is implored probably means that He is thought to have sent the prodigies as a kind of chastisement and to be able to stop them when He wishes. Avitus' references to Sodom

---

19. *Hist.* 2.3.
20. *Hist.* 2.18, 19.
21. *Hist.* 2.20.
22. *Hist.* 2.34. Similarly: *Hist. adv. pag.* 4.4.2.
23. Peiper 1883: 108-12. The events are also described, however, in a letter of Sidonius Apollinaris (*Ep.* 7.1) and in Caesarius of Arles' *Homily* 33 cited in Peiper 1833: 108.

and Nineveh (which Gregory does not mention, however) also indicate this.

But while the citizens of Vienne were gathered in the church to celebrate mass the night before Easter, there was a 'sudden (*subito*)' conflagration of the royal palace within the city walls by 'divine fire (*divinis ignis*)' (a description which also reflects the Roman view of lightning, incidentally).[24] Everyone ran out of the church in fright: only Bishop Mamertus remained at the altar and 'with lamentations and tears pleaded for divine mercy'. His prayer was granted and the fire extinguished. Mamertus thereafter instituted fasts, prayers and almsgiving annually during the period between Easter and Ascension. The terrors having thereupon (*exinde*) ceased, the whole province followed the example of 'what the bishop had done out of faith'. In ancient Rome the gods had been held responsible for exactly the same phenomena as Gregory records both here and later, and appeasement by rituals as well as the search for a significance had been customary there.[25] Evidently, prodigies had already been placed or fitted into a Christian context before Gregory's time. Here earthquakes are definitely labelled as prodigies and regarded as divinely wrought punishments. In a later work Gregory records an earthquake during St Gallus' episcopate in Clermont (525-55) and adds that he does not know *why it happened* (*sed cur hoc acciderit ignoramus*).[26] Gallus was a holy bishop; Gregory probably means that he cannot find any reason for a punishment of the city in this time.

After King Theudebert died, there was a more than usually severe winter (*solito asperiorem*).[27] It is difficult to say whether Gregory intended the sequence and near-juxtaposition (there is only one other story in between) of the events to speak for themselves or not. Theudebert seems to have been a reasonably good king for his time, and there is no indication that his death was untimely.

His son King Theudebald, reported to be of disreputable character, did die young however.[28] During his reign — it lasted not quite seven years — Gregory saw some strange things: grapes growing on an elder tree without any grafting having taken place (he had obviously been alert and observant enough to check the possibility of a 'natural' explanation), and

---

24. Compare Pliny, *Nat. hist.* 2.18. *Hist. adv. pag.* 4.4.3 refers to a similar situation, but without the term 'divine'.
25. Bloch 1963: 120-9.
26. *Vit. patr.* 6.6.
27. *Hist.* 3.36, 37; *Hist. adv. pag.* 3.4.2 is similar.
28. *Hist.* 4.9.

a star moving into the crescent of a five-nights-old moon. He says he believes that these signs heralded the king's death (*Credo haec signa mortem ipsius regis adnuntiasse*). Here are a number of new elements. It is the first time that Gregory records extraordinary natural phenomena which he saw himself. He calls them 'signs'. The fact that he has come to this view only after convincing himself that there was no 'natural' explanation he could discover indicates that he had clear ideas of how natural phenomena could and did behave, but was also prepared to admit that divine action could defy these processes and produce something different. He is consciously interpreting when he says he now believes (*credo*) that these signs were announcing the king's death. This is the first time this pattern of thought appears in the *Histories*.

The next prodigies he mentions are those in 563 which we considered at the beginning of this essay: the collapse of Tauredunum and the events preceding the plague at Clermont. The latter constitute the first instance of prodigies and an epidemic in unmistakable association.

After having related the death of King Chilperic's son Theudebert in a battle with the dukes of the latter's uncle King Sigebert, and before going on to tell the story of Sigebert's subsequent murder in 575, Gregory says, 'In that year a bright light was observed to move about across the sky, just like the one we saw before Chlotar's death (*In eo anno fulgor per caelum discurrisse visus est, sicut quondam ante mortem Chlotari vidimus*)',[29] (though he had in fact not mentioned it in reporting Chlotar's death).[30] This *fulgor* (the Latin word means 'lightning', 'bright light', or 'brilliance') he later described in his treatise *On the course of the stars*, written between 575 and 582 as a comet (*cometes*):[31] 'when a hairy head appears shining with a diadem, it announces a royal death; ...for also before King Sigebert died, it appeared with many hairs (*cum capud crinitum diademate apparuerit fulgorans, regalem adnuntiat letum; ...nam et priusquam Sigiberthus rex obiit, crinita multis apparuit*)'. For Gregory, the 'hair' on the comet's 'head' evidently corresponds to the Merovingian king's traditional long hair. This is the same passage in which, as we saw above, he said that a comet like a bloody sword indicated mass slaughter. Gregory, by then, expected to be able to recognize in a comet the shape of certain future events: this is how it should be 'understood (*qualiter ergo intellegatur, haec est ratio*)'. About the times of its appearance he says: 'it

---

29. *Hist.* 4.50.
30. *Hist.* 4.21.
31. *De cursu stell.* 34. On the date of composition, see Krusch 1885: 855. The first extensive description of a comet is, however, in *Hist.* 6.14 (Krusch's 6.11 must be a typographical error).

appears not always but most often upon the occasion of a king's death or at the time of a regional disaster (*non omni tempore, sed maxime aut in obitu regis aut in excidio apparet regionis*)'. This probably means that when a king dies or there is a severe epidemic a comet usually, but not always, appears. Does *non omni tempore sed maxime* also imply that it can appear unaccompanied by other prodigies or for other reasons? However that may be, it is a credit to Gregory's faith and intellectual honesty that he does not force the facts in order to make his system perfect.

Why had Gregory not mentioned the comet he saw before King Chlotar's death in his description of this event? My conjecture is that, at the time that he was writing about Chlotar's comet, he had not yet seen Sigebert's (in 575), which evidently made him realize that their conjunction in time with both kings' decease, as well as their form, might not be fortuitous. Many royal deaths had occurred, of course, without any signs or prodigies being mentioned then or later: that of Clovis, of course, and those of Childebert and Charibert,[32] to mention only the Merovingians. Were there perhaps special circumstances that made the deaths of Chlotar and Sigebert 'attract' (if one may use that term) a comet? Both in fact had been generally regarded by Gregory as righteous kings, they had both also, not long before their respective deaths, perpetrated or intended to perpetrate a hideous crime. Chlotar had caused his rebellious son Chramn, together with the latter's wife and children whom he had stayed behind to save, to be strangled and burned in a poor man's hut. Within a year he was struck by a fever while hunting, and he died exactly a year after Chramn had been killed, on the same day.[33] Gregory seems to be saying that the murder and burning of his son is requited upon the father, burned to death by a fever, in a significant time-relation: exactly a year later. Here again there is a correspondence of form (burning) with one of time. These two together, as in the case of prodigies preceding the plague or an untimely royal death, indicate for Gregory divine action or punishment.

The assassination of Sigebert at the moment that he seemed to be at the height of his power exhibits a similar pattern.[34] He had taken over large parts of his brother Chilperic's share of the kingdom and was about to besiege Chilperic in Tournai in order to depose him when the saintly (*sanctus*) Bishop Germanus warned him not to try to kill his brother lest the same fate should befall himself: 'He who digs a pit for his brother

---

32. *Hist.* 2.43, 4.20 and 4.26.
33. *Hist.* 4.20, 21.
34. *Hist.* 4. 51.

shall fall therein'.³⁵ But Sigebert, in his sinfulness (*peccatis facientibus*) did not listen. He had just proceeded to let himself be raised on the shield as king of his brother's kingdom when two servants, bewitched (*malificati*) by Queen Fredegunde (Chilperic's wife), approached him pretending to have something to say to him. But they carried large knives, popularly called *scramasaxi*, dipped into poison, with which, once close enough, they struck him down. Only eighteen days, Gregory tells us a little later on, lay between Sigebert's death and that of Chilperic's nephew Theudebert (at the hands of Sigebert's dukes), suggesting that the former was also the retribution for the latter. Again sin has 'attracted' a punishment that is somehow analogical, and closeness in time is essential for the recognition of this pattern, one which I find to be amongst the most basic in the *Histories*.

It looks as though Gregory has come to see extraordinary natural phenomena as participating in this general dynamic pattern. Sudden, unexpected, irregular, incomprehensible and therefore frightening natural phenomena are likely to be signs or prodigies, indications of divine power and anger. It is possible to stop them, perhaps, by cleansing oneself of the sins that brought on the first dislocation of things — sin being, of course, itself a discord in the harmony of the Creation. Signs and prodigies that are not in themselves directly harmful tend to indicate that some major disaster is being prepared or impending; maybe it is even in some way already invisibly present and manifesting its pattern in animate and inanimate nature. Perhaps it is for this reason that extraordinary events which occur more or less closely together in time tend to resemble each other.

BOOKS 5 AND 6. 'FIGURES' AND EVENTS: ANNOUNCEMENTS OF RAVAGES AND THE DEATHS OF KINGS

Book 5 begins with a preface that is sadder than the previous ones to Books 1, 2 and 3. Because of its lamentations about frequent civil wars it has been dated before 584, when the death of Chilperic ended at least the open battles.³⁶ The events covered in this book are those between 575 and 584. (Since there is an indication that there was some kind of pause in Gregory's writing before he went on to Books 7-10 the last four books will be considered separately.)

Viewed as a whole, there are in Books 5 and 6 ten clearly separate lists of more or less simultaneous signs or prodigies (I omit consideration of natural phenomena mentioned within stories); and of these, six are more

---

35. Prov. 26:27.
36. Buchner 1967a xxi.

or less associated with disease (*lues*), one with devastation (*vastatio*), two or three with royal deaths, one or two possibly with both, while only of one cluster are we told that the significance was unknown.

Let us examine first the association with disease. In 577, on the day of the Lord's resurrection, the church in Chinon trembled so violently that everyone was terrified (*conterritus a pavore*) and fled;[37] subsequently the population was decimated by a terrible epidemic (*magna post haec lues populum devastavit*). In 580 there were great rains and floods, causing injury to men, beasts and houses; after these, in September, the trees blossomed anew.[38] Also, a bright light (*fulgor*) was seen moving across the sky at Tours before daybreak, accompanied by a sound like that of falling trees: 'but it can hardly have been a tree, for it was audible over fifty miles and more'. There were serious earthquakes in southwestern Gaul and the Pyrenees, where large boulders killed men and cattle. A divinely caused (*divinitus ortum*) fire burned down villages near Bordeaux: houses and threshing floors suddenly (*subito*) began to burn without having been ignited by any other fire, 'perhaps by divine command (*fortisan iussione divina*)'. In the case of the thunder and in that of what seems to us to be spontaneous combustion Gregory considers the suddenness and the absence of visible 'natural' causes to indicate that an event is a prodigy (the chapter carries this title) and is divinely caused. In Orléans too there was a great fire, in Bourges hailstorms[39] did a great deal of damage, and in Chartres real blood dripped from broken bread (*verus de effracto pane sangues effluxit*). As the latter phenomenon had also occurred in pagan times,[40] it need not be connected with the Eucharist. The following chapter begins: 'A most serious epidemic followed these prodigies (*Sed haec prodigia gravissima lues est subsecuta*)'. While the kings were quarrelling with each other and once more preparing for civil war, dysentery spread through almost all of Gaul. The juxtaposition of the civil war and disease may not be unintentional: Gregory may well see the disease as a punishment for the royal deeds (as Orosius for a Christian persecution). Chilperic's two young sons died of this disease, and Gregory lets Fredegunde cry out that 'the tears of paupers and the sighs of orphans are killing them'. Thereupon repenting of his excessive taxation of these people, her husband Chilperic burned the tax books; but this did not save his sons.[41]

37. *Hist.* 5.17.
38. *Hist.* 5.33.
39. Compare Rev. 8:7; 11:19.
40. *Hist. adv. pag.* 5.18.4.
41. *Hist. adv. pag.* 7.22.2, *Hist.* 5.34, respectively.

Their deaths also had been 'announced' by a sign or vision which confirms their being a divine punishment.[42] While Gregory and Bishop Salvius were standing together and looking at a new roof on Chilperic's residence in Berny-Riviere, Salvius asked him whether he saw something else there as well. Gregory, thinking he was jesting, said he saw nothing else there, but if Salvius did, he should tell him about it. Salvius sighed and said: 'I see the naked sword of the wrath of God hanging over that house (*Video ego evaginatum irae divinae gladio super domum hanc dependentem*) ...' Gregory continues, 'And indeed his prophecy was not a false one, for twenty days later the two sons of King Chilperic died, as I have already told you'. Just as in its appearance before the plague in Clermont, here too the sword is a recognizable indication of what is about to happen, divinely. Nonetheless, Gregory gives us a rather detailed description of the symptoms of the disease in general and reports that many people were cured by leeches and by antidotes consisting of herb potions: it had been rumoured that the disease was caused by 'a hidden poison'. The practical, almost scientific, interest which Gregory exhibits for this and other diseases (especially evident in his record of miraculous cures in the miracle books) seems to contradict his invariably regarding them simultaneously, as divine punishments for sin. Here, as well as in his detailed descriptions of celestial prodigies, Gregory shows that he was interested in the visible world and expected to learn something from observation and analysis. At the same time, however, he was deeply convinced of the reality and power of transcendent, non-physical causation, *which he recognized by its form*. Natural and supernatural causes run parallel, overlap. I strongly suspect that Gregory's seemingly muddled language conceals thinking that is more powerful, clear and sophisticated — on its own grounds — than he has generally been given credit for.

Prodigies followed by disease (*lues*) appeared in Poitiers after the Galician king's envoys to King Guntram were intercepted in that city by Chilperic's men and brought to him.[43] The juxtaposition of these events suggests that Gregory may have seen or suspected a connection between them. The following phenomena are listed: a wolf within the city gates, a fiery sky (*caelum ardentem*),[44] high water in the Loire, an extremely violent (*nimium violente*) storm or cyclone, a darkened (*cumtenebricata*) moon, a comet (*comitis stilla*) not further qualified, and cocks often crowing at dusk instead of at dawn.

42. *Hist.* 5.50.
43. *Hist.* 5.41.
44. As in *Hist. adv. pag.* 4.13.12.

In 582 there were 'portents (*portenta*)'.⁴⁵ This is the only time Gregory uses the term; the content, however, is the same as that indicated by 'signs' and 'prodigies'. In January there were heavy rains, lightning and thunder (*coruscationes atque tonitrua*) and blossoming trees. Also 'the star which I earlier called a comet appeared' with many 'hairs (*comae*)' and 'a long tail that, from a distance, looked like a great pall of smoke over a conflagration'.

Gregory had mentioned a *comitis stilla* in 581,⁴⁶ and it must be to this that he is referring here. The name 'comet' seems to be a relatively recent acquisition for him and he does not expect his readers to recognize it at once. In his *On the course of the stars*, which he probably wrote during this same period, he says: 'This star many have called a "comet" '.⁴⁷ He seems to have found time, then, to do some reading on the subject, and this is the first detailed description of a comet in the *Histories*. The ones before Chlotar's and Sigebert's death Gregory had described only as 'a bright light traversing the sky (*fulgor per caelum discurrisse*).'⁴⁸ If he had had, at the time he wrote this, a fully developed idea of comets, he would surely not have used this inexact description. The detailed story of the sword-like comet above Clermont⁴⁹ must then, if this hypothesis is correct, have been inserted later. Gregory does not say clearly he sees a 'sword' in later comets,⁵⁰ though they are in fact followed by disease (*lues*).

But the list of 'portents' in 592 is not yet complete. On Easter day at Soissons two 'fires (*incendia*)', one larger than the other, burned in the sky; after two hours they merged and disappeared. In Paris 'real blood rained from a cloud and spotted many people's clothes (*verus sanguis ex nube defluxit et super vestimenta multorum hominum caecidit*)'.⁵¹ At Senlis someone woke up one morning to find the whole of the inside of his house spattered with blood. 'This year the people suffered from a terrible epidemic (*Magna tamen eo anno lues in populo fuit*)', Gregory continues. 'Various malignant diseases, boils, tumours and rashes carried off a great number of people. However, many people managed to escape [death or disease] by taking precautions'. Cures, evidently, are possible; and we know from Gregory's other works that these were also sometimes

45. *Hist.* 6.14.
46. *Hist.* 5.41.
47. *De cursu stell.* 34.
48. *Hist.* 4.51.
49. *Hist.* 4.31.
50. *Hist.* 5.41; 6.14.
51. Compare Rev. 8:7.

obtained miraculously at saints' shrines.[52] Again, though divinely sent, the diseases were seen by Gregory as phenomena that could be observed, evaded, and possibly cured by concrete practical measures (or by divine aid).

In the same year, signs appeared again (*Haec in hoc anno iteratis signa apparuerunt*),[53] which Gregory simply mentions without comment, however. They were: a lunar eclipse, blood dripping from broken bread, the collapse of the city walls of Soissons, an earthquake in Angers, wolves devouring dogs inside Bordeaux, the devastation by fire of the city of Bazas, and a fiery light seen moving across the sky (*per caelum ignis discurrere visus est*; in view of the above, perhaps lightning and probably not a comet). He may have considered the time of their occurrence to indicate that they were connected with the previous cluster and with the diseases mentioned there.

Another collection of extraordinary phenomena together with disease entitled 'Of locusts, diseases and prodigies'[54] is mentioned for 584. The locusts are in Spain, the *lues* in Narbonne, where it had returned after three years' absence, and particularly in Albi, though also in many other places (*per loca*). The prodigies mentioned in the title can only refer to the northern lights, which Gregory seems to have seen himself: 'In these days there appeared at midnight in the northern sky many rays which shone with extreme brilliance, coming together and separating again, until they vanished. At the same time the sky towards the north was so bright that one would have believed that day was about to dawn'. The juxtaposition of the locusts, disease and prodigies suggests that Gregory assumed or suspected a connection between them.

In the very next chapter Gregory reports the death, from dysentery, of Chilperic and Fredegunde's son, Theuderic, at the age of two. He adds, 'For this is what the light "figured" which I described above as falling out of a cloud (*Hoc enim fulgor ille, quod superius ex nube dilapsum memoravimus, figuravit*)'.[55] Does this refer to the many moving rays and the quasi-dawn we have just read about? If there was no other possibility, one would be forced to conclude that, even though the descriptions do not seem to correspond, Gregory means the prodigies he has just mentioned. There is another 'sign', however, which comes closer to fitting the description as 'light ... falling out of a cloud', but it takes place at some time in the previous year.[56] Early one Sunday morning at Tours,

52. *Virt. Mart.* 1.37; 2.1, 12, 51; 3.43, 52; 4.9, 47; *Glor. conf.* 24.
53. *Hist.* 6.21.
54. *Hist.* 6.33. Compare *Hist. adv. pag.* 5.11.
55. *Hist.* 6.34.
56. *Hist.* 6.25.

when everyone had come to the church of St Martin for matins, 'while the sky was overcast and it was raining, a large sphere of fire fell from the sky (*globus magnus ignis de caelo dilapsus*) and moved some considerable distance through the air, shining so brightly that everything could be seen as clearly as at high noon. Then it disappeared behind a cloud and darkness fell again'.[57] Gregory adds that there was unusually (*extra solitu*) high water, especially in the Seine and Marne. No other event is there associated with these 'signs', nor does Gregory make any comment upon them. We know from another story, however, that a sphere of fire was sometimes seen when St Martin was 'present'.[58] The dead saint Pelagia had been placed in a church prior to her funeral; at night a large sphere of fire appeared (*globus ignis magnus apparuit*) which came to stand above the church where she lay. It filled the whole church with a 'sudden brightness (*subitus splendor*)' so that it seemed like the middle of the day. And at once (*statim*) many persons who were possessed by spirits (*energumeni* — Gregory often attributes a special divinatory ability to them) cried out saying that St Martin had come to Pelagia's funeral. Although there are certain correspondences between this phenomenon and the one seen before matins, the context is surely not the same: had it been so, Gregory would have said as much and not mentioned the high water directly afterwards. The sphere of fire at Pelagia's funeral is designated as a light phenomenon accompanying the presence of a heavenly being, while the one at matins is presented as one of several 'signs' probably indicating the imminence of some other event or situation. This other event must have been the young prince's death. The similarity of the expressions *ex nube dilapsum* (for Theuderic) and *caelo nubilo... de caelo dilapsus* (before matins) is too striking to be dismissed. How literally did Gregory intend the term 'figured (*figuravit*)' to be taken? He uses it only twice in the *Histories* in the sense of to figure, to represent figurally or symbolically, both times with regard to prodigies.[59] Elsewhere he uses the verb 'show (*ostendere*)'.[60] Is it possible that he saw the child's short life in the 'figure' of a sphere of fire coming out of a cloud, making everything bright as day, and disappearing again into the cloud, after which night resumed? Fredegunde, as Gregory reports in a well-known passage, was wild with grief; she burned all the child's clothes and had his gold and silver treasures melted 'so that nothing would remain intact to remind her of her mourning for her boy'.[61]

57. A sphere of fire preceded the death of Drusus in *Hist. adv. pag.* 5.18.3.
58. *Glor. conf.* 102; see also *Vit. patr.* 12.3.
59. *Hist.* 5.23; 6.34. Compare Blaise 1954: 352.
60. *De cursu stell.* 10, 11, 12.
61. *Hist.* 6.35.

In another case the correspondence of forms in the sky with those of human events is unmistakable and presented as such by Gregory.[62] These phenomena appeared before the violent death of Chilperic's rebellious son Merovech, who had married his uncle's widow, Queen Brunhilde, and had designs on the throne. The year is 577 and Gregory is at Paris together with other bishops for a meeting with Chilperic at which Merovech's treason is a central issue;

> there, signs appeared (*signa... apparuerunt*) in the sky: twenty rays (*radii*) came into view in the north and moved rapidly from east to west. One of them was longer than the others and shone high above them; and when it had risen up to a very great height it disappeared, and the others which had followed it disappeared likewise. In my opinion, they announced Merovech's destruction (*Credo, interitum Merovechi pronuntiassent*).

In fact, Merovech was killed soon afterward and his supporters were apprehended and despatched later.

Later on in the same year, a slightly older son of Chilperic's, Samson, died of dysentery. His mother also fell ill, but recovered. Immediately after these statements, Gregory begins a new chapter, entitled 'About the prodigies that were shown (*De prodigiis ostensis*)',[63] with the statement that after this (*post haec*) he saw (*apparuit nobis*) a star shining in the middle of the moon with stars appearing all around it. 'Also that circle which usually indicates rain appeared around it. But what these may have (pre)figured I do not know (*sed et circulus ille, qui pluviam plerumque significat, circa eam apparuit. Sed quae haec figuraverint, ignoramus*)'. Gregory had earlier interpreted (*credo*) a star moving into the moon as announcing Theudebald's death:[64] why did he not associate this moon and stars with Samson's death? The appearance of the ring around the moon that 'usually indicates (*significat*) rain' — a strictly meteorological and practical observation — is now presented as ambiguous: 'but what all these may have (pre)figured I do not know'. Did the fact that these signs appeared *after* Samson's death preclude their association with it, or was Gregory unable to discover a meaningful correspondence between the form in the sky and that of the small prince's death or another suitable event?

Was it forms or patterns in the sky which he especially expected to resemble earthly events? In the cases of Merovech and Theuderic phenomena in the sky had indeed indicated their impending decease; Salvius' one-man vision of the sword in the sky before the death of

---

62. *Hist.* 5.18.
63. *Hist.* 5.23.
64. *Hist.* 4.9.

Chilperic's sons[65] should, I think, be taken as a special case, almost certainly more a vision than a meteorological phenomenon interpreted symbolically. This leads on to another question. What does Gregory mean by his use of the verbs 'appear (*apparere*)' and 'be shown (*ostensus esse*)' in connection with extraordinary natural events or prodigies? Are they somehow less concretely real than other phenomena, only 'apparitions' like Salvius' vision? There is no indication of this. Roman prodigies and portents too had been 'shown', and in the Bible concrete historical events (such as Christ's life on earth) could reveal, or be 'appearances' of, God's power and purposes.[66] What 'appears' or 'is shown' is therefore probably not the sensory phenomenon as such but its symbolic content as an epiphany or as a divine message about human history. It looks, however, as though the latter is for Gregory so closely bound up with its sensory appearance that these constitute an indivisible whole.

After confessing his ignorance, Gregory goes on to mention other prodigies which are the same as those which will later announce disease: a lunar eclipse (before *lues*) and thunder (also before *lues*).[67] 'Also the bright spots (*splendores*) around the sun appeared which the country folk call "suns", like the ones we mentioned as having appeared before the plague in Clermont. It was said that the sea rose higher than usual and many other signs appeared (*multa alia signa apparuerunt*)': if Gregory is worried about not knowing what they 'mean', he does not say so.

In the same year as the northern lights, locusts and *lues* (584), there is another cluster of diverse signs (*diversa signa*) which Gregory here explicitly connects with ravages among the people (*Hoc anno multa prodigia apparuerunt in Galliis, vastationesque multae fuerunt in populo*).[68] Roses were seen in January, and a large ring of various colours appeared around the sun,[69] 'rather like that in a rainbow when it is raining (*ut solet in illo caelestis iris ambitu, pluvia discendente, monstrari*)'. Frost, storms and drought destroyed vines and crops, and cattle plague decimated the animals. Clearly, the latter are the 'devastations' or ravages.

'Meanwhile (*Interim*)[70] King Chilperic was rounding up a great army to accompany his daughter Rigunth and her treasures to Spain for her wedding. He had many men forcibly recruited from the royal estates.

---

65. *Hist.* 5.50.
66. Bloch 1963: 84-5; Mundle 1971: 316; Gärtner 1971: 317-20.
67. *Hist.* 5.41 and 5.33-4, respectively.
68. *Hist.* 6.44.
69. Compare *Hist. adv. pag.* 6.20.5.
70. *Hist.* 6.45.

Many were reported to have committed suicide rather than be separated from their families; others 'left with deep sighs and curses (*cum gravi gemitu ac maledictionibus discedebant)*'. When Rigunth finally departed, with her fifty carts of gifts and treasures (much of it made up, perhaps, of forced 'gifts' from Chilperic's entourage), an axle broke on one of them and everyone shouted 'Unlucky moment! (*Mala hora!*)'; 'for some took it to be an omen (*pro auspicio*)', Gregory says cautiously but not disapprovingly.

At this point we must digress for a moment. This is one of the three times in the *Histories* that Gregory uses the term *auspicium*, which is the pagan 'omen'. In this instance he seems to agree, but takes care to report it as others' opinion. Elsewhere he describes the looking for omens as a barbarian custom (*consuetudo ... barbarorum*).[71] Clovis too, before his decisive battle with the Goths, had sent messengers to the church of St Martin, saying 'Go and perhaps you will receive some omen of victory in that holy temple (*Ite et forsitan aliquod victuriae auspicium ad aedae sancta suscipitis*)'.[72] According to this story, the king was at that moment a recently baptized barbarian and St Martin indulged him. Just as his messengers entered the church they heard the words of Psalm 18:39-40 being sung: 'Thou didst make my enemies turn their backs to me, and those who hated me I destroyed'. In fact, Gregory reports, Clovis did indeed win at Vouillé because 'the Goths, as is their custom, turned their backs (*terga vertissent*, i.e. fled)'. Gregory evidently disapproves of the barbarian custom of seeking omens. He accepts, however, specific pieces of Bible text, read or sung at a crucial moment, as possible indications from God about the future (this also occurs, without the term *auspicium* being used, in a few other cases).[73]

To return to Rigunth's broken cart, it too did not lie. Gregory's mention of the curses of the departing turns out to be deliberate. On the first night, fifty men disappeared with a hundred of the best horses and as many golden reins, and throughout the journey anyone who could fled with as much as he could carry. The army was supposed to live off the land on its way, and so it did: 'they robbed and plundered to an extent that defies description'. Wherever they had passed, absolutely nothing was left, and so was fulfilled (*impletum est*), says Gregory, what the Lord had said through Joel: 'What the locust has left, the cankerworm has eaten; what the cankerworm has left, the caterpillar has eaten; what the

---

71. *Hist.* 7.29.
72. *Hist.* 2.37.
73. *Hist.* 4.6; 5.14; 5.49.

caterpillar has left, the blight has eaten'.[74] 'Such things happened indeed in this time': what the frost had left, the storm destroyed; what the storm had left, the army carried off. This is truly 'devastation'.

The context of Joel's words is the imminence of the 'day of the Lord', when judgment will take place and Jerusalem will be restored,[75] but which is preceded by chastisements such as the ones mentioned. Thereafter the Lord will restore all that has been destroyed and will pour out his spirit on all flesh. The Lord is speaking:

> And I will give portents in the heavens and on the earth, blood and fire and columns of smoke. The sun shall be turned to darkness and the moon to blood, before the great and terrible day of the Lord comes (*Et dabo prodigia in coelo et signa in terra, sanguinem et vaporem fumi. Sol convertetur in tenebras et luna in sanguinem antequam veniat dies Domini magnus et horribilis*).[76]

In Acts 2:19 this passage is reinterpreted to indicate Jesus' Second Coming. Does Gregory now place the recent prodigies of blood and smoke and the situation in his time — *hoc tempore* may mean 'the present' — in this context?[77]

Directly after he has compared the situation to that predicted by Joel, Gregory begins a new chapter: 'While the army proceeded with their plunder, Chilperic, the Nero and Herod of our time went off to his manor at Chelles and spent his time hunting'.[78] Sulpicius Severus wrote in his *Chronicle* (which Gregory elsewhere mentions) about Nero[79] that he was the worst of men and beasts and that many believed he was the precursor of the Antichrist. Could this passage have been on Gregory's mind? However that may be, Chilperic, as Gregory continues the story, when he returned from the chase in the dark of night, was stabbed and killed while alighting from his horse.

The signs Gregory has been seeing can now be interpreted in four ways: as connected with the ravages or 'devastations', as connected with Chilperic's approaching death, as connected with both, or as indications given by God, together with the 'devastations', that the end of the world is near. The latter would be a new element, if it were there. The pattern in these books up to this point has been to connect — in the late antique pagan manner — prodigies with epidemics or royal deaths if possible, and to see them as indications of momentary divine anger. Gregory had tried to see 'figures' of the announced events in the signs in the sky, but

---

74. Joel 1:4.
75. Joel 3:1-2.
76. Joel 2:30-1.
77. *Hist.* 6.14.
78. *Hist.* 6.46.
79. *Hist.* 1.7 and 2. *praef.*; Severus, *Chron.* 2.28.1.

had not always succeeded. There are signs he cannot explain; and there are calamities that 'defy description'. Is he considering an alternative explanation?

BOOKS 7-10. UNCERTAINTY AND FALSE PROPHETS: SIGNS OF THE APPROACHING END OF THE WORLD

With Chilperic removed from the scene, only King Guntram remained of the quarrelling grandsons of Clovis. Sigebert's son Childebert was about fourteen years old and dominated by his astute Visigothic mother Brunhilde, who could not always keep the restive Austrasian aristocracy in check however. Chilperic had left Fredegunde behind with a baby son, the later Chlotar II. All this meant that the period of civil wars, which Gregory had so deplored, had finally come to an end and that the situation in the Frankish kingdom had, in that respect, decidedly improved. Unfortunately, however, the aristocracy tried to use the situation to its own advantage and there was more disorder than ever. They apparently even invited the self-styled son of Chlotar I, Gundowald, back from Constantinople to make an (unsuccessful) attempt on the throne now that as a result of all the battles and murders within the family, there were almost no Merovingians left. In addition, immediately after Chilperic's death, a long series of attempted assassinations of members of the royal house — which Gregory often explicitly attributes to the machinations of the maleficent Fredegunde[80] — began. Book 7 begins, I think purposely, with a short sketch of the life of Bishop Salvius, whom Gregory knew personally and who died 'in this year' (584 or 585): 'Although I wish to continue the history (*historiam prosequi*) from where I left it at the end of the previous books, my reverence for him compels me to write something first about the blessed Salvius'.[81] It may be that the opening sentence refers not (only) to a pause in Gregory's writing but indeed also to a temporary change of subject, as it says. After the incessant misery in the last chapters of the previous book, this story — told in an entirely different spirit — is more than refreshing. Salvius had been 'in heaven' for four days and thereafter returned to serve in the world: his message was, 'Know that all you see in this world (*mundus*) is without value; as Solomon said, "All is vanity (*Omnia vanitas*)"'.[82] Gregory here seems to play down the 'lesser' calamities that continue to occur in the following chapters. His mood has changed: perhaps he has adjusted himself to the fact that history has not stopped yet after all. He

---

80. *Hist.* 7.20; 8.11; 8.29; 8.44; 9.3; 9.38; 10.18.
81. *Hist.* 7.1.
82. Eccles. 1:2.

does seem to have reconsidered things before continuing his writing.

There is only one set of signs in Book 7 and they are explicitly connected with the coming (violent) death of Gundowald, the pretender.[83] There were withered grapes and blossoming trees in December, and also an earthquake in Angers. A great beacon traversed the sky (*pharus magna per caelum discurrens*) and rays (*radii*) appeared. In the north, a column of fire seemed to hang in the sky for two hours with a large star above it (*columna ignea, quasi de caelo pendens, per duarum horarum spatium visa est, cui stella magna superposita erat*). There is no discernible 'head with long hair' here, but Gundowald, of course, was possibly not a true Merovingian. Gregory adds that many other signs also appeared which, he believed, announced Gundowalds coming death (*quae, ut opinor, ipsius Gundovaldi interitum nuntiarunt*). There is one short separate chapter about the fact that one of his servants was a giant, two or three feet taller than the tallest ordinary man. He was brought to King Guntram and died soon afterwards. This is the only time Gregory mentions a human deformation; in Roman times such 'monsters' (*monstrum*: that which is shown) indicated the anger of the gods.[84]

After all the natural calamities and human destruction one is not surprised to read that in the following year there was a great famine in Gaul. The chapter title 'About the famine this year (*De fame anni praesentis*)'[85] may indicate that Gregory wrote this at the time itself (585) — which would mean that he picked up his pen again fairly soon after the previous book. But the tone is different and there are no signs associated with a biblical situation. Gregory relates concrete facts and consequences: that people ate grass and died, that the poor sold themselves into slavery in order to get food.

Book 8 covers the years 585-586 and contains six sets of extraordinary phenomena, none of which are explicitly associated with any other event. Given that the first five all occurred in 585, the year of the famine mentioned in the previous book, Gregory could have connected them with it, as he had connected signs and ravages earlier.[86] But he lets these stand alone. First,[87] there are the northern lights, such as appear more often (*radii a parte aquilonis, sicut saepius apparere solent*). Also, a bright light traversed the sky (*fulgor per caelum cucurisse*); the terms are too inexact to understand whether this formulation indicates a comet (as

83. *Hist.* 7.11.
84. Bloch 1963: 119.
85. *Hist.* 7.45.
86. *Hist.* 6.44.
87. *Hist.* 8.3.

before Sigebert's death) or perhaps lightning (as in Tours where the same formulation occurs just before what must be thunder).[88] Together with blossoming trees in midsummer, all these are 'signs that were shown (*signi ostensi*)' — presumably by God.

Later, signs appeared again:[89] northern lights (*radius*) brighter than ever and flanked by blood-red clouds (*nubes sanguinae*). Gregory continues,

> And behold! while we were watching them, stunned, similar rays appeared from the four corners of the earth... In the middle of the sky there were glowing clouds and the rays all tended toward it as though it were a pavilion, ... Between the rays there were still other clouds flashing and gleaming brightly. This sign (*signum*) inspired us with great fear, for we suspected that some disaster would be sent upon us from heaven (*super nos aliquam plagam de caelo transmitti*).

We will never know whether Gregory then expected this impressive sign to prefigure only an epidemic (or other calamity sent by God from heaven) or whether he was thinking of another possibility as well, which would account for 'stunned (*attoniti*)' and 'great fear (*magnus metus*)'; he had never before mentioned his personal feelings concerning a prodigy and he does not do so again. The other possibility Gregory may have had in mind is where *fulgor* occurs in an apocalyptic context as indicated in Luke 17:24: 'For as the lightning flashes and lights up the sky from one side to the other, so will the Son of man be in his day (*nam sicut fulgur coruscans de sub caelo, in ea quae sub caelo sunt, fulget, ita erit Filius hominis in die sua*)' (Matthews' version[90] is very similar). Somewhat later, however, when Gregory has recorded that certain islands in the sea had been destroyed by fire divinely (*divinitus*),[91] and thereafter swallowed by the sea, he adds: 'Many even say that the signs which I said earlier that I saw in October when the sky seemed to be on fire (*quasi ardere caelum*) were in fact the brightness (*splendor*) of this conflagration'. The fact that Gregory at the time that he saw these signs, was staying with a friend in the Ardennes, which are by no means close to the sea, need not detain us. It is again a striking testimony of his intellectual honesty that he is capable of considering a partly natural explanation for phenomena which he had at first experienced as a divine message and which as he confesses, had frightened him so much. Again: for him a natural cause does not exclude a supernatural intention and meaning.

Directly before the chapter about the burned islands, Gregory wrote a

---

88. *Hist.* 4.51 and 5.33, respectively.
89. *Hist.* 8.17.
90. Matth. 24:27.
91. *Hist.* 8.24.

short one about floods and a cold summer so wet that it seemed winter rather than summer (*ut hiems magis potaretur esse quam aestas*).[92] Immediately after the account of the burned islands, a short chapter follows about how on another island near Vannes the water in a fish pond had turned into blood.[93] Perhaps because of the fact that he had read about such a possibility in the Bible (although Orosius mentions something similar as well)[94] Gregory shows no trace of doubt that such a thing could happen. We shall see later that he may have adopted the biblical context there as well; here he does not say so. The last cluster of 'signs' (explicitly so designated) in Book 8 also stands alone.[95] Trees blossomed in September and gave a second harvest of apples in December and light(ning?) was seen running across the sky in the shape of a serpent (*fulgor per caelum in modum serpentes cucurrisse visus est*).

It is only in the beginning of the next book that Gregory indicates that he has been missing the apposite events for these signs and that he has been doing some thinking about them. Book 9 covers the years 587-589 and contains only one set of prodigies, explicitly so designated, near the beginning, followed by a chapter on another strange phenomenon; for the rest there are only two descriptions of extreme weather with its consequences, and one detailed factual description of an epidemic (without prodigies).

In 587 household utensils appeared to be inscribed with indelible mysterious characters in the whole region from Chartres to Bordeaux.[96] In October there were new shoots, withered grapes and a second crop of apples. Northern lights appeared again, and many said they saw serpents falling from a cloud (*adserebant nonnulli, vidisse se serpentes ex nube dilapsos*: lightning?). Others were sure that they had seen a whole manor (*villa*) suddenly fall apart (*subitania internicione*) and disappear with houses and men. There was a bad grape harvest and, as a result of torrential rains, very high water in the rivers. Gregory adds that 'many other signs (*signa*) appeared, which usually announce a king's death or the destruction of a whole region (*quae aut regis obitum adnunciare solent aut regiones excidium*)'. Had their meaning now somehow changed? Gregory must have asked himself this question.

In the following chapter,[97] Gregory tells of a strange man who came to

---

92. *Hist.* 8.23.
93. *Hist.* 8.25.
94. Rev. 16: 3-4 and *Hist. adv. pag.* 4.13.12.
95. *Hist.* 8.42.
96. *Hist.* 9.5.
97. *Hist.* 9.6.

Tours that year. He pretended to be some kind of apostle and to heal the sick: not through saintliness (*sanctitate*) but 'by attempting to deceive with the delusion of black magic (*errore nigromantici ingenii quaerebat inludere*)'. No wonder, Gregory says, that he said he was an apostle because 'the author of all evil, from whom all this proceeds, will pretend he is Christ when the world ends'. Gregory discovered his deceit and threw him out of the city. Seven years earlier, he adds, there had been another such impostor who had acquired a following among the people and who worked with witchcraft (*maleficia*): herbal roots, moles' teeth, bones of mice, bears' claws and bear-fat had been found on him. There have been, however, many more of these impostors wandering about lately, Gregory now says, 'of whom I believe the Lord spoke in the Gospel: in the last times (*in novissimis temporibus*) false Christs and false prophets will arise who will do signs and wonders (*signa et prodigia*) so as to deceive even the elect'.[98]

If the men in Gregory's time were the false prophets indicated in the Gospel, then the 'last times' had indeed come. In the Gospel context, *signa et prodigia* are miracles such as healing and raising from the dead, but they may also be signs or prodigies such as we have been looking at (indeed the Pharisees had asked Jesus for a 'sign' in this sense).[99] The prophets were to appear in the time of the worst tribulation the world had ever known. This is part of Jesus' answer to the disciples' asking for a 'sign' of his coming and of 'the end of the world [or world-time] (*quod signum (erit) adventus tui, et consummationis saeculi?*)'.[100] 'Immediately after the tribulation of those days', Matthew's version continues, 'the sun will be darkened and the moon will not give its light, the stars will fall from heaven, and the powers of heaven will be shaken; then will appear the sign of the Son of Man in heaven...'.[101] False prophets, tribulation, solar and lunar eclipses, unseasonable weather, can all be 'signs' of the approaching end. We have seen above that the 'sign' of the Son of Man in heaven was to be spectacular flashing light.[102] Gregory does not say that he now sees the prodigies he has been recording in this context; it is possible, even probable, however, that he expected his readers to make the connection themselves.

Whether the prodigies did in fact cease to appear after this point or whether Gregory only stopped recording them we cannot tell. Twice he

---

98. Matth. 24:24.
99. Compare Moule 1966: 235-8 and Hofius 1971: 1447-52.
100. Matth. 24:3.
101. Matth. 24: 29-30.
102. Matth. 24:27.

reports exceptional weather. In 588 there were great rains and in the spring severe frost, and it was indeed astonishing (*admirabile*) that the frost destroyed everything in places where it had never before done any harm, and yet did not reach the spots where it usually did most damage.[103]. A flood of unheard-of proportions occurred in 589, the trees blossomed again in the autumn, apples were harvested a second time, roses appeared in November,[104] and rivers were so swollen that they covered places which they had never reached before (*quae numquam contingere consuetae fuerant*). Gregory, however, does not explicitly bring all this into connection with anything else or with the 'last times'.

When the plague threatened to invade his kingdom from Marseilles,[105] King Guntram, 'as though he were a good priest', instituted prayers and fasts for three days as 'remedies which might heal the wounds of the sinful people (*remedia, qua cicatrices peccatoris vulgi mederentur*)' — evidently, once these 'wounds' were 'healed' the plague would no longer be necessary as chastisement. The king 'placed all his hope in the Lord's compassion'; this is a phrase which Gregory often uses for those who do so with success. In the next chapter he gives a detailed factual description of the plague's arrival at and progress in Marseilles. One would never, if one had not read the previous chapter, think that an element of divine causation was anywhere even suspected. A ship had entered the port from Spain with its 'usual cargo' (slaves?) which unfortunately carried with it the source (tinder) of this disease (*huius morbi fomitem secum nequiter deferebat*). While they were buying various things from the ship, eight people died immediately (*confestim*) from this contagion (*hoc contagio*). But the consuming disease (*incendium lues*) did not at once (*statim*) spread to all the houses; some time passed and then, like a cornfield set alight, the entire town was suddenly ablaze with pestilence (*urbem totam morbi incendio conflagravit*). Gregory likens the disease and its spread to fire; he sees that it has a carrier and that it is contagious in some way. Nevertheless, he tells us that when Bishop Theodore returned to his city, he thought the best way to combat the disease was to spend the whole time in the church praying for Gods' mercy.

Gregory's observation and analysis of the plague's progress did not prevent him from imitating his friend Bishop Theodore's behaviour when it came to Tours:[106] after prayers, fasting and alms, 'the violence of the

---

103. *Hist.* 9.17.
104. *Hist.* 9.44. Compare Pope Gregory on the inversion of seasons as a sign of the approaching end of the world in Dagens 1977: 98-9.
105. *Hist.* 9.21.
106. *Hist.* 10.30.

divine fury was diverted and [the disease] abated (*averso divini furoris impetu mitigatum est*)'. Appeasing the divine fury, then, is the way to tackle the disease. In Rome in 590, the new pope Gregory combated an epidemic in the same manner.[107] In Book 10 three of the four instances of disease are accompanied by prodigious phenomena such as Gregory had been accustomed to record, and one is placed in another context. These are the only groups of such phenomena in Book 10 and thus the last in the *Histories*. Is Gregory again seeing the correspondence prodigies-disease as he did in Books 5 and 6? Have the tribulation 'like that predicted by Joel' and the false prophets such as those foretold in the Gospel,[108] both indicating some sort of 'last time', left no trace in his thinking?

There were prodigies before the epidemic in Rome:[109] the water in the Tiber rose so high that the city was largely inundated; ancient buildings collapsed, and papal granaries were destroyed. Many serpents as well as a large dragon (*magnus draco*) came down-river. The bubonic plague followed these at once (*de vestigio*), and first of all carried off Pope Pelagius, fulfilling what is written in Ezekiel:[110] 'Begin at my sanctuary'. The context of Ezekiel's words is the Lord's punishment for all the 'abominations' (idol-worship, principally) that are committed by the Israelites, even in the Temple. Those carrying out the slaughter were commanded to begin at the sanctuary (the Temple) where idol-worship had caused the Lord to depart[111] (this is 'the abomination that makes it desolate'). A promise of restoration for the righteous, however, follows.[112] There is no clear indication in Ezekiel's context that this is a sort of 'last time', as in Joel's warning. Gregory has perhaps simply recognized in it an event similar to that in Rome. As will be seen below, it is also possible that because he now tended to see all such phenomena as signs of the end of the world, he made an oblique mental connection — between the reason Ezekiel gives for the punishment, i.e. 'the abomination that makes [the sanctuary] desolate' and the fact that this abomination would be perpetrated by the Antichrist near the end of the world (mentioned in the preface to the first book of the *Histories*).[113]

In the same year the plague reached Gaul[114] and was preceded there by

107. *Hist.* 10.1.
108. *Hist.* 9.6.
109. *Hist.* 10.1.
110. Ezek. 9:6.
111. Ezek. 8:6.
112. Ezek. 11:17ff.
113. *Hist.* 1. *praef.*
114. *Hist.* 10.23.

'signs'; as Gregory lists them: a brightness (*splendor*) at night that made one think it was high noon, spheres of fire often dancing about in the air at night, an earthquake, a solar eclipse, torrential rains, thunder and high water. Chapter 25 begins with the fact that the plague visited Marseilles and that in other cities there was a severe famine. Gregory continues:

> These are the beginning of the sorrows about which the Lord speaks in the Gospel: 'There will be pestilence and famine and earthquakes in many places; and false Christs and false prophets will arise and do signs and prodigies in the sky, so as to lead astray even the elect, as has been happening in this [the present?] time. (*Erunt pestilentia et fames et terrae motus per loca; et exurgent pseudoChristi et pseudoprophetae et dabunt signa et prodigia in caelo, ita ut electos in errore mittant, sicut praesenti gestum est tempore.*)

The earthquake was mentioned in the previous chapter, apparently in connection with the plague, but both it and the plague are now included by Gregory among the 'sufferings' which Jesus mentioned in reply to the disciples' question of what would be the 'sign' of the end.[115] Significantly, Gregory leaves out the wars also mentioned there: for the time being, the civil wars in the Merovingian kingdom had ceased.

But what are these 'signs and prodigies in the sky (*signa et prodigia in caelo*)'? The Gospels of Matthew and Mark both mention false Christs and false prophets who will 'effect great signs and prodigies (*dabunt signa magna et prodigia*)' or 'will effect signs and portents (*dabunt signa et portenta*)'.[116] Gregory, however, has added *in caelo* here. What could he mean? The false prophets in Book 9 had been reported only as attempting to heal miraculously; none had effected anything like the prodigies Gregory has been mentioning. The false Christ whose story follows here[117] is no different; he too did it all by 'devilish arts (*diabolicis artibus*)'. When he began to rob travellers and threaten those who did not believe in him, the servants of the bishop of Puy-en-Velay killed this Christ 'more worthy to be called an Antichrist'. There are very many of these (*plerique*) now in Gaul, Gregory says again, many of whom he saw personally and tried to dissuade from their delusion (*error*). We may deduce from this that the times were certainly troubled and that Gregory was not alone in expecting the Second Coming soon. But still no 'signs and prodigies in the sky' have been mentioned as conjured up, in whatever way, by these men: does Gregory nevertheless now attribute such things as the frequent spheres of fire and the solar eclipse[118] to them? Or did they themselves perhaps claim responsibility for these and other signs?

---

115. Matth. 24:5-8; Mark 13:6-8; Luke 21:10-11.
116. Matth. 24:24 and Mark 13:22, respectively.
117. *Hist.* 10.25.
118. *Hist.* 10.23.

I do not think so. There is another possibility which should at least be considered. In Luke's version of Jesus' answer to the disciples the material is arranged somewhat differently. Like Matthew and Mark, Luke mentions false Christs first, then wars, earthquakes, pestilence and famine (*et terraemotus magni erunt per loca et pestilentia et fames*).[119] Matthew and Mark had mentioned only earthquakes and famines, not pestilence; Gregory then must have had this passage in mind when he included pestilence. Luke adds finally, without any mention of false prophets, that there will be 'terrors from heaven and great signs (*terroresque de caelo et signa magna erunt*)'. (It is not clear whether or not this should be understood as something like signs in the sky.) Matthew and Mark omit these here. Only after mentioning 'the sacrilege that makes [the sanctuary] desolate' (see above) and more tribulations, do Matthew and Mark[120] refer to false Christs again and this time with 'signs and prodigies' intended to lead even the elect astray. Luke makes no second mention of false Christs but repeats, at a later point, that there will be 'signs in the sun, moon and stars'.[121] Did Gregory, paraphrasing from memory as usual, join the first part of Luke's sentence to what Matthew and Mark say about false prophets and their signs and prodigies, adding the qualification 'in the sky' thoughtlessly because Luke had mentioned 'terrors from heaven' as well as 'signs in the sun, moon and stars'? I do not think that Gregory — for all his inaccuracies — is capable of such an unprecedented slip. It seems rather more likely that he intended to place the prodigies he had been seeing and recording into the perspective of the 'last times'. To do this he needed only to complete Luke's sentence and then add what Matthew and Mark said about the prophets. Although I have not found mention of any manuscript of the *Histories* containing either the missing part of Luke or omitting the *in caelo* here, the possibility cannot be excluded that the fault for the omission lies in the manuscript tradition. The combination *prodigia in caelo* occurs only twice in the Bible (Vulgate and Vetus Latina); as we saw above, once as part of Joel's prophecy about the Day of the Lord[122] and for a second time when this passage is repeated in Acts 2:19 in the context of Jesus' Second Coming. It is, of course, the Lord who is speaking, 'I will give prodigies in the heavens...', *dabo prodigia in caelo*. In late Antiquity, however, one tended to look for prodigies in the sky,[123] and it

---

119. Matth. 24:5-7 and Mark 13:6-8; Luke 21:8 and 21:10-11, respectively.
120. Matth. 24:24; Mark 13:22.
121. Luke 21:25. Joel 2:30-1.
122. Joel 2:30-1.
123. Berger 1980 in Haase 1980: 1437 n. 30, 1447-8.

may be this mental habit which lies behind the conscious or unconscious contraction in the text. I find it difficult if not impossible to believe, however, that Gregory himself could have attributed celestial prodigies to the efforts of the deluded and incompetent impostors he describes. The formulation as it stands must be a corruption by an early copyist.

Confused or not, it is nevertheless clear that Gregory is now interpreting not only the signs and prodigies he has recorded but also the false prophets (with their false miracles), the earthquakes, epidemics and famines as 'signs' of the imminent Second Coming.

The last chapter of the *Histories* proper, probably written in 590 at the time the events took place (since it is entitled 'About the weather this year')[124] reports the epidemic in Tours, together with other assorted facts: in Limoges many who had dared to work for the state (*opera publica*) on Sunday (*ob dominici diei iniuriam*) were struck by lightning (*igne caelesti consumpti sunt*); in Tours too some were struck by lightning, though not on Sunday. There was a great drought and the lack of fodder for the domestic animals helped bring about widespread cattle plague with a very high mortality rate. Again Gregory compares the situation with one he had found in the Bible: 'as the prophet Habakkuk foretold: the flock shall be cut off from the fold, and there shall be no herd in the stalls'.[125] The context of Habakkuk's words is trust and faith generally in the power of and deliverance by the Lord in the midst of famine and cattle disease. The fact that the Habakkuk passage is not specifically situated in the context of any 'last time' need not mean that Gregory no longer thought in these terms. He concludes this last chapter of his history by saying that wild animals too had been stricken by the cattle plague, that many corpses had been found in forest thickets, that the hay rotted in the fields because of the great rains and floods, and that, although the vines yielded abundantly, the acorns (on which pigs lived) remained very small.

At that point, for some reason we are not told about, Gregory stopped writing his *Histories*. Two or three years later, in 593 or 594, he added a review of all the bishops of Tours and a computation of the years of the world up to that point[126] (as he had also done at the end of Book 4).

To return to the questions we posed at the beginning of this essay: it has become evident that Gregory at first regarded all extraordinary events — events with no visible natural causes — as prodigies wrought by God and as a punishment in themselves and/or as indications of other punishments

---

124. *Hist.* 10.30.
125. Habak. 3:17.
126. *Hist.* 10.31.

yet to come such as disease, 'devastation' or the death of a king. They do not indicate anything outside of these specific events. Especially in the middle of the *Histories* he tried to see resemblances between the forms or patterns in the sky and the event (pre)figured by them. Later, after many prodigies had appeared without apposite events and Gregory was confronted with a new phenomenon — false prophets — he began to recognize the calamities of his time, and almost certainly the prodigies as well, as divinely wrought 'signs' of the end of the world. Thus his view of the events in his own time was at first relatively optimistic but became increasingly grim as misfortunes continued to accumulate.

From his not inconsiderable knowledge of what 'usually' happens in nature and also from the factual, analytic description he sometimes gives, it is clear that there is for him an accustomed and recognizable order in nature, which appears to work autonomously and whose processes can be analyzed. The Lord of history, however, is also the Lord of nature: God can reveal his purposes with mankind not only through the symbolic value of nature's regular phenomena — as Gregory shows in his *On the course of the stars*[127] —, but also by phenomena ranging from the mildly odd to the very irregular, as we have now seen. The Old and New Testament furnish many examples of this latter category to which can be added those which Orosius and Lactantius carried over from the pagan Roman tradition. All these inevitably sharpened Gregory's attentiveness and extended the limits of his credibility, and they did in any case demonstrably influence his interpretations.

Gregory's manner of recording extraordinary natural phenomena shows him to have a definite 'rational' interest in the visible world and its processes. However, without there apparently being any contradiction for him involved, he combines this with the mental disposition to look for and expect divine, symbolical content: a disposition passed down, as is well known, by the Church Fathers. Today we are accustomed to look for the *how* of events and cannot conceive of any event without an unbroken causal chain preceding it. Gregory, however, saw God as being able to intervene in all human events according to known ethical principles and as communicating the latter in recognizable forms. He was primarily interested in the ethical-spiritual *why*. We now look for evolution and process in historical events; for Gregory history was shot through with discontinuities through divine intervention, and accordingly he looked for consistent patterns or 'figures' he could recognize, especially from the Bible.[128] He also expected to see, where possible, 'figural' correspondences

---

127. *De cursu stell.* 10-16.
128. Compare Thürlemann 1974: 86-94, but also Bolton 1959: 208-11, who compares this to Gregory the Great's similar treatment of hagiography.

between more or less contemporary events in the natural and in the human sphere. In short, he expected the natural world and history — which are causally discontinuous but meet in God — to exhibit (occasional) clusters of congruent, synchronous patterns.

THE PREFACES. GREGORY'S VIEW OF HIS OWN TIME: A BALANCE ATTEMPTED AND LOST

Does Gregory's view of his own time as it emerges from his treatment of prodigies, changing from a moderate optimism to a view that the contemporary misfortunes indicated the approaching end of the world, accord with what he explicitly says elsewhere in the *Histories* about it? His view of contemporary history is revealed in various parts of the work. Beside the well-known General Preface, Gregory has prefaces before Books 1, 2, 3 and 5, in which he reveals something of his attitude toward the subject he intends to deal with. In a few other places too he makes general comments. Finally, his computations of the age of the world also say something about his view of contemporary history. We will now consider the relevant passages.

In the General Preface the picture is somber:

> The study of the liberal arts is decaying and indeed disappearing (*decedente atque immo potius pereunte*) from the cities of Gaul, but a number of things keep happening, some of them good, some of them bad (*vel rectae vel inprobae*): the inhabitants of different regions attack each other savagely, the madness [or rage] of the kings is increasing (*regum furor acueretur*), the churches are attacked by heretics and defended by the Catholics, the faith of Christ burns bright in many men but grows lukewarm in a number of others, the churches themselves are in turn endowed by pious men and stripped bare again by the irreligious. [...]

For those who come after him Gregory will record the bad as well as the good: there still appears to be something like a balance between these. His explicit intention, then, is to write about his own time. In order to place it in the perspective of the history of the world, he will start with the Creation. The mood of this preface is resigned but not one of impending doom. The reference to the increasing madness or rage of kings must almost certainly mean that this preface was written before Chilperic's death; thereafter there was only one adult king, Guntram, for a considerable time, and there were no overt wars between him and Childebert II later.

After a list of the chapter titles of Book 1, there is a lengthy preface to Book 1. It has a twofold purpose: to convince the reader, by an exposition of the Nicene Creed, that its author is a good Catholic Christian (and not an Arian), and after that to make very clear what should be thought about the end of the world.

> Proposing as I do to describe the wars waged by kings against hostile peoples, by martyrs against pagans, and by the churches against the heretics, I wish first of all to explain my own faith, so that whoever reads me may not doubt that I am a Catholic.

The indication of the subject matter here is more optimistic; there are two parties or camps, the good and the bad, and the good are mentioned first — they seem to be in control, or there is at least a balance. It seems likely that this preface was written earlier than the General Preface, which, by contrast, is disillusioned. In the preface to Book 1 nothing explicit is said about describing his own time; his intention, he says, is to add up all the years treated of by earlier chronicles and histories and state clearly how many years have passed since the world began (*quanti ab exordio mundi sint anni*). And this is especially for those who 'are worried about the approaching end of this world'.[129] *Ad proprinquantem finem mundi disperant* can mean either despairing *because* the world is nearing its end or despairing *of* the world's ending soon; in the one case its imminent end, in the other its *not* yet ending induces despair. Whichever Gregory meant, the existence of such thoughts is an indication that the times are troubled. Why it would be a comfort to know the number of years that have passed is unclear unless, although the Church had already in the fourth century forbidden speculation on this point, there were theories about this number still circulating. As will be seen below, Gregory had also encountered them in the writings of earlier Christian historians.

But he himself is not worried in either way:

> Of the end of the world (*finis ...mundi*) I believe what I have learned from my predecessors: that before this the Antichrist will come. First the Antichrist introduces circumcision, proclaiming himself to be Christ. Then he places his own statue in the Temple of Jerusalem to be worshipped; for we read that the Lord has said: 'Ye shall see the abomination that causes desolation (*abhumatio desolationes*) standing in the holy place'.[130] But that this day is a secret for all men the Lord himself makes clear when he says: 'Of that day however and of that hour no one knows. [...]'[131] Our end (*finis*) indeed is Christ himself, who will give us eternal life out of the fullness of his grace, if we have attuned our hearts to him.

Eusebius, Jerome and Orosius with their histories, and Victorius with his Easter tables, Gregory continues, had revealed the calculation of the whole succession of years (*rationem de omni annorum serie*). Gregory will do the same (*usque ad nostrum tempos cunctam annorum congeriem conpotare*) and this is easiest, he says, if he starts with Adam. Everyone

---

129. Hugenholtz 1960: 112.
130. Matth. 24:15.
131. Matth. 24:36.

should remember, however, that the end of the world cannot be known or computed beforehand in any way whatever. The only criterion by which its imminence may be recognized is that of Antichrist having himself worshipped in the Temple. But actually, no one should worry about the end of the world, because the world is not what matters: what matters is our end, our goal (a fine word-play with *finis*) eternal life through Christ.

Here Gregory takes a stand against speculation, which, in a more or less veiled way, occurs in the writings of Severus and Orosius. Severus, writing in 400, says near the beginning of his abbreviated history of the world:[132] 'The world was created by God now almost six thousand years ago'. The idea of a six-thousand year duration of the world had been worked out by a number of early Christian historian- chronographers. Some had reckoned the birth of Christ as taking place in 5500, which would have meant that the world's end was due in 500 A.D. — to which Severus, as well as Gregory, may have been referring. Eusebius, however, corrected this number to 5198, but indicated that speculation about numbers was useless.[133] Severus himself purposely stops counting the world's years after the death of Samson.[134] Orosius places the Incarnation in the year 5199, and elsewhere implies, though purposely refrains from stating, that the Roman Empire, as the last of the world empires prophesied by Daniel, may last only about another 700 more years after this.[135] This would have meant that the end of the world might come around 700 A.D.. Gregory, too, must have had all this in mind but, as a good bishop of the Church, he wishes to silence further discussion. When he makes his own computations at the end of Books 4 and 10, he perhaps purposely does not mention the Incarnation and places the Passion or Resurrection of Christ in the year 5184.

In the preface to Book 2 Gregory apologizes for relating so much that is grievous:

> As we continue to follow the order of the succession of the times (*Prosequentes ordinem temporum*), we record in a mixed and muddled manner (*mixte confusequae* [sic]) the miracles of the saints as well as the slaughterings of peoples. It will not, I am sure, be held unreasonable of me ...since I do it not because it is easier to write like this, but because the succession of the times presents the facts in this way, (*non facilitas scripturis, sed temporum series praestitit*).

But, says Gregory, this mixture occurs also in the histories (*historiae*) of the kings of Israel (about which Severus had written in more detail than

---

132. Severus, *Chron.* 1.2.1.
133. Von den Brincken 1957: 65, 74-5, 80-4.
134. Severus, *Chron.* 1.29.8-9. In *Dial.* 2.14, he does, however, say that the end of the world is near.
135. *Hist. adv. pag.* 1.1.5-6 and 7.2., respectively; Daniel 2:31-45.

Gregory). Let the reader remember the time of Elijah, who did various miracles for the people:

> how many massacres there were of peoples, what famines and what drought oppressed the wretched land...and also in the time of Elisha, who restored life to the dead and performed many other miracles among the people, how much carnage and what misery afflicted that same people of Israel. Just as I have done myself, so Eusebius, Severus and Jerome wove together (*texuerunt*) in their chronicles the wars of kings and the miracles of the martyrs. I have composed my book in the same way, so that the order of the succession of the ages or the whole calculation of the years up to our own times shall more easily be ascertained (*quod facilius saeculorum ordo vel annorum ratio usque nostra tempora tota repperiatur*).

This is a key passage. It shows that at this point in his writing Gregory saw the slaughter, the famine, drought and general misery, which others had apparently taken to indicate that the world was grinding to a stop, as nothing in particular to worry about since they had also occurred under the Old Testament kings (with whom he evidently compares the present Frankish kings) as well. Again, the juxtaposition of kings' wars and miracles of the martyrs implies a balance between these opposites.

But there may be a new element. In the previous prefaces Gregory has consistently spoken of the 'years' of the world (*pro suppotatione* [sic] *annorum; quanti ...sint anni*)[136] or of the 'whole succession' or 'total' of the years (*ratio de omni annorum serie, cuncta annorum congeries*).[137] In this preface Gregory speaks of 'the order of the succession' or simply 'the succession' of 'the times' (*ordo temporum, temporum series*) and of 'the order of the succession of the ages or the whole calculation of the years (*saeculorum ordo vel annorum ratio... tota*)'. The word *ordo*, which means 'order' as well as 'succession', may to be purposely used to form a contrast with 'muddled (*confuse*)'. Gregory is then here giving the chronological order — which is, of course, what he means — a positive value, every bit as good as any other way of arranging his subject matter and, in his view, actually better, even though it may seem 'muddled'. The same attitude to the chronological ordering occurs in a very similar passage in Orosius:[138] 'the more I follow the chronological order, the more confusedly I seem to be writing (*tanto, ut video, inordinatus scripsi, quanto magis ordinem custodivi*)'.

In this way, Gregory says, not only will the number of years be more easily ascertained, but also 'the order of the succession of the ages'. Is this the same as 'the order of the succession of the times' which he mentions at the beginning? *Saeculum* can mean 'age', an indefinitely long period, but

---

136. *Hist.praef. prima* and 1. *praef.*, respectively.
137. *Hist.* 1. *praef.*
138. *Hist. adv. pag.* 3.2.9.

it can also mean 'world', 'world-time' or even 'eternity' as well as 'generation'. (Gregory uses the term elsewhere[139] to mean 'world' but this cannot be meant here.) As for 'times', if there is a succession of them, *tempus* must be in some way a segment of time. Nowhere does Gregory himself say anything more about it, except indirectly, as we have seen, as when he recognized in his own time the 'signs' of the 'last times (*novissima tempora*)'[140] before the return of Christ. These signs (as we know from the Bible passage in question) would announce 'the end of the world (or world-time) (*consummatio saeculi*)'.[141] Without entering into the complicated question of New Testament concepts of time[142] we may, from the little that Gregory *does* say about it, infer that he probably held the more general biblical notion of time as primarily a qualitative, not quantitative, entity determined by its God-given content,[143] which is here the 'sufferings'. The duration of a 'time' or 'age' (which in the Gospels do not appear to be equivalents) would then be the duration of a specific content. Earlier Christian writers had distinguished six 'ages (*aetates*)' in the history of the world, corresponding to the six days of the Creation and each lasting 1000 years. Augustine later, in accordance with the Church's prohibition of speculation about the number of years until the end of the world, reworked the six 'ages' and calculated very different durations, explicitly saying that the duration of the sixth and last age — which, as everyone was agreed, had begun with Christ — could not be known.[144] Gregory however does not use the term *aetates* and does not appear to be acquainted with this conceptual scheme. His large divisions of the world history (which he does not in any way designate as 'ages (*saecula*)') for the purpose of the calculation of the years (see below) do not quite correspond to Augustine's, and in the second version of the divisions (at the end of Book 10) he even reduces their number, which makes it appear as though they were, for him, primarily practical in value, a means of facilitating calculation.[145]

But what about 'times' which appear to be much shorter (if there are a number of them near the end of the 'age')? We have already seen that in a number of places Gregory says that a biblical prophecy of a certain divinely caused situation has been fulfilled (*impletum*) or has been

---

139. *Hist. 7.1.*
140. *Hist. 9.6.*
141. Matth. 24:3.
142. See Hahn 1971: 1457-58.
143. Hahn 1971: 1473-4.
144. Hugenholtz 1960: 115.
145. See Hugenholtz 1960: 116.

actualized (*actum est, gestum est*) 'in this time (*hoc tempore*)'.[146] We may infer, I think, that this situation then determines the quality of 'this time', which Gregory was clearly concerned to recognize. Past 'times' *as such*, do not appear to interest him since he says nothing about them. His own 'time' (*nostra tempus*) or 'times' (*nostra tempora*) and all that happens in it holds his attention:[147] we have seen that in the beginning of his work he wished to regard his own period as perhaps a kind of modified repetition of the age of the Old Testament kings, and that, later, he found himself after all having to agree with those who recognized its character of 'the last times'. Gregory, then, is constantly looking for indications about the inherent *quality*, the God-given content, of his own 'time' or 'times'.

This may be an additional explanation for his strict adherence to the chronological order of events. To be more precise, it may be the reason why he is so concerned with the contemporaneity or simultaneity of events: adverbial phrases indicating contemporaneity abound: 'meanwhile (*interim*)', 'in that time (*tempore illo*)', 'in this time (*hoc tempore*)', 'in the same time (*per idem tempore*)', 'then (*tunc*)', are often used. Except for the explicit indication of the beginning (*initium*) of the sufferings of 'the last times', Gregory nowhere indicates any beginnings or endings of 'times'. Could it be that he himself did not have a really clear idea of this but was rather, as we just saw in the case of the prodigies, simply struck by what seemed to him to be remarkable similarities between a considerable number of events and then took this shared pattern to be an indication of large-scale consistent divine activity (toward man) of a specific kind? Did he perhaps see this activity as constituting a divinely determined 'time'? The example of 'the last times' as qualified by 'sufferings' certainly points in this direction. Since it is (unforeseeable unless specifically revealed) divine action that, for Gregory, decides and constitutes events — an axiom even more evident in his hagiographical works than in the *Histories* — the contemporary context must therefore be for him more essential than its (causal) antecedents. An unmistakable example of this is the sudden truce or peace the constantly quarrelling kings made near Chartres in 574 (see below) which Gregory attributes to the influence of divine power. As we shall see, there too he is more than eager to recognize God acting elsewhere at the same time in essentially the same manner.

The preface to Book 3 consists of one important message: those who

---

146. *Hist.* 6.45; 10.1; 10.30 as well as 9.6 and 10.25.
147. *Hist.* 1. *praef.* and 2. *praef.*, respectively. Vaughan 1986 in Teunis and van Tongerloo 1986: 20-1 sees this rather than any religious view of history as the primary reason for Gregory's presentation of events in their chronological order and his lack of interest in causal development.

confess the Catholic Trinity will conquer and prosper (like Clovis), and those who deny it, the Arians (like the Gothic king Alaric), will lose everything and eternal life as well. Gregory's confidence in this course of affairs is absolute: it is not the nature of the action itself that leads to this outcome — the actual deeds of the Burgundian kings Gundobad, Godigisel and Godomar differ very little if at all from that of their Frankish colleagues — but the support or its opposite by the Lord, which depends on whether or not these kings profess the true Trinity. The Burgundian kings lose their kingdoms because (and only because) they are Arians.

Gregory's lament in the preface to Book 5 can be properly understood only if we digress for a moment to look to the events of the latter part of Book 4. Its last chapters report an unremitting series of wars between the grandsons of Clovis, the brothers Guntram, Sigebert and Chilperic, about their respective shares of the Frankish kingdom (Gregory always uses the singular, *regnum*). Tours and Poitiers had been allotted to Sigebert, but Chilperic had seized them. Sigebert's general Mummolus drove Chilperic's son Clovis out of the region and let everyone swear loyalty to Sigebert. An attempt at reconciliation of the brothers by a council of bishops in Paris in 573 failed;[148] the kings refused to listen to the bishops and the civil war assumed ever greater dimensions. Chilperic, in fact, flew into a rage, and sent his son Theudebert to recapture Tours and Poitiers. There, he slaughtered, burned and devastated everything: 'he burned the churches, stole their holy vessels, killed the clergy, tore down monasteries, raped women and destroyed everything. There was even more weeping in the churches in this time (*tempore illo*) than there had been at the time (*tempore*) of Diocletian's persecution'. Was Gregory thinking of the fact that Sulpicius Severus had said that the tenth and last persecution would be under Antichrist?[149] Immediately thereafter Gregory begins the next chapter with a, for him, unusually lengthy editorial comment:

> And to this day we are still astonished and wondering (*obstupiscimus et admiramur*) why such disasters befall them (*cur tantae super eos plagae inruerint*). But let us think back to what their ancestors did (*Sed recurramus ad illud quod parentes eorum egerunt*) and [compare it with] what they do. By the preaching of the bishops, the former were turned from their pagan shrines towards the churches; the latter daily carry off booty from [these same] churches. The former revered the bishops of the Lord wholeheartedly and listened to them; the latter not only do not listen to them but even persecute them. The former endowed monasteries and churches; the latter destroy and ruin them.

148. *Hist.* 4.47.
149. *Chron.* 2.33.

As an example of the latter, the story of the plundering of the monastery Latta, at the instigation of the Devil (*inimico stimulante*), follows. The monks had warned Theudebert's troops not to touch the place, since St Martin's relics were kept there. On the way back over the river with their booty their boat fell apart and all were killed except one, who had tried to keep them from the plundering. 'In case anyone thinks that this happened by chance (*fortuitu evenisse*)', Gregory says, 'let him consider the fact that among the many guilty ones, only the one innocent person was saved' (St Martin is, of course, understood to have protected 'his' people and possessions). Gregory's reasoning here is clear: because the kings do not listen to bishops' advice and even rob and destroy churches and injure their clergy or, in other words, because they do not honour God, they are therefore afflicted with misfortunes by divine agency.[150]

Then follows the story, referred to above, which more than any other, reveals Gregory's manner of thinking about historical events. Sigebert, after Theudebert's devastations, called in savage tribes from beyond the Rhine to attack Chilperic.[151] Upon the latter's suggestion, however, and lest their kingdom (*regnum*) should be destroyed, they made peace near Chartres and Chilperic returned all the cities that Theudebert had seized. 'But let no one doubt that these kings would never, without a fight, have agreed to make peace if it had not been for the miraculous power (*virtus*) of St Martin', says Gregory, 'for on the very day (*in ipsa die*) they made peace, three paralytics were healed in the saint's church'. In the report of these three healings in his *Miracles of St Martin*,[152] Gregory also mentions that these took place on the same day (*ipsa die*) that Sigebert, the most glorious king (*gloriosissimus rex*), made peace with his brothers, and adds: 'Let no one doubt indeed that this was the victory of the blessed bishop'. This unexpectedly good behaviour of the brothers, Gregory believes, must be the work of (the Lord through) St Martin. The divine character of the event in Chartres is recognized through the simultaneous and essentially similar event in Tours. Three brothers' warped wills are straightened at the same time as three men's warped bodies are 'straightened (*directi*)'. This passage is a trenchant example of the same 'figural' thinking that Gregory displays in his handling of the prodigies: he looks for coherence not in causal connections or development in time, but in the ethico-religious meaning of events, which he recognizes in their form.

In chapter 50, we find the kings' wars continuing despite the truce, and

150. The same reasoning occurs twice in Orosius, *Hist. adv. pag.* 7.8.2 and 7.26.9.
151. *Hist.* 4.49.
152. *Virt. Mart.* 2.5, 6 and 7.

Theudebert is killed on the battlefield by Sigebert's dukes. Gregory begins the chapter: 'Recording these civil wars causes my soul to grieve (*Dolorem enim ingerit animo ista civilia bella referre*)'. How Sigebert subsequently came to be murdered 'because' he had neglected to listen to Bishop Germanus and had intended to kill his brother, we have seen above.

Gregory ends the fourth book in 575 by a computation of the years of the world:

from the Creation to the Flood	2242 years
from the Flood to Abraham	942 years
from Abraham to the Exodus	462 years
from the Exodus to Solomon's Temple.	480 years
from Solomon's Temple to the Babylonian Captivity	390 years
from the Captivity to the Lord's Passion	668 years
from the Passion to the death of St Martin	412 years
from St Martin's death to that of Clovis	112 years
from Clovis' death to that of Theudebert [I]	37 years
from Theudebert's death to that of Sigebert	29 years
	5774 years

For those in Gregory's time who may have thought the world would last 6000 years this reckoning should have been a comfort, and this is probably what he had in mind.[153] As we have seen above, it does not seem likely that Gregory considered *these* time-units of various length as in some way 'ages' or 'times'. Up to the time of Christ there is an apparent resemblance to the later so influential six ages (*aetates*) of Augustine: Adam-Flood-Abraham-David-Babylonian Captivity-Birth of Christ-End of the World, but the number of years in each of Gregory's periods is very different from that found in Augustine's.[154] After the time of Christ, Gregory has repeated here his own, politico-religious, division of the subject matter into 'books', ending respectively with the deaths of St Martin, Clovis, Theudebert and Sigebert.

Book 5 then begins with a preface which seems to indicate that, nevertheless, everyone's worst fears are now being realized:

> It wearies me to record the quarrels and civil wars which are ruining the Frankish people and their kingdom. In these wars, and this is even worse, we see that which

---

153. Gregory and his contemporary Bishop Marius of Avenches must have been using the same 'facts and figures' because their computations more or less agree. In his *Chronica* Marius reckons the age of the world in 567 to be 5768 years. (Mommsen 1894: 238).
154. Hugenholtz 1960: 115.

the Lord foretold about the time of sufferings now already beginning (*tempore illud quod Dominus de dolorum praedixit initium iam videmus*): 'The father shall rise up against the son, and the son against the father; brother shall rise up against brother, and kinsman against kinsman'.[155] They ought indeed to have been warned by the examples of earlier kings (*Debebant enim eos exempla anteriorum regum terrere*) who, when they disagreed among themselves, were promptly annihilated by their enemies. How many times has not Rome, the city of cities and the great capital of the world, been brought low by civil dissensions, and risen again as though from the ground as soon as they ceased. If only you kings would fight battles such as those in which your ancestors exerted themselves, so that the other peoples, afraid of your unity, would have to bow before your power! Remember what Clovis, the founder of your power did. [...] But you, what are you doing? What are you trying to do? Don't you have everything you want [...]? There is only one thing you do not have: because you cannot live in peace with each other, you do not have [the support of] God's grace (*Dei gratiam indegetis*). [...] I beg you, listen to the words of the Apostle: 'But if you bite and devour one another, take heed that ye be not consumed by one another'.[156] Read carefully the writings of the ancients and you will see what civil wars bring forth (*parturiant*).

Gregory concludes by exhorting them, if they insist on indulging in internal discord, to occupy themselves instead with the internal battle of the spirit against the flesh.

This preface appears to contradict itself in tone. The first sentence 'It wearies me to relate the quarrels and civil wars (*Taedit me bellorum civilium diversitatis ... memorare*)' is almost the same as the passage 'Recording these civil wars causes my soul to grieve (*Dolorem enim ingerit animo ista civilia bella referre*)' at the end of Book 4.[157] The sentences pointing to the examples of 'earlier kings', ancestors and Clovis likewise have their parallel in 'But let us think back of what their ancestors did (*Sed recurramus ad illud quod parentes eorum egerunt*)' two chapters earlier in Book 4,[158] although the argument is this time a secular one. There, honouring God and his Church is (divinely) rewarded with power and victories; here, 'history shows' that discord destroys and concord results in great power. More or less abruptly, as if caught up in the emotion brought on by the gravity of the subject, Gregory changes from the third person plural to the second person plural, addressing the kings personally with a passionate plea. God would help you, he seems to say, if only you yourselves would try to improve the situation. All this forms a more or less consistent whole. The reference to the civil wars makes it probable that this preface was written just after the death of Sigebert,

---

155. Mark 13:12.
156. Galat. 5:15.
157. *Hist.* 4.50.
158. *Hist.* 4.48.

whom, as we have seen, Gregory evidently admired (calling him *gloriosissimus rex*).[159]

What, however, is to be made of the reference to 'the time of sufferings (*tempore ...dolorum*)' which has 'now already (*iam*)' begun? Gregory here paraphrases yet another of the 'signs' of the end foretold by Jesus in his answer to the disciples' question: incessant wars. Did Gregory in or shortly after 575 already think of his own time in these terms? The fact that internecine wars have been preordained to take place in the time of sufferings seems to imply that little can be done to stop or relieve them. Gregory, however, urgently pleads for a change in the situation. Is he despairing and at the same time hoping he is wrong about it, still fervently wanting to believe that things could get better if only everyone really tried? Or is it possible that he originally wrote the preface without the reference to the 'time of sufferings' and inserted it later, perhaps around the time of Chilperic's death when he saw the contemporary situation in the context of Joel's words about the 'Day of the Lord'? (Joel's prophecy of portents in this connection is repeated, as we have seen, by Peter in Acts 2:19 in the context of the end of the world.) In an attempt to put false prophets and false Christs into their proper perspective, Gregory, in Book 9 and 10, placed these among the 'signs' of the End; but at that point he does not mention family slaughter as one of those signs. This need not mean, however, that it could not have been at this time that he encountered family slaughter again amongst the 'signs' and inserted this interpretation of them in the preface to Book 5 while revising and inserting additional information in the *Histories*.[160] In fact, the latter possibility seems to be the most likely one.

There are no further prefaces. At the end of Book 10 Gregory affixed a list of the bishops of Tours and a final computation of the years of the world (*summa annorum mundialium*):[161]

from the Creation to the Flood	2242 years
from the Flood to the passage through the Red Sea	1404 years
from the passage to the Resurrection of Christ	1538 years
from the Resurrection to the death of St Martin	412 years
from St Martin's death to the present	197 years
the sum of which is	5792 years
	(in fact: 5793 years)

'The present' has been reckoned as probably being between December

---

159. *Virt. Mart.* 2.7.
160. Buchner 1967a: xxiii.
161. *Hist.* 10.31.

593 and August 594.[162] The periods are fewer and longer than those at the end of Book 4 (Abraham, the Babylonian Captivity, and the Frankish kings are omitted), and again there is no explicit indication of 'times' or 'ages'. The fact that the 'milestones' are now all events of spiritual significance may reflect a diminished concern with and confidence in secular politics.

Reviewing the evidence of the prefaces, comments and computations, the following picture emerges. Gregory undertook to write about his own time and to place it in the perspective of the world's years for those who were in despair about or despairing of its approaching end. The year 6000 is still rather far away, he seems to be saying. He gives clear criteria by which one may recognize the end — Antichrist and his actions — and says all speculation about when this will take place is useless. At the beginning of the *Histories*, slaughter, famines, droughts, wars and general misery are explicitly placed in an Old Testament context: they occurred under the Israelite kings just as they do now under the Frankish kings. There seems to be a balance, at least for Gregory, between evil and good. He started out with the intention of playing down the contemporary miseries and comforting those who saw (in these?) the beginning of the end.

The preface to Book 5 is a passionate plea for peace between the kings. If, at that time, he already saw the current family wars as an indication of the beginning of the end, and thus as inevitable, his urgent tone shows that he still expected to be able to do something about them. It is more likely, however, that he began to think in terms of 'last times' (a viewpoint that is evident to some degree in all Christian writings of late Antiquity) when he turned to the Bible to check on the significance of the false prophets, and this could have been at any time from 580 on, when, as he says,[163] he met (the first?) one. From then on he must have come to see the resemblance of the events of his own time to those unmitigated sufferings that were prophesied to precede the end of this world, and decided to give up his attempt to see and show the balance between good and evil. This development is the same as that which we saw in his treatment of prodigies.

CONCLUSION. SYNCHRONIC SYMBOLICAL PATTERNING AS HISTORICAL COHERENCE

Gregory tends to expect causally discontinuous events in history and

162. Buchner 1967a: xxiv-v.
163. *Hist.* 9.6.

nature to exhibit congruent, synchronous patterns. Modern physical and psychological research has rediscovered the phenomenon of such apparent coincidences, designating it as 'synchronicity' or 'seriality', and has shown that it is far more common than has been generally recognized.[164] Gregory seems to have suspected the informing presence of a certain specific, if not always clearly visible, mode of divine activity toward man everywhere to be responsible for the congruent patterns that are for him the constitutive factor of a coherent period of human history or 'time'. If so, the view of such a symbolical coherence consisting in contemporaneity may have been, beside the practical wish to facilitate the counting of the world's years, a deeper reason for presenting history as a chronological succession of discontinuous events.

For Gregory, events are discontinuous and — in essence — happen not through 'horizontal', causal development in time but through poetic or 'vertical' causation:[165] flashes of divine action from 'above'. God is constantly being called in and at any rate is constantly intervening to stop or alter the course of human affairs according to sometimes recognizable patterns. Biblical events and prophecies are a supratemporal kind of pattern. Synchronous, structurally similar events in nature and in human history or within history itself are another. Although, in Gregory's eyes, certain patterns such as that of the rewarding of faith and the punishment of crime seem to be very clear, he may have ascribed the nevertheless 'mixed and muddled' appearance of history as it happens in 'the order of the succession of times' to man's inability to recognize the larger synchronous pattern in God's manifold ways.

Whereas the surface narrative is purposely chronological, the underlying structure and coherence of the *Histories* is intended to be actually or potentially symbolical: events are connected by their divinely given meaning, which in turn is recognized by its form. In this, too, besides the Christian historians he mentions, Gregory could have been imitating the historical books of the Old Testament. The terminology he uses for extraordinary natural phenomena or prodigies — i.e. 'appeared' and 'were shown' — probably point to the potential or actual revelation of divine power or of a divine message about human history through their being understood as epiphanies and symbols. For Gregory, history and nature are both theophany: roses in January.

---

164. See Jung 1971 and Koestler 1972: 82ff and passim.
165. See Bachelard 1973: 225 on poetic time as 'vertical'.

II

THE WONDERS OF NATURE
models of sudden transformation*

INTRODUCTION. 'THE WORKS OF MEN...HAVE FALLEN INTO RUINS'

But the aforementioned [seven wonders of the ancient world],[1] even though they were sometimes constructed upon divine command, as well as sometimes by human ingenuity alone, still remain works of men, for which reason some have fallen into ruins and others are about to do so. There are other [wonders], however, which our almighty God himself by His own doing in this world either renews every single day or exhibits again after a year has run its course, and which are made manifest in the bounty of a gift, such as the tidal movement of the sea and the fruits of the earth; others are revealed in the manifestation of His heavenly power, such as the sun, the moon, the stars and the phoenix; finally, some of these reprove sinners in that they present a likeness (*figurant*) of the fire of hell, such as Etna and the spring of Grenoble. These are truly wonders which do not grow old with any age, which do not perish by any onslaught, which do not grow less by falling into ruins, except at that time when the Lord should command the world to be destroyed.[2]

---

*This is a somewhat revised version of an article entitled 'The spring, the seed and the tree: Gregory of Tours on the wonders of nature' published in the *Journal of Medieval History* 11 (1985) 89-135 and is reprinted by permission of Elsevier's Science Publishers B.V. (North Holland), Amsterdam.

1. The ark of Noah and the temple of Solomon — Gregory is the first to include these (Krusch 1885: 854); in his *Histories* (1.4) he sees in the ark a figure (*tipus*) of the Church —, the city of Babylon, 'the sepulchre of the Persian kings' (perhaps an amalgamation of the Maussolleion in Halicarnassus with the palace of Cyrus), the colossus of Rhodes, the theatre of Heracles and the lighthouse of Alexandria.
2. *De cursu stell.* 9: *Sed ista, licet quaepiam iussionem Dei, quaepiam autem adinventionem humana constructa sint, ab hominibus tamen constat esse fundata, ideoque et quaedam deruerunt, quaedam autem ruinae sunt proxima. Nam sunt alia quae ipse omnipotens Deus noster proprio opere in hoc mundo vel per dies singulos renovat, vel post transacto anni curriculum repraesentat, quae in locupletatione ostenduntur muneris, ut est commotio oceani et fructus terrae; alia vero in ostensione proferuntur virtutis, ut est sol, luna, stellae, Phinix; et quaedam*

In this rather lengthy preface to his little-known liturgical calendar, *On the course of the stars*, which he probably wrote between 575 and 582, Gregory was the first to posit and describe exclusively natural phenomena as the seven true wonders of the world.[3] As he says, the admirable works of men, even those divinely inspired, such as the ark of Noah and the temple of Solomon, are liable to decay and destruction. The real wonders, therefore, are the constantly renewed and hence indestructible divine works of nature.

This same explicit preference for the permanence of divine works over the transience of human ones also occurs elsewhere in Gregory's works. In the preface to *The glory of the martyrs* he says that since the 'fables' and 'fallacies' of the poets are all 'as though built on sand and look as though they are about to be destroyed, we should turn rather to divine and Gospel miracles (*miracula*)'. Following the instruction of the apostle Paul,[4] Gregory says he wishes 'to write and speak only of that which may build up the Church of God, and which may lead barren minds to the knowledge of perfect faith by fructifying them with holy teaching (*quae mentes inopes ad notitiam perfectae fidei instructione sancta fecundent*)'. Here, too, it is only divine works that are stable and lasting because they are not insubstantial human fantasies but continually renewed facts. Descriptions of these, moreover, (somehow) cause faith to be born in barren minds. This metaphor, as I hope to show later, points to a crucial element in Gregory's thinking.

What is Gregory, who devoted a considerable part of his life to collecting and describing events in which he sees the divine playing a significant role, trying to communicate to his reader? Although almost all his stories are about concrete phenomena and events in the visible world, it is possible to read many of them as being about interior perceptions and events, unconsciously experienced and expressed in terms of the visible. In his *Psychologie der Legende*, H. Günter describes hagiographical stories as 'Seelenvorgänge'. In accordance with early Christian

>   *ex his peccatores arguunt et ignem infernalem figurant, ut est Ethna, fons Gratianopolitanus. Haec sunt enim miracula, quae nulla aetate seniscunt, nullo occasu occidunt, nulla labe minuuntur, nisi cum Dominus mundum dissolvi praeceperit.* I have used my own translation throughout. E. Peters gives an English translation of the whole work in his *Monks, bishops and pagans* (Philadelphia 1975): 207—18.

3. Krusch 1885: 855.
4. Ephes. 4: 29. Sulpicius Severus, in the prologue to his life of St Martin, also rejects 'fables' and chooses instead to present the life and deeds of the saint (*Vit. Mart.* 1.3); he also has a distaste for the present life: *praesentium fastidium* (*Ep.* 2.1).

tradition and like his contemporary Pope Gregory the Great, Gregory reads them as visible manifestations of invisible, spiritual truth.[5] When looked at in this way, his circumstantial descriptions of miracles are statements about the content and morphology of his interior experience and about its values for him. By examining his descriptions of two categories of ordinary and miraculous natural phenomena — water and plant life — in their contexts, I will attempt to look through them to find what he saw that arrested his attention and spoke to his heart, what it was that he wanted others to know about.

Observations and experiences of natural phenomena can sometimes be influenced by the personal and social context in which they take place. The way one perceives nature, however, is even more the result of the cultural and in this case religious tradition in which one grows up and is educated. To understand Gregory it is necessary to look at the inherited ideas about nature that must have determined his categories of perception. Like Pliny, whom Gregory may have read, and Cassiodorus, whom he does not mention, Gregory here uses the word *miracula* for admirable works of men.[6] His list of the seven man-made wonders of the world, however, does not resemble any of the other lists of this kind circulating in Antiquity that are still extant.[7] As we have seen, he also uses the term *miracula* for what we would call miracles, such as those Christ performed in the Gospel stories. Without going into a discussion of terminology,[8] it can be said that the view of natural phenomena and miracles as, respectively, more and less familiar manifestations of the same omnipotent divine will continuously and creatively active in the universe is one found throughout the Old and New Testaments.[9] It is also

---

5. Günter 1949: 9 speaks of legends as 'Seelenvorgänge'. On the visible as a metaphor of the invisible: for instance Prosper of Aquitaine, whose works Gregory may have read, in *Lib. sent.* 134: *Visibile miraculum ad illuminationem vocat; invisibile autem, eum qui vocatus venit, illuminat. Omnia ergo narrat mirabilia Dei, qui credens visibilibus, ad intelligenda invisibilia transitum facit* (based on Augustine, *Ennaratio in psalmis* 9.2). Gregory the Great, *Dial.* 4.6.3: *ex rebus visibilibus cogimur credere quod non videmus*. There are some indications that Pope Gregory may have been acquainted with Gregory of Tours' works (de Vogüé 1976). On the projection of feelings onto other objects, compare Langer 1980: 124.
6. Pliny, *Nat. hist.* 36.30. Gregory mentions this author in *Vit. patr. prol.* Cassiodorus, in his *Variarum* 7.15.4, also makes this equation, but Gregory does not mention him anywhere in his works.
7. Lanowski 1965: 1030; Dawid 1968: 66.
8. See Moule 1966: 235—8.
9. Ross 1966: passim; Grant 1952: 153—81.

found in the writings of the Latin Church Fathers[10] (of whom Gregory, however, mentions very few) as well as in the work of Prosper of Aquitaine, a Gallic writer summarizing the views of Augustine.[11]

He certainly must have read many passages in the Bible with more or less the same meaning, proclaiming the natural world as a manifestation of the power, glory and goodness of God, such as Psalm 19:1: 'The heavens tell of the glory of God ...'. In the Book of Job natural phenomena are explicitly described as *miracula* wrought by God.[12] In the New Testament Gregory could find Paul stating that 'ever since the creation of the world (*mundus*), His invisible qualities (*invisibilia*), namely His eternal power and deity, are seen to have been understood (*intellecta conspiciuntur*) in the things that have been made'.[13] The same apostle told the citizens of Lystra to 'turn...to a living God who made the heavens and earth and sea and all that is in them...[who] did not leave Himself without witness, for He did good from heaven and gave rains and fruitful seasons, filling our hearts with food and gladness'.[14] From passages such as these Gregory could have derived his idea of natural phenomena as wonders, manifesting not only the power but also the generosity of God.

He is also driving at something else, however: he is claiming that in some natural phenomena 'figures' or images of certain specific truths about the spiritual life of men may be discerned. This kind of metaphorical or symbolical thinking is found in Christ's parables (like that of the Kingdom as a grain of mustard seed)[15] as well as in the sayings and epistles of Paul, who sometimes combined it with analogies between events in the Old and those in the New Testament.[16] As we have seen, this use of analogies is usually referred to typological thinking: here, in contrast to symbolical interpretation, both events are historical and concrete. This kind of interpretation was developed in the Greek and Latin patristic writings and by Gregory's time had come to be part of the

10. Taylor 1959a: 74; Augustine also held this view: Marrou 1938: 156. On Gregory's knowledge of earlier authors see Bonnet 1890: 48—76, and Manitius 1896, and Kurth 1919a: 1—29.
11. Prosper, *Lib. sent.* 284, perhaps referring to Augustine, *De civ. Dei* 21.7. Gregory never mentions either author. He may however have looked at Prosper's *Chronica* (see pp. 30-1 n.14) and Quodvultdeus' *Liber promissionibus* which was then attributed to Prosper (see below p. 89). If so, it is not unlikely that he was also acquainted with Prosper's *Sentences*.
12. Job 37: 14, 16.
13. Rom. 1: 20.
14. Acts 14: 15, 17.
15. Matth. 13: 24ff.
16. 1 Cor. 10: 1, 2, 6, 11.

generally accepted Christian tradition.[17] One of Gregory's favourite writers, the poet Prudentius,[18] who lived in the fourth century, wrote: 'In the mirror of the small we mark things that we do not understand, and we are permitted to seek hidden truth (*occultum... verum*) by means of what is at hand'.[19] Augustine, in the fifth century, speaks of extraordinary natural phenomena, that is, prodigies, as 'the wonders (*miracula*) whereby we wish to persuade the unbelievers of the things to come'[20] and mentions the spring of Grenoble as an example. Did Gregory read this? He may also have looked at the exegetical writings of Gallic authors, such as Hilary of Poitiers' *Treatise on the mysteries*, Eucherius of Lyon's *Forms of spiritual understanding* and Quodvultdeus' *Book of promises and prophecies* (until recently attributed to Prosper of Aquitaine)[21], all of which abound in 'figures' and 'types'. In the high and later Middle Ages, nature symbolism was greatly developed.[22] Gregory, however, who was aware of his mutilated Latin and his lack of classical education[23] and considered himself capable only of writing without ornament in 'plain speech (*simplex sermo*)',[24] appears everywhere in his works as practically inclined, more concrete and specific than systematic. Although he sometimes speaks of 'types' and 'figures', much of his symbolism is implicit — perhaps indicating an incomplete conceptualization. As will be seen, he may have experienced the symbol, to a certain degree, as a living, non-verbalized reality.[25]

Gregory says, then, that natural phenomena are constantly being 'renewed', 'recreated' and 'made manifest' by God: revelation is evidently an ongoing process. In addition, natural phenomena may reveal a hidden spiritual truth or mystery and sometimes, as prodigies, announce imminent major events in the human sphere. But what happens in miracles, when the customary course of nature is temporarily abrogated at a specific moment of time in favour of, or to the detriment of one or several human beings? As I hope to show, Gregory — like his namesake

17. On typology: Auerbach 1938: 472. On the patristic tradition: Taylor 1959a: 74—5; Smalley 1964: 1—35. In the third century, Tertullian (whom Gregory does not mention) had said that nature's processes could teach men the truth of such Biblical prophecies as the resurrection (Rees 1930: 213).
18. Bonnet 1890: 64, 70—1.
19. Prudentius, *Hamart.* 83—4; transl. Thomson 1949: 211.
20. Augustine, *De civ. Dei* 21.6.
21. Braun 1964: 19.
22. For instance, Taylor 1959b: 92; Chenu 1979: 1—48.
23. *Vit. patr.* 2. prol.
24. *Virt. Mart.* 2.19. See on this Beumann 1972.
25. Compare Mensching 1957: 6.

and contemporary Gregory the Great[26] — often also sees reflections of definite spiritual meanings in miraculous natural phenomena. His view and experience of nature has up to now been treated only in a brief and general way.[27] A more detailed look at Gregory's ascriptions of meaning to certain ordinary natural phenomena on the one hand and to miracles involving natural phenomena on the other, should reveal an important part of his mental universe.

According to Gregory, which phenomena and which miracles make manifest which spiritual truths and which divine actions? Does this symbolic or figurative view of the natural world make him incapable of appreciating its beauty here and now? Does it leave any room for a conception of an autonomously functioning nature? Furthermore, can some of these experiences and interpretations of phenomena as theophanies and symbols be recognized as elements in the language of universal human spiritual needs or, in Eliade's words,[28] as 'archetypes seeking expression'? On the other hand, might Gregory's interpretations also show in certain respects that 'what a society considers holy and what profane is very much a precipitate of that society's needs and structure'?[29] In the patterns that emerge from an analysis of his treatment of natural phenomena, certain vital contours of the structure and dynamic, as Gregory perceived it, not only of the natural world and miracles, but also of human spiritual and social experience of his time should become apparent.

A. WATER

THE TIDE AS 'THE FIRST WONDER': AN ORIGINAL POETIC IMAGE?

> The first [wonder] of all, therefore, is the tidal movement of the sea and the ocean, in which [the sea] every single day expands so much that, reaching the edge of the land, it covers the beach, and receding to where it came from, leaves [the beach] dry again. An abundant multitude of fish and various weeds is then collected by the people walking on the [now] dry ground. God provided this first wonder for the human race, [one] which is very much to be admired and which corresponds to his power.[30]

---

26. As Boglioni 1974: 34—7.
27. Sprandel 1979. Gautier Dalché (1982) notes that Gregory's descriptions of nature are placed in an abstract, symbolical cadre. Torchio 1982 does not mention Gregory. Stancliffe 1983: 205—27 gives the view of the natural world in Severus' and Martin's time (the late fourth century).
28. Eliade 1958: 453.
29. Brown 1973 in: Brown 1982: 263.
30. *De cursu stell.* 10: *Primum est ergo omnium maris oceani commutio, in qua ita per*

Why did Gregory start with the tidal movement of the sea as the first wonder? Perhaps because the ebb and flow and the bounty it yields is analogous to the rhythm of divine renewal of creative generosity everywhere and with which he shows himself to be so concerned. Judging by what he does with the natural phenomena that follow, this may be the (ultimate) meaning implied in his few obscure and pregnant words, though I do not think that he himself would have translated the analogy into such abstract terms. It may be an original, if not entirely conscious, association for I have not been able to find the image in this context in the works of other writers. If so, he shows himself to have been capable of combining the available biblical and Christian models[31] with a poetical intuition to form powerful thoughts and conclusions of his own.

'THE LIVING SPRING': A SYMBOL OF DIVINE ETERNAL LIFE

The spring or source appears in the mythologies and religious practices of many peoples throughout history as a manifestation of the sacred and a model or symbol of the working of the divine creative power in the world. In what is now France, the cult of springs seems in some cases to have lasted, despite Christian opposition, from Neolithic times until today.[32] A canon of the council of Tours in 567 attests to its presence in Gregory's time.[33] This may be a reason why Gregory did not use the *ordinary* spring as one of his world wonders (the burning fountain will be discussed in the context of fire in the following study). In the chapter titles of his Commentary on the Psalms, however, where he explains their 'truth of spiritual understanding (*veritas spiritualis intelligentiae*)' as prefigurations of Christ's passion and His redemption of mankind, Gregory sums up Psalm 35 by repeating its tenth verse: 'That He (Christ) is the fountainhead of life...(*fons vitae*)'. This could be physical life, since Gregory speaks of God as having created the world through the Word which is Christ,[34] but it can at the same time be spiritual life. The Old

---

dies singulos dilatatur, ut accedens ora litoris repleat rursumque recedens siccum praebeat iter;[a] tunc populis per humum aridam gradientibus piscium sive diversorum liguminum multitudo copiosa colligitur. Hoc primum miraculum Deus humano generi praeparavit, quod et admiratione praeclarum sit et congruum servituti.[b] [a]*iter*: I take this to be a mutilation of *iterum*. [b]*congruum servituti*, which does not make sense, is probably a corruption of *congruum suae virtuti*, as Haase suggests (Krusch 1885: 860 n. cap. 10f.).

31. Compare Oldoni 1972: 610.
32. Vaillat 1932; Eliade 1958: 200. See also Harmening 1979: 49—75.
33. *Conc. Tur.* a. 567, c. 23 in Maassen 1893: 133.
34. *Hist.* 1 *praef.*

Testament metaphor of God as 'the fountain of living water'[35] is in essence repeated by Christ in his meeting with the Samaritan woman at Jacob's well: '... whoever drinks of the water that I shall give him shall never thirst; the water that I shall give him will become in him a spring of water welling up to eternal life'.[36] Here the spring, in its continuous self-renewal, is probably an implicit model of the divine life in Christ. At the same time, its continuous thirst-quenching water, which keeps others alive, physically, is a traditional image of the Holy Spirit.[37]

It is this understanding of the spring which appears in the story that Gregory tells of the vision (*visum*) of an unnamed nun in Queen Radegunde's Convent of the Holy Cross in Poitiers.[38] She told her sisters that, in her vision, she seemed to be making a journey and wished to find the way to 'the living spring':

> Since she did not know the way, a certain man came toward her and said, 'If you wish to find the living spring I will show you'. She thanked him and followed him as he led the way. Thus they walked and came to a large spring, whose waters shone like gold, while the plants around it gleamed like all kinds of gems in the vernal light. Then the man said to her, 'Here is the living spring which you took so much trouble to find! Quench your thirst now from its stream, and let it be for you the spring of living water welling up into eternal life'....

After the nun had thereupon been clothed, by an abbess, with a sparkling royal bridal robe (perhaps she was of royal blood) sent by 'her spouse' (understood to be Christ)', the vision ended; but it so 'wounded her heart (*conpuncta est corde*)'[39] that a few days later she requested to be walled in as a recluse, and this was ceremonially carried out.

The contrast between the idyllic spot and the cramped dungeon she afterwards chose for herself cannot possibly be greater. The decidedly poetic description of nature, in which light imagery predominates,[40] shows how intensely a natural feature could be appreciated, for its resplendence if not for itself. Why, then, should the nun prefer the recluse's cell? Because, in Gregory's time, drinking from the living spring was one way of indicating regeneration into a new, heavenly life and the luminously beautiful spot was almost certainly interpreted as being Paradise. For, as Gregory explains elsewhere,[41] even the most exquisite flowers and plants are perishable and must wilt, while those in Paradise

---

35. Jer: 2.13.
36. John 4:13—4; transl. Rev. Stand. Vers. N.T. 1952: 107.
37. For instance Is. 44:3. Compare Daniélou 1958: 49ff.
38. *Hist.* 6.29.
39. Compare Ps. 108:17 and Acts 2:37.
40. Compare Fortunatus, *Carm.* 8.3.31: *pratorum gemmae*, and 8.7.18: *gemmae*.
41. *Hist.* 1.47.

are eternally fresh. Here again is the deep grief at the transiency of visible phenomena — even though God may be continuously at work in them — and the desperate yearning for permanence we also saw in Gregory's prefaces. The message of Christ's tender delight in the lilies of the field and the birds of the air[42] had in the preceding centuries been overlaid a certain depreciation of the visible world, a view perhaps deriving from Near Eastern dualism, and noticeable in the writings of Paul and John.[43] Tertullian had explained the vagaries and perishability of nature, which was created good and eternal, as due to the devil, demons and original sin.[44] The same view is expressed by Prudentius,[45] who also says: 'For all that the sun looks upon is vain (*vanum*); all things consist of mortal elements and transient matter of creation (*solubilis fluxoque creamine*)'.[46] Gregory himself quotes Salvius as saying, after a vision of heaven, that 'what you look upon in this world is nothing (*nihil*)', 'All is vanity (*vanitas*)'.[47] Hence nature as it was originally intended to be could be found again only in Paradise and, later, in 'a new heaven and a new earth'.[48] In Gregory's time, severe asceticism had come to be looked upon as the summit of Christian attainment: a glorious, if bloodless, martyrdom which, in former times, had been regarded as leading to Paradise instantly.[49] Gregory reports several times that saintly ascetics dying a natural death went straight to heaven.[50] The nun therefore must have chosen physical mortification because it was then regarded as the surest way of attaining Paradise she had seen.[51]

The story of the nun's vision shows how the spring could function in this period as a visionary symbol of Christ, and thus of regeneration into the true, that is, the spiritual life, which is not subject to change and corruption. The spring appears in a similar, but quasi-mythological, context in the story of the phoenix, which Gregory posits as the third wonder.[52] In a similarly beautiful, perpetually green spot at the highest point of the earth — clearly meant to be the original, earthly Paradise[53] —

42. Matth. 5:45 and 10:29.
43. Rees 1930: 211—2.
44. Rees 1930: 214.
45. Ephes. 2:2 and 6:12; Prudentius, *Hamart.* 260ff, 244ff.
46. Prudentius, *Hamart.* 504—5; transl. Thomson 1949: 239—41.
47. *Hist.* 7.1, based on Eccles. 1:2.
48. Rev. 21:1, 4.
49. Graus 1965: 101, 94. Compare, for instance, *Glor. conf.* 104.
50. *Vit. patr.* 10.4; 11.3; *Hist.* 6.29. Compare Severus, *Ep.* 2.4 and *Ep.* 2.9—12 about Martin.
51. Also by Gregory: *Vit. patr.* 11. *prol.*
52. *De cursu stell.* 12.
53. Compare Van den Broek 1971: 305—34, especially 332, and Eliade 1951: 54—5.

there is 'a noble tree' next to which is 'a large and gentle spring'. The phoenix does not drink the water but, after singing 'sweet melodies', bathes three or four times in it. Gregory's source Lactantius[54] also calls it 'a living spring (*fons vivum*)'. Though Gregory does not say so, this can only be intended as a symbol of Christian baptism. Immersion in the water of a spring, accompanied by the appropriate ceremonies (Lactantius, however, places the singing *after* the bathing and just before the conflagration), is regarded as regeneration into eternal life, as is also evident in several of Gregory's stories which will be examined presently. That baptism, however, can also be a kind of 'drinking' Gregory shows elsewhere:[55] 'He [Christ] quenches our thirst with the baptismal ablution'. The thirst in question is clearly that for the eternal life. Eliade regards the symbolism of immersion in water, meaning death and regeneration, as a universal and thus archetypal one, and quotes Paul: 'Know you not that all we who are baptized in Christ Jesus are baptized in his death? For we are buried together with him into death; that, as Christ is risen from the dead by the glory of the Father, so we also may walk in the newness of life'.[56]

There are two stories in which baptismal basins are filled by sources in a special way. In the basin at Embrun, 'water is said to rise up by divine power (*divinitus exoriri*) on the anniversaries of the Lord's birth and of the Last Supper';[57] the associations are unmistakably with Christ and with birth and death/resurrection. At Osser near Seville in Spain[58] the same happens 'by divine power (*divinitus*)' or 'at the command of God (*nutu Dei*)'[59] at Easter every year. On the anniversary of the Last Supper the citizens and the bishop, 'already perceiving in anticipation the scent of a holy fragrance (*jam odorem sacri praesentientes aromatis*)' (see below, p. 121-7) locked and sealed the doors of the building around the empty pool, 'expecting the arrival of the Lord's heavenly power (*virtus*)'.[60] When everyone returned on the third day and the doors were unsealed, the pool was full 'with waves rippling here and there, but the water not flowing away'. As though the water were still not miraculous enough, it was thereupon 'sanctified by exorcism, and chrism was strewn over it'. Then

---

54. Lactantius, *Carmen de phoenice* 25—6.
55. *In psal.* 41. Gregory may also have had in the back of his mind Quodvultdeus' statement in *Lib. promiss.*, *Glor. sanct.* 12: ... *ex ligno vitae sine corruptione cibum sancti capiant et de fonte Christo ... bibant* ...
56. Eliade 1958: 196—7; Rom. 6:3ff. transl. Rev. Stand. Vers. N.T. 1952: 174.
57. *Glor. conf.* 68.
58. Buchner 1967b: 76 n. 6.
59. *Hist.* 6.43 and 5.17 respectively.
60. *Glor. mart.* 23.

everyone started to drink it and take it home in jars to sprinkle on their fields and vineyards for 'protection', almost certainly against evil spirits. In spite of all this, the level of the water did not go down until every child had been baptized. Thereafter 'the waters returned into themselves (*in se reversi*); as I do not know from which beginning they were brought forth (*produntur*), neither do I know how they were brought to an end (*fine clauduntur*)'. When the heretic king Theodegisel, suspecting priestly stratagems, once just before Easter caused deep trenches to be dug around the building, in the hope of exposing hidden aqueducts, he found nothing. He was punished for daring to investigate 'the secret of divine power (*arcanum virtutis divinae*)' and died before this 'mystery' was 'celebrated' again the following year.[61] By 'mystery' Gregory may mean the miraculous appearance of the baptismal water; elsewhere he uses the word *mysterium*, however, to indicate Christ's resurrection which is man's redemption.[62]

Clearly, Gregory accepts the possibility of what looks like an annual divine creation of water *ex nihilo* followed by a return to nothingness. He is content (or even prefers) to be amazed without trying to understand, and castigates the latter as a sinful presumption entailing a deserved death. This heretic people, he says, 'seeing these great things (*magnalia*), is not pierced to the heart (*compungitur*) into [Catholic] belief, but keeps on cunningly attacking the mysteries (*sacramenta*) of the divine precepts with the most wicked chatterings of interpretations'. Speechless wonder and awe at a miracle, admiring without trying to understand, is to be 'pierced to the heart',[63] as the nun also was, and to let the divine message into one's soul unhindered and undeformed by rational thinking. This attitude is perhaps what most fundamentally characterizes Gregory's perception. It makes him accept as possible the frequent and contemporary occurrence of instant new divine creation *ex nihilo* (a persistent theme in his works, as will become evident) for, to God, everything is possible.[64] The intellect that thinks it can explain such things or believes only what it can explain is, for Gregory, pure uncivilized stupidity. Speaking of another miracle elsewhere,[65] Gregory says '... because of the stupidity of my rude (hard) mind (*stultitia mentis durae*) I was in no way inclined to believe these things until the miraculous power (*virtus*) which

61. *Glor. mart.* 24.
62. *Virt. Mart.* 2.29. Ambrose (*De myst.* 3.11) uses it for baptism; Gregory was probably acquainted with this association. See also Blaise 1954: 547—8.
63. See Otto 1936: 15, 29—31, Mensching 1957: 47 and Mensching 1951 in Mensching 1971: 172—5.
64. Matth. 19:26, referred to in *Hist.* 2.3.
65. *Glor. mart.* 5.

had been shown to others, acting in my presence, reproved my brutish slothfulness of mind (*bruta segnities*)'. He concludes: 'And I was silent in astonished admiration (*admiratusque silui*)'. Gregory, then, accepts and even cherishes the fact that God's workings move outside the categories that men's minds have for rational understanding. Elsewhere he says: 'I recall it not without a deep sigh and wonderment. I was rendered speechless (*obstupefactus*) by the miraculous power of the holy liquid'.[66]

Gregory very much makes the impression of *wanting* to be astonished, of experiencing the admiration of every miracle emotionally as an interior meeting with the inexpressible, which is the divine.[67] This experience of divine or miraculous power occurs in most religions. M. Meslin, a modern authority on the subject, has described the experience of the holy as follows: 'Mettant en jeu principalement des éléments affectifs, tels que l'admiration, la crainte, l'étonnement, la stupeur, il a paru apte à définir ce qui ne pouvait guère l'être par une expérience du type cognitif. Pour exprimer l'indicible, seul l'extraordinaire convient'.[68] At the same time, Gregory does try to understand, but in another way: not the 'how' but the 'why'. This he does by analogies. For instance, a thief who took some water from the above-mentioned baptismal pool found, when he came home, that his jar was empty.[69] The water stayed in his jar only when he had given back what he had stolen. The following story shows what is probably the implicit analogy or model here: the water of the River Jordan 'fled (*fugit*)' from a sinful woman who had the habit of killing her babies born of incest.[70] Here Gregory comments: 'The proverb of Solomon is hereby fulfilled, for the Spirit of the Lord flees from falsehood (*fugit fictum*)'.[71] The association of water with the Holy Spirit may also be found, for instance, in Eucherius.[72] Gregory here, as in many other instances, sees a visible event as a metaphor of an invisible, spiritual one.

The other stories in which springs occur are, not surprisingly, those of miracles in which these appear as visible natural phenomena. The

---

66. *Virt. Mart.* 2.32. Compare Gregory the Great, *Dial.* 1.6.2: *obstupesco*. Severus, on the contrary, reports such reactions only to false wonders: *obstupefactus* (*Vit. Mart.* 23.8); *hebetatus* (*Vit. Mart.* 24.5).
67. Like Gregory the Great; see Boglioni 1974: 96. And like Basil the Great; see Petit 1973: 86. I cannot agree with Friedrich 1951: 18 who says that Gregory is never astonished.
68. Meslin 1974: 177. Compare Caillois 1977, especially 454.
69. *Glor. mart.* 25.
70. *Glor. mart.* 87.
71. Wisd. 1:5.
72. Eucherius, *Formul. spir. intell.* 4.

'Christianization' of already existing source cults may sometimes have played a role in the origin of this kind of story.[73] Three times Gregory tells about holy men who, explicitly or implicitly mentioned as following the example of Moses, in one way or another let a spring appear in a previously dry place: a not infrequent motif in Christian hagiography.[74] Since it was an arduous task to carry water up from the bottom of the valley to the cave of the hermit Caluppanus, the holy man prayed to God to 'show' or 'make visible (*ostenderet*)' a spring in his rocky cell:[75]

> And that heavenly power which once brought forth (*produxit*) waters from the rock to quench the thirst of a whole people was present, for, at once after this prayer, drops of water came bursting out (*prorumpens*) of the rock....

Did Gregory also have in the back of his mind Paul's interpretation of this rock as Christ?[76] The term Gregory uses for the act of creating the spring out of nothing is *ostenderet*, the same word he uses to indicate the symbolic character of prodigies.[77] Here, the meaning seems to be the effect of a creation which is at the same time a visible revelation of divine power, or epiphany.

In gratefulness to a woman who, like Rebecca, had given of her water to his ass even though the well was far away from the village, St Martin fell on his knees and prayed to the Lord to 'show' or 'make visible (*ostenderet*)' an enormous spring to the astonished people'. God's creative activity, then, is described in terms of 'revealing' and 'showing' or 'making visible'[79] on the one hand, and of 'bringing forth' and 'bursting forth' on the other. In the third story, Abbot Aredius, after a very long prayer, 'stuck his walking stick into the ground, turned it around two or three times and pulled it out with joy; at once a burst of water followed it, so great that it is still serving the cattle...'.[80] Here the epiphanous quality of the miraculously created source is left implicit, and the holy man's turning the stick around and his joyfully expectation that this would work looks like a magic ritual. The springs in these stories have, in themselves, no unusual qualities, however, and the praise of the saint[81] or of God in His saint is the main point.

In the interesting story of a once abundant spring that disappeared and

73. Graus 1965: 487. Compare Harmening 1979: 48—75.
74. Ex. 17:6; Num. 20:11. See Graus 1965: 486.
75. *Vit. patr.* 11.2. Similarly Gregory the Great, *Dial.* 3.16.2.
76. 1 Cor. 10:4.
77. See pp. 43 and 69.
78. Gen. 24:15ff; *Virt. Mart.* 4.31.
79. Compare Mundle 1971: 310—7; Gärtner 1971: 317—20; Blaise 1954: 586.
80. *Hist.* 10.29.
81. Compare Graus 1965: 488.

then was brought back,[82] Gregory lets us catch a glimpse of various dynamics in nature. The inhabitants of a village in the territory of Limoges, possessing a particularly plentiful spring (*fons erat inriguus*),[83] had made irrigation canals for their gardens and fields 'so that where nature did not supply [a spring], effort might bring one (*ubi eum natura non dabat studium provocaret*)'. This is the only time in his works that Gregory uses the word 'nature' in this sense, as an apparently more or less independent whole.[84] There follows a metaphor: the spring flowed with such sweet abundance 'that one could see the vegetables and cuttings, which were watered by it, rejoicing (*gaudere*)'.[85] Manitius[86] has pointed to *poëtischen Floskeln* (usually reminiscent of Virgil or Prudentius) scattered through Gregory's work, and suggested that he had a tendency toward poetical expression, and perhaps even composed religious poems that have not been preserved. This metaphor of rejoicing plants, even though not entirely original, shows that he had an eye as well as a feeling for plant-life. After such a statement, the next sentence is surprising: 'The grace of the divine Majesty even assisted in it [that is, in the spring: *opitulabatur in eo*] so that in the plants that were watered by it the buds grew (*acciperent incrementum*) quickly'. God's grace (that is, power) is present in the water and is literally giving an extra impetus to the usual growth: this at least is what he seems to be saying. '[Christ] is the innermost inhabitant of everything' Gregory says in another work.[87] His meaning would appear to be that the divine is immanent in the visible world.

When, however, the villagers started to over-extend the range of their canals,

> making, as it were, a game of it, ...[the spring] disappeared into the earth by the envy of the Treacherous One, as I believe, to reappear in the middle of a swamp almost twelve stadia [one and a third miles, somewhat less than two kilometers] away, where it was no longer of use to anyone. At once, the villagers were gripped by fear and expected some new catastrophe to happen in the region. At the same time, they greatly lamented the loss of the benefits that they had been accustomed to have.

Here we see Gregory applying to recent events the view that the devil was allowed to pervert nature because of man's original sin (intellectual pride). Human inventiveness in disregard of God leads to the opposite of

---

82. *Glor. mart.* 36.
83. Compare Virgil, *Georg.* 4.32.
84. See below pp. 111-5.
85. Compare Virgil, *Eclog.* 9.48; *quo segetes gauderent frugibus.*
86. Manitius 1896: 550—3.
87. *In psal.* 82.

what is desired. This is the inverse of: 'to those who believe all things are possible'. The villagers' fear of some imminent disaster probably indicates that they interpreted the disappearance as a portent or prodigy, though Gregory does not use these terms here. If so, this means that in his view at least some of this latter kind of aberration of nature are brought about by the devil, with the permission of God, in order to punish sin or to warn men of greater punishments to come. Not only can God's power, then, assist nature from within, but the devil's, allowed by God, can likewise pervert it. Gregory seems to visualize this power as a kind of separate driving and informing force immanent in the phenomena which may either assist, deflect or suspend their 'natural' qualities or possibilities for action. This view of the dynamics of events will become evident again and again, not only in Gregory's descriptions of the natural world but also in those of human and miraculous events.

In the third year after the spring's sudden disappearance, when everyone's gardens and fields had dried up into barrenness, someone brought relics of the martyr Clement to the priest of the village, Aredius (the same one who had brought forth a spring by prayer and by turning a stick around in the ground). He 'had been besieged night and day by sorrowful neighbours confident that, if he asked God in his prayer, he would be able to make the spring come back in its old place'. Aredius showed himself, this time, to be either very modest or very diplomatic; he said, 'Let's go, dearest friends, and if it is true what their bearer asserts, that these are the relics of the martyr Clement, that will now become apparent when his power (*virtus*) is displayed'.[88] Singing psalms, everyone went to the place where the spring had had originally been. Then

> Aredius placed the relics in what used to be the spring's orifice and prostrated himself in prayer. He asked that the One who had once revealed a bountiful spring in the desert for men condemned to work in the marble quarries, would now, through the intercession of Clement, recall the waters to the same place... At once the spring returned to its orifice, gushing forth (*evomens*) great quantities of water... The astonished (*admirantes*) people expressed great thanks to the Lord, who had both showed the power (*virtus*) of the martyr and deigned to grant the prayer of his faithful servant [Aredius].

This story shows in miniature what Gregory's general view of man and nature was, but also what, according to him, men here and now could do about it: through relics, secure the intercession of a saint to ask God to put things right again. Typological thinking is evident in the fact that God is asked, as it were, to repeat a previous action. In this case the 'power' of the saint is ambivalent in meaning: is it his prestige in heaven

---

88. On relics see Herrmann-Mascard 1975; on *virtus* as miraculous power Hébert 1916: 124—6.

that enables him to persuade God to do this, or is it God's delegated power which the martyr himself is wielding, or is it his prestige that enables him to wield this delegated power? The automatism that is assumed here — that, if they are relics, they *must* work — indicates two things: first, that the 'power' was thought in some way to reside always or to be available upon call in these objects,[84] and second, that the 'power' itself was (in principle and with the appropriate reverence) capable of being, at the least, influenced.

As Gregory describes them, all the springs (except possibly Osser) examined up to now, although 'shown', 'made visible' or 'revealed' upon request, had no other special qualities. The spring in which the martyr Julian's head had been washed directly after his decapitation is the only one to which Gregory attributes a specific miraculous power. It immediately healed Gregory's own sunstroke (headache with fever) when, after a prayer, he had drunk from it and washed his face and head in it: 'as soon as the water fell on me, the pain fled (*fugato dolore*) and I went away cured'.[90] Here the association with Julian's trunkless but already sanctified head (martyrs went straight to heaven) is extremely suggestive and magical: 'like cures like'.[91] In fact, modern scholarship has, on the whole, recognized magic as inseparable from religion, and speaks of 'magico-religious phenomena'.[92] The spring also cures many other kinds of illnesses such as blindness and fevers, however. In fact, 'the violence of fevers is extinguished so quickly as though one sees an enormous blaze above a huge funeral pyre put out by waves that reach out and smother it'. There is a double symbolism here: both the spring (associated, implicitly, with Christ, the fount of life) and Julian's regeneration, into the heavenly life suggest new life, expressed in the metaphor of the extinguished funeral pyre. In other cures, too, Gregory often suggests that a spiritual rebirth took place as well.[93] Meier[94] has observed that the symbolism of healing at the ancient Greek sanctuaries (which in many ways resembles that in the late antique Christian ones) is strikingly similar to that of the mysteries: the cure has the value of a reincarnation. As I hope to show in what follows, renewal through divine power is one of the central elements in Gregory's thinking.

One story shows even more clearly that Gregory thought of the saint's

89. Aune 1980: 1536.
90. *Virt. Jul.* 25.
91. See Brown 1977 in Brown 1982: 228; Meier 1967: 299; Lanczkowski 1960: 1276.
92. Aune 1980: 1510—6.
93. For instance *Virt. Mart.* 1.40: *ut putares denuo renatum*; *Virt. Mart.* 2.13: *renasci denuo fecit*.
94. Meier 1967: 303.

or God's power as actually pulsing in the water of Julian's spring. Aredius had taken a little vial of water from it home with him; later he said to Gregory: 'I call to witness the Almighty God that before I reached home, the colour, the density and the fragrance had been changed (*commutata*) into balsam'.[95] His astute bishop, Ferreolus,[96] later chose only this vial out of other relics to put in the altar of a church newly dedicated to the martyr, saying: 'These are proven (*certae*) relics because the martyr had honoured them with the excellent qualities [being also powers: *virtutes*] of Paradise'. Here again we see a practical concern with the genuineness and efficacy of relics, but also again the association with the transforming force of renewed and eternal life in Paradise, vibrating, as it were, in it; a force which may the more easily be tapped, so to speak, by having it close at hand.

To sum up, when consciously interpreting Scripture, Gregory makes use of the symbolical interpretation of Christ as 'the spring of life'. In the story of the nun's vision, he also interprets, though more implicitly, the spring as the symbol of Christ: imbibing His words or its waters brings about regeneration into eternal life. The spring in the story of the phoenix is probably a symbol of baptism, and hence of regeneration. In the miracle stories, springs occur in various contexts. Through their use, they are also associated with baptism, and thus with spiritual regeneration. Through their manner of appearing, they point to the revelation or 'bursting forth' of God's power in visible phenomena. Their healing qualities seem to symbolize regeneration into the heavenly life. The associations in the miracle stories are sometimes explicit and sometimes implicit and indirect, through the use of verbs or situational structures that are reminiscent of biblical descriptions. I think it is not too much to say that Gregory's presentation of the spring in its various aspects betrays a deep concern with the spiritual regeneration of which it is the symbol. Even when Gregory is not consciously attempting to present it in this way, his veneration of the phenomenon as a divinely produced and sustained refreshment, conditional upon reverential attitude in men, goes a long way in this direction. Gregory was not the only writer in this period who stressed the impermanence of human institutions and was preoccupied with interior regeneration or renewal. In the *Moralia*, his

---

95. *Virt. Jul.* 41.
96. Gams 1873: 564.

contemporary and namesake Pope Gregory the Great exhibits the same concern and in the same context.[97]

The pope lays similar emphasis too on what he calls 'humility',[98] a quality which comes close to the receptive reverence described by Gregory of Tours as 'astonished admiration' at a miracle without any attempt at an explanation. This attitude, the converse of inquisitive, rationalizing self-assertiveness, appears to be a key to Gregory's world-view. Gregory does not only advise a careful, formal etiquette toward the supernatural.[99] As I have tried to show, in his view it was especially the consciously cultivated desire for and surrender to astonished admiration that made possible the affective recognition of the working of divine creative power. The content as well as the presentation of Gregory's writings show that he himself felt renewed and sustained by the experiences of awed reverence when confronted with miracles as theophanies, and that he wished to awaken this reverence in others by recording as many of them as he could find.[100] As we shall see later, Gregory also saw reverence in general, and if necessary fear, as the upholder of the kind of society that he had in mind for his time.

'THE TURBULENT WAVES AND ROCKY CRAGS OF THIS WORLDLY LIFE': SOCIETY OR THE HUMAN MIND?

> The Lord, however, angered by the sins of the people, who were not walking in His paths, sent the Flood and it annihilated every living soul from the face of the earth[101] by its inundation.... But I do not doubt that the image (*species*) of the ark [of Noah] was the model of the Mother Church. For she, passing through the turbulent waves and the rocky crags of this worldly life (*inter fluctus et scupulos huius saeculi*) protects us from imminent evils....[102]

Here the waters called forth by God brought death and dissolution to all earthly and animal forms. But it is primarily a destruction of evil, making a new, purified and regenerated world possible. This is an ancient

---

97. Ladner 1973: 1—17, especially 11. In the latter part of the article Mr. Ladner shows, very significantly in my opinion, that in the dynamic and expansive eleventh century, Gregory VII's concept of renewal, though presupposing the interior kind, centres on that of the church as an institution: i.e. he has sufficient confidence in an earthly institution to reform it.
98. Gregory the Great, *Moralia* 13.32, quoted and discussed by Ladner 1973: 7.
99. Brown 1977 in Brown 1982: 232—3.
100. *Virt. Mart.* 1. *prol.* Ph. Wheelwright 1971: 47 says that awe, meaning wonderment combined with humility, keeps the emotions alive and the mind open.
101. Gen. 7:23.
102. *Hist.* 1.4.

symbolism.¹⁰³ Before Gregory's time, the Church Fathers had seen in the immersion in the Flood a model of Christian baptism.¹⁰⁴ Gregory here, however, chooses to stress the positive contribution of the Church as the ark and therefore points to the negative value (found in the New Testament) of the turbulent deep as a figure of the unstable and dangerous life in this world, which is dominated by the devil.¹⁰⁵ This line of interpretation had also been developed by Christian writers such as Prudentius, Eucherius and Prosper of Aquitaine.¹⁰⁶ Although Pope Gregory speaks of the sea as the human mind,¹⁰⁷ Gregory of Tours does not do so. As we shall see, however, he does visualize the human mind as the (equally turbulent) sky. Today, the sea is regarded by some as an archetypal image of the human subconscious.¹⁰⁸ This being so, it is tempting to see the negative value associated with the sea as 'life in this world' as in part a projection of the manner in which men in the Latin West at that time experienced themselves as well as their society.

Gregory's description of the life in this world as a perilous sea resembles that of Hilary of Poitiers, who wrote: 'The movement and turbulence of this worldly life (*saeculi huius motus atque fluctus*) are compared, according to the prophetic and allegorical understanding (*secundum propheticam et allegoricam intelligentiam*), to the seethings of the undulating sea brought about by the devil's dwelling in them'.¹⁰⁹ More strikingly similar to Gregory's words, however, are those of Quodvultdeus, the then anonymous author of the *Book of promises*, probably thought by Gregory to be Prosper of Aquitaine. In this book he could have found that the Flood 'showed the immersion in the flood of souls in the present time, souls which are drowned by the turbulent waves (*fluctibus*) in the rocky crags of the world (*scopulis saeculi*), in the whirlpool of crimes and by the shipwrecks of various lusts'.¹¹⁰ This

103. Eliade 1958: 194.
104. Compare Daniélou 1958: 97—118.
105. For instance 2 Cor. 4:4 and Gal. 1:4. Compare Orbán 1970: 240. The protective role of the church is evident too in Bishop Nicetius' dream of fishing (for souls) in the sea: *Vit. patr.* 17.5.
106. Prudentius, *Hamart.* 517—20; Eucherius, *Formul. spir. intell.* 4; Prosper, *Expos. psal.* 103.8.
107. Gregory the Great, *Moralia* 29.15, cited and discussed in Ladner 1973:9.
108. As Beirnaert 1950: 272; Schmitt 1945: 114. Compare Blöcker 1981: 121.
109. Hilarius of Poitiers, *Tract. super Ps.* 51.13. *Saeculum* in this period usually means 'this world' or 'the worldly life' in the negative sense of the temporal as opposed to the eternal life (Orbán 1970: 240; Blaise 1954: 732). Compare Severus, *Vit. Mart.* 25.4 and *Ep.* 2.7.
110. Quodvultdeus, *Lib. promiss.* 1.7.13. Jungblut (1977: 345 and 349) notes that Gregory's occasional 'metrical' style also resembles that of Quodvultdeus.

author, who was a pupil of Augustine, sees the Flood's ending in the six hundred and first year of Noah's age as signifying that the end of the world would come after the six ages of worldly life (*aetates saeculi*) and the brief period of the Antichrist's reign. The Church, like the ark, would carry the good and the wicked until the end.[111] Gregory, however, though concerned with 'times', never mentions 'ages', perhaps because he wished to avoid speculation but possibly because he was not acquainted with this theory.[112] The combination, in connection with *saeculum*, of *fluctus* and *scopuli* that occurs in the same context both in the *Book of promises* and in Gregory's work may indicate that Gregory nevertheless read this earlier work; it is also possible, of course, that they had a common source, now lost.

Elsewhere, Gregory seems to point to the positive as well as the negative value of the sea in one and the same chapter. Speaking of the passage through the Red Sea,[113] he says that the partings of the sea[114]

> should be understood spiritually and not literally. For there are in this worldly life, which is figuratively (*figuraliter*) called the sea, many partings, since not all are able to come to the eternal life equally or by the same road.

After allegorically explaining the parable of the vineyard[115] in this context, he continues:

> It is clear that the passage through this sea as well as the pillar of cloud[116] acted as the model (*tipus*) of our baptism; as the apostle Paul said, 'I want you to know, brethren that our fathers were all under the cloud, and all passed through the sea, and in Moses all were baptized in the cloud and the sea'.[117]

Gregory could have found this interpretation also in the works of the Church Fathers but probably read it in Prudentius.[118] He does not try to reconcile the two opposing aspects of the sea as symbol. Eliade states that symbols, since they are used to represent ultimate reality, are by their very nature multivalent and paradoxical: reality can manifest itself only through contradictions and cannot, therefore, be adequately expressed in concepts.[119] The paradox here is that, in baptism as in the initiations of the late antique mysteries, 'death' is necessary for a 'rebirth' to be

---

111. Quodvultdeus, *Lib. promiss.* 1.7.13.
112. See pp. 60-1.
113. *Hist.* 1.10, referring to Ex. 14:21.
114. Ps. 136:13.
115. Matth. 20:3.
116. Ex. 14:19.
117. 1 Cor. 10:1, 2.
118. Prudentius, *Cathem.* 12.165—7. Compare Daniélou 1958: 119—35.
119. Eliade 1952: 17. Compare Meslin 1975 in Ménard 1975: 28 on the 'plurivocité' of symbols.

possible; the water must destroy the 'old' before it can bring about the 'new' life.[120] The *Book of promises* however, says the following about the Red Sea passage:[121]

> Behold the water as revenger, sanctified by the Word, reddened by blood, struck by the Cross in the symbol (*in mysterio*) of the rod[122] brings salvation to those coming to seek the Saviour, and it drives sins, with their author the devil, into the deep like the Egyptians with their king.

In other words, Christ, through His Passion, has overcome the devil and death in water as well as in the world and made it an instrument of salvation.[123] Elsewhere, Gregory writes: '... [Christ] carries the Church, redeemed by His blood, on His neck above the turbulence of the life of this world (*fluctus saeculi*)'.[124] The sea, then, can destroy but can also renew, depending upon one's spiritual quality, and one may be carried above the sea-like turbulence of the world by Christ in His Church.

'Thou rulest the raging of the sea; when its waves rise, thou stillest them'.[125] The text of Gregory's interpretative title for his (lost) commentary on the psalm in which this quotation occurs is corrupt and obscure but probably means something like: '[Christ] rules all things mightily through his power over water (*cum potestate aquae omnia potenter dominetur* [sic])'.[126] In the New Testament, Christ's victory over the demonic powers in the sea was indicated by his stilling of the storm on the Sea of Galilee as well as by his walking on the water.[127] These are some of the model events or paradigms behind a number of stories that Gregory tells about danger at sea. In these stories, however, Christ remains in the background; what Gregory lets us see of the role of the saints and their relics reveals a by no means unambiguous interplay of power between man and the supernatural, which tells us something about the art of survival as practised in his time. The following story about a storm on the Lake of Geneva is typical.[128] A priest, entrusted with carrying the relics of the martyrs of Agaune to King Guntram crossed this lake on this journey. No sooner had he and his travelling companions set sail, than

---

120. Hopfner 1935: 1323; Beirnaert 1950: 255—70.
121. Quodvultdeus, *Lib. promiss.* 1.38.
122. Ex. 17:6.
123. Compare Beirnaert 1950: 267.
124. *In psal.* 23.
125. Ps. 88:9, transl. Rev. Stand. Vers. O.T. 1952: Ps. 98:9, p. 622.
126. *In psal.* 88.
127. Matth. 8:23—7 and 14:25ff. respectively. Similarly Prudentius, *Apoth.* 664—71.
128. *Glor. mart.* 75. Similar stories are: *Glor. mart.* 68, 82; *Glor. conf.* 94; *Virt. Mart.* 2.17; *Vit. patr.* 17.5. Compare Severus, *Dial.* 3.14.

> suddenly a storm arose that lifted up the sea into turbulence: waves high as mountains rose up to the stars, and now the stern of the little boat was raised up high while the prow seemed to be swallowed up; then again, the stern was submerged while the prow was lifted into the skies.[129]

The sailors prepared themselves for death. But the priest, covered with foam from the waves, took from his neck the little case with relics,

> held it out full of confidence against the boiling waves, and invoked the aid of the saints in a loud voice, saying 'Glorious martyrs! I beg for your power [to save me] lest I perish in these waves; stronger still, you who never fail to give aid to those who are about to perish deign, I pray, to extend to me your right hand of salvation. Subdue the turbulence and lead us by the power of your aid to the shore we wish to reach!' And while he was saying this, the wind ceased blowing, the waves died down and they were carried to the shore.

If the suddenness of the storm and perhaps the 'boiling' waves imply demonic agency, this is here not made explicit. In another similar story[130] Gregory says: 'The wind was called forth at the instigation of the Tempter (*tentatoris impulsu commoto vento*)'. The priest's calm confidence, his opposing the relics to the waves and his invocation which, in spite of its reverential formulation, posits the almost coercive 'fact' that the martyrs 'never fail' in their aid — all this shows that 'in prayer the boundary between magical formula and supplication remains fluid'.[131] The terms '(miraculous) power (*virtus*)' and 'oppress (*opprimite*)', as well as the fact that the storm and waves abate upon hearing, as it were, these words spoken, also indicate that one power is overcoming another.

The demonic element in turbulent water (also an archetypal image)[132] actually becomes visible in Gregory's report of the flooding of the Tiber at Rome in 590:[133]

> A multitude of serpents and a huge dragon, as large as a massive beam, went along the river-bed down into the sea; but the beasts were drowned in the salty waves[134] of the turbid sea and thrown onto the shore. Immediately thereupon, the plague came which is called bubonic...

Serpents and dragons are, of course, traditionally associated with the devil. The sea, in the Old as well as the New Testament, is the home of

---

129. Compare Virgil, *Aen.* 1.103.
130. *Virt. Mart.* 1.2. Severus, by contrast, never implies demonic agency in storms; the latter are indications of the power of God: *Dial.* 3.8. Compare Fontaine 1968: 755.
131. M. Weber, quoted in Aune 1980: 1551. Similarly Hamman 1980 in Haase 1980: 1230—1.
132. As Beirnaert 1950: 272ff.
133. *Hist.* 10.1.
134. Compare Virgil, *Aen.* 5.182.

demonic monsters.[135] In the above report, it drowns them, like the demonically-possessed Gadarene swine.[136] The same (or other) demons were probably assumed to have then immediately set about causing the plague.[137]

There is one story about a man who is described as 'envious', 'contrary' and 'proud', the qualities by which the devil is always recognized in Gregory's stories. This proud man tried to prevent people who were transporting columns for St Martin's Church from using his part of a small river for this purpose and was punished by drowning.[138] Gregory says: 'When the proud man struck his horse, he was thrown into the little stream and died in the bosom of the eddy of waters, suffocated by his own attack (*ictibus suis suffocatus interiit*)'. Drowning in 'a little stream' implies malicious agency; Gregory indicates that the man's attacks upon the saint have boomeranged upon himself, but it is not clear whether it is because he got entangled in his own obstructions in the stream or because the demonic power in the water has been allowed to overcome him on account of his overweening pride. The meanings could also overlap. The main point of the story, however, is that any disparagement of St Martin will be severely punished.

Gregory also tells stories, on the other hand, in which relics of saints seem to function as power objects without the saint having being called upon. Constantine's mother, the Empress Helen, threw one of the nails of the Cross into the Adriatic Sea, in which up till then so many ships and men had been drowned that it had been called a 'whirlpool and abyss for sailors'. She did this

> trusting in the mercy of the Lord, which can easily subdue the savage turbulence of the waves. When this had been done, the sea was made calm, and since that time there are only breezes favourable to navigation. And to this day the sailors worship the sanctified sea (*sanctificatum mare venerantur*) when they have entered upon it and give themselves over to fasting, prayers and psalm-singing.[139]

It looks as though it was thereafter not a question of asking God for aid but of venerating the sea itself as a holy object! Doubtless because, as Gregory says, 'all that has touched the sacrosanct Body becomes thereby itself sacred (*sacratum*)'.[140] Likewise, a woodsman who had given hospitality to a priest for the night and had eaten bread blessed by him

---

135. As in Job 7:12, Dan. 7 and Rev.13:1.
136. Matth. 8:32.
137. As in *Vit. patr.* 17.4.
138. *Virt. Mart.* 1.2.
139. *Glor. mart.* 5.
140. *Glor. mart.* 6. Compare Helgeland 1980 in Haase 1980: 1297 and Vauchez 1975: 29.

for breakfast, could not be pulled into the water of a stream by its demons because, as he overheard them saying, 'a sacred thing (*res sacra*)' prevented them from doing so. He was 'protected' by the bread that had just been blessed, that is, by the priest's unintentional 'Eucharist'.[141]

Another example of this kind of thinking is the 'great miracle' that the power of God (*virtus Domini*) accomplished when, late one night at Coblenz, when a boat, which Gregory suddenly found himself sharing with a huge crowd of various uninvited people, filled to the rims with water yet did not sink. In fact, Gregory says, 'could not sink', 'for we had with us relics of the blessed Martin as well as of other saints, by whose (miraculous) power (*virtus*) we believe ourselves to have been saved'.[142] Gregory does not say he invoked either the saints or God. Nevertheless, God's power performed the miracle, and it was at the same time the saints' power (*quorum virtus*) that saved him. One can only conclude that the very presence of the saints' relics 'automatically' brought divine power into action. A similar case, when a martyr's ashes floated so that the people could collect them,[143] he calls 'a new miracle (*miraculi novitas*)', probably because it had no precedent in the Gospels. In all these examples 'power', operating virtually 'automatically' through holy objects, temporarily changed the natural properties of water or of the object in the water, or offered protection against the demons in water.

Saintly power is seen to operate in a very different manner in another story.[144] When a sudden storm caused a boat to be severely tossed about upon the waves, one of its passengers, Bishop Baudinus of Tours,[145]

> prostrated himself in prayer with tears; holding his joined hands up to the stars,[146] he beseeched the aid of the blessed Martin and asked him to deign to come at once.
> One of the treacherous ones [sic] however, said: 'That Martin whom you are calling upon has left you already, and he won't save you in this hour of need'. I believe in truth that this utterance was brought forth by the devil so as to dislodge the blessed bishop from his praying. But he, repelling this javelin with the cuirass of his faith, entreated more and more the help of the holy man and at the same time exhorted all to pray. While they were thus praying, suddenly a most delightful odour as that of balsam came over the ship, and as though someone were walking around with a censer, a smell of incense spread everywhere. At the moment that this fragrance came, the savage fury of the winds ceased, the mountainous masses of water on each side of the ship were shattered, and the sea became tranquil again. All aboard who had prepared themselves for death, were astonished at the peace of

---

141. *Glor. conf.* 31. Compare Graus 1965: 219—20.
142. *Hist.* 8.14.
143. *Glor. mart.* 96.
144. *Virt. Mart.* 1.9.
145. Bishop of Tours between 549 and 555 according to Gams 1873: 639.
146. Virgil, *Aen.* 1.92.

the waves, and in the calm they soon reached the shore. No one need doubt that this storm was calmed by the arrival of the saint.

Here the devil, implicitly active in the sudden storm also works through a human agent, trying to put an end to the totally concentrated confidence and prayer which, certainly in the absence of relics, appear to be the way to get things done supernaturally. Elsewhere, Gregory says this explicitly, often referring to Christ's injunction, 'Ask, and it shall be given to you...'.[147] Quoting the Gospel, he makes this an excuse for 'importunity'[148] or even outright pressure, such as that of supplicants who refuse to eat or to leave the church until their request is granted.[149] Although Gregory elsewhere insists on reverent astonishment he is also convinced, or wishes to be, that the divine power has certain obligations towards those who call upon it in faith. He shows that when a patron saint, for instance, does not appear to fulfil his obligations of protection and healing, he can be threatened with abandonment by his 'clients'.[150]

That the saint was thought to be present in person during his action is corroborated by another story in which a holy man is seen at night in a church with garments still dripping because he had just saved some people in a storm.[151] Is this saving power, then, purely personal? When, in another saving action, St Martin had let a gentle breeze and 'an obedient wave (*unda famulans*)' bring those already drowning safely to the shore, Gregory comments:

> Here that same power was present that divided the waters of the Jordan so that the people [of Israel] could walk on the dry ground between the mountainous masses of water;[152] that [power] which rescued the perishing Peter by lovingly extending its right hand, lest he should drown;[153] and that which brought the sailor who called upon the Lord of St Martin up from the bottom of the sea to the shore where he wished to go.[154]

Gregory seems to be saying that it is all God's power, whether exerted by the Father, the Son or St Martin or by all these together.[155] Here, however, the purely intercessory role of Martin is explicitly mentioned, in

---

147. Mark 11:24, mentioned in *Vit. patr.* 16. *prol.*; *Hist.* 2.3, 8.10; *Glor. mart.* 6.
148. Luke 11:8: *si perseveraverit pulsans*; cited in *Glor. mart.* 13. Similarly Severus, *Dial.* 3.14.
149. *Glor. mart.* 13; *Virt. Mart.* 3.39.
150. As in *Glor. conf.* 70; *Virt. Mart.* 3.8.
151. *Glor. mart.* 33.
152. Josh. 3:16.
153. Matth. 14:30—1.
154. *Virt. Mart.*1.2.
155. Compare *Virt. Mart.* 1.32: *tribuente Domino et juvante patrono*; *Virt. Mart.* 4.12: *fides nostra retinet in multorum sanctorum virtutibus unum Dominum operari*.

contrast to the previous story. In other stories, the formulation can point in a different direction. When a boat-bridge had broken, for instance, Gregory lets the drowning cry, 'Most blessed Genesius, rescue us by the power of your own sanctity (*propriae sanctitatis virtus*)'![156]

In all these stories the emphasis is upon the divine power working in the water to save one who calls upon it from being swallowed up and annihilated in the treacherous deep, rather than upon any association of death and (spiritual) resurrection. What we see in these stories are the outlines of a power structure in which the role of the saint is not always unambiguous, and in which the human supplicant believes he can sometimes, through prayers and power objects, exert strong pressure upon a power greater than himself.

There are two stories which, at first sight, appear to be ordeals by water. A woman whose husband accused her of a crime which, however, 'could not in any way be proved, was condemned by the judge to be thrown in the water (*ut aquis immergeretur dijudicata est*)'.[157] This formulation can be understood either as an ordeal or as a punishment. The next sentence, however, makes the interpretation as an ordeal highly unlikely: she was thrown from a boat into the Rhône with a huge stone tied around her neck. In the original Germanic ordeal by cold water the person in question was bound only, and the earliest extant rules of procedure for Christian cold water ordeals date from the eighth century.[158] The woman began to call upon the martyr, crying, 'Holy Genesius, glorious martyr, who sanctified (*sanctificasti*) these waters by the act (*pulsu*) of swimming in them, rescue me according to my innocence!' and 'at once she began to float upon the water'. This, too, is evidence against the view of the incident as an ordeal: in the early Germanic version as well as in the later version, those who float are the *guilty*.[159] When the people saw this, they took her back into the boat and brought her to the saint's church. Thereafter, according to the contemporary custom of asylum, she was no longer disturbed either by the judge or by her husband. If this event was in fact a (pagan) ordeal, Gregory does not recognize or describe it as such. When he reports other cases of condemned persons being saved by a saint, from prison or from the gallows, this is more an indication of forgiveness than of innocence,

---

156. *Glor. mart.* 68.
157. *Glor. mart.* 68.
158. Leitmaier 1960: 1131; Michel 1931: 1143, Vauchez 1975: 28—9. Compare Fontaine 1968: 657 (n. 2), Harmening 1979: 269, 271 and Mensching 1957: 50.
159. Leitmaier 1960: 1130.

since some of these were by their own admission guilty.[160] They too, however, were thereafter left in peace by the judge. Noteworthy in the story of the woman is that, again, water is considered to have been made 'holy' through contact with a holy person or object. Here this seems to mean only that the water is able to co-operate in the rescue: it is not revered for itself. In the later Christian ordeals, a prayer was said over the water beforehand. The circulation of this kind of story may have played a role in the development of christianized ordeals.

Another woman, unjustly accused by her husband of adultery (an easy way of getting rid of an unwanted wife?) was also condemned to be thrown into the water (*dijudicatur immergi*).[161] She, too, was thrown from a bridge with a millstone tied to her neck into the Saône, while her husband shouted some unkind last words about washing off her sins after her. 'But', says Gregory, 'the compassion of the Lord, which does not allow the innocent to perish, provided a beam under the water which men could not see'. This formulation seems to indicate that it was an invisible, supernatural beam. The millstone fell on one side of it, the woman on the other; in this way she did not sink to the bottom. At sunset, her family requested and received permission from the judge to fetch her body from the river. When they had retrieved her from under the water and found she was still breathing, they hurried her to a nearby church, fearing that the judge would order her to be drowned again. This, too, indicates that — in Gregory's eyes, at least — this immersion was *intended* as a punishment and not as an ordeal. At the same time, however, he makes of her being saved the equivalent of an ordeal, saying: 'the faith of a pure conscience saved her, as well as the Lord, whom she had constantly called upon', and especially: 'the compassion of the Lord does not allow the innocent to perish'. If he means to say that innocence, in a sense just like a relic, somehow constrains God into rescuing it, then he is already thinking in terms of a Christian ordeal.[162] In his *Histories*, in fact, he tries whenever possible, to show God saving the innocent.[163]

Gregory reports one martyr's death by drowning[164] in such a way that it supports these ideas, or rather hopes, about the innocent. After repeating the essentials of the story he found in Jerome's translation of

---

160. For instance *Virt. Mart.* 3.53. St Martin emphasized forgiveness: Severus, *Vit. Mart.* 22.4.
161. *Glor. mart.* 69. See on the position of women in Frankish law Wemple 1981: 27—50.
162. See on this Radding 1979.
163. For instance *Hist.* 3.28.
164. *Hist.* 1.35.

Eusebius' *Chronicle* and in Prudentius'[165] story about Bishop Quirinus of Siscia being thrown with a millstone around his neck into the river during the persecution of Diocletian, he adds a comment of his own. Although it seems insignificant, this comment in fact betrays a whole manner of thinking. At first the bishop, he says, was 'for a long time borne on top of the water by divine power'. Prudentius says: 'the river did not allow him to be submerged' and 'the underlying depth (*substrata profunditas*) did not dare to swallow of its own accord the stone, the noose and the man'.[166] In other words, the bishop's holiness brings about an attitude of veneration even in the element of water. Gregory, however, says: '...and the waters did not swallow one who was not weighed down by the heaviness of crime (*nec sorbebant aquae, quem pondus criminis non praemebat*)'. Why would he bring up the, here irrelevant, notion of 'crime', unless he was thinking, in general terms, of some kind of possible indication of guilt or innocence through the action of water?[167] What Prudentius regards as a proof of *sanctity*, Gregory presents as a proof of *innocence*. At the same time he interprets the visible as a metaphor of the invisible: the absence of the physical quality of heaviness indicates the absence of the moral quality of criminality.[168] Thus, for Gregory, natural phenomena do not only present figures of prophetic truths, but also visible indications of the moral quality of persons — which is indeed a presupposition underlying the institution of ordeals. Quirinus nevertheless attained his fervently desired martyrdom by asking God just before the people were about to rescue him, to let him sink and thereby go to heaven.

In this context, Gregory's story about an ordeal by boiling water[169] is relevant, although of course it has little to do with deep water. When, after a long theological debate, a Roman (Catholic) Christian and an Arian found that neither could convince the other by arguments, the former, considering that 'wisdom will not enter a malevolent mind',[170]

165. Hieronymus, *Chronicon* 2:A.D. 312 in Migne 1866: 495—6; Prudentius, *Perist.* 7.
166. Prudentius, *Perist.* 7.28, 48—50.
167. Prudentius, *Perist.* 7.56—7 on the contrary, describes this miracle as a manifestation of Christ's power over water.
168. This seems to contradict what he reports elsewhere about objects that increase in weight after they have been in contact with relics (*Glor. mart.* 27; *Virt. Mart.* 1.11). That is one of the many times that Gregory sees *das Ideelle als Materielles*, a more general characteristic of medieval thinking according to Gurjewitsch 1978: 85.
169. *Glor. mart.* 80.
170. Wis. 1:4.

suggested that the talking be stopped and 'the truth be proved by facts (*factis rei veritas approbetur*)'. If the Roman should succeed 'with the help of the Holy Spirit' in extracting a ring from a cauldron of boiling water (a recognized Frankish judicial ordeal in that time, which could, however, also be bought off)[171] he should be acknowledged as having the truth on his side. The next day the Roman party indeed succeeded in bringing up the ring 'after searching for it [at the bottom] for about an hour' and said that he had felt the water to be at most lukewarm. The heretic thereupon boldly thrust in his hand, wishing to prove the truth of his faith in the same easy manner — and found the flesh cooking off his bones. 'And that', Gregory concludes with evident satisfaction, 'was the end of the debate'. I suggest that the Catholic's maxim 'Let the truth be proved by facts', that is, by visible, material indications, was also Gregory's own. God's power influencing the behaviour of water could thus be used to resolve social and religious conflicts.

In the following story the interpretation of a swollen river as a divine action hinges entirely upon the social and political context in which it occurs. We see Gregory seizing upon it as one of a cluster of signs to convince himself and others of the rightness of his political action. In its two mutually complementary versions,[172] it shows how such extraordinary natural phenomena, when effectively interpreted and presented, could be an ultimate weapon sorely needed in his time by an unarmed bishop against predatory Franks.

In 576, after the murder of King Sigebert, the city of Tours and its territory, through rightfully belonging to Sigebert's son and heir Childebert, was annexed by the latter's uncle, King Chilperic. The king sent a certain Roccolenus with troops to pry Duke Guntram Boso, whom he suspected of murdering his son Theudebert,[173] out of his asylum in the church of St Martin in Tours. From the opposite side of the Loire, Roccolenus sent messengers to Gregory to say that if he did not hand over the duke, the city and the suburbs would be razed. Having heard this, Gregory was very distressed and went to St Martin's church to ask for his aid. Then three things happened in rapid succession (I am making a synthetic reconstruction of events by fitting Gregory's two versions of the story into each other). First, while he was praying in the church, a woman who had been paralyzed for twelve years was suddenly healed. Gregory took this to be the saint's answer. He sent Roccolenus the message that the holy church had never been violated in this manner and

---

171. Balon 1965: 621—6; *Pactus legis Salicae* tit. 53 in: Eckhardt 1962: 200—3.
172. *Hist.* 5.4; *Virt. Mart.* 2.37.
173. *Hist.* 4.30.

that it could not be allowed to happen now. If in spite of this, Roccolenus were to attempt to do it anyway, things would go well neither for him nor for the king who had given such an order: 'he would do better to fear the holiness (*sanctitas*) of the saint, whose miraculous power (*virtus*) yesterday straightened paralytic limbs'. A miraculous act of mercy is here presented under its aspect of power. The saint is present, listening and active. Gregory lets the cure function as an intimidation directed at Roccolenus: sanctity is effective power.

The second thing that happened is that Roccolenus, while he and his army were devastating the properties of the church as well as of the poor on the other side of the Loire, 'was struck by God (*a Deo percutitur*)' and suffered an attack of jaundice as well as of the same ailments that Herod had once had. This is a 'typical' interpretation: it makes of Roccolenus 'a new Herod'[174] — which is useful propaganda. What Gregory here left to be understood, he says explicitly elsewhere:[175] Roccolenus was 'struck by the power of the blessed Martin for the many evils he had perpetrated'. Again the power of God and that of the saint seem to be two aspects of the same thing.

Meanwhile, and this is the third event that took place (the *Histories* omit it, however), 'at the command of God and also by the power of the holy man (*nutu Dei vel virtute beati viri*) the river bed became full without there having been any rains to fill it, and prevented the enemy from crossing it, lest he should harm the city'. Gregory is aware of the abrogation of a 'natural' causality here and therefore attributes the event to God's *command* as well as the *power* of St Martin. Have we to do here with power as prestige in heaven or power as effective energy in the dynamic of events? This remains ambiguous. The swollen river is a purely practical barrier which temporarily protected the city; it is not a sign or symbol of some other spiritual truth, but acquires its significance from its timing.

Though ill, Roccolenus did eventually come into the city for the mass of Epiphany. Gregory reports that once Roccolenus had entered St Martin's Church his 'threatening fury' cooled down: the juxtaposition implies the influence of the saint here. Thereafter, though he could not eat or drink that day, he left for Poitiers without, it seems, making any more trouble. Gregory may have invited him, as the king's representative, to a meal after mass (how else could he have known Roccolenus did not eat or drink that day?), and persuaded him, by describing examples of St

---

174. Gregory later also calls King Chilperic 'the Nero and Herod of our times' (*Hist.* 1.46).
175. *Hist.* 5.1.

Martin's power that took away any appetite he may still have had, that it would be better for his health if he were to give up the idea of extricating Duke Guntram from the church or burning down the city. Roccolenus died shortly afterwards, on the last day of February, the day before he planned to 'afflict' the city of Poitiers (possibly by the imposition of taxes).[176] Here too, the chronological juxtaposition of two apparently unrelated events implies a direct spiritual connection. Throughout his works, Gregory mentions taxes only in the context of misfortune or death befalling those who order or collect them.[177] In his view, the kings should support the poor, not 'rob' them (as he lets Queen Fredegunde say).[178]

To return to the subject of this section and to review the evidence: the deep water in the Loire was only a timely miracle to prevent the destruction of the city of Tours. The sea as a symbol, even though it can have the regenerative value of baptism, for Gregory usually represents the turbid demon-infested 'life of this world', whose dangers can be overcome only by Christ through His Church. If such stories can be understood as *Seelenvorgänge*, the manner in which it is spoken about may reveal a contemporary attitude to society and perhaps also to the human mind. The stories of miraculous rescues at sea would then take on a symbolic value: the answer to fear and powerlessness is divine aid. Gregory's stories show in what manner this divine power could be called upon and exerted: the exact role of the saint, for instance, seems to vary and remains ambiguous. At the same time, while carefully maintaining a reverential attitude, those asking for help could, by their use of certain formulations, of insistent prayer and of saint's relics, in fact believe that they were exercising some measure of constraint upon the supernatural power. This attitude has been described as an answer to insecurity.[179] Gregory's treatment of three cases of punishment by drowning and one ordeal reveals his tendency to look upon a visible event as the materialization of a metaphor expressing an invisible truth. In the personal and social sphere, this kind of thinking prepared the way for the later Christian ordeals. His interpretation of a swollen river as an act of divine assistance becomes understandable when one remembers that,

---

176. Possibly by imposing taxes: see Buchner 1967a: 286 n. 1.
177. For instance *Hist.* 3.36.
178. *Hist.* 5.34.
179. Van Baal 1960. Van der Lof 1974: 237 argues, however, that Gregory's attitude is spiritual and not magical: 'un monde tout différent de celui de la magie'. As I hope to have shown, I think 'completely different' is an exaggeration. In a future study, I intend to explore this and related subjects in Gregory's writings.

being an unarmed bishop in a violent time, he felt himself to be utterly dependent upon whatever could be interpreted as divine help or could be used as an intimidation.

An analysis of Gregory's treatment of deep water has revealed some of the ways in which he tried to understand and, when possible manipulate, a natural and human environment that seemed and indeed was arbitrary and dangerous. He expected, as is evident everywhere in his works, divine power — whether or not upon request — either to help or to strike just as suddenly as the Merovingian battle-axes that not infrequently cleft from behind the heads of unsuspecting guests at a party.[180] In a society that was insufficiently ordered and contained by human rule, an unconditional confidence in the effective justice of divine government was for him the only alternative to despair. He therefore wished to read this divine justice into concrete, visible phenomena.

'SUDDENLY A MOST HIDEOUS RAIN-CLOUD': THE DIABOLICAL MENACE

> One cannot believe that he [Abbot Aredius of Limoges] could possibly be darkened by a cloud of falsehood since God often protected him from a cloud of pelting rain so effectively that, while his companions were drenched, he felt not a single drop.[181]

In defending Aredius' credibility as a witness to the life of another saint, Gregory here sums up his own view on bad weather: those placing their trust in God are spared. At the same time, as we have seen him doing before, he tends to see a visible event or phenomenon as a metaphor expressing a spiritual condition. A 'cloud' as a metaphor of the mind (reminiscent of Prudentius and Fortunatus)[182] has been concretized by Gregory into a visible sign by God. Prudentius also mentions clouds (quoting the apostle Paul) in the following passage:[183]

> ...it is with spirits of darkness that we contend night and day, which bear rule over the damp and heavy-clouded air.[184] All this middle region, you must know, which stretches between the heavens above and the earth beneath and suspends the clouds in its great empty space, upholds the government of diverse powers and is the gruesome seat of wicked rulers under the command of Belial.

As will become evident when we look at his stories, it was probably this view of the sublunar sky that Gregory associated with the human mind.

---

180. As in *Hist.* 8.36; 9.9; 9.19.
181. *Vit. patr.* 17. *prol.*
182. Prudentius, *Hamart.* 89; Fortunatus, *Carm.* 10.1.1: *nubs erroris*. Similarly however, Severus, *Vit. Mart.* 19.3. Compare Fontaine 1968: 885—6.
183. Prudentius, *Hamart.* 514—20, transl. Thomson 1949: 241.
184. Compare Ephes. 6:12, 2:2.

Elsewhere he describes Christ and his Church as the sun and the moon of 'the sky of the human mind'.[185] Both, though created good, are for the duration of 'this world' subject to the devil and his agents.[186]

Not surprisingly, Gregory tells more stories besides the one quoted above in which rain-clouds are miraculously diverted compared with only one story in which a saint prays for and gets rain.[187] An analysis of the context and of the manner in which this occurs reveals Gregory's view of the dynamic of the natural and the human world from another angle. 'To this day', he says, 'the Lord has prevented any savage rain-cloud from coming near the roofless house at Ephesus where the apostle John wrote the Fourth Gospel'.[188] A heavy storm died down when the aged Bishop Euphronius went out, at the command of two saints appearing in a dream, to consecrate a new chapel.[189] A novice of a monastery in Bordeaux, who was watching the sheaves of grain laid out to dry, saw the sky suddenly clouding over and a heavy rain accompanied by a roaring wind (*imber validus cum rumore venti*) approaching the spot.[190] Since there was no time to call the others to help gather it in, the novice prostrated himself on the ground and prayed God not to let the rain fall on the sheaves. As he lay there, the rain-cloud divided in such a way that, while the rain poured down all around them, not one ear of grain got wet. After this, the young monk was severely chastised by the abbot in order to suppress any tendency he might have to be proud of such a miracle (*miraculum*). Gregory knew what he was talking about. He tells us that once, on a journey from Burgundy to Auvergne, 'a great storm came up against us (*oritur contra nos magna tempestas*)', lightning flashed and thunder rumbled.[191] When Gregory then straightaway took the relics he wore in a gold capsule around his neck and held them out against the cloud, it at once divided into two parts, one passing to the right and the other to the left of the company, leaving them unharmed. Demonic agency seems implied in the formulation 'against us', just as it was in the 'sudden' appearance of the clouds in the previous story. The fact that in both cases the cloud itself was divided, in the latter by Gregory's holding out relics 'against' it, seems to indicate that the demonic power was thought of as more or less localized there.[192] This miracle elated the

185. *Vit. patr.* 18. *prol.*
186. Ephes. 2:1—2; Rom. 8:19—21. Similarly Prudentius, *Hamart.* 543ff.
187. *Vit. patr.* 4.4. Compare *Vit. Nic. Lugd.* 6 and *Vit. Caes. Arel.* 26.
188. *Glor. mart.* 29.
189. *Glor. conf.* 18.
190. *Hist.* 4.34. Comp. *Virt. Mart.* 1.9: *cum violentia venti nimbo teterrimo.*
191. *Glor. mart.* 83.
192. Compare Blöcker 1981: 119.

youthful Gregory, who considered it a reward of his merits — that is until, shortly afterwards, he experienced a very painful fall from his horse. This he then understood to be a punishment for his vanity. Since that time, he says, he has always regarded any miracle of the saints that he was considered worthy enough to see as 'a gift of God on account of *their* faith'.

In the following story, a dark storm appears to be almost personified as a malign power.[193] As the festive procession that welcomed the relics of the martyrs Agricola and Vitalis 'with crosses and candles' and escorted them for the last five miles to the city of Clermont, 'suddenly (*subito*) the sky clouded over and a dark and most hideous rain-storm came upon them...(*imber umbrosus atque teterrimus super eos descendit*)'. This resembles Gregory's description of another storm: 'suddenly a most hideous rain-cloud arrived with a violent wind (*subito adveniente cum violentia venti nimbo teterrimo*)'.[194] The adjective 'hideous (*teter*)' occurs in Gregory's works only for something associated with evil (for instance, an eclipsed sun (*sol teter*) because of a ruler's crimes and 'a most hideous shade (*umbra teterrima*)' for the devil himself).[195] So much rain thereupon fell from this dark and perhaps diabolic rainstorm that the roads were turned into rivers. However, around the relics not a drop was seen to fall. As the procession moved on, the rain followed it at a distance, 'as it were, paying deference, drenching the people but not touching those who carried the relics'.[196] Elsewhere Gregory reports that a hailstorm which used to ravage one of the family's fields annually, avoided it 'as though it were afraid' after Gregory had put some wax which had fallen on St Martin's tomb into the tallest vine.[197] This makes the function of relics and objects that have (even indirectly) touched relics very clear indeed: they are depositories of 'power' that could work, 'automatically', as it were, upon atmospheric phenomena.[198] As we saw earlier, a general consensus of belief in the efficacious power of relics was for Gregory a vital necessity: stories such as these worked to bringing about this consensus. If even clouds feared the relics, how much more should men do so!

Gregory goes even further. He lets us see how in several cases atmospheric phenomena impinge upon human history. In 555, when

---

193. *Glor. mart.* 43.
194. *Virt. Mart.* 1.9.
195. *Hist.* 2.3; *Vit. patr.* 9.2 and 17.3.
196. Gregory the Great tells a similar story in *Dial.* 3.11.5.
197. *Virt. Mart.* 1.34. Compare Severus, *Dial.* 3.7. and see Stancliffe 1983: 221—2.
198. Similarly *Vit. Nic. Lugd.* 10 and *Vit. Caes. Arel.* 27.

Chramn had seized control of territories belonging to his father Clothar, the latter sent two of his other sons, Charibert and Guntram, out against him with an army.[199] Just as the two armies were moving towards each other to give battle, 'a suddenly arisen storm prevented them by frightful lightning and thunder from fighting'. When everyone had returned to their tents, Chramn sent a messenger to his brothers with the false report that their father had just died in a battle with the Saxons; this sent them hurrying back to Burgundy without attempting anything more against him. Why does Gregory describe this non-battle in such detail? To us, Chramn clearly seems to be the guilty party, and in the light of the stories just looked at one might almost be excused for attributing this storm, so opportune for Chramn, to the agency of, if anyone, the devil.

A comparison with the following incident which takes place earlier, in 534,[200] will show what Gregory was probably thinking of. The kings Childebert and Theudebert mustered their armies to go and attack their brother Clothar. Hearing this, Clothar fled into a wood with his army and 'placed all his hope in the compassion of God'. At the same time, in Tours, their mother Queen Clotilde, having learned of their plans, went to the tomb of St Martin and prayed there the whole night that a civil war between her sons might be averted. The following morning, when the brothers were about to attack Clothar,

> a storm arose over the place where they had gathered, which tore down their tents, blew their baggage away and turned everything upside down; lightning, thunder and hailstones came down all together on top of them. The brothers lay face down on the hail-covered ground and, having no other protection left than their shields, were badly beaten by the pelting hail; their greatest fear was that they should be struck by lightning. Their horses were so scattered that they were later found twenty *stadia* [three and a half kilometers] away, and some were never found again. While they were thus being beaten by the hailstones, as I have said, and were lying prostrate on the ground, they repented and prayed God for forgiveness that they had ever wished to undertake this battle against their own blood.
>
> Upon Chlotar, however, not one drop of rain had fallen[201] nor had the sound of thunder been heard in the place where he was; not even the slightest breath of wind had been felt. The brothers then sent a messenger to him and asked for peace and concord. When this had been granted, they returned home. No one will doubt that this was a miracle (*virtus*) of St Martin at the request of the queen.

The purpose of both storms is now clear: to avert civil war or war between next of kin.[202] Gregory more than once bitterly deplores the civil

---

199. *Hist.* 4.16.
200. *Hist.* 3.28. See p. 105.
201. Similarly Gregory the Great, *Dial.* 3.12.5.
202. Compare Fontaine 1968: 755 and Blume 1970: 71.

wars taking place in his own time and often shows that this kind of war ends in self-destruction.[203]

If Gregory implies that a storm's behaviour may be either divinely or demonically activated, it is the wind which Gregory sometimes explicitly designates as a diabolical instrument. In a story examined earlier we saw that a storm could suddenly get up on the river because 'the wind was brought into motion by the instigation of the Tempter (*tentatoris impulsu*)'.[204] On a smaller scale, Gregory reports several cases of a sudden violent wind (*subito commotus cum impetu ventus*)[205] gathering dust and/or chaff (*subito orta super se violentia venti cum pulvere*)[206] which then caused blindness, especially in children. It becomes clear from the following story[207] that this sudden movement is understood as being diabolical. While a boy of three was being tenderly carried by his mother, perhaps as she walked through the fields, working there or bringing lunch to her family, (suddenly),

> stirred up by diabolic instigation (*commota per immissionem diabolicam*), a violent wind lifted the dust and chaff from the earth and rushed upon the mother and child like a great whirlwind. The rustic and incautious woman, however, did not think of protecting herself and her son with the sign of the Saviour, wherefore the treachery prevailed and the eyes of the child filled with dust and were closed... When he was grown, he was given to beggars so that, travelling with them, he might receive some livelihood, for his parents were very poor.

In yet another story,[208] a man was working in the fields when 'the wind started blowing and he, terror-stricken, began to tremble, to feel all his limbs paralyzing, and cried that death was upon him'. When his neighbours came running they saw him, while groaning and crying, become completely paralyzed, deaf and blind. Fortunately, both the afflicted people described in these stories were later healed at St Martin's tomb in Tours. The point here is not whether we might be able to think of some other explanation, but that Gregory and perhaps the people in question attributed the events to a malicious agency in the wind.

In the stories about rain, clouds and wind, we have seen Gregory interpreting the behaviour of these phenomena in terms of demonic or diabolic agency, to which divine agency could, by means of prayer or the invocation of a saint through his relics, be opposed. This view made

203. *Hist.* 4.50 and 5.*praef.*; *Hist.* 2.40; 3.6.; 4.51; 5.49 respectively.
204. *Virt. Mart.* 1.2.
205. *Virt. Mart.* 4.17. Similarly *Virt. Mart.* 4.18.
206. *Virt. Mart.* 3.20.
207. *Virt. Mart.* 3.16.
208. *Virt. Mart.* 4.22.

suffering comprehensible and, in principle, avoidable. Sometimes, however, God or a saint could use the devil's destructiveness in a storm to accomplish his own purpose: to prevent civil war. Atmospheric phenomena are thus experienced and interpreted by Gregory as, on the one hand, amenable to influence, and, on the other, as tending to uphold the social and moral order.

What is striking in these stories, however, is again the prominence of the experience of a sudden, violent assault of power. This power is countered and overcome by the equally lightning-like[209] power of God through his saints, either at once or later. At least this is how Gregory presents it. Reality did not (as modern historians tend to imagine it) slowly evolve 'horizontally' and comprehensibly from one condition or situation to another. Divine and diabolic power were never far away and could flash out at any moment to bring about a radical change in the situation.

WATER: DESTRUCTION AND REGENERATION

Although he is prepared to recognize purely human and natural causal processes as such, Gregory is more concerned with divine and diabolic purposes. He tries to decipher God's messages and intentions by carefully observing visible phenomena and looking for possible analogies with specific spiritual truths applicable to a given situation. In contrast to Pope Gregory the Great's more refined 'interiorisation' of the spiritual lesson of the miracles,[210] he expects the structure of the physical situation to reflect or even be a materialization of the spiritual one. This clearly observable tendency in his stories points, in my opinion, towards their having been to a certain extent consciously experienced, as presenting truths of and for the soul. In our terms, such an experience is also an 'inner event'. The preoccupation with the spiritual meaning of the constant divine activity in sensory-concrete phenomena must have been the reason for the circumstantiality of Gregory's miracle descriptions. This, and what he perceived to be the symbolic as well as the epiphanous quality of visible reality, are almost certainly responsible for his frequent use of the biblically derived verbs 'showing', 'making visible' and 'revealing' to indicate the creative activity of divine power.

In Gregory's works, water is sometimes thought of as the turbulent and dangerous life in this world, and sometimes as a visible manifestation of the divine which is at the same time a symbol of renewal in nature and in man. The miraculous behaviour of water can also fulfil human needs

---

209. Compare Mensching 1957: 83 and Meslin 1974: 175.
210. Van Uytfanghe 1981: 219.

such as curing illness and preventing civil war. The stories about water in its natural state seem to concretize Gregory's deepest fears about society in this period of extreme insecurity and perhaps also about the human spiritual state. Water in its theophanous appearance or action functions as a remedy for individual or social ills. Stories about springs particularly seem to make visible in concrete reality a symbolism of individual spiritual regeneration. Gregory did his 'abstract' thinking in images of visible events.

B. PLANT LIFE

'THE SPROUTING OF SEEDS': AN IMAGE OF REBIRTH

The second [wonder] is similar to this [first one], being the sprouting of seeds and the fruits of trees. When the seeds are sown in the earth and covered by the furrows, they rise up high with the coming of the summer, adorned with leaves, nourished inside by sap and fat. This the Lord, Sower of the spiritual doctrine, turned into a parable about the advance of His words which He scattered among the people, saying:

'The word of God is as if a man should scatter seed, and should rise night and day...[Gregory omits a verse here]; for the earth produces of itself, first the blade, then the ear, then the full grain in the ear'.[211] The apostle Paul, however, gives an image (*figuravit*) of the resurrection in this way, saying: 'What you sow does not come to life unless it first dies'.[212]

So is it with the resurrection of the dead: 'what is sown in weakness rises in power (*virtus*)',[213] and so on.

The same is true indeed of the nature (*natura*) of trees, which, as I believe, is a sign (*signat*) of that same resurrection, when in the winter, denuded of leaves, they seem to be dead, and in the time of spring they are adorned with leaves and embellished by flowers, while in the summer they are full of apples. Which wonder, notwithstanding its being used in this way as a likeness (*similitudo*), exhibits a favour to the peoples [of the earth] here and now, so that man should know that he receives food from the One Who created him out of nothing (*creavit ex nihilo*).[214]

---

211. Is. 55:10—11; Mark 4:26, 28.
212. 1 Cor. 15:36.
213. 1 Cor. 15:43.
214. *De cursu stell.* 11: *Secundum est simile huic, de granis scilicet frugum et de fructibus arborum, cum iacta terrae simina* [sic] *et sulcis operta, adveniente aestate eriguntur in culmina, ornataque comis et spicis lacteo intrinsecus adipe saginantur, quae Dominus spiritalis doctrinae sator de profecto verborum suorum, quae in populos iaciebat, parabolice commutavit, dicens: 'Sic est verbum Dei, quemadmodum si iactet homo semen, et exurgat nocte et diae* [sic]*, ultro enim terra fructificat primum herbam, deinde spicam, deinde plenum granum in spicam'. Paulus autem apostolus de resurrectione hanc rationem figuravit, dicens: 'Quod seminas non vivificatur, nisi prius moriatur. Sic est,' inquit, 'et resurrectio mortuorum: seminatur in infirmitate, surgit in virtute,'*

'... and the seed should sprout and grow, he knows not how'.[215] This passage, which Gregory — characteristically — omitted (perhaps because he thought it self-evident), gives the essence of the wonder. It is a widely recognized epiphany of the sacred: divine creation visibly at work,[216] generously producing an unceasing renewal of life, as well as beauty and nourishment for men. At the same time, an analogy is made between the (miraculous) birth and growth of a seed and the dynamic of the 'words' of God in men's hearts. Gregory has substituted Isaiah's 'word of God' for Mark's 'Kingdom of God'. Perhaps he was quoting from memory. It seems more probable, however, that he was deliberately referring to something like the creative power of the Word or Logos, as the fourth Gospel calls Christ,[217] and carrying this creative quality over into the actual words spoken by Him. It is possible that his expectation, as we saw earlier, that words about miracles would cause faith to sprout in barren minds,[218] is based on a more or less unreflective association of word with Word. If so, it is another instance of Gregory's tendency to translate abstract concepts into concrete phenomena and events. It also betrays, however, an experience of reality resembling, in an unconscious way, that of a meditation upon the content of Scripture which forms the soul into the likeness of its content, as it is described for instance by Cassian. The experience itself seems to be close to, if not identical with, that which Gregory describes as his 'astonished admiration' and awed reverence when confronted with miracles. This latter attitude is also comparable to that of the adepts of the ancient mysteries toward the 'revelations' presented there.[219] Much of what Gregory has to say and the manner in which he says it becomes recognizable when this experience and attitude are understood.

The way in which seeds germinate is the 'figure' of another special

> etcetera. Aequa est enim arborum natura, quae, ut puto, ipsam resurrectionem signat, cum in hieme nudatae foliis tamquam mortui habentur, verno vero tempore ornantur foliis, decorantur floribus, pomisque aestate replentur. Quod miraculum quamquam hac utatur similitudinem, ad praesens tamen beneficium populis praestat, ut cognoscat homo, ab illo se accipere victum, qui eum creavit ex nihilo.

215. Mark 4:27.
216. Eliade 1958: 278.
217. John 1:3. Compare Mensching 1957: 14.
218. *Glor. mart. prol.*; *Vit. patr. 2. prol.*
219. On Cassian's view of meditation see Chadwick 1968: 102. Gregory mentions Cassian's works, implying that he is acquainted with their content, in *Hist.* 10.29 and *Vit. patr.* 20.3. On meditation in modern psychotherapy, for instance: Assagioli 1965 and Singer 1974. On mysteries and Christianity: Nock 1952. Leonardi also states that 'contemplation' was the ideal of the early Middle Ages (Leonardi 1982: 451—4). Compare also Smalley 1964: 27 and Ohly 1977: 20.

truth: the resurrection requires that one dies first. Gregory here seems to mean regeneration in heaven after actual, physical death, and not the interior spiritual event during this life that Paul sometimes means.[220] The symbolism of the seed had been used in the ancient mysteries of Eleusis and Osiris to indicate a psychical pattern of withdrawal and return that has been called the Rebirth archetype.[221] The same image, but indicating the resurrection, is found in the Greek and Latin Church Fathers, including Augustine.[222] Gregory's friend, the poet Fortunatus, who also uses the image,[223] elsewhere associates the rebirth of plant life in the spring with the resurrection of Christ at that time.[224]

However, to combine the three aspects of germination — as wonder of generosity, proof of the resurrection and likeness of the growth of the words of God in men's hearts without an association of 'death' as a prerequisite — seems to be Gregory's own idea. It shows, in any case, that he could entertain associations at various levels simultaneously. In Eucherius' *Forms of spiritual understanding*[225] he could also have found the following: 'The tree is Christ when He is risen, and when He dies He is the grain'. Gregory's qualification 'as I believe' may however indicate that, as far as trees are concerned, he wishes the reader to regard the association as made more or less on his own authority: that is without a Bible quotation to back it up. Not only Eucherius' statement but also, as we shall see below, the ancient pagan tree symbolism and the current association of the tree with the Cross may have influenced Gregory's thinking on this point.

In his report of a dispute he once had with one of his priests who doubted the resurrection,[226] Gregory uses the same two arguments (in very similar words) for the resurrection, but in reverse order. Here, however, he calls these phenomena 'evidence supporting this matter (*testimonia, quae hanc causam adfirmant*)': 'Why', he continues, 'even the elements (*elementa*) that we see indicate it ...'. The trees, that lose their leaves in the fall, 'as it were rise anew (*quasi resurgunt*)' in the spring when they clothe themselves again with foliage. He goes on:

220. Rom. 6:3—4.
221. Hopfner 1935: 1323—4; Brede Kristensen 1949: 143, 160; Bodkin 1963: 272—5. Compare Nock 1952, Eliade 1959 especially 241—8, and Meslin 1974.
222. Beirnaert 1950: 275. Augustine, *De civ. Dei* 20.20.
223. Fortunatus, *Carm.* 11.1.42: *Ergo moritur homo quasi granum in sulco, ut resurgat cum spico et multiplicetur in fructu, assimiletur et angelo.*
224. Fortunatus, *Carm.* 3.9.31—4. Compare Ganzenmüller 1916: 201 and Koebner 1915: 59—60.
225. Eucherius, *Formul. spir. intell.* 4.
226. *Hist.* 10.13.

The seeds that are sown in the earth also show this; having been entrusted to the furrows,[227] they rise anew, if they have died, with much fruit.[228] As the apostle Paul says,[229] 'You foolish man, what you sow does not come to life unless it first dies'.

All these things are shown to the world so that it may believe in the resurrection.

Despairing of the permanence and vitality of human institutions, Gregory chose to keep his gaze steadily on every phenomenon of creative renewal, as revelations of the divine and a promise to men. The image of the seed that must die before it can live again appears in many cultures as a symbol for the experience of interior renewal. Is Gregory thinking only of the future resurrection, or does what he says about the words of God in men's hearts point, indirectly, to an interior renewal in the present life as well?

'NATURE', 'MYSTERY' AND THE VIRGIN BIRTH: THE PATTERNS OF MIRACLE

When Gregory speaks of 'the nature' of trees, he means their essential character.[230] Only once does he use the term 'nature' for the whole of the natural world: when, as we saw, he says that the inhabitants of a certain village, by their irrigation canals, distributed water 'so that where nature (*natura*) did not supply [a spring], effort might bring one'.[231]

Elsewhere, to indicate what we would now call 'nature' (i.e. earth, sky, vegetation) Gregory uses the word 'elements', as in: 'He created all the elements that we see'.[232] What these elements do *not* include appears in a passage in which Gregory speaks of the Creation: 'After all the elements of the earth had been created, God took a clod of frail earth and moulded man in His own image and likeness...'.[233] The 'elements' are thus probably the antique four: water, earth, air and fire.[234] In a story about a poor hermit who, for years, successfully cooked his vegetables in a wooden cooking pot,[235] Gregory, speaking of the saints, says that 'the Redeemer, who created all out of nothing..., even commands the very

---

227. Compare Virgil, *Georg.* 2.57.
228. John 12:24.
229. 1 Cor. 15:36.
230. Compare Grant 1952: 3—18 and Blaise 1954: 549—50.
231. *Glor. mart.* 36. *Hist.* 9.39: (about Radegunde and her nuns) *quam matrem facit gratia, non natura* is a quotation from a letter written by a number of bishops.
232. *In psal.* 73. Compare Stancliffe 1983: 207, 221—3.
233. *Hist.* 1.1.
234. Compare Blaise 1954: 303.
235. *Glor. conf.* 98.

elements to obey them'. This was a commonly held view in Gregory's time.[236] The elements in this case may be the fire, which did not consume the wood, and perhaps the wood (as earth?), which 'one would have thought to be bronze'.

'Nature' as a (consistent) whole does not seem to have held Gregory's attention.[237] As will be seen in the following story, for him it is not 'nature' that has 'elements', but the other way around. Since he here has a lot more to say on the subject, it is worth looking at the story as a whole.[238] In expectation of the ceremonial deposition of the relics of St Julian the next day in a new church in Tours built in the martyr's honour, the monks who had just built it invited Gregory as their bishop and perhaps the notables of the city to drink some of their wine and then spend the night in vigil there, singing hymns and 'heavenly melodies'.[239] The next day, when mass had been celebrated and the relics installed, the monk in charge thanked those who had kept the vigil with him and invited them, as he had done before, for a meal. When he entered the cellar, however, he found the small wine cask which he had left almost half empty the evening before, now overflowing with wine so that it ran in a rivulet to the door. Surprised, he decanted many pitchers full from it, but it remained full until the next day. This happened on the third of May. Gregory continues:

> O wonderful power *(virtus)* of the martyr! He brought forth wine from the cask without the vines having blossomed, whereas usually one has to harvest the wine before putting it in casks. The cask produced new wine derived not from grapes but from power (*virtus*) alone: the cask filled up with liquid, the fruit not being brought to it but created there. The Lord did this to glorify the martyr, just as He filled the womb of the Virgin without seed, making her a mother while remaining chaste... Truly, a wine that was not cultivated came without being pressed: a wine that is found not in the shoots of the vine but in hidden mysteries (*in occultis mysteriis*)...the One who once at the wedding[240] made wine from water, now generously offered the same to his people without [its partaking in] the nature of any element (*sine ullius elementi natura*)...

A wine created spontaneously, not partaking in the 'nature' of any 'element': Gregory the Great tells similar stories (*vinum non augeretur, sed nasceretur*), and Fortunatus describes how St Marcellus caused 'mystic wine (*vinum mysticum*)' to 'be born (*nasceretur*)' out of Seine water.[241] In

236. Likewise, for instance, Fortunatus, *Vit. Hil.* 35. Compare Fontaine 1968: 766, 774, 777 n.1.
237. Compare Radding 1979: 959.
238. *Virt. Jul.* 35.
239. *Virt. Jul.* 34. Similarly: Severus, *Ep.* 3.20—1: *hymni caelestes.*
240. Of Cana: John 2:1—10.
241. Gregory the Great, *Dial.* 1.9.3—4 and 14: *vinum non augeretur sed nasceretur*; Fortunatus, *Vit. Marc.* 21—2: *vinum mysticum ... nasceretur.*

both cases, the verb 'to be born' may point to the same dynamic pattern. But of these only Gregory of Tours (like Augustine, also, however)[242] mentions the association with the Virgin Birth explicitly, in this case as the model of the possibility of an entirely new creation *ex nihilo* (a phrase he likes to use, as we have seen)[243] of a mystic nature, which looks, feels and tastes like ordinary wine, but which sprang out of the 'mystery' and 'power' of divine creation. Here 'mystery' is the secret of divine creativity. Elsewhere Gregory uses 'mystery' to denote the secret of a saint's miraculous power which is, of course, the same thing. This equation is also made by Fortunatus.[244] As we have seen, Gregory left this mystery (which, characteristically, he perhaps did not like to verbalize) out of his quotation about the word of God as a seed.

In a similar story, concerning a monastery in Jerusalem dedicated to her, the Virgin herself 'produces' grain.[245] Twice, possibly as a result of bad harvests, the sizeable congregation of monks found themselves without anything to eat and threatened to leave, in order to be able to survive elsewhere. The abbot persuaded them that God would give them food if they would spend the night praying and singing psalms in the church. The next morning they found their granaries so full of wheat that they could hardly open the doors. Several years later, there was again no food, and the monks started grumbling once more. The abbot again led them in 'lying on the floor of the church' the whole night, praying and singing 'psalms, hymns and spiritual songs'. After matins, while they were sleeping, 'an angel of the Lord came' into the locked church and put 'a countless multitude' of gold coins on the altar. Gregory concludes: 'It is not to be wondered at (*Nec mirum*) that the blessed Virgin, without any effort, produced (*protulit*) food for her dependants, since she conceived without the participation of a man and remained a virgin even after she had borne a child'. This is the only other time that Gregory specifically mentions the Virgin Birth as the model for a miracle. Considering, however, how attentive and receptive he shows himself to be to the dynamic of sudden leaps in the process of natural and of human reality, it looks although he always had it in the back of his mind as it were as its model. Images like that of the spring bursting forth from a dry rock and the plant arising through the death of the seed point to the same *discontinuous dynamic*. This for

242. Augustine, *Bon. coniug.* 2, cited in Grant 1952: 216.
243. For instance in *De cursu stell.* 11; *Hist.* 10.13; *Glor. conf.* 98. Compare Martin's (indirect) demasking of the supernatural white tunic of Anatolius as a diabolic apparition: Severus, *Vit. Mart.* 23.6—11.
244. *Virt. Jul.* 35. Similarly Fortunatus, *Vit. Hil.* 48, and *Vit. Germ.* 132. Also: Isidorus Hisp., *Etym.* 6.19.42.
245. *Glor. mart.* 10.

Gregory and his contemporaries unreflected and self-evident truth about reality is one of the things that most fundamentally separates their thinking from ours.[246]

The abbot in this story had said the first time — though we may be sure it is Gregory speaking — 'Let us pray, most beloved brothers, and the Lord will give us food; for it cannot happen (*nec enim potest fieri*) that wheat be lacking in the monastery of the one who brought forth from her womb the grain (fruit) of life (*frugem vitae*) for a perishing world (*mundo pereunti*)'. Here Gregory is making the same analogy, but in the opposite direction and with a different emphasis. 'It cannot happen' stands in the place of 'it is not to be wondered at', but is much stronger, indicating a necessity. What is necessary here is the correspondence between the pattern of the metaphor of the Virgin's actions towards the world as a whole — bringing forth Christ, who is the 'food' for the life of the spirit — and the pattern of an analogous physical, material situation: her providing grain for starving dependants. Gregory might have done no more than indicate that one should always trust in the never-failing support of one's patron saint, a common attitude at that time.[247] Instead, he chose to emphasize the necessity of a spiritual pattern, to be apprehended in the repetition of itself in an image (something which we look upon today as a purely mental phenomenon of human construction, a metaphor) in visible, material reality.[248] I suggest that this is because he experienced the image as possessing a degree of inherent independent and active reality: it looks as though he did not distinguish completely between the mental image and the reality which it represented. All this seems to indicate that to him, as to present-day 'archaic' thinking,[249] the spiritual and the material appear as more of a continuum than they do to us today.

At the same time, Gregory's formulation has something almost coercive about it. He is doing more than just seeing existing correspondences. Sulpicius Severus shows traces of the same kind of thinking, which Fontaine has called 'inverse allegorism' and 'magic literalism'.[250] Of Gregory's contemporaries, neither Gregory the Great nor Fortunatus go

---

246. Augustine regarded the Creation as having occurred in a leap or *ictus* (Auerbach 1958: 42). A similar discontinuous dynamic, that of spontaneous generation, was however recognized by pagans and Christians alike (Grant 1952: 217).
247. Brown 1981: 126.
248. *Glor. mart.* 28, about the apostle Paul's martyrdom is similar: *Nec mirum si lac ejus manavit ex corpore, qui gentes incredulas et parturivit et peperit, ac lacte spiritali nutritas....* [sic]. Compare Gurjewitsch 1978: 85.
249. Eliade 1952: 233.
250. Severus, *Vit. Mart.* 4.5; see Fontaine 1968: 530.

this far. The former, however, reports one particular incident in such a way that it resembles sympathetic magic: Benedict's sister, wishing him to stay the night, prayed with tears 'by which she led (*traxit*) the cloudless sky to rain'.[251] This resembles Gregory's description of Bishop Mamertus at Vienne: 'the river of his flowing tears extinguished the fire'.[252] Less clear but also suggestive is what Fortunatus writes about Bishop Hilary of Poitiers' resuscitation of a child: 'the bishop lay down in the dust until they both rose at the same time, the old man from his prayer and the child from death'.[253] Gregory of Tours sees another mental image become physical reality in the story of a fruit merchant[254] who refused to give alms to a poor old man, saying he had only stones in his ship. The poor man (almost certainly understood to be Christ or a saint) replied that if he said the fruit were stones, they would indeed all be turned into stones:

> And at once the whole cargo of the ship, which had been edible, was converted into stone. I myself saw a date from this cargo as well as an olive, harder than marble. For, while they had been turned into the hardness of stone, they had not lost their colour: they had kept their form (*forma*) and their appearance (*species*).

Here Gregory accepts the possibility of a change that may be apprehended through sensory experience. The transforming power of the old man's words is for him, obviously, more probable than any idea that he may have about the workings of the natural world. Words and divine power can, in an instant, change the 'nature' of the 'elements'.

Besides the Virgin Birth, one suspects that the Eucharist, to which Gregory elsewhere refers to as a 'mystery',[255] and the story of the wedding in Cana, were also models influencing his expectations about and perceptions of constancy and sudden change in the natural world. Roman religion had recognized the discontinuities in natural processes, such as growth. Following the Biblical and early Christian tradition,[256] Gregory sees nature as a regular pattern that is not only essentially miraculous to start with, but also liable to exhibit sudden, recognizably patterned transformations, both of which express the omnipotence of God.

---

251. Gregory the Great, *Dial.* 2.33.3.
252. *Hist.* 2.34.
253. Fortunatus, *Vit. Hil.* 45.
254. *Glor. conf.* 109.
255. For instance *Virt. Mart.* 2.1, 40; *Vit. patr.* 16.2.
256. Brede Kristensen 1949: 219; Grant 1952: 263.

'THE TREE OF LIFE' OR ITS 'PLEASANT SHADE': SYMBOL OR OBJECT OF AESTHETIC PLEASURE?

The first 'psalm shows (*ostendit*) that He [that is, Christ] is the tree of life (*lignum vitae*)'.[257] In accordance with patristic tradition,[258] this is Gregory's interpretation of what he in his preface calls 'the truth of spiritual understanding (*veritas spiritualis intelligentiae*)' of the first Psalm's statement[259] about the righteous man whose 'delight is in the law of the Lord': 'He is like a tree, planted by streams of water, that yields its fruit in its season, and its leaf does not wither'. Genesis,[260] of course, placed the Tree of Life in the midst of Paradise, which is watered by a river. Revelation[261] describes 'the river of the water of life' and 'the tree of life' as close to the throne of God and the Lamb. This association of tree and water appears in the Upanishads, as well as in the Nordic and Jewish-Christian traditions.[262]

Because the tree, with its roots in the earth and its branches in heaven, tended to be experienced as an axis joining earth with heaven, it was often near a tree that theophanies took place (as they had with Abraham).[263] Such a spot was thenceforth experienced as 'the centre of the world' or of absolute reality, as a microcosm, and *imago mundi*.[264] As we saw above, it is exactly in this context that, the 'large and gentle spring' and the 'noble tree (*arbor nobilis*)' appear in Gregory's description of the phoenix's evergreen pleasance in the highest place of the earth.[265] Gregory there gives neither of them the qualification 'of life', however, perhaps because he experiences this symbolism[266] as implicit in the whole situation. He may also have had another dimension of this symbolism in mind. His friend Fortunatus follows the early Christian tradition[267] when he calls the Cross 'the one noble tree (*arbor una nobilis*)'.[268] Here again is the fundamental notion, similar to that of the ancient mysteries,[269] of true, eternal 'life' being

257. *In psal.* 1.
258. See Reno 1978: 79—123. Compare Ladner 1979 on the tree as a symbol in the Middle Ages.
259. Ps. 1:2—3, transl. Rev. Stand. Vers. O.T. 1952: 563.
260. Gen. 2:9—10.
261. Rev. 22:1—2. Compare James 1966: 259—61.
262. Eliade 1958: 276, 282.
263. Gen. 12:6—7, *Hist.* 5.43. Compare Eliade 1958: 269—70, 273.
264. Eliade 1958:282, 271.
265. *De cursu stell.* 12.
266. Reno 1978: 124—86.
267. Eliade 1958: 292—4.
268. Fortunatus, *Carm.* 2.2.22; similarly 2.1.9 and 11.1.27.
269. Brede Kristensen 1949: 217.

achieved in man, as in the natural world, only through 'death'.

The trees mentioned in Gregory's miracle stories all carry explicit or implicit connotations of death and resurrection or of revival. Either they are themselves revived by a saint or, through their association with a saint, they revive others by curing them of their ills.[270] A mulberry tree grew on the spot where Genesius was martyred (by decapitation) in Arles; people later took so much of it away on account of its healing properties that only part of the trunk remained, still living and healing.[271] A laurel tree that sprang up above the martyr Baudillius' grave in Nîmes, which often gave 'a heavenly remedy' to the ill, was plucked so bare, however, that it was unable to survive.[272] Another Genesius, martyr of Bigorre, was able by his prayers to make a chestnut tree which had long been dead come back to life (*in viriditatem redire*).[273] An interesting story about the saintly priest Severus of Béziers gives us another glimpse of Gregory's view of the operation of nature.[274] When the branch of a medlar tree hit his face as he rode to church one Sunday, this priest cursed it, saying: 'Let God, by whose order you have come out of the earth, command you to wither!' This incident, of course, resembles Christ's cursing of the fig tree.[275] (Gregory mentions at the beginning of the story that Severus came from a noble family, which may also explain his tone in this incident.) The tree withered at once. Four days later, when the priest returned along the same route, he regretted having cursed (*maledixi*) the tree, prostrated himself at its roots and prayed:

> 'Almighty God, according to whose decision all things are directed, at whose command what is not born is created (*creantur*), what is created lives, and what is dead is renewed (*reformantur*): [...] order that this tree may live again and that it be as it was before'. And at once, as though [sucked up] by some disposition of its vessels, the sap rose up from the earth and spread as an abundant refreshment through all the branches of the wide-spread tree, loosening the withered buds and causing leaves to burst out [from them], [causing it] to come back to life (*revixisse*), to the astonishment of those standing around it.

The general formulation here shows very clearly how Gregory thought of divine power as the omnipresent and immanent principle of all creation, life and growth in the natural world, operating by quite 'natural' means as,

---

270. *Glor. mart.* 46; *Glor. conf.* 7. This is definitely not the case in Severus' stories about St Martin, who cuts down trees venerated by pagans: Severus, *Vit. Mart.* 13.
271. *Glor. mart.* 67.
272. *Glor. mart.* 77.
273. *Glor. mart.* 73.
274. *Glor. conf.* 50.
275. Compare Mark 11: 13—4, 20.

in this case the sap.²⁷⁶ Gregory concludes that he believes the divine pity to which this miracle (*miraculum*) testifies would also have restored the dead to life upon the prayer of the hermit. Here the association with the resurrection is explicit. On another occasion we are told that a gardener converted the dead trunk of a tree once planted by the Breton hermit Joannes into a garden bench.²⁷⁷ Two years later, Gregory says, the gardener 'touched by remorse, — as I believe through divine inspiration —', reverently buried the trunk. When it had been buried ('as it were, put in a grave (*ut ita dicam, sepulta fuerat*') it produced new shoots and leaves and, when Gregory saw it, it stood 'five or six feet high, still growing — by God's will — every year'. Divine power has again effected a resurrection from the grave. Gregory must have expected his readers to recognize this 'truth of spiritual understanding' in the story.

In all these accounts, however, the tree is more than only a symbol of the resurrection. Beside flowers, which will be discussed below, the tree is the only phenomenon of plant life which receives repeated attention in Gregory's miracle stories, as well as in his lists of prodigies.²⁷⁸ It is possible that this is connected with the ancient Celtic and Germanic cult of trees, to whose presence in Gregory's time a canon of the council of Tours testifies,²⁷⁹ and with a conscious attempt by the church authorities to put a Christian version of this in its place.²⁸⁰

Like his choosing to regard germination and growth as a divine wonder, Gregory's emphasis on trees may be an attempt to claim this sector from the ancient popular deities. At the same time, however, it does not seem too much to say that these stories betray some real feeling on Gregory's part towards trees. His attention to roots, sap, bark, buds, shoots, blossoms and fruits as well as grafting, which is also evident in his lists of prodigies,²⁸¹ shows careful observation. Friardus's 'pity (*misericordia*)' for the blown-down tree and the gardener's 'remorse (*dolor cordis*)' about Joannes' tree serving as a garden bench indicate a certain degree of empathy. Two of Gregory's descriptions of trees betray real aesthetic pleasure and are reminiscent of poetry. In another place he writes that Abbot Martius, as an old man, used to sit in the shade of the trees in the monastery garden, 'their

276. Compare *Vit. patr.* 10.3. A revived stick also appears in Severus, *Dial.* 1.19 and Cassian, *Instit.* 4.24.
277. *Glor. conf.* 23.
278. *Hist.* 4.9; 5.33; 6.14; 7.11; 8.8; 8.42; 9.5; 9.44.
279. *Conc. Tur.* a.567, c. 23 in Maassen 1893: 133. See also Severus, *Vit. Mart.* 13 and on this Fontaine 1968: 737—66, especially 741—2 and 751. Further: Harmening 1979: 49—75.
280. Compare Graus 1965: 187 and Fontaine 1968: 745.
281. *Hist.* 4.9.

leaves whispering in the breeze (*susurrantibus aurae sibilo foliis*)'.[282] The above-mentioned hermit Joannes, Gregory says, used to sit and read or write under his laurel trees in 'the pleasant shade of their delightful branches (*jucundarum frondium amoenitas*)'. This expression speaks for itself. Gregory's symbolical view of nature by no means precludes his appreciating its beauty.

'IT FLOURISHED AS THOUGH IT WERE PAINTED': THE TRANSIENCE OF EARTHLY GARDENS

Describing at one point the beauty of a vine-covered arcade in front of St Martin's Church 'in Galicia', Gregory makes an interesting comparison: 'with grapes hanging in it, it flourished as though it were painted (*quasi picta vernabat*)'.[283] He probably means: more beautiful and perfect than one would expect it to be, reminding one of the decorative wall-paintings in houses. Did he look at nature with a 'perfect' example in mind? Was, for Gregory, plant life as it occurred in nature, with its blemishes and its transiency, not good enough, for the same reasons that the works and the fables of men were not good enough? Of the grapes hanging in the arcade we are told that when King Miro's jester dared to try to pick a bunch of them, he found his hand and his arm suddenly paralyzed, for the vines were 'consecrated to the saint (*ipsi consecrata*)'. Was it then this sacred quality that made them more than naturally beautiful — perhaps like a bit of Paradise showing?

Certainly, as distinct from descriptions of Heaven in which mansions or spacious halls figure large,[284] Gregory describes Paradise in terms of a pleasant shady spot: 'the grove of Paradise (*nemus paradisiacum*)'.[285] The following description may indicate what Gregory was thinking of when he described St Martin's vine:

> ... the love of God lifts man from the things of the earth, calls him to the heavens, places him in Paradise, in which the souls of the happy, having drunk the new wine of the vine of life are feasting in the Kingdom of God. Men should therefore desire to drink the mystery of this vine, so that they may be able to go to that most pleasant and delightful home. If the vine which we now see extending its branches, on which the leaves and hanging grapes intertwine with the tendrils, delights us with a pleasant sight, while it not only bears abundant fruit but also protects us as a useful shady

---

282. *Vit. patr.* 14.2. Compare Fortunatus, *Carm.* 6.6.7: *molli blanda susurro/aura levis, semper pendula mala quatit.*
283. *Virt. Mart.* 4.7. Compare Severus, *Dial.* 2.10 in which a meadow full of flowers is compared to a gobelin.
284. *Hist.* 4.33; 7.11.
285. *Vit. patr.* 19. *prol.* Huxley 1959: 86 thinks that horticulture has its roots in men's visionary experience of 'the other world'.
286. *Vit. patr.* 12. *prol.*

arbour from the burning rays of the sun in the summer, [and] of which we know that, after having produced fruit in its season, it will become bare by the falling of its leaves — how much more ought we to desire that vine which knows no seasons and does not droop through the heat of any disease, which, when we no longer hope for anything, gives that which we had hoped for and lets us enjoy it.

The perfect vine is seasonless and permanent: it is the 'vine of life', like the spring and the tree a symbol of Christ[287] and existing in Paradise. The wine, as *mysterium*, is doubtless associated with the wine of the Eucharist, which effects mystic participation in the true, eternal life through Christ. Paradise is like sitting in the cool shade: Gregory here suggests but does not use the traditional Christian term *refrigerium* for the experience of Paradise.[288] If there is any passage in Gregory's works that proves that he took delight in nature, it is this one. Nevertheless, he sees it at the same time as but an imperfect reflection and foretaste of Paradise.

His description of gardens and pleasances on earth seem to show that these could also be appreciated for themselves, however. Abbot Bracchio, for instance, wished to be buried in 'the place near the river, where I have been thinking of building a chapel, [and which] is very delightful (*jucundus est valde*)'.[289] The saintly Monegunde had a small garden near her cell, in which she used to go' for a bit of refreshment (*pro quadam relevatione*), [...] looking at the plants there and walking around'.[290] The hermit Joannes, as we saw, liked to sit in the pleasant shade of the 'delightful branches' of his laurel trees.[291] The monks in the city of Clermont had 'a garden full of a multitude of vegetables and fruit trees, pleasing to behold as well as delightful in its fertility (*et amoenus visibus et fertilitate jucundus*)'.[292] But when a counsellor of King Alaric (an Arian heretic and an enemy of Catholics) advised him to have the church of St Felix in Narbonne lowered a little so that the king might enjoy a better view of the countryside from his palace, the man became blind as soon as it had been carried out.[293] The honour of a saint was more important than any view in the world, just as it was more important than the harmless enjoyment of a beautiful bunch of grapes.

The yearning for Paradise, which some hold to be universal,[294] was so

287. Eucherius, *Formul. spir. intell.* 4.
288. See Mohrmann 1961: 81—91.
289. *Vit. patr.* 12.3.
290. *Vit. patr.* 19.1.
291. *Glor. conf.* 23.
292. *Vit. patr.* 14.2.
293. *Glor. mart.* 91; *Hist.* 2.37.
294. Eliade 1952: 70.

strong in some of Gregory's contemporaries, such as the nun in Poitiers, who saw it in her vision, that they were willing to give up all that reminded them of it on earth in order, as they thought, to be able to enjoy it later in heaven forever. The hermit Joannes probably interpreted this 'death to the world' in a more spiritual manner and saw nothing wrong in planting his laurel trees. Gregory, as we saw above, could be decidedly poetical about a natural world in which he delighted, but he could never forget its transience. Paradise was the image-model through which gardens in this world were perceived.

'ROSES AND LILIES': THE INEXPRESSIBLE AS FRAGRANCE

> One night when the deacon [Urbanus] was lying awake in his bed, he heard a sound as though the church door were being opened. Many hours later, he heard it being shut again. After this, he got out of bed, took a lamp and went to the tomb [of St Julian, in the church]. There he saw — wonderful to relate — that the floor was covered with glowingly red roses, very large ones with a strong, sweet fragrance. He was astonished to see, through the openings in the lattice-work, that they also lay inside the tomb. Although it was then November, they looked so fresh that one would have thought they had been cut from their living stems that very moment.[295]

Gregory calls this 'a wonderful thing...that appeared (*mira res...apparuit*)', and probably took the association of red roses with martyrdom[296] to be self-evident. The appearance of the flowers, whether culled and brought from Paradise or perhaps created on the spot, is pure poetry. The practical-minded deacon, however, collected them reverently and made healing potions out of them. Gregory does not even attempt an explanation.

Flowers occur more often in Gregory's works than one might expect. In his lists of prodigies occurring in or on trees, it is their unseasonable blossoms that excite his astonishment, and he also records roses blooming in November and in January as something akin to prodigies.[297] In his miracle stories, however, he associates flowers as well as their fragrance in various ways with Paradise.

The priest Severus (of the medlar tree) used to gather lilies at the time when they began to bloom — 'to be born' Gregory says (*nascuntur*) — and hang them on the walls of the villa's that he had converted into churches.[298] When he died, he was buried in one of these churches. A lily, hanging there, which had let fall its petals and for a whole year seemed so dried up that it would turn into dust if one touched it, revived (*in rediviva viriditate*

---

295. *Virt. Jul.* 46b.
296. Eucherius, *Formul. spir. intell.* 4.
297. *Hist.* 9.44; 6.44.
298. *Glor. conf.* 50.

resurgit) on the anniversary of the day that he had 'migrated from his body':[299]

> One could see the leaves slowly becoming green again and the flowers arising; without any moisture of water or from the earth it was renewed so that it looked exactly as it did before. And so the blessed confessor, who together with the other saints, flourishes like a palm in heaven, brings forth (*profert*) new flowers from his tomb.

The emphasis, here, is not so much on the lily itself as on its resurrection (*resurgit*) on the very day that Severus is supposed to have begun his new life in heaven. Again we see a visible event annually representing an invisible one that occurred in the past, and yet is in a sense repeated every year.[300] This is the 'mythical' time of all the holy days of the Church, in which past and present coalesce. Severus' new life, moreover, is associated with the growth of a palm, a traditional image.[301] Gregory seems to intend this image of the parallel plant in heaven as, in some way, an *explanation* of the phenomenon of the revived lily. This is the same kind of thinking as that which explained the miraculous grain for the starving monks by reference to the Virgin's having produced the 'grain of life' for the world.[302] Deeply convinced of the symbolic character of reality, Gregory saw the participation of an ideal image in a concrete event, or its repetition in a material configuration, as one of the self-evident structuring principles of reality.[303] Possible material causes of an event may be mildly interesting but are in fact irrelevant.

Certain traditional Christian events and images were the models through which Gregory perceived contemporary events. This perceptual organisation made it possible for him, despite his practical sense, powers of observation and intellectual honesty[304] to explain the thrilling discovery of lilies near a tomb as having been 'brought forth' by the saint. In a similar story,[305] the trees in front of the martyr Eulalia's tomb in Merida produce (*proferunt*) every year on the anniversary of her death sweet-smelling gem-like blossoms (*flores gemmei*) in the form of doves, because her soul had gone up to heaven in the form of a dove (a symbol of the Holy Spirit).[306] The association of flowers with gems is reminiscent of their

299   *Glor. conf.* 51. On the lily as a symbol in the Bible see Goldmann 1975.
300. Similarly *Glor. mart.* 73.
301. See Fontaine 1969: 1228 and *Glor. mart.* 95. Compare Severus, *Ep.* 2.10.
302. *Glor. mart.* 10.
303. On theories of medieval symbolism see for instance: Chydenius 1975, Chenu 1979 and Ladner 1979: 223—33.
304. Evident in his examination and evaluation of such extraordinary natural phenomena as prodigies; see pp. 33-4.
305. *Glor. mart.* 90.
306. As in Matth. 3:16.

description in the nun's vision: 'gleaming like all kinds of gems in the spring light'.[307] There is, however, another dimension here as well: the timing and the number of the flowers are taken to indicate the fruitfulness of the coming year. Gregory saw analogy as the language by which God speaks to men.

Roses and lilies are the flowers that are especially associated with Paradise. Fortunatus calls them 'eternal flowers' that have the scent of Paradise.[308] Gregory compared the appearance of the saintly Bishop Gregory of Langres on his deathbed to roses and lilies, 'so that one would have thought he was already prepared for the glory of the future resurrection'.[309] Elsewhere, he speaks of a crown of 'beautiful lilies' as a heavenly reward for the predestined.[310] The lily is probably also what he, in another prologue, calls 'the flower of chastity'.[311] It is these heavenly flowers that Gregory lets a tearful bride speak of to her husband on their wedding night: she prefers them above all the flowers of this world:[312]

> ... behold, having been deserted by the immortal Christ, who promised me Paradise as a dowry, fate has made me the spouse of a mortal man; and instead of imperishable roses, a garland of drooping roses now does not adorn but disgraces me [...]. Earthly beauty makes me shudder, for I see the hands of the Redeemer pierced on account of the life of the world. [...]

When the bridegroom countered that their parents wished for heirs to continue the family and inherit their properties, for they were both only children, she continued,

> The world is nothing, wealth is nothing, the glory of this worldly life is nothing, the very life that we enjoy here is nothing. Instead, we should seek that life which is not shut off by the end of death, which is not destroyed by any illness or finished by any old age (*quae labe ulle non solvitur nec aliquo occasu finitur*), in which man remains in eternal blessedness, lives in a light that never diminishes, and, what is greater than all these things, rejoices with inextinguishable delight as an angel in the contemplation of the presence of the Lord Himself.

Gregory is here retelling a traditional story about events that occurred before he was born, and Bonnet has expressed doubt as to whether the words of the conversation are his own.[313] This is, however, the same bridal *mystique* as in the vision of the nun at Poitiers:[314] to merit the beauty of Paradise, one must give it up in the world. As Gregory also lets Salvius

---

307. *Hist.* 6.29.
308. Fortunatus, *Carm.* 6.6.2; 8.4.11—2.
309. *Vit. patr.* 7.3.
310. *Vit. patr.* 1. *prol.*
311. *Vit. patr.* 7. *prol.*
312. *Hist.* 1.47.
313. Bonnet 1890: 707 n.2.
314. *Hist.* 6.29.

say,[315] the world — even its beauty — is vain, nothing. Why? Because it is transient. The formulation here closely resembles that which we have already seen in the treatise *On the course of the stars*[316] about the wonders of God contrasted with the works of men: 'which do not grow old with any age, which do not perish by any onslaught, which do not grow less by falling into ruins (*quae nulla aetate seniscunt, nullo occasu occidunt, nulla labe minuuntur*)'. All these parallels seem to indicate that Gregory himself is the author of the bride's lament. As we have seen, however, in his preface to *The course of the stars* he describes the constant renewal of plant life in this world as a divine wonder. What the bride here says does not take this into account: it would have seriously weakened her argument. To his credit, Gregory is prepared to leave room for the strictly ascetic world as well as for the view that earthly beauty and renewal may be appreciated in their pointing to their Creator and to Paradise.

All the flowers in the above stories were either seen in Paradise (in the vision) or 'brought forth' (from there?) by a saint.[317] Sometimes, however, as we have already seen in Gregory's story of the ship in the storm,[318] a fragrance of incense could appear without any visible source. Elsewhere, like his namesake Pope Gregory,[319] he reports that an enrapturingly sweet smell of flowers could suddenly be perceived and likewise interpreted as an indication of the presence of a saint. Although this could be in part a Christian version of the classical tradition that associated these fragrances with the presence of the pagan gods, the symbolism is a widespread one.[320] A story Gregory tells about his own experience of this shows how it could be perceived.[321] One day he went with Bishop Avitus of Clermont to a church in the village of Mauzac which contained a relic of St Germanus:

> When the holy bishop, still fasting, entered this church around the tenth hour [about four o'clock in the afternoon], all of us who were with him smelled the fragrance of lilies and roses. This, we were sure, was produced for us by the merit of the blessed bishop [Germanus], for it was the month of November.

One cannot help wondering whether everyone had been fasting and if this did not increase their suggestibility and tendency toward hallucination.[322] This does not, however, explain the *content* of the experience. In fact,

315. *Hist.* 7.1.
316. *De cursu stell.* 9.
317. Dead saints were thought of as living in Paradise, as for instance in *Vit. patr.* 6.7; 7.8.
318. *Virt. Mart.* 1.9.
319. Gregory the Great, *Dial.* 3.30.5.
320. See Lohmeyer 1919, Lilja 1972 and Kötting 1982: 168 and passim.
321. *Glor. conf.* 41.
322. Compare for instance Huxley 1959: 120—1 and Ludwig 1966 in Tart 1969: 10—13.

Gregory lets us see that the sensation of the immediacy of the holy could often bring about a sudden, rapturous bliss that was verbalized as and mentally associated with the fragrance of flowers or herbs. About the main church in Clermont Gregory says: 'the awesome presence of God (*terror Dei*) and a great brightness are perceived (*conspicitur*) in it, and in the spring the devout often smell a most beautiful scent, as though of herbs, coming there'.[323] As we saw, when Bishop Ebregisil of Cologne, looking for the body of St Mallosus under the floor of his chapel, had dug seven feet deep,[324] 'he was suddenly overwhelmed by a tremendously beautiful smell (*odor immensi aromatis*) and cried: "I believe that Christ is showing me his martyr when he surrounds me with such sweetness!" ' Continuing to dig, he found the perfectly preserved body.

What Gregory has his friend Bishop Salvius say about his vision of heaven lets us see how this 'being in heaven' is assimilated to the effect of fragrance. While he stood there, he says, 'an exceedingly delightful fragrance enveloped me (*operuit me odor nimiae suavitatis*), so that, nourished by this sweetness, I no longer wished for food or drink'.[325] This odour came back with him to earth and stayed with him, so that there he did not eat or drink for three days. As soon as he told others about what he had seen however, it immediately left him; he interpreted this as a punishment for revealing so great a mystery (*mysterium*). In the description of Salvius' previous career, in the same story, Gregory also mentions odour in what looks like a metaphor: 'But when the fragrance of the divine breathing reached the innermost part of his soul (*cum divini spiramenti odor interna viscerum attigisset*), he left the service of the world (*saeculum*) and entered a monastery'. The indescribable experience of the Holy Spirit was like the poetry of fragrance. A spiritual experience is again perceived as or expressed in a sensory one.[326]

A delightful smell, inspiring reverence or perhaps love, could be perceived whenever the presence of the holy was suspected. When the hermit Friardus died, the cell trembled and 'was fragrant with divine odours (*divinis aromatibus effragare*)'.[327] As we saw, the inhabitants of Osser went with their bishop to lock the doors of the empty baptismal pool on Good Friday, 'already sensing the imminent arrival of the holy

---

323. *Hist.* 2.16.
324. *Glor. mart.* 62.
325. Compare Isidorus Hispal., *Etym.* 17.10.2.
326. Similarly Kötting 1982: 169. Compare Meslin 1974: 169. Lilja 1972:28 states that, in the classical tradition, the sons of Aphrodite are frequently presented as creating the feeling of love by means of their breath.
327. *Vit. patr.* 10.4.

fragrance (*iam odorem sacri praesentientes aromatis*)'.[328] A similar fragrance could be noticed around objects: in the wax dripping from unseen candles on saints' tombs,[329] or in the 'manna' and oil exuding from St Andrew's tomb, which also indicated the fertility of the coming year.[330]

It seems almost certain that these fragrances were associated with Paradise, but, apart from the story of Salvius, Gregory only twice specifically says so. The reader will remember that he ascribes the balsamy qualities of the water taken from St Julian's spring to 'the excellent qualities [or powers] of Paradise'.[331] What he says about fragrance in the context of the historic event of King Clovis' baptism is unmistakable however:[332]

> ...the church was decorated with white draperies, the baptismal chapel made ready, balsamy odours wafted about everywhere, fragrant candles burned with shimmering light, and the whole baptismal chapel was filled with a divine scent; God gave such grace to those present there, that they believed themselves to have been transported into the odours of Paradise (*se paradisi odoribus collocari*).

To return to flowers, there is one passage in which Gregory seems to speak about them in a rather different way. In their funeral plaint at Radegunde's death,[333] the nuns of the Convent of the Holy Cross in Poitiers bewail their lot as 'orphans' now that their 'mother' Radegunde, for whom they left behind family, homes and riches, has gone from them. Up to now the convent has seemed larger to them than villas or cities;[335] through the contemplation of her 'glorious face' they found gold and silver there, and

> received flowering vines, crested grain and meadows bright with all kinds of flowers. In you we gathered violets; you were for us the glowing rose and the luminous lily; your words shone for us like the sun. [...] Now, however, the whole earth is dark for us, and this place is cramped, because we can no longer look on your face. [...]

One wonders whether this is Gregory's own poetry[336] or perhaps a rendering of that of one of the nuns, or even of that of Fortunatus, Radegunde's frequent guest and admirer. The latter sometimes sent her the above-mentioned flowers accompanied by poems and his words in the poem on virginity, dedicated to the nuns, resemble these.[337] In another

328. *Glor. mart.* 23.
329. *Glor. conf.* 18.
330. *Glor. mart.* 30.
331. *Virt. Jul.* 41.
332. *Hist.* 2.31.
333. *Glor. conf.* 104.
334. Likewise Severus, *Ep.* 3.10.
335. Compare Gautier Dalché 1982: 413—4.
336. Bonnet has — on general grounds — doubts about this: Bonnet 1890: 707. n. 2.
337. Fortunatus, *Carm.* 7.8, 8.6, and 8.3.30—3: *ista legit violas carpit et illa*

poem, addressed to Radegunde herself, he says that when she secluded herself (as she used to do periodically) it was for him as though the sun ceased to shine (*te celante mihi stat sine sole dies*).[338] Perhaps Gregory here wanted to be 'ornate' and did some (unconscious?) borrowing. Not only do the expressions of the exuberant love of worldly beauty for its own sake[339] seem foreign to Gregory, but also the manner in which the metaphor is used. His own metaphors, as we have seen, tend to become a description of spiritual reality.

This becomes clear when he describes what he saw when he came into her cell and first looked at the dead Radegunde: 'her holy face shone so brightly that it was more beautiful than roses and lilies' (the flowers, more than any others, associated with Paradise). This moment was recorded too by one of her biographers, the nun Baudonivia,[340] who however adds something that Gregory himself omits. Because the bishop of Poitiers was absent visiting in his diocese, Gregory was summoned to officiate at her funeral:

> When he came to the place where the holy body lay — as he was later wont to tell it, with an oath and weeping — he saw, as it were, in a human being the face of an angel shining like roses and lilies. He was so awe-struck (*metu concussus*) and reduced to trembling (*tremefactus est*) by this that the devout man, wholly in God (*Deo plenus*), stood there as though he were in the presence of the Lord's blessed Mother.

This almost fortuitously preserved description of Gregory at a poignant moment shows what a speechless awe and intense emotion a few, seemingly poetical as well as symbolical, written words can conceal. I strongly suspect that similar emotional depth may lie behind more of his descriptions of the experience of the holy than he himself indicates.

Using a widespread symbolism, Gregory often describes the inexpressible, perceived as the immediacy of the holy, in terms of flowers or fragrance. Moreover, the new creation of flowers as well as their reviving and healing properties as documented in his miracle stories, also exhibit what was imagined to be the quality of the new life in Paradise, of which one may occasionally be fortunate enough to catch a faint scent on earth.

---

rosas/pratorum gemmas ac lilia pollice rumpunt/et quod odoratum est flore comante metunt. Quodvultdeus (*Lib. promiss.*, *Glor. sanct.* 17) calls the violet the flower of (married) continence: Radegunde had been married to King Clothar before she entered the monastic life.

338. Fortunatus, *Carm.* 11.2.6; on her seclusion *Carm.* 8.9.
339. On this in Fortunatus see Ganzenmüller 1916: 220—3 and Koebner 1915: 59.
340. Baudonivia, *Vit. Radeg.* 23. Severus, *Ep.* 3.17, compares St Martin's face at death to that of an angel.

PLANT LIFE: PARADISE LOST AND SOMETIMES REGAINED

To sum up the evidence on Gregory's attitude to plantlife, it can be stated clearly that nature as a system of regularities did exist for him. He looked at it primarily, however, as a miracle of divinely sustained creation, in which God could at any moment intervene to change the existing situation or to create something new. Like regular natural phenomena, these sudden transformations were generally structured according to what he thought of as pre-existing models or image-patterns of spiritual truth: God's actions in the past and His promises for the future. It is only at this level that explanation may be desirable or necessary; God's omnipotence makes all inquiry into material causes and effects irrelevant and even sacrilegious. Gregory is inclined to see what we would call metaphors rather as images or patterns of objective spiritual reality which are liable to materialize into visible phenomena and events. All this indicates that for him the visible world is more or less directly shot through with divine power expressing itself in forms, qualities and perhaps even substances. The meaning of each phenomenon or event is recognizable in its form, or as Gregory would express it, in its 'figure'.

In much of what Gregory writes about seeds, trees, gardens and flowers, the association of the resurrection, of the new life, keeps recurring. The obverse of this association, however, is that, notwithstanding Gregory's lively interest in and appreciation of the beauty of nature, he cannot forget that it is subject to disease and decay: in short, that it is transient. In fact, what nature does is to remind men of a Paradise — lost long ago and now yearned for in the future life — in which the poetry of a beautiful fragrance represents new, 'real' life of perpetual fulfilment that is beyond words and notions.

The verbal emphasis in Gregory's stories is usually upon the new life as the resurrection after physical death. The less reflective use of certain verbs and images, however, gives us a glimpse of the inexpressible mystery of the dynamisms of new, divine life revealing itself in nature and in man already during this earthly existence.[341]

CONCLUSION. 'IMAGE-LOGIC', THE MIRACLE OF RENEWAL AND SOCIETY

In describing God's wonders of nature, Gregory is trying to convince his readers that at a time when society, institutions of culture and learning, architectural and artistic monuments and human literature[342] all seem to be

---

341. Compare Hébert 1916: 131 who speaks of Gregory's view of reality as 'dynamism'.
342. *Hist. 5. praef.*; *Hist. praef. prima*; *De cursu stell.* 9; *Glor. mart. prol.* respectively.

in the process of being destroyed, a man can find permanence, stability and hope in the awed contemplation of the mystery and miracle of the holy as continuous visible creation, renewal and rebirth into permanence. Man can become a part of this process in two ways: by believing that, as God promises in the Bible and shows in His wonders of nature, He will make this rebirth happen to the deserving at death, and by living so as to deserve it at that moment. But this is not all. As I have tried to show, Gregory everywhere implicitly or explicitly alludes to or shows the mystery of divine renewal happening in those who are receptive to it in this world *now*: in the spiritual 'rebirth' of baptism; in the physical, but also spiritual 'rebirth' of a miraculous cure; for some, in an asceticism that achieves spiritual 'life' through physical 'death'; in the seed and the tree, which die in order to live; and in the miracles of the revival of trees and flowers or even of the entirely new creation *ex nihilo* of a spring and of wine and grain. The latter may obliquely refer, on another level, to the daily 'mystery' of participation in the divine life through the Eucharist.

Gregory sought out these various experiences and collected them. Where he was not directly involved, he experienced, in watching or hearing about such experiences afterwards, a sense of awed wonder as well as an exhilaration at its impact on himself. Possibly this was not unconnected with the fact that the experiences contained in Gregory's stories about plant life clearly express what has been called the Rebirth archetype.[343] An authority on the subject has written:

> Les catégories symboliques des Pères, Jung l'a bien remarqué, sont celles-lá même que la psychologie profonde a décelées dans la structure de la psyche. Elles sont archétypiques. [...] La reprise par le Christ et par l'Eglise des grandes images que sont le soleil, la lune, le bois, l'eau, la mère, etc. [...] signifient une évangélisation des puissances affectives désignées par lá. [...] C'est par leur médiation que le salut inauguré à la fine pointe de l'âme pénètre jusque dans les profondeurs de la psyche.[344]

For this to happen, however, an attitude of what Gregory describes as 'astonished admiration' must have been a necessary condition: such symbols have nothing to do with rational thinking. For Gregory, miracles were symbolic expressions of spiritual truths in concrete, visible reality.[345] He intended his collections of stories to be a lively kind of practical theology. We can see that he tended to apprehend not only general spiritual truths but also interior experience (which often coalesced with the former) in terms of concrete, visible phenomena and events. What he

---

343. Compare Bodkin 1963: 34, 72, 272—5, 325.
344. Beirnaert 1950: 284—5, citing Jung 1944: 32.
345. I owe this idea to Kee 1983: 250 who says that the Gospel of John views miracle as 'a symbol of divine transformation'.

describes as the holy, therefore, also seems to stand for the inexpressible element of interior experience: the moment of renewal.

This is evident when he says that he expects the divine renewing and creative power that worked in natural phenomena and in nature miracles to work in the same recognizable patterns or models in men. Divine power can turn even the 'barrenness' of his own understanding (*sterilis sensu*) and his language (*lingua sterilis*)[346] into fruitfulness. As he says in the general preface to the *Miracles of St Martin*:

> I am afflicted with the torment of a double fatigue, of grief as well as of fear. Of grief that so many miracles which happened in the time of our predecessors are not recorded in writing; of fear that I, an unlettered man, should undertake such a distinguished work. But, encouraged by the hope of divine compassion, I shall undertake to do that which I have been instructed to do [by a vision]. For, as I believe, He is able to bring it forth out of the barrenness of my language, who, by producing water from a dry rock in the desert, quenched the burning thirst of a whole people. [...]

Gregory expected such divinely inspired descriptions of miracles, in turn, to 'cause faith to sprout in inert minds (*mentes inopes ad notitiam... fidei...fecundent*)'.[347] A contamination of meanings between Word and words may not be the only model for this event. Gregory says elsewhere (using as metaphors of the visible phenomena he describes in his miracle stories) about some of Christ's sayings, that they are the 'seeds of eternal life (*vitae perpetuae semina*), which the heavenly Sower, in the field of the uneducated mind, waters from the divine spring with his precepts and makes fruitful with his teachings ...'.[348] Spiritual truths expressed in words, then, can be 'seeds of eternal life' and as such sprout in men's hearts. Gregory hoped that his own imaged stories would transmit these truths that generate new life.

It has been said that the early Christian habit of meditative reading, of contemplating the events in the Bible as charged with a deeper spiritual meaning, contributed to the rise to dominance of a way of understanding human experience, such as Gregory's, through images derived from biblical events. The fact that he found himself in a society with a by then largely oral culture may also have predisposed him to express himself in terms of visible events.[349] Although Gregory is capable of understanding and using abstract concepts to generalize experience, he prefers to do this

---

346. *Vit. patr.* 9. *prol.* and *Virt. Mart.* 1.11.
347. *Glor. mart. prol.*
348. *Vit. patr.* 2. *prol.*
349. On allegorical interpretation see Smalley 1964: 27 and Ohly 1977: 20. On oral culture see for instance Sas 1955; Vauchez 1975: 7, 147; Ropert 1976; Ariès 1976; and Vollrath 1981.

in images which have the quality of as yet incompletely verbalized emotive experience. It is this that makes him unable to reflect on his own thinking:[350] he is immersed in it. For him, internal and exterior reality tend to become one.[351] It is this, too, that explains his structuring of experience by clusterings and 'networks' of metaphors[352] rather than by circumstantial causality. His thinking follows the laws of imagination[353] rather than the logic of reason: images are not conceived of and thought about abstractly but are seen and related to each other through their visible form.[354] As in poetry, reality consists of discontinuous images joined by 'leaps' of 'emotional logic'.[355] Hence it is certain image-models, and not circumstantial causality, that generate even concrete reality in sudden pulses of transformation. This discontinuous, leaping 'image-logic', so long unrecognized because it exists alongside his practical common sense and keen psychological insight, is responsible for Gregory's creviced presentation. It is also the essence of his belief in miracle and his desire for 'astonished admiration' at the wonder of renewal or instant creation in nature and in men. Gregory's reality is that of poetry: 'La poésie est un émerveillement' in which 'le temps ne coule plus. Il jaillit'.[356] Gregory's reality, also, notwithstanding the fact that he was literate, almost exactly resembles that described as 'la mentalité primitive' by L. Lévy-Bruhl.

If divine renewal, also in men, may be considered to be an essential part of that which Gregory regarded as 'the holy', can it also be said of this renewal that it 'is very much a precipitate of [...] society's needs and structure?'[357] Not in any *direct* way, as I hope to have shown. The notion of natural renewal as the symbol of human interior renewal was part of a tradition that was by then perhaps a thousand or more years old, persisting through many social changes. Renewal seems to be a need of each individual in the realization of his spiritual potential more than a strictly social need. What we do see is that the form in which this need or wish is projected, and the human reality with which it is associated, are influenced by cultural and social needs and structures, however much the latter (in the sixth century) may have needed creative renewal. The helpful and

---

350. Compare Hartmann 1979: 23.
351. Compare Smalley 1964: 5; Ricoeur 1975a: 308.
352. As Ricoeur 1975b: 157, on metaphors as the hermeneutics of reality.
353. Described by Langer 1953: 241—4.
354. As Müller 1957: 241—4.
355. Lewis 1961: 35.
356. Bachelard 1961: 77 and 1973: 227; Lévy-Bruhl 1922a, 1922b and 1963.
357. Brown 1973 in: Brown 1982: 263. Compare Fontaine's critique of Brown's too exclusively sociological approach in Fontaine 1982.
358. Ladner 1973: 2—17.

punishing figure of the saint as such is indeed in many important ways (though not in essence, as I hope to show in the fourth essay) a 'precipitate' of the needs and structure of late antique society. But that which the saint and his miraculous 'power' represent — the new, divinely given, true life — cannot be reduced to social needs or structures. Gregory did not think of renovating society as such (although circumstances in fact compelled him to innovate much of the time). Like his contemporary, Pope Gregory the Great, who was in a very similar position, he thought of 'renewal' only in individual, interior terms. Because tradition prescribed it. Probably also because society did not seem to offer sufficient opportunities to realise this ideal life, which was — anyway — projected into a 'Heaven' or 'Paradise' after the earthly life. The contrast between the imagined ideal life in the future and the actual, earthly one became too great in this period. Men were too busy saving their souls by trying to 'merit' Heaven to get around to thinking systematically about earthly society as such in a constructive manner. Gregory's practical dependence on saints was, in important ways, influenced by contemporary social needs and structures, but his ultimate goal and desire was a harmonious relation to the divine cosmos, which transcended any earthly society. Its values — forgiveness, regeneration — cannot be derived from contemporary social practice, neither in Jesus' time nor in Gregory's. We are left with an irreducible residue: man's spiritual life, a 'factor' that may have its own manner of action and influence in what could be termed 'happening reality'.

Gregory's models of sudden transformation, the images that structure his view of reality, have a social function, but they do not derive from his society. They are part of the late antique Christian world-view in which he was brought up.

III

LIGHT AND FIRE IN A 'DARK WORLD'
metaphors and reality

INTRODUCTION: 'THIS DARK PLACE, THE EARTHLY HABITATION'
When Abbot Salvius opened his eyes after his seeming death (which it turns out later was in fact a night during which he had made a visionary journey to a heaven filled with 'inexpressible light') 'he stretched out his arms and said, "O merciful Lord, what have you done to me? Why did you let me return to this dark place, the earthly habitation, when I would so much have preferred your mercy in heaven to the absolutely worthless life of this world?"'[1]

Why was life in this world experienced as 'dark'? Is it the contemporary violent and half-barbaric social reality of sixth-century Gaul that Salvius is referring to? Or is he simply reiterating a by then traditional view that had arisen in a relatively prosperous and peaceable Mediteranean society already in the first century before Christ? In that case, is there simply no relation at all between the state of society and certain persistent patterns of thought and feeling, such as that which finds the world to be 'dark'? Gregory's 'dark' world turns out to be patched with sudden flashes of unearthly light. Is it possible to relate this not only to his — more or less inherited — manner of thinking but also to the state of the society in which he lived?

In late Antiquity the world may have seemed 'dark' because both pagan philosophy and Christian theology were dominated by a traditional ideal of a higher, spiritual world with which a great deal of light imagery was associated.[2] The preoccupation with light has been (speculatively) connected with a spread of the Greek preference for the

---

1. *Hist.* 7.1.
2. Van der Aalst 1962: 90, 105 and passim; Camelot 1976. Dörrie 1975: 10, 13, 18. Oeing-Hanshoff 1961: 1023-4. Aalen 1960: 357 speaks of 'Hellenistic light-mysticism'. Huxley 1959: 75 says that the perception of light is the prime feature of visionary experience.

visual mode of perception on the one hand,[3] and with the influence of widespread adherence to Near Eastern solar and astral religion on the other.[4] At a more popular level, Christian hymns as well as funerary inscriptions celebrated the ever-recurring victory of light over darkness,[5] an originally dualistic theme that had been developed in its Christian form especially in the Gospel of John. Metaphors of light and darkness had come to designate, if not opposing cosmic powers, at least opposite qualities of life.[6] Since the late fourth century, moreover, collections of stories about Syrian and Egyptian hermits had been circulating in which perceptions of (fiery) light, already a Biblical phenomenon, accompanied holiness and prayer.[7]

In the late sixth century we find Pope Gregory I using a certain amount of light imagery in his theological works as well as in his popular miracle stories, where he also describes reports of spontaneous effulgence.[8] Of other western writers in this period only Gregory of Tours and his friend Venantius Fortunatus use light imagery with conspicuous frequency. They too describe what they present as ordinary, non-mystical, experiences of spontaneous effulgence. Whereas Fortunatus at the same time carries on the antique tradition of light imagery as poetic ornament, Gregory handles it in a way that not only reveals more of his image-models of divine activity in the created world but also brings us squarely up against the problem of his imprecision or 'obscurity'. The following analysis of one of his stories of miraculous cures of blindness will reveal the kind of complexities and ambiguities we will have to deal with.

Queen Ultrogotha was the widow of Childebert I, one of Clovis' sons, and the following miracle[9] took place before Gregory became bishop of Tours in 573:

> When Queen Ultrogotha heard about the miracles that were happening in the place where the holy body [of St Martin] lay, she wanted with all her devout heart to come and see them — it seemed to her that this would be equal to listening to Solomon's wisdom. After she had fasted, stayed up nights praying and sent generous gifts ahead of her, she came to the holy place and entered the church fearful and trembling. She did not dare to approach the blessed tomb, saying that

3. Van der Aalst 1962: 84, 93.
4. Aalen 1960: 357.
5. Van Biezen and Schulte Nordholt 1967: 9. Sanders 1965 a and b passim.
6. Maclean 1915: 52-3; Aalen 1960: 358-9; Closs 1961: 1022-3; Schnackenburg 1961: 1025-6: Hahn 1976: 493; Matthieu 1976. Sanders 1965b: 758-9.
7. See Edsman 1940: 154-74 and n. 277.
8. See Dagens 1977: 173, 347-52 and, for instance, *Dial.* 2.3.5: *contemplationis lumen*; *Dial.* 2.35. 2-7: *lux creatoris, Dei lumen*; 2.37.3: a vision of innumerable lamps along the way to heaven; 3.29.3: *lampades accensae*.
9. *Virt. Mart.* 1.12.

she was not worthy to do so, that her sins stood in the way of her doing this.

The morning after she had spent another night in vigil, with prayers and unceasing tears, she again made gifts to the church and asked for mass to be said for the blessed confessor [Martin]. During the celebration of this mass, three blind men who had already spent a long time praying for their recovery at the feet of the blessed bishop [that is, at St Martin's tomb] were suddenly surrounded by a dazzling brightness and received again the eyesight they had formerly lost. At once, a great shout, praising God, rose to the sky. The queen as well as the people hurried to see this miracle. Everyone was awed by the faith of the lady and by the glory of the confessor. But above all everyone praised our God who gives such power to his saints that through them such things may be done: who gave to this world, among other lights, the huge star, which is the blessed Martin, through whom its darkness becomes bright. Like a bountiful olive tree in the spring, he presents the Lord every day with fruits, the conversions of those who suffer.

The first analogy made here shows where Gregory stands. It expresses his most fundamental attitude and conviction, evident throughout his works: *seeing* a miracle is equivalent to *hearing* words of wisdom uttered. This statement almost seems to indicate that Gregory was conscious of a shift towards the primacy of visual perception having taken place between Solomon's and his own time. Wisdom now entered the heart through the eyes. Equally essential is the notion that miracles, and not the verbal expression of Christianity, are the true wisdom: not intangible words but visible deeds, action. At the same time, there may have been an indirect comparison between the basilica of St Martin and Solomon's Temple.

Gregory seems to have assumed the connection between fasting, keeping vigils, praying with tears and commissioning masses on the one hand, and the incidence of miracles on the other, to be self-evident. In fact, he describes many cures of persons who have themselves performed these actions. In a sense, the latter resemble the contemporary monastic practice (as it had been described, for instance, by Cassian) of ascetic penitential actions and 'unceasing prayer' in order to achieve the 'purity' of soul necessary for the contemplation of the divine truth.[10] As I hope to show, Gregory's stress on tearful repentance prior to cures may also be part of a 'purificatory process'. J. Schlick has interpreted it as a pastoral policy of creating a kind of individual, private penitence in the period after the custom of public penitence had fallen into disuse and before Irish tariffed private penitence had made its appearance.[11] Modern psychological research has indicated that fasting, lack of sleep and continuous praying, singing or meditation can lead to an altered

10. Chadwick 1968: 79-80, 102-9. See also Fontaine 1967: 206. On the Christian use of meditation practices derived from antique philosophy see Hadot 1981.
11. Schlick 1966: 281.

perception, a decreased awareness of sensory stimuli and an increased awareness of imaginative processes.[12] It will be seen later that the latter as well as the interior 'purification' alluded to above probably played a not insignificant role in the process of miraculous cures.

In the present story, however, it looks as though the Queen's concrete, visible indications of faith and humility, combined with what must have been tearful and insistent requests for a miracle, are regarded at the same time as somehow almost obliging the dead saint to perform one upon others in her presence. Her combination of self-mortification and prayer as a manner of formulating a request to God resembles that of St Martin when, on a certain occasion, he desired to speak to the emperor and was not admitted.[13] Gregory's confidence in the saint's performance, which was founded upon Christ's promise that everything asked for in prayer and in the firm belief that it would be received, would be in fact given,[14] is very great. What to us seems to be an assemblage of incongruities — purification by a (consciousness-modifying) act of penance, a humble appeal to a personal agent of power, and the realization that one exerts by these and other more clearly manipulative symbolical actions some kind of constraint — all this was clearly a harmonious whole to Gregory and his contemporaries. These elements were seen as being able, in some way, to work together to produce sudden inexplicable transformations in individuals: miraculous cures. The statement that everyone 'marvelled' points to the beholders' affective participation in the event. It must have strengthened not only individual faith but also group solidarity.

The second 'cluster' of thoughts, this time in the form of light images, takes us into what seems to be a flux of visuality, imagery and affectivity at the heart of the miracle itself. (In the following, where the Latin terms can have various meanings, I have given them in addition to my English translation.) Let us look again at what happened. During mass, a ritual of affective participation in which symbols of light, renewal and liberation play a central role, the blind men were suddenly surrounded by a dazzling brightness (*subito... fulgore nimio circumdati*) and received back their eyesight (literally: light) (*lumen...receperunt*). Everyone admired the saint's glory (*gloria*) and praised God who gives such power (*virtus*) to his saints, giving to this world (*mundus*) — among other luminaries

---

12. Huxley 1959: 121. Ludwig 1966 in Tart 1969: 9-22 gives a full description of altered states of consciousness, their causes, characteristics and effects.
13. Severus, *Dial.* 2.5. Kolenkow 1980: 1497, 1502-3 seems to suggest that the combination of abstinence or ascetism with magical powers derives from the attitudes and practices of later antique philosophy. Compare on these Hadot 1981.
14. Mark 11:24.

(*luminaria*) — the huge star (*immensum sidus*), which is the blessed Martin, through whom its darkness becomes bright (*tenebrae refulgeant*).[15] Unmistakable here too is the world's being experienced or thought of as 'dark'. Without some kind of (heavenly) light, living in it is comparable to blindness. But *what* kind of heavenly light? It is not Gregory's fault that all the terms for light and heavenly bodies that he uses have traditional metaphorical as well as literal meanings. Are 'luminaries', 'star' and 'becomes bright' no more than vivid metaphors for the action of the holy? This would be an unproblematic interpretation had not Gregory mentioned the 'dazzling brightness' that 'suddenly surrounded' these men.

His use of the term *fulgor*, also used elsewhere for lightning, implies that this was a supernatural kind of light, brighter than that of day. Was it the sensation of returning eyesight that dazzled these men's eyes or did everyone else see a dazzling, supernatural light appearing around them? It is possible that Gregory had in mind another image of illumination: Ambrose and others had spoken of the newly baptized as shining with (heavenly) light,[16] and Gregory (though he rarely, as here, uses the word 'conversion'), often presents cures as initiating such a change of life.[17] Alternatively, is the dazzling light perhaps reminiscent of Paul's experience on the way to Damascus,[18] visible to the men themselves alone? Or is it an indication of the presence of the 'star' St Martin, giving 'light' simultaneously in the literal as well as the metaphorical sense? Church dignitaries could traditionally sometimes be described as 'stars' and the word 'glory', here associated with the saint, also has traditional connotations of heavenly light.[19] It must be said at once here that, as for instance Ambrose's description of the newly baptized shows, the tendency — natural enough, perhaps — to blur the distinction between physical and metaphorical light was not new.[20] Augustine, who is

15. Compare Gregorius Magnus, *Moralia* 9.8 in Migne 1849: 863 A): *praedicatores sancti ut sol...et velut stellae in tenebris lucent...; et velut stellae in nocte resplendent.*
16. Camelot 1976: 1149-51; Edsman 1940: 163.
17. See below, p. 200ff. The metaphor of St Martin as an olive tree also points in this direction; the latter was a symbol of eternal life (Cumont 1949: 34).
18. Acts 9:3.
19. Sanders 1965b: 792-5; Aalen 1976: 46. Compare Hahn 1976: 485. Severus however, had also used it to describe St Martin's apparition after death (*Ep.* 2.16. See Fontaine 1969: 1253).
20. Van der Aalst 1962: 110; Aalen 1951: 77, 85, 314; Cumont 1949: 363; Sibum 1962: passim. Sanders 1965b: 859 'het reëel en/of metaforisch-gedachte "christelijk licht"'; 860: 'het heiligheidsaureool...dat soms tot reëel licht verdicht' and Sanders 1965b: 778.

described as having a rich personal experience of light mysticism,[21] explicitly distinguished the 'intelligible' light from that perceivable by the senses.[22] Prudentius (348-415), however, who seems to be one of Gregory's favourite poets[23] and who uses a great deal of light imagery in his hymns, tends, although he does make a distinction between them, to regard visible light as somehow an extension of the metaphorical.[24] At the end of the sixth century, Pope Gregory reports luminous phenomena, yet explicitly distinguishes exterior and interior light.[25] In Gregory of Tours' presentation, however, no clear distinction is made. Whether the light is visionary, imaginary or physical remains ambiguous.

As the above story shows, not only is light an image with a meaning of central importance for him, but also if we try to follow him when he mentions it, we are plunged into ambiguities and obscurities. Alongside the initial query of why the world was experienced as 'dark', this raises two questions. First, given that Gregory was above all a visually-oriented man who was inclined to avoid extensive conceptual thinking, what was he trying to express with his light imagery?[26] Second, what is the nature of his apparent imprecision or obscurity as it appears in the context of light? Put another way: what is it that he is describing with light metaphors and how, for him, are these metaphors related to sensory reality?

For Gregory, light was inseparable from fire because, directly or indirectly, it was always produced by something burning. It will therefore be necessary in this study, to take account of experiences and imagery of fire which, though often close to and merging into those of light, can also represent an opposite quality: that of scorching or consuming. I shall begin by examining Gregory's descriptions of the perception of fire, that is visible fire and lightning, as will as his apparent metaphors of fire and imaginings of infernal fire. Most of these phenomena and metaphors turn out to be interpreted in such a way as to support the church's idea of how men should behave in society. Then I

21. Camelot 1976: 1156.
22. Oeing-Hanhoff 1961: 1024.
23. Bonnet 1890: 64. Gregory quotes Prudentius in: *Glor. mart.* 40, 92, 105 and 112, and *Vit. patr.* 6. *prol.*
24. As in *Cathem.* 5.29-30: *quis non rapidi luminis arduam manantemque Deo cernat originem* and 5.153: *tu lux vera oculis, lux quoque sensibus.* On light imagery in Prudentius in general, cf. Van Assendelft 1976 passim.
25. As in *Dial.* 4.11.2: *exteriores tenebrae...interna lux* and 4.11.3: *corporis lumen... cordis lumen.* There is one ambiguous case, however: in the twilight preceding the end of the world, *tenebrae quadam iam rerum spiritualium permixtione translucent.*
26. On religious symbols see, for instance Meslin, 1974 (in the context of psychology) and Holte 1979 (in the context of society).

shall turn to consider the perception and imagining of light and show how the various qualities he attributed to it are often metaphors of transformational interior experience as well as of certain aspects of the social life of his time. From all this, the contours of the relation of Gregory's metaphors to sensory reality will begin to emerge. Next, the influence on perception of what must be pre-existent, wish-expressing mental imagery will be explored through an examination of Gregory's description of various kinds of spontaneous effulgence seen around holy persons or objects. These too have unmistakable functions for the individual as well as for society. In a final section I shall relate light imagery and perceptions connected with physical cures to imaginal thinking, purification and the experience of holy power. In the conclusion, the evidence on Gregory's understanding of the relation of metaphor to reality will be placed in the general perspective of his experience of himself and his world, and an answer to the more general question of the relation between his world-view and his social circumstances is attempted.

A. FIRE AS BURNING HEAT

> Cham's first-born son was Chus. Instructed by the devil, he invented all the arts of magic and idolatry, setting up a statue so that it could be worshipped and letting men see stars and fire fall from heaven by false power (*falsa vertute*). This man went to the Persians, and they called him Zoroaster, that is: 'living star'. From him they even learned to worship fire, and they venerate him, who was [eventually] divinely consumed by fire (*divinitus ignem* [sic] *consumptum*), as a god.[27]

Gregory's tone here is derisive. Elsewhere, he reports that the contemporary Armenian Christians living near the Persian border rejected friendship with the Persians because the latter insisted on their worshipping fire.[28] Their bishop answered the Persian envoys: 'What kind of deity (*deitas*) is there in fire that it should be worshipped? God created it for the use of men; it is lighted with tinder and extinguished by water. When one fans it, it burns; when neglected, it goes out'.

Does Gregory regard this matter-of-fact position as being his own as well? If so, it is far from being the whole truth. If not deity, some other kind of definitely immaterial dynamics becomes visible in his descriptions of various kinds of fires. In reporting the Armenian stand, did he want to play these down or was he not entirely conscious of his attitude?

---

27. *Hist.* 1.5. Similarly Isidore, *Etym.* 14.3.12.
28. *Hist.* 4.40.

'TREACHERIES OF SATAN'?: NATURAL FIRE AS VISIBLE VIOLENCE

In his *Histories* Gregory, like Livy, Eusebius, Jerome and Orosius, includes some large-scale fires in the lists of extraordinary natural phenomena he calls 'signs', 'portents' or 'prodigies', and in which he tries to discern a divine message.[29] Many 'prodigies' preceded (in Gregory's view probably 'announced') an epidemic of dysentery whose victims included two of King Chilperic's sons.[30] Among these were two fires. One was 'a divinely-started fire (*divinitus ortum incendium*) [which] destroyed a village near Bordeaux: a house and a granary containing the harvest burned down — as he says 'perhaps by divine command' — having been suddenly seized (*subito conpraehensi*) by a fire that had no origin anywhere else'. The other fire, in Orléans, left almost everyone destitute, even the rich, because thieves looted whatever little had been spared. The ascription of the former fire, which was probably in fact a case of spontaneous combustion, to divine action is a clear case of filling the gaps in the knowledge of causes and effects with the assumption of interference from without, common to all primitive societies. The observation that the other fire had left everyone destitute appears to carry a connotation of punishment. Gregory even seems to see a significance in the more or less simultaneous occurrence of these and other calamities: the implementation of a programme of divine chastisement.[31] Elsewhere, not in a list of prodigies, Gregory also actually explains a fire that destroyed the church of St Martin at Tours as caused 'by the sins of the people and the outrageous activities which Wiliachar [who, as the father-in-law of a rebellious prince, had sought asylum there] perpetrated in it'.[32]

When 'divine fire (*divinus ignis*)' (probably lightning[33]) caused the royal Burgundian palace in Vienne to catch fire on the day before Easter, its bishop Mamertus, as we saw, 'with sighs and tears implored the mercy of God, ...and the river of his flowing tears extinguished the fire of the palace'.[34] In his *Homily on the Rogations*, however, Avitus of Vienne compares the event with the divine punishment of Nineveh.[35] Clearly,

---

29. For instance *Hist.* 6.21 and below. For his treatment of prodigies see chapter I.
30. *Hist.* 5.32-3.
31. As in the Bible: see Bietenhard 1976: 655-7.
32. *Hist.* 4.20.
33. *Hist.* 2.34. Compare *caelestis ignis* in Pliny, *Nat. hist.* 2.18.82.
34. When he had, thereafter, instituted prayers, fasts and almsgiving, the other 'terrors (*terrores*)' also ceased. This programme of action resembles the traditional appeasement of the gods after the occurrence of similar prodigies. See on this Bloch 1963: 119-29.
35. Jon. 3:5-10; Avitus, *Homilia in rogationibus*, 1.30-32 in Peiper 1883: 111: Gregory mentions this as his source of information.

real, visible fire is sometimes being interpreted as an instrument of divine chastisement, however it may have been started. The citizens of Vienne no doubt tried to extinguish the fire in the palace with material means, but for Gregory it is in this case God who started and who stopped it, whatever the actions of men. Gregory's bold use, among a number of matter-of-fact statements, of the metaphor 'river of tears' makes it look as though he visualized a literal flood of tears as (perhaps on another level of reality) actually extinguishing the fire.[36]

In a few cases, Gregory explicitly attributes a fire to the agency of the devil. One fire, which a bishop stopped with the sign of the Cross, is described by Gregory as 'treacheries (*insidiae*) of Satan'.[37] Thus diabolic envy (*invidia tentatoris immissum*)[38] and instigation of the devil (*instinctu maligni*)[39] can constitute causes. A piece of wax scraped from St Martin's tomb (a relic by contact)[40] cast into flames previously described as 'voracious (*voraci*)' extinguished the whole fire at once: Gregory says it was a new kind of miracle (*novum miraculum*) that wax, which usually (*erat solita*) feeds the flames, 'stifled their violence by the force of its holiness (*violentiam ignis vi sanctitatis oppressit*)'. 'Violence' and 'savageness' are words Gregory always uses for destructive, evil power,[41] which he often attributes to the agency of the devil. Once in the context of a martyrdom and once in the context of an ordeal, Gregory speaks of 'savage fire (*incendia saeva*)'.[42] 'The force of holiness', an expression he does not use elsewhere, is very revealing, reminiscent of the phrase 'powerful in all kinds of sanctity'.[43] It is a power that can more than counter that of the devil, who is in a few cases explicitly designated as being responsible for a fire.

During his life, St Martin had 'commanded fire'[44] and in a number of

---

36. In a similar case, the flames started to fall (*decidere*) as soon as St Martin's aid was invoked with tears (*Virt. Mart.* 4.47): *restinxit plebs per lacrimas quod nequiverat superare per undas.*
37. *Glor. conf.* 55.
38. *Virt. Mart.* 1.2. Gregory is paraphrasing Paulinus Petricordiensis' *Vita Martini* (whom he, however, calls Paulinus of Nola): in Migne 1961: 1072C. Compare: *Hist.* 2.3.: *in maiore insania...episcopus [Arrianus] invidia inflammante succenditur. Insania* and *invidia* are always diabolical qualities; for instance *Hist.* 7.36; 8.15.
39. *Glor. conf.* 54; 14.
40. Compare Helgeland 1980: 1297.
41. Of human action with an evil intention: *Hist.* 1.48; 2.3; 3.7; 4.12; 5.14; 5.36; 6.41; 7.29; 9.27; 10.2; 10.15. *Water*: *Hist.* 4.30; 4.31. *Wind*: *Hist.* 5.41; 10:13.
42. *Glor. mart.* 95; *Glor. conf.* 14.
43. *Hist.* 1.37.
44. Severus, *Vit. Mart.* 14.2; *Dial* 1.25.1; *Ep.* 1.10-15.

stories Gregory lets us see that his and other saints' relics can also extinguish or contain fires. Let us look at three of them. On one of his journeys, Gregory himself saw a fire, which had been consuming a poor man's hut with its roof of leaves, 'die out (*obstupuit*) as though it had never been kindled at the sight of (*in aspectu*) the holy relics' (of the Virgin, the apostles and St Martin) that he 'held up against it (*contra ignem*)'.[45] Similarly, as Gregory's mother once lay sleeping in her house, the beams of the ceiling caught fire through sparks from the hearth. But, Gregory says, 'through the power (*virtus*), as I believe, of [saint Eusebius of Vercelli], whose relics were kept nearby, the flame — against its nature (*contra naturam*) — retreated by being driven downward. Instead of reaching towards the roof, as it usually does (*ut mos est*), it ran downward'.[46] After his mother had awoken and called the servants, the fire was finally extinguished with water. In the third and more spectacular story taking place at harvest time on one of his mother's estates, the south wind fanned a small fire of chaff into a large conflagration, threatening the corn that had just been harvested and threshed. Gregory's mother rose quickly from the table and 'held up the relics [which she evidently always had with her] against the balls of fire (*elevatis sacris pignoribus contra ignium globos*) so that the whole fire stopped at that very instant (*de momento*) and hardly a spark could thereupon be found among the heap of burned chaff'.[47] These three stories have several features in common: in each a discernible origin of the fire is mentioned or assumed; in none is the fire experienced as a divine punishment for which mercy must be asked or earned; and finally, in all three, the flames can be 'turned back' or stifled instantly and completely by holy power through relics. It is not clear whether Gregory is here thinking of fire simply as an 'element' which is 'commanded', or whether, somewhere at the back of his mind, he is also thinking of a diabolic power possibly active in it, as in the first stories examined earlier.

The following story about a great fire in the city of Paris in 585[48] shows more clearly than many other stories that even when Gregory does not explicitly say so, he conceives of reality as happening on various levels at once. Immediately after concluding a description of the outrageous murder of Bishop Praetextatus as he prayed in church with the comment 'In truth (*enim*) many evil deeds were done in this time',[49] Gregory begins

---

45. *Glor. mart.* 10. A similar case: Bishop Gallus with the Gospels in *Vit. patr.* 6.6.
46. *Glor. conf.* 3. Gregory the Great tells a similar story in *Dial.* 1.6.2.
47. *Glor. mart.* 83.
48. *Hist.* 8.33.
49. *Hist.* 8.31, 32.

a new chapter with the words: 'Accordingly (*igitur*) there was in these days in the city of Paris a woman who said to the inhabitants, "Flee from the city, for I tell you it will be consumed by a fire!"' The words *enim* and *igitur* may indicate that Gregory is connecting the evil deeds with the fire, and in all likelihood with the latter as their punishment. When the citizens did not believe the woman, she protested she was speaking the truth 'for I saw in a dream a luminous man (*vidi in somnium virum inluminatum*) coming out of the church of St Vincent, holding a lighted candle in his hand and setting the merchants' houses on fire, one after another'.[50] Thereupon, surprisingly, Gregory proceeds to describe a completely 'natural' cause of the fire: three days after the woman's prophecy, one of the citizens had gone at the crack of dawn to his storage cellar to get some oil with a lighted lamp or candle in his hand. When he had taken the oil, he went out and left the burning light standing next to the oil barrel. This dangerous proximity caused the house to catch fire and the wind soon spread the fire over the whole city, sparing only the churches (perhaps built of stone). Gregory makes no attempt to reconcile the two versions of the fire's origins.[51] One must conclude that the two versions relate the same physical event, one as it took place on the visible plane and one as it took place on the spiritual plane. Three chapters earlier, before the murder of the bishop, Gregory had let King Guntram deliver a kind of sermon to the assembled bishops and magnates, saying that the current lawlessness and lack of respect for the church would have to stop if they did not wish 'God's anger to come upon the whole...country'.[52] Gregory apparently expects the reader to make the connection himself: he may also have expected them to remember that fire had been the divine punishment of Sodom.[53]

Notwithstanding the fact that Gregory probably considered this fire to be a punishment from God through one of his saints, he graphically describes how the 'power (*virtus*)' of another saint, St Martin, saved his own chapel and 'did not permit the ruling flames (*flammi dominantes*) to harm the surrounding houses'. The expression 'ruling flames' seems to suggest a kind of power in the fire. Whose power? That of God, of

50. This 'luminous man' is probably a saint, perhaps St Vincent or possibly St Germanus, former bishop of Paris, whose tomb Gregory says to be in this church, and who later liberates prisoners threatened by the fire.
51. There is one other story in which Gregory says that a saint is responsible for the burning of a house, in that case to avenge his honour (*Glor. conf.* 80). The man had lighted this fire himself, however.
52. *Hist.* 8.30.
53. As also Avitus, *Hom. in rog.* 1.18-9 in Peiper 1883: 109: *Quis enim in crebris ignibus imbres Sodomiticos non timeret?*

another saint, of the devil or simply that of fire as an 'element'? Gregory leaves all this unexpressed: he is not interested in or troubled by superficial contradictions. The flames are overcome by the evidently stronger power of the saint — and this is where his real interest lies. The saint's power is brought into action by, as Gregory describes it, 'the strongest possible hope (or trust: *spes firmissima*)' in this power[54] on the part of the man who had built the chapel and then sought refuge in it during the fire. Here Gregory again suggests something without explicitly stating it: that this strongest hope itself worked as a kind of power obliging the saint to action. The relations between the fire, the man and the saint are thus formulated in terms of power. In fact, implicitly or explicitly, power relations tend to play a large if not dominant role in everything Gregory has to say about human events.

Natural fire, in conclusion then, may sometimes be started by God or a saint in order to punish men for their sinful behaviour. It may also come about by the agency of the devil. Regardless of their origin, Gregory tends to ascribe violent and 'dominating' qualities to the devouring flames. He seems to see it as a visualization of the quality of a violent power. Fire may be stifled and driven back instantly by holy power brought into action through personal prayer, firm trust in a saint or the holding out of the sign of the Cross or relics 'against' it. He seems to imagine the holy power as an instant, invisible wind that blows the fire away or out. Gregory is more interested in the extinction of the fire than in its ontological nature, which can remain ambiguous. In certain stories we seem to get a glimpse of another level of reality on which visible earthly events are brought about through what we would call metaphors, images and dreams. It has been observed that even today there are few scientific, 'objective' studies of fire as a phenomenon: its appearance is so suggestive that the imagination at once tends to take over.[55]

'FIRE FROM HEAVEN': AN INSTRUMENT OF JUSTICE

In his lists of prodigies, Gregory sometimes mentions phenomena, such as 'light (*fulgor*) running across the sky like serpents'.[56] This may simply be lightning but he naturally suspects some further significance in it, perhaps having in the back of his mind Christ's description of his Second

---

54. See p. 243-4.
55. As Bachelard 1949: 10-1.
56. *Hist.* 8.42. Similarly *Hist.* 5.33 and 8.8: *fulgor per caelum cucurrisse visus est*; 6.14: *coruscationes et tonitrua*; 6.21: *per caelum ignis discurrere visus est*; 9.5: *serpentes ex nube dilapsi* (?)

Coming: 'like flashing light(ning) (*fulgor coruscans*) that lights up the sky from one side to the other...'[57]

In the Old Testament as well as in Roman tradition,[58] lightning, as a natural phenomenon, was fire from heaven or from God, and consumption by it could be regarded as divine punishment. Accordingly, Gregory reports that in the city of Limoges several people had been 'consumed by heavenly fire (*igne caelesti*)' for performing public services on the day of the Lord; others in the region of Tours were also consumed, but not on Sunday.[59] The same threat is evident in his other stories about lightning, where it is also clearly being exploited as a means of enforcing the conduct the church demands. St Julian shows himself able by his 'power (*potentia*)' to 'command' lightning not to hurt those who had sought refuge in his church from a storm; he also, however, lets 'the splendour of divine power', in the form of lightning, destroy an idol.[60] Someone who entered the saint's church by the window in order to let the rest of his war-band plunder it, later died 'consumed by fire from heaven (*igne de caelo consumptus*)'.[61] A man who had seized some of the saint's properties was later, while he was enjoying good cheer at the table, suddenly struck down 'by a fiery dart that had fallen from the sky (*jaculo igneo de coelis elapso*)...and was slowly consumed like a flaming funeral pyre'.[62] Finally, to convince any doubters, Gregory points out, that this could not have happened by chance, for in the midst of innocent people, the violator (*sacrilegus*) of Julian's properties was the only one who was struck.

Another story concerns an arsonist who thought he could clear himself of suspicion by swearing his innocence upon the relics of a saint.[63] This practice, of which Gregory gives other examples as well,[64] shows again how the authority imputed to a saint could be used to fill gaps in the contemporary administration of justice. Since it seemed obvious that the man had set his neighbour's house on fire, he was told that he would not

---

57. Luke 17:24. See p. 000.
58. Bietenhard 1975: 654; Pliny, *Nat. hist.* 2.18.82; 2.55.145. Gregory cites Prudentius on this in *Glor. mart.* 40. Isidore (*Etym.* 19.6.4) distinguishes the human and the divine use.
59. *Hist.* 10.30: *plerique igne caelesti consumpti sunt.*
60. *Virt. Jul.* 27: *fulgura, imber igne mixtus et grandine*; 6: *splendor divinae potentiae*. St Hilary also protected against a thunderstorm: *tempestas cum tonitruo et coruscatione* (*Glor. conf.* 2).
61. *Virt. Jul.* 13.
62. *Virt. Jul.* 15.
63. *Hist.* 8.16.
64. For instance *Hist.* 7.29; 8.16; *Glor. mart.* 20, 33, 34, 39, 52, 53, 57; *Virt. mart.* 1.31; *Glor. conf.* 29, 93, 94; *Virt. Jul.* 19; *Vit. patr.* 8.9.

be admitted into the church, and had better do his swearing outside, 'for God is everywhere, and his power (*virtus*) is outside as well as inside'. The man then swore 'by the almighty God and by the power (*virtus*) of his bishop, the blessed Martin', that he had not started the fire. As he turned to walk away, however,

> it seemed to him as though he was surrounded by fire (*visum est ei quasi ab igne circumdare*). Falling to the ground at once, he began to cry out that he was being violently consumed (*vehementer exuri*) by the bishop. The unhappy man shouted: 'I call God to witness that I saw a fire fall from heaven (*ignem de caelo cadere*) which now surrounds me and melts me with its terrible heat (*validis vaporibus*)!'. And as he was saying this, he died. This incident was a warning to many people not to risk any perjuries in this place from then on.

A saint is seen punishing again, here by what is probably understood to be lightning. Gregory obviously accepts a bolt of lightning seen and felt by only one person as equally real, in its own way, as one seen by everyone, and expects his readers to do the same.

Individualized perception was evidently more acceptable in his day than in ours — as long as it more or less conformed to certain generally accepted image-models. Gregory loves what we call 'poetic justice': Chus, who made men worship natural fire, was killed by heavenly fire; an arsonist, who abused natural fire, and on top of that committed perjury, was also struck down by heavenly fire. Lightning is being interpreted in a way that it supports the church's conception of justice. Beliefs here work for the cohesion of society: they are themselves social institutions.[65]

'FLAMING HELL': A FEAR-INSPIRING IMAGE

> The fourth (wonder of the world) is Mount Etna on the island of Sicily, which boils up with living fire (*vivi ardores*), spits out huge flames (*flammae*) and belches forth fiery (*ignea*) brimstone in a terrible way upon the inhabitants of this region... And if something is thrown into the opening from which these flames come, it is soon vomited forth again...
>
> The fifth (wonder) is the spring of Grenoble, that gives forth water and fire (*ignis*) at the same time: for one can see flames (*flammae*) hovering above the water; one can draw water from the middle of the fire (*focus*) and not be seared (*ureris*); one can drink it and not be burned (*incenderis*), carry it and not be consumed by the fire (*ab igne comprehenderis*); if one puts a candle or torch to it, it catches fire as soon as the flames touch it, while if one puts one's hand in it, it will not be burned...
>
> O astonishing mystery of divine power (*O admirabile potentiae divinae mysterium*)! One spring produces both fire and water, so that all men would perceive that both the refreshment of the life in glory (*refrigerium gloriosae vitae*) and the judgment of eternal death are in his power, and would understand that

---

65. Compare Douglas 1966: 89.

permission was not given to the fires (*incendia*) to hurt that same human body which, if after the Judgment it should be found guilty of sin, they will receive for the purpose of perpetual burning (*exurendum*).[66]

In his introduction to God's seven wonders, Gregory says that Mount Etna and the spring of Grenoble 'reprove sinners in that they present a likeness of the fire of hell (*ignem infernalem figurant*)'.[67] A hundred-and-fifty years earlier Augustine, writing his *City of God*, had also mentioned this spring but as one of the many wonders of the world indicating God's omnipotence and power to do what seems impossible: namely to resurrect the dead and to torment the guilty in everlasting fire.[68] The distance between the two men is evident in this one example. Augustine sees the spring in an *abstract* manner, as a non-specific proof of divine omnipotence in general; Gregory sees an *image* of the as yet hidden reality of heaven and hell as already visibly present in the created world. The searing fire and the cool refreshment of Paradise, the latter a standard Christian phrase,[69] are here mentioned in, as it were, static opposition; there is no suggestion of any progression through the fire to refreshment as in the works of Paulinus of Nola, which Gregory may or may not have known.[70] The brimstone coming out of Etna was, of course, associated with divine punishment.[71] Was Gregory aware of the fact that there were some in his time who believed that this volcano might resemble or in fact be the earthly entrance to hell? In this context, his contemporary Pope Gregory the Great, relates a hermit's vision in which

66. *De cursu stell.* 13-4. I have omitted Gregory's quotes of other authors because they are purely descriptive. Respectively, on Etna: Vergil. *Aen.* 3.570-4: *Portus ab accessu ventorum inmotus et ingens Ipse, sed horrefecis iuxta tonat Ethna ruinis, Interdumque atra prorumpit ad aethera nubem Turbine fumantem piceo et candente favilla, Adtollitque globos flammarum et sidera lambit*. Julius Titianus (see Krusch 1885: 862 n. 1): *Montes maximi in Sicilia quattuor, Ericus, Nebrodes, Neptunius et Ethna, quem videns saepius flammas e vertice volvere, idque sentire orbis prope fide credentium, quamquam id: cum primum Romae nuntiatum est, arsisse Ethnam, in monstris procuratum est*. And on the spring of Grenoble: Hilary of Arles' poem is mentioned in *Vit. Hil. Arel.* 11.14 (Migne 1859: 1232B) but lost (see also Krusch 1885: 862 n. 3): *Si vere exurunt ignes, cur vivitis undae? Si vere extinguunt undae, cur vivitis ignis? Limpharum in gremiis inimicus condidit ignis, Communesque ortus imperat alta manus.*
67. *De cursu stell.* 9. Compare Edsman 1940: 179.
68. *De civ. Dei* 21.7.
69. See on this, Mohrmann 1961: 81-91.
70. *Epist.* 28 and *Poema* 7.32-43, cited in Le Goff 1981: 91. Also *Poema* 8.30-3. Gregory confuses him with his namesake of Périgueux (*Virt. Mart.* 1.2), but shows knowledge of his life of St Felix of Nola (*Glor. mart.* 103) and of Paulinus' own life (*Glor. conf.* 108).
71. Bietenhard 1975: 657.

he saw King Theodoric of Italy being thrown into its crater by Pope John and the patrician Symmachus, both of whose deaths he had just caused.[72] What Gregory of Tours says about this king is that he 'was suddenly struck by God' as a 'vengeance' for the deaths of Christian martyrs and that he 'perished exhausted by immense agonies, and at once began to suffer the perpetual fire of flaming hell (*suscepit protinus perpetuum gehennae flammantis incendium*)'.[73] Was King Theodoric so obviously guilty that he did not need to await Judgment before being punished? This is what Gregory seems to be saying explicitly, on one occasion, in a theological debate, but also in a few other stories of the notoriously wicked. There, even when he does not mention fire, he says something like 'he rapidly descended to hell (*velociter descendens ad infernum*)'.[74] Gregory's visceral hatred of heretics is again evident in what he says about the death of Arius, their prophet, who 'after his intestines (*interiora*) had fallen out, was subjected to infernal fires (*infernalibus ignibus subditur*)'.[75] It may be that Gregory also visualized Christ in action here who, as he says in his *Commentary on the Psalms*, 'himself hands over the wicked who are about to be consumed (*consumendi*) to the infernal oven (*clibanus infernalis*)'.[76] As J. Le Goff suggests, this is good pastoral psychology in a society in which only fear of power[77] is able to contain violence and immorality, a feature which emerges very clearly from all Gregory's writings about his own time.[78]

72. *Dial.* 4.31.3. It later came to be associated with Purgatory: Le Goff 1981: 130-1. Isidore also associates it with divine punishment: *Etym.* 19.6.4.
73. *Glor. mart.* 39.
74. *Glor. mart.* 47. Similarly, *Hist.* 2.23; *Glor. mart.* 30; *Glor. conf.* 63: *descenderunt viventes et vociferantes in Tartarum.* Compare *Hist.* 10.13: while Lazarus 'rests in the bosom of Abraham, the rich man is tortured in the flames'.
75. *Hist.* 3. *praef.* Elsewhere, too, Gregory associates latrines, faeces and their repulsive odours with extreme wickedness or the devil: *Hist.* 9.6.; *Vit. patr.* 11.1 and 17.3. Compare on this Fontaine 1968: 850-1 and 1969: 1037). Gregory notes that a priest who dared to plot against his own bishop suffered the same punishment as Arius: *Hist.* 2.23; this is an indication of how fundamentally threatening such an event would be for someone in Gregory's position (see also p. 280). Equally threatening were the robbers of such property. The canons of church councils are more concerned with this than with other affairs: Stancliffe 1979: 59. Gregory's writings are full of stories of how saints punished such injuries: *Hist.* 2.37; 4.16; 4.48; 6.10; 7.21, 35; 8.12; *Glor. mart.* 58, 60, 71, 78, 104; *Glor. conf.* 79; *Virt. Jul.* 13, 14, 15, 16, 17, 20, 39; *Virt. Mart.* 1.17, 30, etc.
76. *In psal.* 20.
77. Le Goff 1981: 121.
78. For instance, *Glor. conf.* 86: *rex exterritus*; *Glor. mart.* 72: *iudex, timore perterritus* and 85: (Gregory himself) *pavore perterritus.*

In one of his diatribes against avarice, Gregory asks: 'Why, O man, do you gather mounds of ruddy gold (*aurus rubiginosus*), when you will be burned with them in hell (*cum iis arsurus in gehenna*)'?[79] The ruddy gold here seems to merge into the image of the flames. How literally Gregory meant this equation of gold and flames to be taken, a story of what he calls 'a stupendous miracle (*stupendum miraculum*)' shows.[80] A certain woman, who had seemed to be pious, received money as alms. However, instead of giving what she did not need for herself to the poor or for the ransom of captives, she put the silver and gold into a huge earthenware pot which she hid under the floor of her cell. Gregory sighs: 'O thrice and four times and always accursed avarice (*cupiditas*), that cheats men of light (*lux*) and submerges them in darkness (*in tenebras*)!' When the pot was full, she died and 'dead to God, and migrating into hell (*migrans in inferno* [sic]), she was buried'. After her burial, the priests asked the woman's servant what her mistress had done with the money and whether she had had time to distribute it. The girl said that she had never seen the woman give away money to anyone. The pot was soon found under the pavement. When the bishop heard of it he flew into a rage, and ordered the lid to be taken from the tomb and the contents of the pot to be thrown over her dead body, shouting: 'Keep what you have amassed! The poor of Christ will not lack sustenance!' That same night voices, cries and wails were heard coming from the tomb; the loudest one cried that it 'was consumed by the fire of gold (*auri consumebatur incendio*)'. When after three days the people could no longer bear this and asked the bishop to come, he let the tomb be opened again and everyone saw 'the gold as though molten in a furnace entering into the mouth of the dead woman with a sulphurous flame (*flamma sulphurea*)'. Then the bishop prayed to the Lord asking, now that her wickedness had been shown to the people, that 'he would order the punishment to depart from the body (*poenam cessare juberet a corpore*)'. Thereafter, the tomb having been covered again, the voices were heard no more.[81] A stream of fiery metal is a

---

79. *Glor. mart.* 57. Compare the rich man suffering in flames in Luke 16:24, as also in Gregory the Great, *Dial.* 4.30.3 (punishment by fire also in *Dial.* 4.32.5), and see Gehenna in Michel 1924: 2198 and Bietenhard 1975: 655-6. Gregory further highlights avarice as the root of all evil (1 Tim. 6:10) in: *Hist.* 4.46 (citing Vergil, *Aen.* 3.56-7), *Vit. patr.*6. praef. (citing Prudentius, *Hamart.* 257), *Glor. conf.* 63, 78 (*inflammante concupiscentia*), 82, 112 (citing Prudentius, mentioning *Tartarus* and *gehenna*), *Vit. patr.* 6. prol. (citing Prudentius), *Virt. Mart.* 1.30 (*Tartara*), and *Hist.* 6.36 (citing Prudentius)
80. *Glor. mart.* 105.
81. Pope Gregory tells a few similar stories: *Dial.* 4.53.2; 4.56.1, and mentions expiatory or purifying fire (*purgatorius ignis*): *Dial.* 4.41.3.

purificatory theme in ancient Persian religion;[82] but Gregory appears to see fire only as a punishment. Sulphur, of course, is associated with the punishment of Sodom.[83] Presumably, Gregory takes for granted that the dead woman's soul continues to be tormented after the visible signs have disappeared from her body.

Even a community of monks in these days, as Gregory tells us explicitly,[84] needed to be governed not by 'humble request (*supplicatio*)' but by 'fear (*timor*)'. A too gentle abbot, Sunniulf, himself needed a vision to frighten him into being 'much stricter' with his monks. In this vision, a motif appears which is similar to one which the Church Father Origen, in the third century, had presented as a kind of purgatory.[85] Gregory writes:

> As he used to tell people, he was led in a vision (*visum*) to a certain fiery river (*flumen igneum*). People came running into it from one shore, as bees to the hive, and became immersed (*mergebantur*), some up to the waist, others to their armpits and many up to the chin, all crying and weeping that they were being fiercely burned (*vehementer aduri*). There was also a bridge over the river but it was so narrow that it could hardly carry one foot's breadth. On the opposite shore, however, a large house could be seen which was white on the outside. Then he asked those who were with him what all this meant.
>
> They said to him: 'From this bridge anyone will fall who is found to have been slothful in enforcing the discipline of the flock entrusted to him. One who has been strict crosses without danger and is led rejoicing into the house which you see on the other side'. This answer shocked him into waking up, and from then on he was much stricter with the monks.

Though the people are described as running towards the river from the shore, once they are in it they appear to be immobilized. If there were some indication that, after a time, they could get to the other side, the river could be interpreted as a purgative experience. But the narrow bridge is presented as the only way to cross it. The whole scene, the juxtaposition of fire and a place of repose accessible only by a narrow bridge, resembles images of an older visionary tradition.[86]

To review the evidence on infernal fire: Gregory looks in natural phenomena and in miraculous phenomena around dead or dying

---

82. Bietenhard 1975: 653.
83. Bietenhard 1975: 657.
84. *Hist.* 4.33.
85. Mangenot 1932: 357; Le Goff 1981: 81-7; Patch 1970: 84-8, 91-3, 95-7. Cumont 1949: 455 says it derives from the Avesta.
86. Le Goff 1981: 134. Compare 2 Esdras 7: 6-9. See also Mangenot 1932: 357, Edsman 1940: 3, Cumont 1949: 455. Gregory the Great, perhaps because he could associate fire with purification, tells a very similar story in which the river, however, is stinking mud: *Dial.* 4.37.7-10.

notorious sinners for visible representations of the torture of perpetual fire in hell. Those — and only those — guilty of serious crimes against the church, such as heresy, sedition or avarice at its expense are said to go there at once after death, just as the saints go directly to heaven, without waiting for the Day of Judgment. The threatening image of infernal fire, made visible in specific circumstances, is used by the church as a weapon to protect her interests as well as to uphold moral values.

'BEDEWED IN THE MIDST OF FIRE': SPIRITUALITY AND MATERIALITY

Le Goff has shown that the twelfth-century doctrine of a fiery purgatory combined into a systematic whole a number of motifs of fire and ice-cold water from older traditions that had been transmitted more or less separately in the Bible and early Christian literature. In the early Middle Ages, though purifying fire is mentioned by some, it is not yet localized anywhere.[87] What is the evidence on the notion of purification by fire in Gregory?

In his version of the story of the phoenix, which he mentions as the third of the true wonders of the world,[88] Gregory says only that fire from the sun reduced the bird, together with its nest, to ashes. Its new formation out of an egg-shaped globule of these dusty ashes is a 'figure' of human resurrection on the Day of Judgment. And here lies the emphasis: this 'miracle (*miraculum*)' proves that human resurrection is possible. The fire, it seems, is for Gregory primarily the means by which the bird is reduced to dust, not itself anything causing regeneration. What about the martyrs who died by fire, however? During a persecution, Gregory reports, 'Polycarp...was consecrated to God through fire as the purest burnt offering (*velut holocaustum purissimum per ignem Domino consecratur*)'.[89] Elsewhere, Gregory also uses *holocaustum*, which in the Old Testament means burnt offerings in the literal sense, in a for him rare metaphorical sense of offering 'the incense of his prayers and the burnt offerings of his praises on the altar of a pure heart'. His words strongly resemble those of Quodvultdeus, however,[90] and both may be based on

---

87. Le Goff 1981: 19-23; Mangenot 1932: 357-60; Michel 1924: 2258-9. Edsman (1949: 175) says that the theme of rejuvenation by fire does not appear in western literature until the tenth century.
88. *De cursu stell.* 12. Compare Edsman 1949: 178-203.
89. *Hist.* 1.28. Compare Edsman 1949: 166-70 on the martyrs and Edsman 1940: 139-40 on the sacrificial fire (holocaust) in the Temple. At the prophet Elijah's request, God sent fire from heaven to consume the altar offering (1 Kings 18:38); but Gregory does not seem to refer to this.
90. *Vit. patr.* 14.1; Quodvultdeus, *Lib. promiss.*, *Glor. sanct.* 18. Fortunatus, too,

Revelation 8:3-4. The meaning in these cases seems to be 'sacrifice', and not purification.

In a story about miracles in a church in which the martyr Laurentius' relics were kept Gregory himself again says nothing significant about fire.[91] Assuming the story of his passion to be known, he nonetheless quotes Fortunatus as saying: 'O Laurentius, you who were deservedly consumed by the life-giving flames (*merito flammis vitalibus uste*) since you came out of them as victor because of your ardent faith (*fervente fide*).'[92] Are these 'life-giving flames' an echo of an old tradition of regenerating fire?[93] The terms 'victor' and 'ardent faith' seem to imply an opposition, however: it was the fire of his faith which caused him to be regenerated into eternal life, not the physical fire which he overcame. Nevertheless, in good poetic manner, something which is denied on the surface is suggested at another level[94] by the collocation 'life-giving flames'.

Although Gregory quotes Fortunatus, he does not quote the latter's comment on the martyr's passion: 'You, sacred Levite, were purified (*purgate*) by the punishment of the faithful believer; through being burned by the flames, you now live in [or possess] the light (*unde prius flammas, hinc modo lumen habes*)'.[95] It is possible to read this statement as expressing a purification by (the punishment of) fire. Gregory is not interested enough to include it, perhaps because it is a rather abstract thought, or perhaps because the idea was not quite congenial to him. One of Gregory's favourite authors, Prudentius, whose version of the story Gregory must also have known, mentions the fact that Laurentius' face shone with light while he was being roasted and comments, 'So God is an everlasting fire (*ignis aeternus*); for Christ is the true fire (*ignis verus*): it is he who fills (*conplet*) the just with light (*lumen*) and consumes (*urit*) the guilty'.[96] What he may mean is that the martyr, being filled with light, did not feel the physical fire — an interpretation that would accord with Fortunatus' 'burning faith' and 'victor'. There is no hint of any possible purification, however: Prudentius says the guilty are simply consumed.

uses *holocaustum* to mean the sacrifice of the Eucharist: literally in *Vit. Mart.* 3.54; metaphorically in *Carm.* 3.6.53 and 5.5.127. There does not seem to be a deeper level of meaning.
91. *Glor. mart.* 41; nor in *Glor. mart.* 82.
92. *Carm.* 9.14.1-2.
93. Compare Salin 1973: 202-6.
94. Wheelwright 1959: 72.
95. *Carm.* 9.14.19-20. Compare *Carm.* 1.2.13: *haec sua tecta replet Laurentius igne sereno cui pia flamma dedit luce perenne diem.*
96. *Perist.* 2.393-6.

Gregory also tells us about the Armenian martyrs[97] who were exposed to a frozen lake and thereafter to 'the savage fire (*incendia saeva*)' or 'the boiling vapours of fire (*aestuantes ignium vapores*)' of an overheated bath. If he is thinking of this as a model of purification, he gives no hint of it, saying only that they suffered their tortures (*supplicata*) patiently in order to receive a larger palm in heaven. One of them, whose faith could not stand the test, gave up and, Gregory says, would later suffer the torture of perpetual fire (*perpetui ignis supplicium*).

The alternation of extreme heat and cold occurs as a motif of purification in the ancient religions that preceded Christianity.[98] Gregory's younger contemporary, Isidore of Seville, possibly reflecting current church tradition, also specifies that hell (*gehenna*) consists of the double torture of fire and extreme cold.[99] Gregory the Great, drawing on the writings of Augustine, seems to be the only one in the late sixth century who explicitly believes in purgatory fire (*purgatorius ignis*). Nevertheless, he also reports two remarkable cases of departed souls being observed as it were to expiate their, relatively minor, sins as servants in the Roman-style public baths,[100] which also involve the hot and cold principle. These people disappeared after someone, at their request, had interceded for them with God by prayers and daily masses for a certain length of time. With one possible exception,[101] Gregory of Tours nowhere even hints at such masses for the dead in Gaul. In the story of the Armenian martyrs (which will be looked at in the next section), he does not seem to see the fire as a divine purification. The adjective *saeva* for the flames seems rather to suggest the opposite:[102] the agency of the devil. We have to conclude then, that for Gregory, fire remains a punishment only, possibly carried out by the devil.

As we have already seen, saints were thought to be able to 'command' a fire to stop. In a number of stories Gregory lets us see what happens when a more or less 'holy' person or object is exposed to fire at close range: each time the fire is unable to do any harm. In the case of persons, the

---

97. *Glor. mart.* 95.
98. Le Goff 1981: 128. Compare Edsman 1940: 176 and 1949: 165.
99. *Etym.* 14.9.9.
100. *Dial.* 4.41.3: *ante iudicium purgatorius ignis credendum est*. This expiates minor offences, but only if these are balanced by sufficient good deeds. Baths: *Dial.* 4.42.3-4, 4.57.3-7. See Le Goff 1981: 124-9. Caesarius of Arles, too, believed in purgatorial fire (Le Goff 1981: 118ff).
101. He mentions what may be a mass for the dead King Sigismund at Agaune in what is now Switzerland (*Glor. mart.* 74): see below, p. 204-5.
102. Compare *Glor. conf.* 7: *saeva daemonis invidia*; *Glor. mart.* 55: *auctor invidiae*; *Vit. patr.* 15.3: *daemonis saevi livore*; *Virt. Mart.* 2.18: *saevi daemonis... audacia*.

story of the three Hebrew youths in the furnace, which Gregory thinks worth mentioning in his extremely brief sketch of Old Testament history, is probably his image-model for the relation between fire and the holy.[103] He says they were 'bedewed in the midst of the fire'. Likewise, when a Jewish boy, who had just taken the Eucharist together with his Christian schoolmates, was thrown into a furnace by his irate father and later taken out unhurt, Gregory explains:[104] 'that same compassion (*misericordia*) was present that once sprinkled the three Hebrew youths who had been thrown into the Chaldaean furnace with a dewy cloud. It did not permit this boy, lying on the heap of burning coals and surrounded by fire, to be in the least consumed (*prorsus consumi non patitur*)'. When his father was later thrown into the same furnace by the furious crowd, 'the fire consumed him so completely (*ita totum absorbuit*) that hardly any trace remained of his bones'. The child later said that the Virgin had covered him with her cloak. Here, clearly, the same fire that cannot harm one who has just taken the holy Eucharist[105] completely consumes one who is guilty of a serious crime. This seems to be a paradigm. Elsewhere, relics are rescued from a burning church by one who, 'being told about the power (*virtus*) of the martyrs, was more protected by his faith than by his shield... (and) not harmed by the fire...'.[106] Trust in a saint's power through his relics then could also bring this power into action to protect oneself or one's house[107] from fire.

In other stories it is the relics themselves which prove to be impervious to fire. For example, a band of brigands, who have robbed a traveller of relics in the hope of finding gold, throw them into a fire in disgust when they find they have been disappointed; the badly beaten traveller later finds them lying undamaged on top of the burning embers; even the cloth in which they are wrapped looks as though it has come out of the water rather than out of a fire.[108] In another story, Gregory says explicitly that it is the power (*virtus*) of the saint which has preserved, on the occasion of a large-scale fire at his church, not only his relics but the altar cloth and

103. *Hist.* 1.15, as well as in *Virt. Jul. praef.*, referring to Dan. 3:13ff. Severus' story of the fire in St Martin's cell is similar (*Ep.* 1.10-5) and Fontaine surmises that he uses the same model of the three youths (Fontaine 1969: 1171-5). Compare Edsman 1949: 170.
104. *Glor. mart.* 9. Compare Gregory the Great, *Dial.* 3.18.2-3.
105. Compare *Glor. conf.* 31.
106. *Glor. mart.* 30. Compare Severus, *Ep.* 1.12-3.
107. *Hist.* 7.31.
108. *Glor. mart.* 18. Similarly, a saint could cook in a wooden cauldron whose bottom, in the flames, remained wet 'as though continuously moistened by someone' (*Glor. conf.* 96).

even the herbs placed on it[109] (for their sweet smell or for medicinal purposes: to increase their effectiveness?)[110]. Elsewhere he reports that a silver box with relics survived a church fire that 'would have been able to melt a thousand pounds of silver or iron instantly' and was found 'unburned' under the ashes: 'gleaming, it looked like a bright star'.[111] Gregory has visualized the scene again and the physical appearance of the casket coincides with his mental image of the saints as 'stars' (about which more will be said in a subsequent section).

In three cases, he adds a moral dimension. A book containing the story of St Martin's life, inadvertently thrown into a fire together with the chaff someone had used to sleep on, was found completely unmarked under the ashes. Gregory sees a symbolic truth in this event: 'Thus divine power (*virtus divina*) deigned to protect his praises by someone who was in a way his own disciple, so that the flame did not devour (*ureret*) the book of the one whom, in this life, the sting of lust had not consumed (*adussit*)'.[112] In the Bible too, sexual desire is associated with fire.[113] Not surprisingly, Gregory associated the latter kind of fire with darkness rather than light, as the following example shows.[114] A married man from a senatorial family became converted and was appointed bishop. When he assumed his office, his wife took up a separate and religious life. However, at a certain moment, she was moved by the devil to desire him again as 'a new Eve': 'fired (*succensa*) by lust and covered by the darkness of sin (*operta peccati tenebris*) she hurried through the dark of night (*per tenebras noctis*) to the bishop's residence'. Typically, Gregory seems to see the darkness of her soul symbolized in the darkness around her. In the third story, fire functions as an ordeal.[115] A bishop who was accused of having fathered a child proved his innocence to the multitude by carrying burning coals in his cloak up to the tomb of St Martin. When he had thrown them down there, his clothes proved to be unburned and he said: 'Just as you see this robe to be undamaged (*inlesum*) by these live coals,

---

109. *Hist.* 7.12: *Sed virtus beati adfuit ut...pallolae...non consumentur ab igne.*
110. Compare *Glor. mart.* 70: a sage leaf on the floor is *pro honore martyrum in crypta conspresum*, but heals illness when taken home. Similarly *Glor. conf.* 92: *Vit. patr.* 6.7; 8.6. Compare *Glor. conf.* 54 and *Vit. patr.* 2.3; similarly *Hist.* 10.24.
111. *Glor. mart.* 51: *tanquam sidus praeclarum apparuit.*
112. *Virt. Mart.* 3.42.
113. Compare Bietenhard 1975: 655 and Gregory, *Vit. patr.* 6. prol.: *juvenilis fervores flammae*; 15. prol.: *nullus libidinum aestus exussit*; and *Glor. conf.* 75: *se uri non posse ab incentivi ignis ardere.* Compare Prudentius, *Hamart.* 253.
114. *Hist.* 1.44.
115. *Hist.* 2.1.

so is my body undefiled (*inpollutum*) by the touch of union with a woman'.[116] Physical fire can burn only those who are already 'burning' with some unclean passion anyway.

In the above examples we see symbolic thinking functioning in society. Gregory records two other ordeal-like occurrences by heat, both intended to prove the truth of the Catholic faith against the Arian heresy. In one case a ring was to be extracted from a cauldron of boiling water, in the other from among burning coals.[117] In the latter event, the Catholic party said, '...if my faith is true, these savage flames will not hurt me (*nihil mihi praevaleant haec incendia saeva*)'. These *de facto* ordeals have the same structure as that of the three young men in the furnace and the same function: to convince opponents of one's righteousness and of one's version of the truth. Fire consumes the sinful but cannot harm those who put their trust in God or a saint.

In one case, however, a fire turned out to be an illusion brought about by the devil (*diaboli fallacia*).[118] When the devil saw he could not deceive (*illudere*) a saintly abbot by lascivious mental suggestions, 'he attacked him with visible battles (*visibilibus proeliis*)': one night the abbot suddenly woke up and 'seemed to see (*vidit...quasi*) his cell being consumed by fire'. Not being able to get his door open, he prostrated himself in prayer and made the sign of the cross upon and around himself: 'at once, the phantom flames (*phantasia flammarum*) which had appeared, vanished...'. Since contemporary hymns sometimes mention and more often seem to hint at lustful[119] thoughts at night as a typical diabolic temptation, it may be that Gregory and his contemporaries understood this phantasmal fire to be an extension or visible representation of the interior fire of concupiscence.[120] Here it is described, however, as appearing from without: just like the 'fiery darts of the devil (*ignita diaboli tela*)' — presumably temptations — which a saint could ward off with 'the armour of God and the sword of the Holy Spirit', as Gregory says in another story.[121]

116. Compare Michel 1931: 1139-43.
117. *Glor. mart.* 79 (see also p. 98-9); *Glor. conf.* 14: Gregory lets the Catholic party call it a 'miracle'.
118. *Vit. patr.* 5.3. Similarly, Gregory the Great relates how the devil produced *phantasticus ignis* out of an idol thrown into the kitchen fire (*Dial.* 2.10.1-2). Compare Severus, *Ep.* 1.11 and Fontaine 1969: 1158-9.
119. For instance, *Anal. hymn.* 51.34, n. 33:1-4 and 51.19, n. 19:11-2. Similarly, Prudentius associates nighttime with sinful thoughts (*Cathem.* 1 and 2) and also advises the sign of the Cross to drive them away (*Cathem.* 6.133). See also Bietenhard 1975: 655.
120. Compare Bachelard 1949: 89-118.
121. *Vit. patr.* 14.1; Eph. 6:16.

So far, then, Gregory shows no interest in connecting fire, or fire and ice, with any kind of purification. He either does not even recognize the possibility of such a thought in Fortunatus' words or he rejects the idea. His model-image is the three youths in the furnace, the principle inferred from this model being that those who have faith, and those who have avoided or resisted sexual desire (which is spoken of as fire and associated with impurity), but also holy objects, are all immune to the ravages of natural fire. This notion is in keeping with Gregory's unreflective conviction that physical events must necessarily reflect moral or spiritual content. Again, an image which we would regard as metaphor is thought of as determining visible, sensory-concrete events.

'DIVINE FIRE': PUNISHMENT OR PURIFICATION?

Gregory does describe something, however, that seems to oscillate between punishment and a terrestrial kind of purification. Following the Old Testament and Christian tradition, Isidore of Seville says of the heat of fever that it is 'as if from a fire (*quasi ab igni*)'[122] and sometimes Gregory seems to be saying something similar. The story of a woman slave who went to hoe in the field on the feast of St John the Baptist, when everyone was expected to be in church,[123] is an obvious piece of propaganda for the observation of the church's holy days, directed at the apparently not completely converted country folk.[124] As the woman started to work

> at once her hands were seized by divine fire (*divino igne sunt apprehensae*), her face also seemed to give forth flames (*quasi emittens flammas*) and all of it boiled up (*ebullivit*) with swellings and sores. At the same time, the unhappy woman was burnt (*urebatur*) by the pain of shame no less than by that of her body...

Typically, action again takes place on two levels at once: 'divine fire' is causing the inflammation, shame makes her 'burn' inside. Are the flames that seem to come forth from her face a metaphor, or is Gregory thinking of divine fire as an invisible but very real fire? This 'fire', however, leads to insight and repentance, and she is later cured. Similarly, a woman who, on Sunday, has just placed a loaf of bread to be baked among the hot ashes found that her right hand 'was suddenly inflamed by divine fire (*divino igne*)' — initiated or not by 'natural' fire? Gregory is apparently not interested in or sees no essential distinction here. The 'flames were put out (*restinctis ardoribus*)' when she had vowed henceforth to spend

---

122. Job 30:30. Compare Isidore, *Etym*. 4.8.4. See Solle 1975: 652 and Bietenhard 1975: 656.
123. *Virt. Mart.* 2.17. Similarly *Hist.* 9.22: *incendium lues, morbi incendium*.
124. See Wood 1979: 63-4.

the Sunday in prayer and had spent a whole night in church praying, holding a candle as tall as herself which she had made with her own hands.[125] Divine fire also has the quality of physical reality in the story of the soldiers who plundered and set fire to a church: they found that their hands 'were being burned by divine power (*divinitus urebantur*), giving forth a great deal of smoke, such as usually arises from fire (*sicut ex incendio surgi solet*)'.[126] Was Gregory really not acquainted with the cause and nature of burns by fire or was he so sure that any harm that came to these people *must* have been a divine punishment, that he regarded any phenomenon as spiritually caused, whatever its physical antecedents?[127] In the two stories just discussed, something like a continuum between physical and spiritual reality seems to emerge. Gregory's conviction of the reality of divine fire is so strong that it overrides his practical common sense. It looks as though, for him, divine fire is not a metaphor but a concrete though invisible reality.

Divine 'fire' could become visible in a physical condition but it was also possible to feel it only internally. A slave who was possessed by a demon[128] and was brought to the church of the martyr St Victor of Marseille cried out, when he got there, that 'he was being burned by the power of the saint (*se exuri ejus virtute*)'.[129] As is evident in Gregory's other stories, however, it is not the man himself who is being burned, but the demons in him, who are also considered to be doing the shouting.[130] After having run around raving through the whole building for two days, the man left on the third day 'cleansed (*mundatus*)'. Here a fiery kind of

125. *Glor. mart.* 15. Similarly *Virt. Mart.* 1.18, 2.11. See on this theme p. 198 ff.
126. *Hist.* 7.35.
127. There is some evidence for this: his surprise, for instance, that poison in the Eucharist actually worked. This could only happen, he says, because it had been consecrated by a heretic, whence the devil could have power over it (*Hist.* 3.31).
128. His behaviour resembles what we would call epilepsy. Gregory was also acquainted with this term and says the illness is caused by *saevi daemonis audacia* (*Virt. Mart.* 2.18).
129. *Glor. Mart.* 76.
130. For instance *Hist.* 6.6: *Multi autem ex ipsis a daemonibus correpti clamabant, 'Cur nos, sancte beatissime, sic crucias et incendis?'*; *Vit. patr.* 17.2: a demon confesses the crimes of the king and others. *Vit. patr.* 9.2: the devil confesses his own crimes; *Hist.* 6.29: a possessed person cries: '... *Princeps vero noster, quem vos diabolum nominatis, ...*'; *Hist.* 8.12: a possessed woman cries that a living bishop *'nos cotidianis incendiis conflat'*; Gregory comments, *'Et licet daemoniis credi non debeat...'*; *Hist.* 9.21: ...*ego ipse saepius larvas inergia famulante nomen eius invocantes audieram ac criminum propriorum gesta, virtute ipsius discernente, fatere* (about King Guntram's miraculous power); *Virt. Mart.* 1.2: *multas voces emittere...ac lingua gentium incognitarum saepissime loqui, venturaque fateri et crimina confiteri*. See also *Virt. Mart.* 2.15, 3.39.

power of the saint had tortured and driven out the demons, thereby purging the man. In other, similar, cases Gregory does not always use fire or purification imagery however, but rather verbs indicating torture such as *cruciare* and *torqueri*.[131] The slave was subsequently freed, as was usual in such cases,[132] and later even became abbot of a monastery, a fact which shows how such a cure could be a breakthrough in every way for the least fortunate and most restricted group in Merovingian society.

In the case of a serious crime, however, the 'fire' of a saint's power could be fatal. A man who had requested a vigil to be held for St Nicetius of Lyon[133] and had then proceeded to spend the night in drunken revelry, found himself 'seized by fever, burned as much by wine as by divine fire (*sicut vino ita divino incendio*)'[134] — a fine word-play, to be sure, but once again we see action with a double quality: physical and spiritual. The furious priest, who came the following morning to suspend him from communion, refused his request for penitence and told him he deserved to be 'burned by the power (*virtute exureris*)' of the saint whose vigil he had neglected. While this *de facto* malediction was being uttered — the timing is no doubt significant — the unhappy drunkard died. This shows how dead saints had their own weapons with which to avenge their honour. Propaganda such as this story was then the unarmed church's most effective defence in a violent society.[135]

Similar to the above is the case of a former deacon who had entered the service of the 'fisc' or public treasury.[136] Besides perpetrating many other illegal and rapacious deeds, he once carried off by violence some sheep belonging to the church of St Julian. Many years later, when he happened to be in the same town on business, he stopped in at St Julian's church for a quick, insincere gesture of devotion. But 'as he lay there on the ground in front of the tomb, he was suddenly seized by fever; and it attacked him with such violent heat (*tanta vi calore opprimitur*) that he was unable to

131. *Vit. patr.* 8.11: *cruciari; Virt. Mart.* 3.39: *torqueri; Hist.* 8.34: *torqueri, peruri, cruciare; Hist.* 5.36: *exuror; Hist.* 6.6: *crucias et incendis.* Similarly, *Virt. Mart.* 2.20; 4.21; *Virt. Jul.* 14, 32; *Vit. patr.* 8.4; *Glor. conf.* 3. Brown has suggested that these terms, as well as the 'burning', may be reminiscences of Roman judicial torture (Brown 1981: 108-9).
132. As, for instance, especially in *Virt. Mart.* 1.22; also, for instance, in *Virt. Mart.* 1.26; 2.4, 6, 9, 13, 15 and often.
133. This saint is notable for his vindictiveness after his death: *Hist.* 4.36; *Vit. patr.* 8.5.
134. *Vit. patr.* 8.11. Similarly *Virt. Mart.* 2.32. See also n. 123.
135. Explicitly, for instance, in *Virt. Jul.* 21: *multa quidem et alia* [St Julianus] *in praevaricationibus ostendit; sed satis sint ista ad coercendam desidiam eorum; Virt. Mart.* 1.29: *audite haec omnes potestatem habentes.*
136. *Virt. Jul.* 17.

get up or even to call a servant'. When his servants came at last to see what was taking him so unusually long in church and could not get answers to their questions from him, they carried him to a nearby house. There the fever increased and the unhappy man cried out that 'he was being burned by the martyr (*se...incendi per martyrem*)':

> As the torches of the trial of his soul were thus applied (*admotis animae juducii facibus*), he confessed his crimes, which he had not done before, and asked as loudly as he could for water to be poured upon him. When many buckets of water had thus been emptied over him, smoke started to come out of his body as though out of a furnace. Meanwhile his miserable body, as though it had in fact been burned (*ceu combustus*), turned black and started to give off such a vile smell that those standing around him could hardly endure it.

Soon after this he died. Gregory concludes: 'From all this it is quite clear to which place the man went who departed with such a trial (or judgment: *judicium*)'.[137] A nasty smell, in Gregory's stories, always indicates the presence of the devil;[138] the blackness too indicates, in Gregory's opinion, that the ruler of the infernal world was already burning this man.[139]

Gregory's conviction of the concrete though invisible reality of 'divine fire' overrides his commonsense experience: spiritual and physical reality tend to overlap or merge.[140] Divine fire punishes either the demons in an innocent man or else a guilty man himself. When this punishment results in a 'cleansing' of evil spirits or in a repentance of one's sins, one could speak of an earthly purification. Belief in the reality of 'divine fire' was essential for the enforcement of the Church's notions of justice and moral behaviour. Though it looks to us as very obviously imaginative, it made a great deal of sense — albeit another kind of intelligent, practical common-sense than our own — in the whole structure of the Church's adjustment to an all but barbaric society.

Natural fire, then, is an ambiguous phenomenon. Besides being an element of creation, it can be started by the devil as well as by God or a saint. Regardless of its origin, however, it can be perceived as exhibiting the violent power that is associated with the devil. Wicked passions are likewise spoken of in terms of fire or as being punished by fire. God or the saint can, if requested, stifle and stop any fire instantly; such a request is often made in what looks like a magical way. Incidences of being struck

---

137. Compare Baudonivia, *Vit. Rad.* 13.
138. *Vit. patr.* 11.1; 17.3; *Hist.* 9.6. As also Severus, *Vit. Mart.* 24.8. This is a motif from the Egyptian monastic world: Fontaine 1968: 850-1 and 1969: 1037.
139. See, however, Brown 1981: 108-9.
140. Fontaine has also observed this occasionally in Severus' writing (Fontaine 1968: 526-30).

by lightning are interpreted in such a way as to support the church's conception of her rights, rules and properties. The frightening image of infernal fire is associated with the deaths of those who have in some way despoiled the church, insulted the saint or plotted against the lawful church authority — which probably means that for Gregory these were the most pressing problems.

For Gregory, fire always punishes the guilty. The righteous or the holy are impervious to it, according to the image-model of the three young men in the Chaldean furnace. Hence fire can be used as an ordeal. Of Gregory's contemporaries, Pope Gregory and perhaps Fortunatus referred to purifying fire, without, however, stressing it. Gregory himself, following Severus and Prudentius, seems simply to skip the passages about it which he found in the Bible[141] and in his sources. He nowhere hints at any purificatory qualities of fire except in the 'divine fire' that can, on earth, either cleanse a man of evil spirits or cause a fever or infection that leads to repentance. In these cases — as a punishment or chastisement — it does effect a purification, but on earth. In certain stories, 'divine fire' is described in such a way that physical and spiritual reality seem to overlap. Here, imaginative analogies and Gregory's conviction of the concrete, though invisible, reality of a 'divine fire' are stronger than his knowledge through common sense observation: metaphor and reality coincide.

B. LIGHT, AND FIRE AS LUMINOSITY

LIGHT AND DARKNESS: METAPHORS AND SENSORY PHENOMENA

> ...while the vigil before [St. Julian's] feast was being held, [a man] stealthily took the horse of another man who had, by chance, come to the same ceremony, mounted it and rode away quickly. He who had lost the light of truth (*lumen veritatis*) hoped thereby that he would not be discovered before [the arrival of] daylight (*lux*), and that the night (*nox*) would conceal the stealthy crime of him whose heart was filled with the darkness of greed (*cupiditatis tenebrae*). For about such people the Lord speaks in the Gospel, saying, 'All those who do evil, hate the light (*lux*)'.[142]

Here opposite ethical qualities are indicated by metaphors of light and darkness as in Paul's saying, which Gregory quotes in another story: '...For what partnership has righteousness with iniquity? Or what fellowship has light (*lux*) with darkness (*tenebrae*)?'[143] In classical Greece

---

141. Collected, for instance, by Quodvultdeus, *Liber promiss. Dimid. temp.* 20.32.
142. John 3:20; *Virt. Jul.* 18.
143. 2 Cor. 6:14.

physical darkness had been associated with danger and anxiety, and metaphorical darkness with secrecy and deceitfulness; while light had then been associated with the opposites of these.[144] In late Jewish writings, the Qumran literature and in the Gospel of John, darkness is a cosmic force striving to dominate man, but is subject to and overcome by the light of divine power.[145] It is only in first and second-century Gnosticism and its later derivatives that darkness is represented as an independent power and the ruler of the material world. The spiritual world, on the other hand, is one of light. Man's soul is a spark of this light and he can attain liberation from the darkness by 'enlightenment' through *gnosis*, knowledge of the truth.[146] It will be obvious that, in the context of an ethical rather than a metaphysical dualism, John puts all this in Christian terms: it was, after all, the religious idiom of the time. Through John, but also Paul, it became an important part of the Christian symbolical tradition.[147] In late Antiquity, neo-Platonist philosopher-mystics also 'parlent une langage imagé où la lumière physique est le symbole de l'illumination psychique'.[148] There are indications, however, that from Hellenistic times on, symbolic and physical light could merge in what has been called a 'geistiger Realismus'.[149] The symbol participates in, is immediately experienced as, the reality it signifies. As I hope to show, there is a great deal of evidence that much of Gregory's light imagery should be understood in this way.

In his writings, sometimes the older association of darkness with insecurity reappears, but it has a demonic quality which is typical for the late antique period. This is evident in his description of dusk falling while a company was crossing the Loire: 'frightful night (*nox horribilis*) had already seized the world with its onrushing darkness (*irruentibus tenebris*), when suddenly the wind changed', separated the boats supporting the bridge and filled them with water; everyone would have been drowned if St Martin had not been invoked for aid.[150] In another

---

144. Hahn 1975: 420-2.
145. Hahn 1975: 423.
146. Hahn 1975: 422. On Gnosticism in general see Rudolph 1977 and van den Broek 1986. Compare Edsman 1949: 214-5 and Tardieu 1975 on the 'divine spark'.
147. Compare also Pulver 1944. Eucherius summarizes it in *Formul. spir. intell.* 3 in Migne 1859: 738-42.
148. Cumont 1949: 363.
149. Aalen 1951: 95, 77.
150. *Virt. Mart.* 2.17. Compare Prudentius, *Cathem.* 5.3.: *merso sole chaos ingruit horridum*, and *Cathem.* 1.17-8: *tectis tenebris horridis*. On light and dark in Prudentius: Van Assendelft 1976: 22-4 and passim, and Herzog 1966: 52-92. On

case of such a sudden storm Gregory says explicitly that the devil was responsible.[151] Not only in Gregory's writings but also for instance in Prudentius' hymns, the darkness of night is thought to give the devil and his demons the opportunity for the free exercise of their powers. It is not surprising, then, that Gregory designates the devil as 'the prince of darkness (*princeps tenebrarum*)'.[152] Compared to the light of heaven, Gregory lets Salvius say, the world itself is 'dark', and also 'squalid (*squalidum*)', suggesting impurity, which is equated with sinfulness.[153] But the night is especially so. Quite often in his works, when Gregory seems to be giving a traditional description of the 'quiet' of night, we find that this nonetheless turns out to be the setting for some heinous crime.[154]

Paul's association of metaphorical with visible light and darkness mentioned above, is quoted two more times by Gregory and in similar contexts.[155] It is as though he visualizes a kind of continuum between the darkness within and the darkness outside of man; the darkness of greed is at the same time an ignorance of the truth, which is light. A crime is carried out 'in the obscurity (*obscuritas*) of night',[156] rushing 'through the gloom of dark night (*per obscurae noctis tenebrae*)' or by one hurrying 'through the dark night (*per tenebras noctis*)' herself 'benighted by sin (*operta peccati tenebris*)'[157]. In this last case, the sin was sexual desire. Elsewhere too, Gregory speaks of 'the darkness of lust (*tenebrae concupiscentiae*)',[158] implying that the 'fire' also associated with it is thought of as something 'dark'. Likewise, physical blindness is regarded, in one case, as the punishment for an avarice that had blinded someone's

'night' in the Christian background: Sanders 1965a: 157-64, and on light and dark in the antique background: Bultmann 1940 in Dinkler 1967: 323-55. Brown 1972 describes the late antique preoccupation with demons.

151. *Virt. Mart.* 1.2. See also p. 102 ff.
152. *Hist.* 8.34. Compare Prudentius, *Hamart.* 514: *spiriti tenebrosi*, and Matth. 9:34: *princeps daemoniorum*. Late antique conceptions of light and dark, with sources and literature, in Sanders 1965a: 164-83, 758-60.
153. *Hist.* 7.1. Compare Fortunatus, *Carm.* 4.7.7-8: *tristis orbis, lacrimosa dies*. See on this in late Antiquity, Sanders 1965a: 138-57, and for the earlier tradition, Cumont 1949: 48-9.
154. As in *Glor. mart.* 88: *cunctos sub alta noctis silentio sopor arripuit et omnes blandiente somno dedissent membra quieti*; compare Prudentius, *Cathem.* 6.11-2: *blandus sopor vicissim fessos relaxat artus*. Further: *Virt. Jul.* 20: *data cunctis nocturna quieta silentio, vel operiente umbrosa caligine mundum*.
155. 2 Cor. 6:14, in *Vit. patr.* 14.2 and *Glor. mart.* 37. Compare on *nox*: Sanders 1965a: 157-64.
156. Compare Bonnet 1890: 260-1.
157. *Hist.* 10.21 (reminiscent of Vergil, *Aen.* 6.286); *Glor. mart.* 21; and *Hist.* 1.44 respectively.
158. *Vit. patr.* 18. *prol.*

judgment.[159] Gregory expects the physical condition or circumstances to be a materialization of the spiritual quality of a person or event.[160] This resembles his attempts to recognize the 'figures' of imminent or simultaneous human events in natural phenomena. It seems as though congruence was for him a fundamental law of reality.[161]

The return of daylight, which figures so large in contemporary hymns as a symbol of the return of the light of Christ to human hearts heavy with the sins of night,[162] is sometimes the moment of a sudden cure after a night of prayers: 'as the day began to light up (*lucescente die*),...he deserved to see the light (*lumen*)' (i.e., he was cured of his blindness).[163] In

159. *Glor. conf.* 13.
160. For instance, *Glor. mart.* 12 (*claritas - obscuritas*); *Virt. Mart.* 3.16 (*tenebrae criminum*); *Hist.* 1.20 (*tenebrae* upon Christ's crucifixion). Compare Bolton 1959: 211 on Gregory the Great's view: 'the visible world is a metaphor of the invisible'.
161. For instance, Gregory says that the lamps and candles that symbolically indicate the veneration of a saint sometimes themselves have miraculous qualities: for instance, *Glor. conf.* 68, 69; *Vit. patr.* 8.8; *Glor. mart.* 5, 15. When those in charge of a shrine think a saint is not fulfilling his obligations, they threaten to or actually do put out the lights and even break the lamps: *Glor. conf.* 70; *Virt. Mart.* 3.8; *Glor. mart.* 99.
162. Notably, *Christus qui lux es et dies*, *Anal. hymn.* 51.21 n. 22; further, 51.8 n. 5; 51.9 n. 6; 51.10 n. 7; 51.11 n. 8 and, for instance, Prudentius, *Cathem.* 1.37-44. What Gregory says in the title for his (lost) commentary on Psalm 62 may be connected with this. Unfortunately, the text has not been completely established and may be corrupt. There he says: *Quod ipse* [i.e. Christ] *sit in quem per splendorem me...is debeamus in matutinis meditationibus exercere*. In the Vulgate, Ps. 62:2 and 7 reads *Deus meus, ad te de luce vigilo...; ... si memor fui tui supra stratum meum in matutinis meditabor in te ...* The only thing mentioned in Psalm 62 which approaches *splendor* is God's 'power and glory (*virtus et gloria*)' seen in the sanctuary (3). In this context, this power and glory is associated with light or even fiery light, sometimes through lamps or torches (Aalen 1976: 45; Hahn 1975: 485). In the hymns of the time Christ is often associated with the morning star or the returning sun- or daylight (Dölger 1920: 293-318. For instance: Prudentius, *Cathem.* 2.77-78; 1.15.-16 and passim). Dölger (294) cites one hymn in which the word *splendor* occurs (*Anal. hymn.* 50.11-12): Splendor paternae gloriae/ De luce lucem proferens/ Lux lucis et fons luminis/ Diem dies illuminans/ Verusque sol illabere/ Micans nitore perpeti/ Jubarque Sancti Spiritus/ Infunde nostris sensibus. For Gregory's *me...is* Krusch (1885: 876) has *memores*, probably referring to *si memor fui tui*. Another solution may be *mentes* as the object of *debeamus exercere*; Hilary of Poitiers says in his comment on this psalm (*Tract. in Ps.* 62.9 in Migne 1844: 405C): *Meditatio Dei nocturna et matutina. Verum haec non tam verborum officia quam mentis sunt...* But he continues: *Meditationem matutinam recordatio nocturna consummat*. For *si memor fui tui* he has *si memoratus sum tui*. It seems clear that this is private, interior meditation, probably accompanying prayer.
163. *Virt. Mart.* 2.19. Similarly *Glor. conf.* 82, 83; *Vit. patr.* 2.4; *Virt. Mart.* 1.18, 2.34;

another case, after he and his parents had persisted in prayer and fasting, a crippled child is healed 'on the third day...when the light of mercy appeared (*exorto misericordiae lumine*)'.[164] Here daylight could be a metaphor for the saint's healing power, derived from Christ who, as Gregory in his *Commentary on the Psalms*, says, quoting the Gospel of John, is 'the Light of the world, the Way, the Truth and the Life (*lux mundi, via, veritas et vita*)'.[165] Here, Gregory says a great deal more about Christ being light: He is 'the eternal Light (*lumen aeternum*)' and 'the Light of those who believe (*credentium lumen*)'. Also 'he gives light to our eyes (*oculos nostros inluminat*) lest they should sleep in eternal death'[166] and especially: 'He is the illumination, the protection and the salvation (*inluminatio, protectio et salus*) of his servants who believe in him'.[167] Divine protection against physical attack — something with which Gregory and his contemporaries were also much concerned — is a recurring theme in the Psalms, light imagery in connection with the Lord less so. But Gregory, in his (traditional) attempt to explain how the Psalms prophesied the coming and the actions of Christ, seems to magnify the light imagery. For him, evidently, Christ was traditionally imagined in terms of light.

Nevertheless, the one around whom most of Gregory's light imagery revolves is not Christ but the saint or his relics. What is Gregory trying to express with his light imagery and what does this tell us about Gregory's and his contemporaries' experience of the saint?

METAPHORS

'*A large flame*': *metaphors of interior illumination*

...After I had joined Abbot Aredius [in Limoges] and had been educated by him, I [Wulfilaicus] travelled with him to the church of St Martin [in Tours]. When we departed from there he took a little bit of dust off the saint's tomb so that it might bless us (*pro benedictione*), putting it in a small capsule which then hung around my neck.

> *Glor. conf.* 15. Other miracles at dawn: *Glor. mart.* 10, 90. Cures, however, also often happen at night: for instance, *Glor. mart.* 30; *Glor. conf.* 65, 87; *Virt. Jul.* 25, 36, 37; *Virt. Mart.* 1.33; 2.4, 31, 56.

164. *Virt. Mart.* 3.6.
165. *In psal.* 42; John 8:12, 14:6.
166. Again a blurring of metaphysical and physical light. Compare: *Glor. mart.* 91: *lumen caruit oculorum* (died); *Virt. Mart.* 4.22: *lumen caruit oculorum* (blindness); *Hist.* 2.7: *lumen caruit oculorum* (died). See on this expression, Sanders 1965a: 119-28. Compare further: *Vit. patr.* 1.6: *ab hac luce migrare* (die); *Virt. Mart.* 1.15: *lumen* (eyesight); *Virt. Jul.* 10: *lumen* (eyesight).
167. *In psal.* 35, 66, 12 and 26 respectively. Compare John 1:9.

> When we had arrived at his monastery in the region of Limoges and he took the capsule to put it in his chapel, [we found that] the dust in it had increased so greatly that it not only filled the capsule completely but even spilled out from all the cracks. Through the brightness of this miracle (or: through this splendid miracle) my soul lit up (or: glowed with desire) more than before to place all my confidence in his power (*Ex hoc mihi miraculi lumine animus magis accendit totam spem meam in eius virtute defigere*).[168]

Ostensibly, these are Wulfilaicus' own words, but an admixture (at least) of Gregory's is not unlikely. It is possible to read the last statement in the passage as pure metaphor. There is no suggestion of any experience of visible light. Brightness or splendour is a highly positive value-judgment. The fact that St Martin had been miraculously at work in the dust as it hung against Wulfilaicus' breast[169] cannot but have impressed the young disciple. Metaphors of light and of fire that glows but does not burn are used for an event that 'captured' his heart. For him from now on, as for Gregory too, St Martin's power was one of the most stable, and at the same time most dynamic, facts in his life.

In the preface to the *Miracles of St Julian*, Gregory also speaks of a spiritual desire as an interior 'fire'. He takes his cue from a psalm:

> Somehow, the divine kindness kindles in us a large flame (metaphorically, desire: *magnum...igniculum... succendit*) to enter upon the path of his righteousness when he says: 'The eyes of the Lord are on the righteous and his ears hear their prayers'. This shows that whoever loves righteousness with his whole heart (*cor*) will be heard by the Lord when he prays. By following this path...the blessed martyrs were glorified...in that they cure the sick, revive the dead, disdain the present life, long for the future one, are indifferent to torture, do not feel pain and aspire only to the heavenly kingdom. All of this they doubtless would not have been able to do by their own strength alone; but because they walked in the path of righteousness unswervingly, [their prayers] were answered by the Lord...
>
> So the renowned martyr Julian too, ...ablaze with this fire (*ab hoc igne succensus*), longed for these things and desired them with his whole heart...[170].

Here fire is again associated with the glow of desire, in this case for being heard by God. As Gregory tells it, this desire has more to do with being able to work miracles, and with eventually attaining heaven later than with any experience of closeness to God in this life. The present life existed only to be transcended in one way or another. Again, there is a strong suggestion of constraint: if one is righteous, the Lord *must* answer one's prayers. An explanation for this may be that belief in the supernatural in those times was not a private luxury, as it were, but part of a social system: if socially constructive attitudes and respect for

---

168. *Hist.* 8.15.
169. Helgeland 1980: 1295, 1297, 1305.
170. *Virt. Jul. prol.*; Ps. 33:15.

authority were to be stimulated, it was necessary to believe in a supernatural power that rewarded and punished in predictable ways.

Another metaphor of interior fire bears a superficial resemblance to a Gnostic (and, earlier, Stoic) image of the soul. It is not Gregory's own however, and occurs in his quotation of a letter which a number of bishops wrote to Queen Radegunde to pledge their support for her establishment of the Rule of Caesarius in her convent at Poitiers.[171] The bishops say that they are joyful that, through the example of St Martin, the love of heavenly things rises anew in her.

> For, although the time (*tempus*) is getting worse through the decrepitude of the age (*saeculi vetustas*), faith flowers anew through the effort of your heart (*sensus*); that [faith] which was growing cold through the slothful cooling of old age, at last becomes warm again through the ardour of [your] glowing heart (*ferventis animi...incalescat ardore*)...
>
> With the brilliance of [St Martin's] renown lighting up before you (*Cuius opiniones radio praemicante*), you cause the hearts of those listening to you to be so suffused by a heavenly glow (*caelestis fulgor*) that the souls of the virgins called forth from everywhere, ablaze with the spark of divine fire (*divini ignis scentella* [sic] *succensi*), come in great haste, longing to be refreshed in Christ's love at the spring of your heart; having left their families, they prefer to be with you, whom grace, not nature, made their mother.

Remarkably, the light and fire imagery seems to refer to St Martin rather than to Christ, whose love is here almost certainly thought of as water, perhaps as the 'living spring'. Although fire and water are usually contradictory images, they do not seem to conflict here: because they both stand for the spiritual life, there is a higher, symbolic unity between the two. In this case it is Radegunde's words, coming out of an ardent, glowing heart, that cause a heavenly glow or spark of divine fire — reminiscent of the Gnostic image of the soul — [172] to arise in the women's hearts. Equally noteworthy is the fact that her ardour is not inspired by any thought of temporal rewards or miracles. Fortunatus' poems also indicate that she had a warm, even passionate, heart and that family and motherly feelings were very strong in her. There are only two male saints to whom Gregory attributes the quality of heavenly love: St Quintian was 'aglow with the flame of heavenly love (*charitas igniculo fervidus* [sic])', and St Nicetius (Gregory's maternal great-uncle, with whom he spent some time in his youth) did so many works of love that 'God, who is true love (*vera caritas*), was seen to live in his heart'.[173]

In the following story, which Gregory probably took from a popular

---

171. *Hist.* 9.39.
172. On the soul as part of cosmic ethereal fire or deity see: Aalen 1960: 357; Edsman 1949: 214-5; Cumont 1949: 113, 176, 274 and Bietenhard 1975: 654.
173. *Vit. patr.* 4.1; *Hist.* 4.36.

tradition, this love becomes light, not fire. In a lengthy lament on their wedding night a tearful bride confesses to her brand-new husband that she prefers, as a virgin, to be the bride of Christ. The man answers:

> 'Through your most sweet words eternal life illumines me like a great star (*aeterna mihi vita tamquam magnum inluxit*), and therefore, if you wish to abstain from physical desire, I will share your resolve'.[174]

Here it is not fire (which, in this situation, would perhaps call to mind too easily the flames of sexual desire) but the radiance, as it were, of a star lighting up within. This radiance is the experience of the 'eternal life' as interior light; the new wife has just glowingly described it as 'eternal beatitude...light that never fails (*lux non occidens*)'[175] and as 'the contemplation of the presence of the Lord [in] unending joy'. Here again, and this cannot but be significant, Gregory lets words produce, transmit or magnify (this remains ambiguous) the glow or spark. Using another metaphor, as we have seen, Gregory says that divine precepts can make eternal life sprout in men, and divinely inspired descriptions of saints' miracles can create faith in barren minds.[176]

In the stories we have just looked at, Gregory lets us see that words as well as miracles can produce, transmit or enlarge an interior fire or light that strives toward or participates in heavenly fire or light. Although Christ is described in John's Gospel as the true Wisdom, the light of the Truth, the Word or Logos through which all was and is created, and who 'enlightens every man'[177] Gregory does not mention him here. The titles of his *Commentary on the Psalms* show that he was capable of making these associations, but he and his flock were probably more immediately concerned with miracles, confidence in a saint, and the expectation of heavenly life. It is to these that ostensibly metaphorical light-qualities are attributed.

'Stars' and 'a new sun': more than metaphors?

Late antique inscriptions show that the use of light imagery denoting light to describe moral or social distinction[178] (as also in our use of terms such as 'illustrious' and 'luminary') was well-known in Gregory's day. Church functionaries could also be described in this way, but here the background must additionally be Christ's saying to his disciples 'You are

---

174. *Hist.* 1.47 and, more briefly, *Glor. conf.* 32.
175. Similarly *Vit. patr.* 13.prol..
176. *De cursu stell.* 11 and *Vit. patr.*2.prol.; *Glor. mart. prol.*.
177. John 1:1, 3, 9.
178. Sanders 1965b: 67-69.

the light of the world'.¹⁷⁹ In fifth-century Gallic hagiography there is one instance of light imagery describing a previous worldly career,¹⁸⁰ and there are several which refer to eminence in the religious sphere: two saints are described as 'brilliant lights (*lumina*) of religion', and one is 'surrounded by the light (*lux*) of authority', which made it impossible for him to avoid meeting people, as he, in his modesty, wished to do.¹⁸¹ Similarly when, in the early sixth century, St Caesarius of Arles tried to hide behind tombs at the time when the people sought to make him bishop, it is said that 'the brightness (*claritas*) of his way of life revealed' him.¹⁸² This could be a sixth-century version of the same theme, but something remarkable has happened. The brightness of his way of life is clearly a metaphor, yet in its revealing his presence behind tombs it refers to light perceived by the senses. There is a blurring of the distinction between a mental and a physical phenomenon.

In Severus' fourth-century *Life of St Martin*, which was an important model for western hagiography,¹⁸³ there is another kind of light imagery. It occurs in a well-known description of the glorified saint appearing to the author in a dream-vision or apparition, reminiscent not of secular praise but of the God-man in the visions of the books of Daniel and Revelation:¹⁸⁴ he was 'clothed in a white toga, with a flaming face, starry eyes and shining hair (*vultu igneo, stellantibus oculis, crine purpureo*)'. As we shall see, Gregory's descriptions of the personal appearance of saints when they have just died or as they are seen in dreams or visions after their death also tend to stress a strong luminosity.¹⁸⁵ These few scattered instances of light imagery around saints, though suggestive, are the only ones in Gallic hagiography until Gregory's time.

Gregory's predilection for light imagery, nourished by reading Prudentius' and Fortunatus' work, may have derived from the already-mentioned current of popular devotion that is evident in late antique inscriptions and hymns¹⁸⁶ and which in turn may be connected with the important role played by light symbolism in Christian liturgy from the fourth century on. According to some scholars, the Gallican liturgy of

179. Matth. 5:14. See Sanders 1965b: 768.
180. Constantius Lugdunensis, *Vit. Germ.* 1.1.
181. Constantius Lugd., *Vit. Germ.* 3.12; 4.21. Fortunatus however twice praises his subject in terms of *light*: *Vit. Germ. praef.* and 1.
182. *Vita Caes.* 1.14.
183. Aigrain 1953: 162; Hugenholtz 1960: 130-1.
184. Severus, *Ep.* 2.3; Daniel 7:9, 10:6; Rev. 1.14.
185. For instance *Virt. Mart.* 1.6; *Glor. conf.* 18.
186. See n. 5.

Gregory's time shows the influence of the Eastern churches, in which light symbolism was decidedly central.[187]

A number of Gregory's adjectives and verbs denoting light in connection with saints and their lives and works possibly mean no more than 'distinguished' in the traditional sense: Abbot Martius of Clermont, for instance, is said to have 'shone like a huge star (*tanquam sidus egregium...fulgeret*) in this city through his 'religious way of life'.[188] Less clear are: Bishop Irenaeus of Lyons 'shone brightly through virtue [or miraculous power] (*admirabile virtute enituit*)' and Paulinus of Nola 'was resplendent in the power [or virtue?] of many gifts of spiritual grace (*in virtute multiplicata gratiarum spiritualium charismata resplenduit*)'.[189] The meaning of the word *virtus*, which in Gregory's stories often means miraculous power or the miracle itself, is ambiguous here. Holiness, however, is often very closely assimilated to miraculous power, as for instance in the description of Bishop Maximus of Trier: 'powerful in all kinds of holiness (*potens in omni sanctitate*)'.[190] It will become clear below that holiness, power and light tend to be treated as different aspects of the same phenomenon.[191]

But when Gregory calls St Martin 'a new sun (*sol novus*)',[192] or says that 'our sun rose and Gaul was shot through with new rays of light (*...lumen nostrum exoritur, novisque lampadum radiis Gallia perlustratur*)' by St

---

187. On light symbolism in Christian liturgy, see Maclean 1915: 55 and Pax 1961: 1026; on oriental influence, Fischer 1961: 1091, 1094, and Camelot 1976: 1154. Compare, however, Griffe 1951 and Gy: 1976. Ewig 1979 in Atsma 1979: 393-410 notes not inconsiderable evidence of contacts with Syria and the East in the sixth century. Fontaine speaks of Gnostic or illuminist preachers in the fourth: Fontaine 1969: 996-7, 1021, Fontaine 1967: 232-3. Baudonivia, *Vita Radeg.* 23. Edsman 1940: 183 notes that the perception of light and fiery phenomena (which will be looked at in the next section) at baptism were a Syrian tradition.
188. *Vit. patr.* 14.1; see, also, *Hist.* 1.45 and *Vit. patr.* 4. *prol.: Fructus autem spiritus est omne quod in Deo pollet ac nitet, quod in hoc saeculo, mortificatur carne, animam exsultere facit, in futuro autem gaudiis donat aeternis.* Likewise: *Glor. conf.* 94. Compare *Vit. patr.* 20. *prol.: cum non floreret natalibus, gloriosis meretis praefulgebat.* Compare Gregorius Magnus *Moralia* 9.8 in: Migne 1849: *fulgens vita praedicantium. Vit. patr.* 7.2 and *Hist.* 3.19. Similarly, *Vit. patr.* 15.4.
189. *Hist.* 1.29; *Glor. conf.* 110. Similarly: *Hist.* 2.21, *Hist.* 1.33. Similarly, *Glor. conf.* 85. Compare *Glor. conf.* 38: *Magna quondam fuerunt mundi luminaria quae, ut sol radiis, ita mundum virtutibus illustrabant.* A clear case of *virtus* as miraculous power is, for instance, *Glor. mart.* 76: *Est ad sepulcrum...mira virtus.* A rare instance of *virtus* as moral virtue in *Hist.* 5.1.
190. *Hist.* 1.37.
191. This is an O.T. tradition. See Aalen 1951: 173-8; Sibum 1962: 11-7.
192. *Decedente jam mundo sol novus exoriens* (*Virt. Mart.* 1.3).

Martin's *preaching* there, it may be a different kind of light from that with which 'he shone (*refulgeret*) through his miracles (or virtues: *virtutes*)'.[193] As Gregory could have read, for instance, in Prudentius' writings, the sun was an early Christian symbol of Christ.[194] About the 'light' of true doctrine more will be said below.

The following description may indicate what Gregory has at the back of his mind. Abbot Martius of Clermont, 'shining in the world as a beacon of true light (*velut jubar veri luminis in orbe resplendens*), continuously dispelled (*pellebat*) illnesses by the efficacy of his miraculous powers (or deeds of power?) (*virtutum efficacia*)'.[195] 'The true light' is, of course, Christ, as in the Gospel of John 1:9. Not insignificantly, this light is here associated with the 'driving out' of illnesses, which were in that time thought to be the work of demons,[196] who were associated with 'darkness'.[197]

Elsewhere Gregory, on the authority of his 'predecessors',[198] calls Christ and the Church the two 'great luminaries', being the sun and the moon[199] of 'the sky of the human mind', given by God

> so that they should shine (*luceant*) in the darkness (*tenebrae*) of ignorance and illumine (*illuminent*) our lowly intelligence, as the evangelist John has said about the Lord himself, because he is the light (*lux*) of the world, who 'illumines (*illuminat*) every man coming into this world'. He [Christ] also placed stars (*stellae*) in it, that is to say, patriarchs, prophets and apostles, to teach us with their doctrines and illumine (*illuminent*) us with their wonders (*mirabilia*), as He [Christ] has said in the Gospel: 'You are the light (*lux*) of the world' and 'Let your light so

193. *Hist.* 1.39. Compare Gregorius Magnus, *Moralia* 9.8 in Migne 1849: 864B): *ipsi [predicatores] sol esse memorantur; ...quia praedicando vim luminis ostendunt*.
194. For instance, in *Cathem.* 2.3-4; see Dölger 1920: 259-318; Herzog 1966: 52-4 and Van Assendelft 1976: 34 and passim, *Vit. Mart. praef.* 48-9, *Vita Hil.* 6: 19, *Virt. Hil.* 2, *Vit. Marc.* 5, *Vit. Alb.* 18: 21.
195. *Vit. patr.* 14.3. Compare Constantius Lugd., *Vit. Germ.* 15: a blind girl is cured by placing relics on her eyes: *quos statim evacuatos tenebris lumine veritatis implevit*. The coalescence of metaphorical and physical light is unmistakable here.
196. As in *Vit. patr.* 17.4 and often.
197. Sanders 1965b: 860; and, for instance, *Anal. hymn.* 51.28 n. 26: 5-6; Prudentius, *Cathem.* 2.17-20.
198. See Sanders 1965b: 775-807 with the sources in the notes; of these, Gregory (elsewhere) mentions Jerome, Sedulius, Paulinus of Nola, Prudentius, Sidonius Apollinaris, Lactantius, and Paulinus of Périgueux (see Bonnet 1890: 64-5). Ambrosius, *Hexaem.* 4.2 in Migne 1845: 190) also speaks of Christ and the church as sun and moon. Gregory's whole passage shows great similarity, however, to Eucherius, *Form. spir. intell.* 3 in Migne 1859: 739D-740A).
199. Gen. 1:16-7. In his *De cursu stell.* 15-6 Gregory uses no symbolism and says that the sun, as sixth wonder of the world, brings light and fruitfulness to the world, while the moon, as the seventh wonder, indicates the months.

shine (*Sic luceat lux vestra*) among men that they see your good works and glorify your Father who is in heaven...'. Thanks to the teaching of these men, therefore, there are up to our own times [men] who in this worldly life (*saeculum*) are like the beacons of stars (*quasi astrorum jubar*), not only shining with the light (*radiantes luce*) of their merits but even dazzling (*coruscantes*) through the greatness of their teachings, who lit up (*illustraverunt*) the whole world by the beam (*radius*) of their preaching...teaching men to abstain from worldly cares and leave the murkiness (*tenebrae*) of lust behind to follow the true God by whom all things were made...[200].

As in the description of St Martin, light is here associated with *knowledge* imparted by the *preaching* of true doctrine,[201] as well as with *miracles* and *merit*. The first two save men from the 'darkness' of ignorance, worldly cares and lust (illness is not explicitly mentioned); the latter pair seem to radiate their own kind of effulgence, exciting praise and imitation. Their source is Christ, just as the sun is the source of all light in the world. This prologue exhibits the most elaborate and sustained use of light imagery in Gregory's works. It presents a coherent, if imaginatively structured, whole: luminaries are to the sky (above a dark world) as Christ and his saints are to the — by implication also 'dark' — human mind.[203] Everything the saints say and do radiates an ostensibly metaphorical light.

In Prudentius' 'Hymn for the lighting of the lamps', one of the many early medieval hymns on the theme of light,[203] he distinguishes between the light within and that outside of man and says that both come from God.[204] Whereas Pope Gregory makes the inside-outside opposition (*intus-foris*) one of his most frequent and fundamental distinctions,[205] Gregory of Tours nowhere says or even implies anything like it. On the contrary: he mentions something that seems to be a kind of visible radiance in those who mortified their bodies and lived only by Christ:

> In them shone (*fulgebat*) that same signal light (*lumen insigne*) of the resurrection with which the angel shone (*refulsit*) who moved the stone from (Jesus') sepulchre... With this [light] Jesus also shone (*resplenduit*) when he came, through closed doors, into the apostles' meeting unexpectedly...[206].

200. *Vit. patr.*18.*prol.*, quoting John 1:9 and Matth. 5:14.
201. Van der Aalst 1962: 109ff.
202. This metaphor also in Eucherius, *Form. spir. intell.* 3 in Migne 1859: 738D): *Sunt etiam coeli omnes animae sanctae et justae*, and in Prudentius, *Hamart.* 89-92.
203. For instance, *Anal. hymn.* 50.85 n. 71; 51.38-9 n. 40; 51.28 n. 26.
204. *Cathem.* 5.29-30, 153.
205. Dagens 1977: 25.
206. Mark 16:5; *Vit. patr.*2.*prol.*; John 20:22. Compare Prudentius, *Perist.* 2.361-72 (Acts 7:55, Exod. 32:29-30). Sometimes Gregory seems to describe this 'light of the resurrection' as already visibly present: *Hist.* 6.29. Compare Gregorius Magnus, *Dial.* 4.16.5-6.

In contrast to Severus' description of the apparition of the luminous St Martin, Gregory is referring here to living saints. However, he also describes dead saints as luminous: when Bishop Gregory of Langres had died 'his face was so glorified (*glorificata*) that it looked like roses...while the rest of his body shone like a white-gleaming lily (*tanquam candens lilium refulgebat*), so that one would have thought that he was already then prepared for the glory (*gloria*) of the future resurrection'.[207] In these descriptions the suggestion of a continuity between interior and visible light is very strong.

Sometimes Gregory also uses verbs or phrases denoting light to describe objects regarded as possessing holy energy or miraculous power. A bed, for instance, that had belonged to a holy bishop and through which many cures had been effected after his death, is said to 'sparkle with similar miraculous power (*simili virtute nitescit*)'.[208] Considering what Gregory had said earlier in connection with the healing of the three blind men, this is an interesting statement: does he mean 'similar' in degree or in nature? Is the bed, as object, doing the healing, or the saint, through it?[209] As almost everywhere in Gregory's writings, beneath a deceptively simple appearance the words are often ambiguous, the boundaries fluid, the meanings multiple, unconfinable or even contradictory — what he seems to want to say will scarcely let itself be pinned down by words.[210]

Elsewhere he describes how men perceived and reacted to a gem set in a crucifix that was standing in a dark church: 'it shone like a star (*tanquam iubar coeleste refulgebat*)', causing 'speechless astonishment (*obstupefactus*)' and 'fear (*timor*)'.[211] Why did holy objects tend to be perceived with magnified luminosity? The reactions of the observers show that, as we saw earlier, holiness and light suggested holy power.[212] When Gregory says that a saint's body 'shines bright with miraculous powers (*virtutibus pollet*)' or that the church of St Julian 'shines bright (*refulget*)' because of

---

207. *Vit. patr.* 7.3. Compare *Glor. mart.* 21 and Aalen 1951: 320, Sanders 1965b: 772-3.
208. *Glor. conf.* 85.
209. Compare on this, Helgeland 1980: 1290-8.
210. Compare Gurjewitsch 1978: 390: '... amorphes, äusserst ungegliedertes, fliessendes Weltempfinden'.
211. *Virt. Jul.* 20. Compare *Glor. mart.* 51: a silver box containing relics *tanquam sidus praeclarum apparuit*. Huxley 1959: 83ff. suggests that gems are reminiscent of the quality of visionary experience. Compare Severus' report of pearls being seen to sparkle on St Martin's hand while he celebrated the Eucharist (*Dial.* 3.10).
212. Compare Fortunatus, *Carm.* 2.1.1 and 2.3.11.

its miracles,[213] the evidence seems to point to his having imagined something like visible light radiating from these objects. Some of his contemporaries seem to have shared this mental picture. When, for instance the archpriest of Néris wanted to have the body of the hermit Patroclus, who had just died, as a relic for his church, he assembled a band of priests to help him carry it off by violence from the funeral service in the monastery. Gregory says,

> As he approached it in a fiercely determined manner (*furibundus*), he saw from afar the cloth which covered the holy limbs gleaming white with the utmost brilliance (*eximio albere nitore*), and God let him be so overcome by fear (*metu perterritus*) that he at once put the plan which he had so incautiously conceived out of his mind, and joined [the monks] in the singing of the funeral service...[214].

As Gregory tells it, the white cloth is perceived as actually radiating light, and the appearance of light around a saint's relics evidently indicates the presence of his heavenly power. Here a visual impression again calls up and coincides with a mental image having a strong affective quality: it changes behaviour. In cases such as this, one can say that the visualization of the light metaphor as a physical phenomenon modifies the information received through the senses: one 'sees' the 'dream' image in sensory reality. As G. Bachelard has described this kind of experience: 'on rêvait, on ne regardait plus' and 'le rêve est plus fort que l'expérience'.[215] The late antique (Plotinian) theory of vision may also help to explain this experience however. According to this theory, as described by A. Cazenave, all light that was perceived emanated from the objects themselves; furthermore, men did not think of themselves as in the act of seeing, but participated affectively in what was being seen.[216] This would accord with the tendency, noted earlier, to experience a visible symbol as participating in that which it symbolized, and explain the strong emotional impact of seeing light. Gregory, evidently, is emotionally involved in his mental images in a similar manner. The evidence indicates that, for him, light metaphors tended less to be ornaments of style than visualizations of what he regarded as powerful spiritual reality.

Gregory, then, attributes ostensibly metaphorical light-qualities — ultimately derived from Christ as 'the Light of the world' — to personal

213. *Glor. conf.* 71; *Virt. Jul.* 9.
214. *Vit. patr.* 9.3.
215. Bachelard 1961: 42; 1949: 46. Compare S. Tomkins 1962: 13: 'What is consciously perceived is imagery which is created by the organism itself'.
216. Cazenave 1981: 870. She applies this notion to explain the perspective from within in early medieval frescoes.

holiness or merit, divine grace, the holy power to perform miracles as well as the miracles themselves, and preaching and its content. In short, everything a holy man is, says and does is said to radiate light: he is, like the disciples of Jesus, a 'light of the world', a luminary or a 'star'. When he manifests himself in some way after death, he is described as shining with the visible light of heavenly 'glory'. Gregory's light-imagery turns up in many forms — often elusive, fluid, many-levelled — around what seem to be matter-of-fact statements. But its diffusiveness is perhaps only apparent. It may have been held together by the dominating metaphor of the human mind as the sky, illuminated by Christ as the sun and his saints as the stars.

If there is one thing about Gregory on which everyone has always agreed, it is that he is 'un visuel':[217] he describes events with dramatic and visual detail. His tendency to present things in visible, concrete terms instead of by abstract notions has been taken to indicate that he lived in the concrete part of reality only. Without intending to minimize his very evident eye for visible phenomena, I wish to suggest, on the basis of the evidence so far, that his manner of 'abstract' thinking has not been recognized up to now because a large part of it takes place through images that are directly *seen* rather than in concepts as abstractions from experience, that are rationally put together. Alongside the more or less conscious conceptual organization of sensory information, he also orders the latter in a less reflective, more metaphoric and poetic way. Designating these thought processes as 'secondary' and 'primary' respectively, modern psychology has discovered that they coexist twenty-four hours a day in contemporary European adults as well: it is the primary thought process, designated variously as 'iconic', 'imagist' and 'imaginal' thinking, that appears in our dreams.[218] While awake, most adults pay little if any attention to it: it is therefore usually unconscious. What makes Gregory different from us is that he paid less attention to words than we do and was more conscious of these 'dream' images than we are. A number of recent poetic theorists and philosophers insist that actual human experience of reality is better expressed through images than through concepts: the manner in which images can relate to each other is infinitely more subtle and complicated and more closely approaches the quality of this experience than the logic of what now turn out to be rational simplifications.[219]

Gregory's upbringing did not include the rational alternative, and this

217. Latouche 1963: 20.
218. As for instance, Jung 1952: 9-51; Singer 1974: 171-200; Cartwright 1978: 65-66; Rycroft 1979: 151; Leuner 1980b in Leuner 1980a: 9-56; Epstein 1981: 157-8.
219. As for instance, Wheelwright 1959 and 1968; Langer 1980 (1942) and 1953;

is part of his charm. He is not able to take a self-conscious, critical distance from his own mental phenomena. On the contrary, he is immersed in what he sees or visualizes: he thinks more often in immediately experienced, affect-laden images rather than in words. Suzanne Langer has called the imaginative mode 'the naive mode of experience in which action and feeling, sensory and moral value, causal and symbolical connections are still undivorced'.[220] It is in this sense that Gregory may be called 'naive'.[221] His mode of thought to a certain extent resembles what in present-day archaic societies has been called 'optic thinking', thinking in visual units.[222] In Gregory, these visual units tend to coalesce with the pre-existent mental or 'dream' images, so that he often 'dreamed while thinking, and thought while dreaming'.[223]

In Gregory's thought, then, the late antique habit of analogical understanding of reality often becomes the recognition of the congruence of a visible event with a metaphorical image, and vice versa: the visualization of a metaphor as a sensory-concrete phenomenon or event. It is not surprising that, as we shall see in the next section, his imagination and sensory perception sometimes tend to coalesce, to become indistinguishable.

PERCEPTIONS OF SPONTANEOUS EFFULGENCE

'The brilliance of a new light': the desire for illumination

> On the Friday before the holy day of Easter, when people were holding the vigil without any light, there appeared before the altar around the third hour of the night a very small light like a spark (*lumen parvulum in modum scintillae*) which grew larger and larger, scattering brilliant rays (*comas fulgoris spargens*) to all sides, and slowly began to extend itself upwards. It became a great beacon in the dark night (*pharus magna obscurae nocti*) giving light to the people keeping the vigil and praying. But when the sky began to grow lighter (*illucescente coelo*) it slowly diminished and as daylight returned (*data terris luce*) it vanished from the sight of those who were watching it with awed astonishment (*mirantium*).[224]

> Bachelard 1960; Singer 1974. On recent developments in theories about images and human knowledge in general, see for instance, Vidal 1983. Compare E. Cassirer, *An essay on man* (New Haven 1944): 11: quoted in Epstein 1981: 151: 'Rational thought, logical and metaphysical thought can comprehend only those objects which are free from contradictions, and which have a consistent nature and truth. It is, however, just this homogenity which we never find in man'.

220. Langer 1953: 217.
221. Auerbach 1946: 91.
222. See Müller 1957.
223. Bachelard 1961: 21.
224. *Glor. mart.* 5. The third hour of night was then about 9 p.m. (Strubbe and Voet 1961: 15).

Like the theme of spontaneous generation through divine power,[225] that of spontaneous effulgence or luminosity in the context of the holy occurs frequently in Gregory's works. The above event may somehow be connected with the office of the Paschal candles that symbolized the resurrection of Christ as the return of light.[226] Contemporary hymns, as we saw, often centred on Christ as light.[227] Or is this spontaneous luminosity somehow connected with the relic of the true Cross, kept in this church? Fortunatus had said (perhaps also in visionary terms) that it 'shone' and even 'flashed with the flame of its miraculous powers'.[228] Gregory's relatively numerous reports of spontaneous luminosity suggest that, like the sudden renewal or creations out of nothing, this luminosity was the way in which an important interior event was thought of and experienced.

The perception of spontaneous light is attested from the early classical and Biblical world up to and including the present day. The interpretations of it, however, can differ. In the Temple at Jerusalem but also in the temples of pagan gods, such luminosity could indicate the presence or the 'glory' of the divinity.[229] In the mysteries, a sudden light appearing in the darkness was supposed to symbolize as well as effect the birth of divine life in the candidate: as will be seen below, something like this image continues to be experienced as effective reality in Gregory's day. The same image is used by Plato, Plotinus and later, in a Christian adaptation, by Augustine, to indicate the sudden moment of intuitive, true understanding of cosmic reality.[230] The evangelist John's 'light [that]

---

225. See p. 113.
226. Prudentius mentions a lights vigil on the eve of Easter and identifies Christ with light in *Cathem.* 5.149-56. On this light symbolism in connection with the risen Christ at Easter: Davy 1976: 163; Sanders 1965a: 164 and Sanders 1965b: 779-91; Pax 1960: 108; Maclean 1915: 55.
227. As Prudentius, *Cathem.* 1, 2 and 5; the office of the lighting of the lamps at dusk, described in the latter hymn, fell into disuse after the eighth century according to Davy 1976: 166. See further, Schulte Nordholt 1964: 7-8; Pax 1961: 1026; Dölger 1920: 293-303.
228. Fortunatus, *Carm.* 2.1.1: *crux benedicta nitet*; 2.3.11: *virtutum flamma coruscat*; 2.6.2: *fulget crucis mysterium*.
229. Edsman 1940: 175; Hahn 1976: 485; Aalen 1960: 357; Pax 1960: 108; Closs 1961: 1023; Leipoldt 1957: 202-4. See also Sanders 1965b: 860 and note 258.
230. von Ivanka 1959: 350-51, who cites Plato, *Symp.* 210E, *Ep.* 7.341C; and Plotinus, *Enn.* 5.3.17; 5.5.7; 6.7.34 and 36. Veuthey 1971: 1331-3, 1336-8. Similarly Bultmann 1967: 340-42, Cumont 1949: 266 and 357-8, Hedwig 1980: 41ff. and Dörrie 1975. On modern light mysticism, see Eliade 1958.

shines in the darkness' may also refer to the mystery tradition,[231] and in any case gave this light central place in Christian thinking. What is Gregory's interpretation of the ancient image and phenomenon of spontaneous luminosity in the exigencies of his new, Christian-barbaric society?

Sometimes, spontaneous effulgence seems to be interpreted as a manifestation of a saint's honour: 'The great brightness (*magna claritas*) which fills that crypt is, as I believe, a sign (*signat*) of the martyr's merits'.[232] In another case,[233] in which Gregory explicitly says that he saw the light himself, he gives another explanation. Once, in the middle of January, he was hastening 'through the dark night' to the chapel of Marsat, which contained relics of the Virgin, in order to celebrate the vigil on the eve of her feast. From a distance he saw 'such an immense brightness (*immensa claritas*) shining through the windows that one would have thought a multitude of lamps and candles to be lighted in it'. Thinking that others had preceded him, Gregory knocked at the door; but all was silence and no one answered. While he then waited outside for a servant to fetch the key and meanwhile lit a candle, the door suddenly opened by itself and

> as we entered the chapel — I believe it was through the darkness of my sins (*a caligine peccatorum meorum*) — the brightness, which we had been looking at with awed astonishment from the outside, disappeared upon the appearance of our candle. We could find nothing from where that brightness could have come (*unde...exorta*) except the holy power (*virtus*) of the glorious Virgin.

As we shall see below, Gregory uses the same word (*virtus*) to indicate the source of another luminous phenomenon: here only the notion of saintly power as the cause or source of light is relevant. The notion that the perception of this supernatural light depended upon one's visual faculties not being clouded over by 'the darkness of sin' — again a visual expression to indicate a spiritual condition — is, however, extremely important.[234] If one could catch a glimpse of something divine it meant that one's status was improved, on earth as well as in heaven. Quite apart

---

231. John 1:5. See Hahn 1976: 488.
232. *Glor. mart.* 49. Compare with this Sanders 1965b: 773-4 and 826, where this lightglow seems to be a metaphor, which is definitely not the case with Gregory. In Gregory the Great's stories, spontaneous luminosity in churches always consists of lighted lamps (*Dial.* 3.29.3; 3.30.6; 3.31.5). Compare Gregory of Tours, *Hist.* 2.16. Perhaps a similar divine lightglow is mentioned in inscriptions in Sanders 1965b: 813-14 and 824. On God as light: Sanders 1965b: 775-78.
233. *Glor. mart.* 8.
234. Compare *Glor. mart.* 1 and 12. As in *Glor. mart.* 85 and 101, and *Hist.* 5.50.

from the considerable emotional impact that such a perception is likely to have had, this 'prestige-factor' will certainly have been an incentive toward perceiving such things at all. Seen from another angle, the notion of differences in 'purity' between individuals may partly explain the ease with which Gregory often accepts different perceptions of the same situation or event.

On a number of occasions the appearance of luminous phenomena leads to the discovery of a holy body in an unsuspected place and so to a cult for this new saint.[235] The following story[236] shows which elements could play a role in such an event. Near a monastery that was situated on top of a hill and surrounded by the ruins of old buildings

> they say...there was a hidden crypt which had not yet been revealed to any of the Christians. Every Saturday night a bright light (*lumen accensum*) was seen there by the inhabitants, but no one knew what this mystery meant (*quod sibi hoc vellet mysterium*): they suspected, however, that there was something divine about it (*aliquid ibidem retineri divinum*). Then two possessed men came out of the church of St Martin and, clapping their hands, began to cry out, saying, 'The most blessed Solemnis rests here in a hidden crypt. Uncover his tomb, friends of God! And when you have found it, lay cloths over it, light a lamp (*lumen*) and offer him the veneration (*cultus*) he deserves; if you do what we say it will be a benefit to this region'. Saying this with much shouting, they tried to dig out the earth with their nails.

When the inhabitants, upon digging, found the crypt and a large tomb in it, the possessed men cried that this was Solemnis' tomb and were healed soon thereafter. Many other people, afflicted with various illnesses, then began to come to the tomb and to be healed there. Pagans had been accustomed to worship springs, trees and often natural phenomena by placing lighted candles there.[237] There seems to be a persistence of this pagan kind of thinking and a transference of the gesture of placing lighted candles onto the cult of the saints.

The use of lights (oil lamps and candles) has been said to dominate the liturgy of the period.[238] Gregory shows us that mysterious luminosity, spontaneously lighted candles or lamps and lamps that keep on burning without refill long after the oil should have been consumed, are also associated with existing cults of saints.[239] Though I don't think he would have stopped to reflect on this, it is possible for us to distinguish at least

---

235. *Glor. conf.* 18, *Glor. mart.* 50 (dream) and *Hist.* 6.37 (*ferunt...lumen ibi divinitus apparere*).
236. *Glor. conf.* 21.
237. Harmening 1979: 55, 61, 63.
238. Pax 1961: 1026.
239. Spontaneous light: *Glor. mart.* 54 and 56; *Glor. conf.* 102; long-burning light: *Glor. mart.* 5; perpetual light: *Glor. mart.* 31.

two aspects in this symbolism. On the one hand, the light is clearly a token of men's veneration of a powerful heavenly figure, on the other, its miraculous kind of luminosity seems to be experienced as in some way a manifestation of the saint's 'power (*virtus*)', as we have seen above in Gregory's own experience in the chapel at Marsat. The connotation of 'power' may approach that of Biblical 'glory'. In the Old and New Testaments the Lord's glory (Hebrew: *kabod*, Greek: *doxa*, usually translated in the Vulgate as *gloria*) is associated with supernatural brightness, and also symbolized in that of man-made luminaries.[240]

Gregory apprehends the general in the image of the particular. He writes as though he and the men of his time found their true inspiration in specific, visible events.[241] The light that is experienced as shining forth spontaneously, seems to exhibit the quality of the new spiritual life in the light that is given from without. The fact that the following story may show formal traces of the Germanic belief of *nodfyr*[242] does not detract from its spiritual content: new Christian notions could be assimilated only by understanding them through some of the old forms. If Gregory took a story such as this seriously, we will never begin to understand him unless we are also prepared to do this and thereby to try to experience its internal effect.

A case similar to the discovery of Solemnis' tomb, is that of the tomb of Amarandus, which lay covered by spiky brush before being, 'at the command of the Lord (*Domino jubente*), revealed to the Christian people'.[243] Either before or after this discovery (it is not clear which), the crypt in which he lay 'shone with brightness (*resplenduit*)'. After the original inhabitants of that place had been dispersed or killed during hostilities, new people came from afar and 'tried to venerate the blessed martyr as their own guardian (*quasi custodi proprio*)'. Once, someone who had come a long way found himself without fire to light the candle he intended to 'offer' at the tomb. After he had tried for a long time, without success, to light it by means of striking flint with iron,

> the candle, which had already been set upon the tomb, was lit by a heavenly torch (*coelesti lampade...illuminatur*); and so it happened that what human effort could not achieve was accomplished by the majesty of the divine power (*divini numinis*

---

240. Hahn 1976: 485; Aalen 1975: 45; Sibum 1962: 11; Aalen 1951: 73-78. There is one explicit association: *gloria virtutis* (2: Thess. 19). Prudentius also associates God and his power (*vis*) with *lux, lumen, fulgor, splendor, claritatis numen* (*Perist.* 10.318-23). Compare *Glor. mart.* 6.
241. Explicitly in *Glor. mart.* 80: *Factis rei veritas approbetur*. Elsewhere, he himself refuses to believe until he sees with his own eyes (*Glor. mart.* 5).
242. Bachelard 1949: 68-69. On *niedfyr*: Harmening 1979: 151, 198.
243. *Glor. mart.* 56.

majestate). Heavenly honour was shown (*officiat ministrantur*) when man was not able to show it, and the candle was lit by the brilliance of a new light (*luminisque novi fulgore cereus clarificatur accensus*). When this had been shown (*manifestum*) to the people, no one from then on dared to take fire from elsewhere to light his candle. Later, when the area came to be inhabited by men again, and there were homes in which fire was made, this particular miracle (*miraculum*) was no longer performed for the people, but [the shrine] was frequently brightened [or honoured: *illustretur*] by other miracles.

If one tries to put aside, for the moment, all modern, preconceived notions about the causality of sensory phenomena and simply to experience something of what this first observer, and after him others, could have experienced, two constituent elements appear. The first is the evidently deeply-felt need of the community for a 'guardian' or, as Gregory more frequently says, a 'patron': someone near enough to be approachable and powerful enough to protect and aid his clients.[244] Recent research has shown that this need was a general one in late Antiquity and that it had to do with the inadequacy of governmental institutions at 'grass roots' level.[245] Gregory's stories, as we have already had occasion to see, often show the saint experienced as functioning not only as a healer but also as a heavenly version of the secular patron in an aristocratic society.[246] The second element is connected with the first and is in various ways an answer to it: what even the most concentrated human effort cannot achieve, divine grace will supply. This supernatural 'answer' functions at the same time as an indication that the martyr has accepted the request for patronage. The attitude that man cannot achieve anything without God is evident throughout Gregory's writings and is sometimes explicitly formulated, as when he quotes the Psalm: 'Unless the Lord builds a house, those who work on it labour in vain'.[247]

Gregory must have known as well as we do that candles simply do not light themselves. Why was he willing, even eager, to accept the report that such a thing had nonetheless happened? Clearly, because he wanted and expected to find evidence of the active presence of divine power as the intrinsic dynamic of reality suddenly bursting into visibility, in this case as light. Such a phenomenon was possible because, for God, there are no limits to the possible.[248] If one now simply tries to experience what the man in the story and, indirectly, Gregory experienced, it becomes clear

244. For instance, *Hist.* 1.48; 7.29; *Virt. mart.* 1.32 and 38; 4. *prol.*; *Glor. mart.* 106. See Corbett 1981.
245. Brown 1971: 36-37.
246. See, for instance, Irsigler 1969: 221-52.
247. Psalm 127:1; *Vit. patr.* 10.*prol.*; *Hist.* 1.15.
248. As he says in *Hist.* 2.3: *omnia possibilia sunt credenti*. This was also the view of Augustine, as Grant 1952: 217, 263.

that the 'brilliance of a new light' is the breakthrough of the divine quality of life into the visible, physical world.[249] The man and his neighbours, as well as Gregory, influenced by having heard about models of such events in stories they had been told, perceived or wished to perceive and believe that the candle lighted itself. I suggest that this is because, on the one hand, for them the modern distinction between an interior and an exterior event was much less clear. On the other hand, it is evident that men and women in that period intensely wished for and somehow expected the breakthrough of heavenly light. Today the metaphor of the sudden appearance of a light indicates a sudden insight or the recognition of any less than obvious truth. In Gregory's time, the image of (sudden) spontaneous light still had the connotation of the revelation of and participation in divine truth and/or life.[250] As his stories show, light was experienced emotionally: it banished the fearsome darkness in which demons were ever on the prowl. As such it seems to be something which cannot quite be verbalized, only directly experienced. The perception of some kind of sudden or 'new' light is mentioned by Gregory in connection with a significant number of experiences of the holy, including various kinds of miracles. The adjectives 'sudden', 'new' and 'brilliant' indicate the intense quality of the experience. Illumination in all its forms seems to be the image of an unconscious wish.

One story shows more concretely what could be a reason for supernatural brightness in a church during the night. In the cemetery of the city Autun, 'a mysterious psalm-singing (*occulti psallenti mysterium*) was frequently heard', and those who were singing these praises to God often appeared to men.[251] One night two persons heard the sound of psalms in the church of St Stephen, which adjoined the cemetery. 'Wondering at the sweetness of the melody (*admirantes dulcedinem moduli*)' and assuming that some devout people were celebrating the vigil there, they went in.

> After having spent a very long time in prayer, they rose and saw that none of the lamps were burning and that everything shone with its own kind of brightness

249. Compare the expression 'new light' in funeral epigraphy in Sanders 1965b: 848.
250. As Bultmann 1940 in Dinkler 1967: 348-50 on the mysteries, and Pulver 1944: 256 on John's Gospel, Paul's experience (Acts 9:3) is also, of course, paradigmatic. According to Gilson (1960: 77-88, esp. 78), light, in Augustine's doctrine of illumination, is a metaphor for the infused divine grace by which alone man may know the truth. The creative as well as noetic quality of this light is stressed in his view that God is to the spirit what the sun is to the earth (Davy 1976: 230; Oeing-Hanhoff 1961: 1023). Gregory the Great associated *interna lux* with the true life in Christ (*Homiliae in evangelia* 1.2.1, cited in Dagens 1977: 173). See also chapter III, n. 5. Compare further Huxley 1959: 75.
251. *Glor. conf.* 72.

(*propria claritate...splendere*); they also saw the choir of psalm-singers but did not recognize a single one of them. While they were therefore standing there, stunned and dumbstruck (*attoniti et stupore perculsi*), one of the psalm-singers came up to them and said, 'You have done a cursed thing by presuming to be present while we are offering to God the secrets of our prayers. Go away, therefore, and leave our homes, or you will die!'

One of the men left; the other, who stayed, died in a few days.

The mentioning of 'our homes (*domus nostrae*)' may indicate that these singers are the dead who have been accepted into heaven; in any case, they are heavenly beings with whom mortals may not associate.[252] That the supernatural brightness in churches could be associated with the presence of heavenly beings honouring God at night in the churches of men must have been a reassuring thought.

To review the evidence so far: spontaneous luminosity was perceived in the vicinity of the remains of holy persons in a lamp or candle burning 'without fuel' or 'without having been lit by man', or as a great, local brightness without any visible source. In line with antique tradition, this brightness seems to be experienced primarily as the 'presence' of the divine: God or heavenly beings, but especially — and this seems to be new with Gregory — of the heavenly *power* connected with a holy person's material remains. The experience seems to take place as the fulfilment of an unconscious wish in image-form. Often this wish takes the more practical form of the desire for the protection and aid of a saint as a heavenly patron.

'Suddenly a terrifying blaze': visible 'virtus'

> When the king [Clovis] had come to the region of Poitiers and was staying in his tents at a distance from the city, it seemed to him that (*visa est ei*) a fiery beacon (*pharus ignea*) rose out of St Hilary's church and came to rest over him (*super se advenire*), so that, aided by the light (*lumine... adiutus*) of the blessed confessor Hilary, he might more easily overcome the army of the [Visigothic] heretics, against whom that same bishop had often fought in matters of the faith.[253]

Not only Gregory, but also Fortunatus interprets the night-time appearance of this light (*lumen*) as a sign (*signum*) telling the king to ask for and then expect St Hilary's aid in the battle.[254] Fortunatus then goes on, however, to compare this 'image of light (*figura lampadis*)' with the pillar of fire (*columna ignis*) that led the Israelites through the desert, but also refers to Clovis as another Constantine who, of course, conquered

---

252. Compare *Glor. mart.* 33; again (coincidentally?) in a church of St Stephen.
253. *Hist.* 2.37.
254. *Virt. Hil.* 20. Gregory, on the contrary, uses the terms *signum* and *prodigium* almost exclusively for the equivalent of portent (see p. 000).

after he saw 'a cross of light' in the sky.²⁵⁵ Gregory says elsewhere about this pillar of fire that 'it prefigured (*praetulit typus*)the Holy Spirit'.²⁵⁶ Has he too, albeit silently, associated the beacon with the Old Testament phenomenon and thus with visible holy energy? He does not, however, make any explicit distinction between the nature of these light phenomena and of those which he sometimes records as 'portents', 'signs' and 'prodigies'.²⁵⁷ These phenomena, always perceived in the sky at a great distance, clearly have a different kind of function: they only 'announce' some other major event in the human sphere, whereas Hilary's 'fiery beacon' and the Israelites' 'pillar of fire' seem to be interpreted as somehow exerting an immediate influence on the situation in which they appear.

Perceptions of fiery light occur regularly in Gregory's writings however and, when observed at more or less close range, are taken to indicate the presence of some aspect of the holy. In this Gregory may be continuing a Biblical tradition: in the Old Testament meteorological but also man-made or supernaturally-appearing fiery light symbolizes the radiance of the Lord's presence, or 'glory'.²⁵⁸ In the New Testament, such fiery light indicates heavenly glory generally, but also the presence of the Holy Spirit. The latter interpretation continued into Gregory's time and beyond.²⁵⁹ Egyptian monks in the patristic age tell of fiery light seen around or above praying monks whose 'pure' hearts are illumined by God or the Holy Spirit.²⁶⁰ This changing interpretation of fiery light seems to exhibit a certain parallelism with the overall shift of focus in religious experience from the patriarchal Old Testament age to an early Christian prophetic period (in which the Holy Spirit determined the concept of holiness) and then to the late antique period, in which the holy man as such was the central figure.²⁶¹ Gregory, however, gives yet

255. Eusebius Caes., *Vit. Const.* 1.28-30 in Migne 1857: 943 B-C quoted and discussed in Kelsey 1968: 125-6.
256. *Hist.* 1.10.
257. See *Hist.* 5.18, 7.11 and *Hist.* 8.17. Christ's Second Coming was to be announced by flashing light in the clouds: Luke 17:24; compare Prudentius, *Cathem.* 102.
258. Compare Ex. 24:17: *species gloriae Domini quasi ignis,* and Hahn 1976: 485; Bietenhard 1975: 655; Seebass 1976: 228; Aalen 1951: 73-78; Aalen 1976: 45; Sibum 1961-62: 11, 24-25, but also Prudentius, *Perist.* 393-4.
259. Acts 2:3; Prosper Aq., *Expos. Psal.* 103.4 in Migne 1861: 289-90 and Eucherius, *Formul.* 3 in Migne 1859: 738D. Compare Bietenhard 1975: 656; Aalen 1976: 46-7.
260. As indicated by Edsman 1940: 154-74; Daniélou 1969: 789; Pax 1960: 109, Veuthey 1971: 1334. Gregory mentions them in his own *Vit. patr.* 20.3.
261. Seebass 1976: 228; Brown 1971: 103.

another meaning to this phenomenon, one which I have not been able to find in any of the earlier or contemporary sources that are extant: it reveals an aspect of his experience of the holy that has not yet received the attention it deserves.

In a description of 'natural' fire Gregory twice uses the expression 'spheres of fire (*ignium globi; globi flammarum*)';[262] the latter expression also occurs in Severus' life of St Martin, as well as in Virgil's *Georgics*,[263] from either of which Gregory may have borrowed it. They are all described, explicitly or implicitly, as ordinary fire being carried by a strong wind and are not regarded as anything very extraordinary. Two other 'spheres of fire' however, that can not be traced to a 'natural' fire, are classified as 'signs (*signa*)' in the sense of portents.[264] Iranian religion, Neo-Pythagoreans, and later the Stoics and Plotinus all had conceived of the soul as a fiery sphere.[265] In the late sixth century Pope Gregory reports Benedict's vision — from a tower — of Bishop Germanus of Capua's soul 'being carried in a fiery sphere (*in sphera ignea*) into heaven by angels'.[265] The specific connection of a fiery sphere in the sky with the presence on earth of a dead saint, however, seems to make its appearance with Fortunatus and Gregory. Gregory mentions three other instances of light descending out of the sky, of which only one, however, is explicitly described as fiery. I will mention here two of them. In the first incident a 'pious [or trustworthy] man said...he saw it (*referebat...vir fidelis...vidisse se*)', while Gregory himself, inside the church, had seen nothing.[266] At the very moment that Gregory had, unknown to anyone, entered St Martin's church at night to place some relics of St Julian on the altar there before installing them in a new chapel dedicated to that saint the next day, the man (who must have been standing or walking outside), as he told Gregory the next morning, saw 'an enormous blaze of light descend out of the sky (*pharum immensi luminis e coelo delapsam*) and, as it were (*quasi*), enter the church'. (Because it is here seen at relatively close range, the translation 'blaze' seems more appropriate than 'beacon'.) Gregory continues: 'I conjectured (*conjicimus*) that it must have come forth out of the martyr [Julian's] *power (a virtute martyris processisse)*'. This seems to

262. *Glor. mart.* 83; *Hist.* 8.33.
263. *Vit. Mart.* 14.1, reminiscent of Vergilius, *Georg.* 1.473.
264. *Hist.* 6.25 and 10.23. Compare, however, *Hist. adv. pag.* 5.18.3. See also p. 41. Another sphere of fire resembles that of Clovis: *Glor. mart.* 12. Supernatural aid in battle is a common motif in Gregory's stories: as, for instance, *Hist.* 2.7 and 3.28.
265. Cumont 1949: 176, 274, 355; Ménard 1975: 40; Gregorius Magnus, *Dial.* 2.35.3.
266. *Virt. Jul.* 34. It was during this same night that Julian's *virtus* created new wine in the cellar, as Gregory relates in the next chapter (see p. 112).

be a new image. In the New Testament heavenly beings are also accompanied by a blaze of light, which is associated with their 'glory',[267] however, not with any *power*. Or does perhaps Gregory's *virtus* include 'glory' as one of its many overlapping meanings?[268] Surprisingly, Gregory then goes on to relate how, when Julian's relics had been placed in their new chapel the next day, one of the possessed men in the church there cried out that not only the martyr but also St Martin was present, and was subsequently cured. This cure may be one reason why the accent was laid on the saint's miraculous power.[269] Here Gregory probably takes it to be self-evident that the sphere of fire was recognized as the one that, according to his biographer Severus, once shone forth from St Martin's head as he was blessing the Eucharist at the altar.[270]

In the second incident, we catch a glimpse of what may sometimes have been imagined in these light phenomena; Gregory calls it 'a mystery of light (*mysterium luminis*) which revealed (*patefecit*) most clearly the faith of (Bishop) Trojanus as well as the glory (*gloria*) of Martin'.[271] Here the association of light is not with 'power' but with 'glory' (luminous power as a heavenly being?)[272] and the light this time is not explicitly described as fiery. One night when the bishop, accompanied by a subdeacon, was walking around in the cemetery outside the city, 'there appeared to him a large sphere of light (*apparuit ei globus magnus luminis*) that looked as though it were (*quasi*) descending out of the sky'. The terms describing the perception indicate again that Gregory understood this to be a 'manifestation to the spiritual faculties rather than to the senses'.[273] This must be what he means by saying the event showed the 'faith' of the bishop: he often associates such perceptions with piety and merit.[274] There then follows a surprising phrase: 'Recognizing what it was...', the man of God told his companion to stay where he was and hastened to the place where the light was coming down in order to meet it. What he recognized, as he later told the stupefied (*attonitus*) and trembling

---

267. Aalen 1976: 46; Hahn 1975: 486. Compare Fortunatus, *Vit. Germ.* 23 and *Vit. Pat.* 46 and Gregory's own descriptions of dead saints in the following chapter.
268. Glory and power are, in the New Testament, associated only with God, as in: Col. 1:11, 2 Thess. 1:9 and Rev. 19:1 (Aalen 1976: 46).
269. *Glor. conf.* 102.
270. Severus, *Dial.* 2.2. The same incident is mentioned in Paulinus Petric., *Vit. Mart.* 4, in Migne 1861:1039B. Fortunatus, *Carm.* 10.6.9-10; *Vit. Mart.* 3. 55-6.
271. *Glor. conf.* 58.
272. As in *Vit. patr.* 7.3.
273. As formulated by McComiskey 1967: 489.
274. *Glor. mart.* 85: *sed haec videre non merui*; *Glor. mart.* 8: *credo a caligine peccatorum meorum, claritas... discessit.*

(*tremens*) subdeacon, was St Martin. After reciprocal blessings and kisses, followed by a prayer, they spoke for a very long time together. The subdeacon was warned, however, not to divulge 'the secrets of God (*arcana Dei*)', for he would die on the day that he did.[275] Accordingly, when the subdeacon felt he was about to die anyway (as Gregory himself tells it), he called together the bishop, all the men in clerical orders and the notables of the city and told them the story. His dying immediately afterwards was, of course, interpreted as proving its veracity.

Following the tradition that describes heavenly beings in terms of light, Gregory often mentions luminescence in connection with the appearance of dead saints; some of these experiences will be examined in the next section, others in the subsequent essay on dreams and visions (Chapter IV). Twice, however, he reports luminous phenomena around living persons, and these too resemble earlier descriptions. His story of what happened to a monk who was praying and silently reciting psalms in a lonely place[276] resembles those about certain Egyptian ascetics circulating in his day,[277] but also reminds one of the 'sphere' and 'hairs' of fire above St Martins' head:

> ...from each side of his mouth a flame (*flamma*) came forth which, gradually growing in length, rose up above him as a light vapour (*quasi fumiculus*) and, joined together there, turned into a great blaze (*pharus magna*) that was seen (*videbatur*) to ascend to the sky; and although his hair was being pulled upwards by this, it did not hurt his head.

Gregory calls this 'a great miracle (*miraculum*)', and introduces the story with the sentence: 'Formerly there were great luminaries (*luminaria*) in the world who brightened (*illustrabant*) it with their *virtutes*, just as the sun does with its rays (*radii*)'. The context here seems to suggest that Gregory interprets the 'great blaze' as visible *virtus*, again visualizing a metaphor. If he connects this phenomenon with the 'tongues as of fire (*linguae tamquam ignis*)' above the apostles' heads, which were associated with the Holy Spirit,[278] he does not say so.

Gregory, evidently, could think of fiery blazes and spheres as travelling

---

275. Similarly *Hist.* 2.7.
276. *Glor. conf.* 38.
277. Cited and discussed in Edsman 1940: 154-74, especially 157. See also Davy 1976: 218-26, 260-61 and Veuthey 1971: 1334-5. Severus, *Dial.* 2.2: *ita ut in sublime contendens longum admodum crinem flamma produceret*.
278. Acts 2:3-4. Also Eucherius, *Formul.* 3 in Migne 1859: 738D. Compare Fortunatus about Bishop Avitus of Clermont: *diffuso interius spiritus igne micans* (*Carm.* 5.5.126). On prayer as a pillar of fire constituting the link between heaven and earth in monastic tales, see Edsman 1940: 157-8 and Daniélou 1969. Compare Gregory the Great on Benedict's death in *Dial.* 2.35.3: *vidit...animam in sphera ignea ab angelis in caelum ferri*. See n. 265.

between heaven and earth in both directions. He interpreted them either as divinely-caused prodigies or as manifestations of a holy person's *virtus*, a term in which spiritual virtues and a heavenly life seem to coincide with spiritual power and its effects. His emphasis in the descriptions of fiery light is not on spiritual 'love' or 'purity of heart' but on a heavenly state of being which is at the same time holy energy. This view is almost certainly connected with his pastoral responsibilities.

Whereas reports of fiery light around heavenly persons coming down to earth and around living persons praying to heaven may be found in the works of previous and other contemporary writers as well, Gregory is the first one to describe such 'fire', on one occasion, as we shall see, from his own experience, as visibly rising out of dead saints' relics. Although the phenomenon resembles that of the spontaneous effulgence examined earlier, its specific source and its description as fire rather than as light seem to indicate that its quality is different enough to warrant separate treatment.

> One night when Abbot Bracchio was keeping vigils in the church of St Martin in Tours, he saw at about midnight what looked like a sphere of blazing fire shining forth (*vidit quasi globum ignis immensi...emicare*) out of the holy relics [placed on the altar] and ascend with great brilliance (*cum lumine magno*) up to the vaulted ceiling of the church. This was doubtless something divine (*aliquid divinum*), for out of all those who were present it was shown (*ostensum*) only to him.[279]

Gregory gives no further comment here but elsewhere devotes a separate chapter to a discussion 'About the fire (*ignis*) that has often burst forth (*saepe prorupit*) from the relics of the saints':

> In my opinion (*ut opinor*), this fire contains a secret truth (*continet mysticum sacramentum*) and my murky intelligence cannot understand how it can appear and give off so much light (*lumen praebet*) and yet not consume (*adurit*) anything. I only know this much: these things appear (*apparent*) to the righteous or above (*super*) the righteous. For it appeared to Moses in the thorn bush and to the other Fathers in the burnt offering (in the Temple: *in holocausto*). Bursting forth (*prorumpens*) also from the top of the blessed Martin's head it made its way into the heights of the heavens.[280]

Gregory then briefly reiterates Abbot Bracchio's experience and mentions one of his own (which will be looked at below). It is worth noting that he presents statements here as his own opinion and not as backed up by the writings of 'predecessors'. He does not appear to see an essential difference between the fire issuing from persons or relics and going towards God, and that which appeared to Moses as the visible

---

279. *Vit. patr.* 12.3.
280. *Glor. conf.* 39; *mysticum sacramentum*: see Blaise 1954: 215, 730.

manifestation of God himself.[281] Although, in the *Histories*, Gregory says that the 'pillar of fire' that led the Hebrews through the desert was the 'figure (*typus*)' of the Holy Spirit,[282] he does not explicitly associate fiery light phenomena with the Holy Spirit.

What he does associate with fiery light at close range he was, as he tells it, compelled to formulate to check panic in his community in a moment of crisis. It is one of his most amazing — and revealing — stories.[283] For the instruction of the faithful, he says, he will tell something of how in his chapel 'the *virtus* (power? heavenly quality? both?) of the blessed Martin manifested itself by a revelation (*se revelatione revelavit*) in such a way that that frightening fiery sphere appeared (*appareret ignitus globus ille terribilis*) to many people...'. When Gregory had just ceremoniously consecrated the altar in what used to be a storage-room in his residence in order to convert it into a chapel, probably for his private use, he went back with his following to St Martin's church to bring the relics of Martin and other saints from there

> solemnly, with crosses and burning candles. There was a large choir of priests and Levites in white robes and a distinguished group of citizens honoured by various dignities as well as a large crowd of people of the next highest rank. Carrying on high the sacrosanct relics, which were decorated with cloths and incense, we came to the door of the chapel.
>
> As we entered it, however, suddenly a terrifying blaze filled the room (*subito replevit cellulam illam fulgor terribilis*), so that those present were forced to shut their eyes out of fear (*timor*) and because of the exceeding brightness (*splendor nimius*). The light flashed like lightning (*discurrebat...tanquam fulgur*) around the whole room, inducing a great fear (*metus*) in us: for no one could know what it was and all lay, terror-stricken (*pavore prostrati*), on the ground.
>
> Then I said, 'Don't be afraid. For what you see is the *virtus* of the saints. Remember the book on the Life of the blessed Martin and recall how when he recited the sacred words a sphere of fire was seen (*globus ignis... visus*) to come out of his head and rise to heaven. So don't be frightened but believe that he has come to visit us together with his holy relics'.
>
> When everyone's fear had subsided, we praised God, saying 'Blessed be he who comes in the name of the Lord. The Lord is God and He has given us light (*illuxit nos*)'.
>
> But that earlier miracle (*miraculum*) was seen only by a few, while this one appeared (*apparuit*) to all the people; in the former [the saint's] *virtus* was manifested (*in illo fuit virtutis indicium*), in this one his fullness of grace; the former was then hidden in order to avoid pride, this one was shown (*manifestum*) to all to indicate his glory (*ad gloriam*); there ceremonial rites were devoutly pronounced before God, here a new chapel which would serve for the praises of God was

---

281. The latter interpretation in Prudentius, *Cathem.* 5.31-2 (referring to Ex. 3:2ff.). Compare *Cathem.* 5.37-40.
282. *Hist.* 1.10.
283. *Glor. conf.* 20.

consecrated by the brightening/honouring (*illustratio*) of holy relics.

Let us therefore, as we ought to, devoutly hope and pray that the saint, who often carried the people's wishes to heaven by this sacred fire (*per hunc sacrum ignem sustulit in excelsum*), will visit (*visitet*) them. This fire (*ignis*) — which I mentioned in the story about the praying monk as well as in that in which Abbot Bracchio saw fire coming out of holy relics — I hold to be a mystery (*mysticum esse puto*), since it does not consume but only gives off light (*illuminet*). It cannot come forth (*se prodere*), however, or appear (*apparere*) to anyone without the grace of the Divine Majesty.

Gregory says, '...what you see is the *virtus* of the saints': not (as with Moses) God (though it is through His grace that the phenomenon is seen), nor Christ (Paul's experience of blinding light on the way to Damascus could have been paradigmatic here),[284] nor the Holy Spirit (once visible as fire above the apostles' heads).[285] The context in which Gregory places his own and others' perception of ethereal fire indicates that for him the *virtus* of the saint is the central point of reference in his religious perception, that which he could most recognizably experience as its active, dynamic element. Now, what then exactly does he mean here and elsewhere by *virtus*?[286] Whereas Gregory sometimes uses the plural of this term in such a way that it can only mean something equivalent to 'miracles' or, more accurately, 'acts of heavenly power',[287] here he uses the word *miraculum* for this kind of event, and says that in this *miraculum* the saint's *virtus* was manifested. What he seems to mean here is the heavenly quality of true spiritual existence, which includes a holy power, possessed by saints already in this life and now 'revealed' through the 'visit' of the already 'glorified' saint. If Gregory sees distinctions between these three phenomena — the 'terrifying blaze', the 'sacred fire' that carried Martin's and the monk's prayers to heaven[288] and the fire which arose from the relics (which could be imagined to have come down from heaven temporarily, as in some of the stories we have looked at), he does not say so.

An immediate perception of spontaneous, intensely brilliant or fiery light had been for centuries an important if not central form in which men had visualized and experienced the meeting with that which seemed

---

284. Moses: Ex. 34:29-30. Paul: Acts 9:3: *et subito circumfulsit eum lux de caelo*. For Gregory's words on illumination, compare Ps. 117:26-7.
285. Acts 2:3. Late antique hymns also mention this fire; as for instance: *Anal. hymn.* 51.98; *Perist.* 2.393-6.
286. On the meanings of *virtus*, see Blaise 1954: 851 and Vermeer 1965: 62-4.
287. For instance: *de virtutibus beati Martini quas in eo loco operatus est* (*Hist.* 8.16); *tantae virtutes quae sub antecessoribus nostris factae sunt* (*Virt. Mart. 1.prol.*). Compare Moule 1966: 237-8.
288. As Edsman 1940: 154-74.

to be 'the heart of life'.[289] It was, obviously, still being so experienced in Gregory's day. What makes the event under consideration so unique is the large number of people present who, if we are to believe Gregory, *all* saw this sudden flashing light. There were, of course, factors conducive to visionary experience — for some people perhaps, the lack of certain vitamins in the diet; for the clerical party, a largely sleepless night keeping the vigil; for everyone: the singing or hearing of sacred (Gregory sometimes says 'heavenly') melodies',[290] the warm, shimmering light of many candles, wafts of incense. Of similar circumstances on another occasion Gregory says that people had believed themselves to be in Paradise.[291] But the most significant factor was a consequence of the reason for the whole ceremony: the awe and excitement at the presence of objects in which, as Gregory's stories amply demonstrate, tremendous holiness and active power were believed to reside. The relics were at that moment the focus of everyone's attention. To associate the light experience with them was natural as well as most understandable for those present. By identifying as a manifestation of his patron-saint's *virtus* an inexplicable phenomenon that had produced paralyzing fear, Gregory could vindicate the power of his saint, reassure his shaken community and strengthen as well as focus its solidarity around such a glorious heavenly patron.[292]

A last story shows that even this fiery light could even have practical survival value.[293] When night fell and a heavy thunderstorm 'with great shafts of lightning (*fulgura*)' descended upon a company travelling with the relics of St Martin,

> two lances, carried by servants, began to shine forth with fiery beams (*emissas flammeas pharos*), giving light to those following. Blazing forth (*fulgurantes*), the lances went ahead, conferring a miracle (*miraculum*) as well as a benefit (*beneficium*) upon the travellers and manifesting the holy power of the saint (*virtutemque beati antestiti ostendentes*).

Is this again an instance of *virtus* manifestating itself as fiery light? The phrasing seems to indicate this. Would it have made an essential difference to Gregory if he had known that this is an atmospheric phenomenon capable of a 'natural' explanation?[294] I don't think so. This

---

289. 'Eine Berührung des Zentrums des Alls mit dem eigenen Seinszentrum' (von Ivanka 1959: 355 on Plotinus' light-mysticism; on the same in Plato: 351).
290. *Virt. Jul.* 35.
291. *Hist.* 2.31.
292. Compare Brown 1977 in Brown 1982: 222-50.
293. *Virt. Mart.* 1.10. As a protection against enemies: *Virt. Mart.* 1.14.
294. So-called corposant or St Elmo's fire, a luminous electrical discharge sometimes seen on a ship or aircraft during a storm.

incident resembles the one of the hands giving off smoke near an ordinary fire, according to Gregory because they were burned by 'divine fire'. All of nature, as divine creation, was essentially miraculous; here too, saintly power and a natural phenomenon could have coincided.

Gregory lets us see that the forms of traditional imaginative perceptions of light and fiery light are experienced in a new context and with a new content. In the sky, they can 'prefigure' human or cosmic events or indicate the presence and aid of a saint's heavenly power. Around the person of a living or dead saint, they make visible his *virtus*, the heavenly state that radiates miraculous power. Gregory is the first to describe perceptions at close range of light, fiery or not, around relics. Here, too, (fiery) light is equated with visible holiness, described as the saint's *virtus*.

Whatever may have been the reasons for the incorporation of the language and symbolism of the mysteries into Christian liturgy in the fourth century,[295] it is clear that in the sixth their symbolism of divine illumination in an environment of darkness expressed a deep emotional need of individual men and women. Gregory's stories of spontaneous effulgence also seem to confirm the observation that in a predominantly oral culture thinking may be carried out in visual units and wishes expressed in the perception of images such as these.[296] They can function as metaphors of abstract truths, not in a conscious way but, as Bachelard put it, with 'une épaisseur onirique, une brume d'imprécision'.[297]

These stories also show that, as Bachelard has observed, 'les rêves et les rêveries ne se modernisent pas aussi vite que nos actions. Nos rêveries sont des véritables habitudes psychiques fortement enracineés'.[298] Traditional metaphors of sudden illumination by truth or by a divine presence reappear in the cult of the saints as waking dreams of spontaneous luminosity. In Gregory's interpretation, the truth they make accessible to experience is not the structure of the universe, but the terrifying and yet reassuring miraculous power of these saints. Gregory's truth is immediate, personal and emotional. Holy power is the central fact in his life.

---

295. Maclean 1915: 55; Schulz 1961: 1087; Bultmann 1940 in Dinkler 1967: 354-5; Lanne 1976: 890. See especially Nock 1952: 210-1 and passim.
296. As in Müller 1957.
297. Bachelard 1961: 20-2.
298. Bachelard 1961: 6. See also Gaus 1975: 428-9.

C. LIGHT AS PURIFICATORY POWER

'THE CONTEMPLATION OF THE FLAME': FROM METAPHOR TO REALITY
Gregory uses light imagery only for persons, objects and events with a spiritual dimension and tends to visualize this imagery as light visible to the senses. In apparitions of spontaneous effulgence, image-models of the holy as light or illumination also influence and merge with perception. Most of his miracle-stories, however, concern cures, and in a number of these cures perceptions of luminosity coincide with the moment of instantaneous healing. This suggests that the experience of light may be even more vital than has become evident up to now. Sometimes the light is seen immediately after the cure, sometimes at the moment of the cure itself. It is the visible manifestation of the holy power that drives out illness and sin: the holy power that, in other words, purifies. There is one story in which the contemplation of physical light effects a cure: Gregory identifies it with the saint's *virtus*. Here, a metaphor has become reality. First, I shall consider these cures and then, in a final section, look at what Gregory has to say about the dynamic of the saint's power in the context of purification.

Sometimes Gregory reports what seems to be more-than-natural light being perceived during or just after the healing, as, for example, 'while he stood at the feet of St Martin, suddenly it seemed to him as though something like lightning flashed around him (*subito visum est ei circa se tanquam coruscatio resplenderet*); and at once he opened his eyes and saw everything'.[299] Although it may have been no more than the returning daylight to eyes that were no longer accustomed to it, Gregory's formulation suggests something supernatural. In fact, it resembles the New Testament's description of Paul's experience on the road to Damascus: 'suddenly a light from heaven flashed around him: (*subito circumfulsit eum lux de coelo*)'.[300] Gregory concludes his account of the healing: 'When he had received holy orders immediately thereafter, the man went home cured'. Likewise, he writes of two blind men from Bourges: while on St Martin's feast day 'the miracles from his Life were being read to the people, ...a brilliance like lightning appeared above them (*factus est super illos splendor corusco similis*), and the ties which had held their eyelids closed were broken, blood flowed from their eyes...'

299. *Virt. Mart.* 2.15. Some modern psychologists see a connection between the intensified sensory experience of light and the liberation of energy upon the resolution of an unconscious conflict: Deikman 1966 in Tart 1969: 38: 'Liberated energy experienced as light may be the core sensory experience of mysticism'.
300. Acts 9:3.

and they were able to see.[301] This seems to be an instance of the report of one miracle inspiring another.[302] Elsewhere, Gregory suggestively clusters the imminence of Christmas (the feast commemorating the birth of 'the Light of the world'), approaching dawn, a burning candle, renewed eyesight, 'external light' and 'the light of your [i.e.St Martin's] holy power':

> ...When the vigil before Christmas was ended and everyone had left, [a fifteen-year-old blind beggar boy] lay kneeling at the feet of the saint, not moving. Then he seemed to feel as though someone pricked his eyes with a sharp point; suddenly blood burst forth and started flowing from them onto his knees. When he lifted up his face, he saw above him a candle shining forth (*elucere*), and shouting out loudly, he cried: "I thank you, holy confessor of God, that I was worthy to receive [my] eyesight (*lumen*) through your power!'
>
> O wonderful grace (*gratia*)! O immeasurable power (*virtus*)! Truly you scatter your gifts among the people for all sorts of ailments. For the one who had asked for alms, received eyesight (*lumen*) and, long deprived of external light (*extera lux*), his face is now adorned with the light of your holy power (*virtutis tuae lumine vultus ornatur*). O if the darkness of our many sins did not hide you from our sight (*a nostris visibus*) you would certainly come in a visible way (*visibiliter*) and you would cry out to the sick the words of Peter: 'Gold and silver I do not have, but what I have, I give to you: in the name of Christ, depart in good health'.[303]

The whole story reads like a poem in which light and darkness, visibility and invisibility, interior and sense experience, sensory and spiritual reality intersect, mingle, and stand in tensive relation to each other in an undefinable way. The composition of the latter part indicates that Gregory is consciously using oratorical rhythm and artistic devices. The poetical 'obscurity', however (here the 'soft focus', 'the complex tension among variously related plurisigns', as Philip Wheelwright called them) seems to be largely unconscious. For Gregory, too, such experience was 'too subtle and elusive to allow exact delimitation'; his ambivalent expressions correspond to his experience of 'a real ambivalence in the nature of things'.[304] The only definite explanation he could verbalize was that of the saint's power and he applied it to whatever he could not adequately describe or understand.

Not only illumination but also the resurrection is an image-model that Gregory visualizes in miraculous cures. The notion of a cure as a revival from death and as a new birth in the spiritual as well as physical sense is found in the New Testament but also, earlier, in the records of the ancient sanctuary of Epidauros, in which cures were ascribed to the god

---

301. *Virt. Mart.* 2.29. On these 'ties', see chapter IV, p. 240.
302. Compare Brown 1981: 80-4.
303. *Virt. Mart.* 3.16; Acts 6:3.
304. Wheelwright 1959: 62, 66, 63.

Asclepius.³⁰⁵ In Gregory's stories we can sometimes catch a glimpse of images through which people experienced the saint infusing his holy energy (his *virtus*) in one man's inner being to precipitate this birth into a new life.³⁰⁶

The following story is illustrative. Marusa had been disabled by gout as well as by blindness and had lived as though she were dead (*tanquam mortua*). Two years after she had been cured of her gout, she returned to pray at St Martin's tomb: 'soon her eyes were opened and she rose in renewed light (*mox apertis oculis, in rediviva luce surrexit*)'.³⁰⁷ The adjectives 'dead' and 'renewed' as well as the verb 'rose' have the connotation of the Resurrection: the ultimate rebirth into the heavenly life. Another story³⁰⁸ tells us in more detail what Gregory could mean by such a 'rebirth'. Ursulf had fasted and prayed for two months in St Martin's church to be cured of his blindness. One Sunday (the day on which light was created and on which Christ rose), 'as he was standing at the feet of lord [Martin] and listening to the solemnities of mass with the rest of the people, suddenly (*subito*) his eyes were opened and he began to be able to see everything so clearly that he came to the holy altar to receive communion without help from anyone'. The consecration and consumption of the Eucharist was an intensely holy moment and it may have helped to 'trigger' the cure.³⁰⁹ Gregory continues:

> On that day, at the same moment that (*dum*) the grace of the Lord's body was being given to the people, the blessed bishop (Martin) deigned to give him back his sight (*lumen*), and while the sun shone, the stars of his eyes reflected the light (*elucente sole luminum suorum refulserunt stellae*).

Gregory also sees a connection between the distribution of the Eucharist and the cure, and expresses it in a visual way: the sun functions as the symbol for Christ,³¹⁰ shining into the hearts of those taking communion and at the same time as visible light into the eyes of the healed man as though the latter were stars.³¹¹ At the same time, however, the sun could refer to St Martin.³¹² The tension between these two meanings is not

---

305. As in Matth. 9:2. On Epidaurus: Meier 1966: 315-6: further, for instance, Kelsey 1963: 46; Kee 1983: 78-104.
306. Other cures in Gregory: for instance, in terms of rebirth or resurrection: *Virt. Mart.* 2.8,13; 3.27, 43; 4.34; body and spirit: *Virt. Mart.* 3.60; 4. *prol.*
307. *Virt. Mart.* 2.3. Compare *Virt. Mart.* 2.8. *Redivivus*: Blaise 1954: 704.
308. *Virt. Mart.* 2.13.
309. Other cures occurring during liturgical rites: *Virt. Mart.* 2.14, 25, 30, 33, 47, 49; 3.19; 4.18; *Virt. Jul.* 47.
310. See p. 171.
311. Compare Prudentius, *Cathem.* 5.29-30, 153 and Dölger 1920: 293-318.
312. *Hist.* 1.39; *Virt. Mart.* 1.3. (Similarly Gregorius Magnus, *Moralia* 9:8 in Migne 1849: 863 A, based on Matth. 13:43).

resolved. St Martin, and not Christ, is explicitly designated as 'illumining' the heart of the man he cured physically:

> Who else, I ask you, could ever be found to be such a doctor that he applies two remedies to one illness? Behold, in one blind man two acts of power were manifested (*virtutes ostensae*): one that first opened his eyes so that he could see earthly things and then one that illumined the eyes of his heart (*cordis oculos illuminavit*) so that he should not desire them. For the saint deigned to dedicate to his service the one whom he, so to speak, had caused to be born anew in the world (*renasci denuo fecit in mundum*).[313]

Gregory may have had another association in the back of his mind as well. In a morning hymn which Gregory must have known, Prudentius compares the light of the rising sun dispelling the world's darkness to that of Christ cleansing the stains out of men's consciences (*sunt multa fucis inlita, quae luce purgentur tua*).[314] Does Gregory also associate (St Martin's) light-giving qualities with such a purification?

In a few cases, light appears at the moment of healing to men suffering other diseases. Gregory describes the cure of a certain Landulf as 'infested by a demon of lunacy' and suffering from 'the illness that experienced doctors call epilepsy':[315]

> as he was standing at the feet of the glorious lord [Martin], a state of ecstasy came over him (*factus est in stupore mentis*) and he saw the blessed church ablaze with a new light (*vidit...novo lumine effulgere*). Out of this light the saint came and said to him,
>
> 'Your prayer is granted. Behold, you will recover from the illness you suffer'. And after he had made the sign of the cross over the man's head, he went away.
>
> Then the man came to himself (*in se reversus*), realized that all the demonic trickeries (*insidiae*) had gone and that he was completely cured.

The 'new light'[316] here authenticates the personal presence of St Martin, just as his making the sign of the Cross, but it also seems to express the quality of this presence as the man experienced it. A certain luminosity was in fact characteristic of many apparitions of saints; these apparitions will be examined in the following essay.

Driving out demons was an exorcism, hence a purification.[317] We saw earlier that the saint could be experienced as performing it invisibly by

---

313. Manumissio . tering the service of the saint after a cure also in *Virt. Mart.* 1.40; 2.4, 57, 58, 59; 3.46, 47; 4.30, 36. Compare Brown 1981: 113. The phrase 'eyes of the heart' derives, ultimately, from Ambrosius and Augustine (Fontaine 1968: 887). Gregory also emphasizes the saint's spiritual healing alongside the physical in *Virt. Mart.* 3.60; 4. *prol.*; *Glor. Mart.* 99 *Virt. Jul.* 29.
314. *Cathem.* 2.59-60. Compare Dölger 1920: 293-318.
315. *Virt. Mart.* 2.18.
316. Compare *Glor. conf.* 86.
317. See Brown 1981: 108-12.

sensations of 'burning' as well as of 'torture'.[318] Here, in an 'altered state of consciousness', a light-giving presence and the sign of the Cross are experienced as transmitting a stream of purifying, healing energy which should probably be identified with one aspect of what Gregory understands *virtus* to be.

A very different case is that of Gregory's good friend Salvius. At the moment that he seemed to 'die',[319] 'the cell was suddenly lit up with a bright light (*magno lumine...clarificata*) and shook'; when he later revived, he told his monks that he had then been taken up by two angels and carried to heaven. In his description of the journey, the quality of light seems to express the essence of his experience. These are his words, as Gregory records them:

> Listen, O beloved, and know that what you see in this world is nothing; as the prophet Solomon spoke, 'It is all vanity'. Happy is he who can live in such a way in this life that he deserves to see the glory (*gloria*) of God in heaven...I was carried by two angels into the heights of the heavens so that I seemed to have not only this squalid world (*squalidum saeculum*) but even the sun, the moon, the clouds and the stars under my feet. After this, I was led through a door brighter than this light into that dwelling-place in which the whole floor gleamed like gold and silver, and in which there was an inexpressible light (*lux ineffabilis*) as well as an indescribable spaciousness.[320]

He was led through a multitude of men and women in clerical and secular attire (the saints) to a place

> over which hung a cloud lighter than all light (*omne luce lucidior*) in which neither sun, nor moon, nor star could be seen since it shone beyond all these more splendidly than natural light (*naturali luce splendidus*); out of this cloud proceeded a voice like the sound of rushing waters...[321]

Compared with the description of the heavenly Jerusalem as a city built of transparent jewels in the Book of Revelation,[322] this description lays more accent on the supernatural quality of the light experienced. This light must be understood to be the 'glory of God' mentioned earlier: the Book of Revelation explicitly says about the heavenly city that 'the brightness (*claritas*) of God is its light'.[323] In contrast to this light, the world now seemed 'dark', 'empty' and 'squalid' (*tenebrosus, vanitas, squalidus*).[324] In Salvius' case, the experience of this inexpressible light

---

318. See p. 157 ff and n. 131. A similar story is *Virt. Jul.* 42.
319. *Hist.* 7.1. Compare Patch 1970: 97-8.
320. Compare Rev. 12:1; 21:21, and *Anal. hymn.* 51.12 n. 9.
321. Compare: Ex. 24:15-18: *Et habitavit gloria Domini super Sinai, tegens illum nube...*; Rev. 21:23, 1:15 and 14:2 respectively.
322. Rev. 21:10-23.
323. Rev. 21:23.
324. A late antique as well as early Christian tradition: Sanders 1965a: 150-4.

suddenly and completely cured his almost-fatal illness. Moreover, after waking up, he remained for three days without food or drink and without speaking to anyone, breathing in an odour of such intense sweetness that he had need of nothing else.[325] The experience of seeing Heaven and being drenched in its light had cleansed, inspired and revived him, bringing him temporarily even into a kind of heavenly life on earth.

There is one story, finally, that in its compactness seems to present the essence of what Gregory has to say about the significance of light and fire as light in human experience.[326] When his brother-in-law Justin once came down with a high fever and pain all over his body (influenza?) and felt he 'was about to expire' (a motif Gregory also uses elsewhere[327] and which, though it may be a cliché, suggests the resurrection image-model), Gregory sent him one of the small candles (candle-ends?) that he had taken with him from the tomb of St Martin, with the following message:

> 'Light it in front of him and let him pray to the Lord in the contemplation of its light (*in contemplatione luminis*) and ask the omnipotence of the saint to save him (*et deprecetur omnipotentiam antestitis ut ei succurrat*)'.
>
> The servant brought to the sick man what I had given him. When the candle had been burning a while beside his bed, they cut off the part of its wick that had already been burned and gave it to him to drink diluted in water. The moment he drank it he was immediately cured (*ut hausit sanitatem protinus recepit*) and recovered from his illness.
>
> Later, he told us how the power of the holy bishop relieved him (*qualiter sibi virtus beati antestitis subvenit*). As he used to tell it, at the first moment that the beam of light from the candle dispelled the darkness of night from his eyes, immediately upon the contemplation of the flame, the fever departed from his body (*ubi primum oculis ejus jubar luminis progressuma cereo pepulit tenebras noctis, protinus in contemplatione flammae febris recessit a corpore*)... These things were brought about by the saint's power (*facit haec virtus antestitis*), which often, in an outpouring compassion (*proflua miseratione*), gives aid (*opem tribuit*) to the unfortunate and remedies to the sick.

Here again we have a Brownian movement of ambiguous, apparently contradictory images. For instance, was it the potion or the light which drove out the illness? A possible, rationalistic interpretation is that first, as he says, the contemplation of the flame caused the fever to subside, and then the drinking of the potion dispelled the aches and discomfort all over his body. Gregory, however, does not seem to be interested in

---

325. Compare Isidorus, *Etym.* 18.9.10: *primum homines oleribus alerentur, antequam fruges et carnes ederent.* Moses on Sinai was nourished by God's glory (Ex. 47:9; cited in Aalen 1951: 316).
326. *Virt. Mart.* 2.2. On this subject generally, see Bachelard 1949 and 1961, Gogaud 1953 and Lautman 1981.
327. For instance, *Virt. Mart.* 1.32: *amissa omni spe vitae praesentis.*

clarifying the temporal sequence: it is the saint's power itself which is central for him.

His instructions are intriguingly mysterious. 'Pray to the Lord in the contemplation of its light' — a consciously practised meditative absorption in the candle-light as the way to reach God? Or to reach the saint? Is this perhaps also what others do when, praying to be cured, they hold a lighted candle in church all night long?[328] In church tradition, the candle flame had been associated with the pillar of fire, which, of course, represented the Holy Spirit.[329] If God, as Prudentius had said, is 'the true light of our eyes as well as of our minds', is this light, like the fiery light arising from living and dead saints, also experienced as the visible manifestation of divine power? Can it also be the 'light shining in the darkness' that imparts something of the quality of divine life to the beholder? Is it at the same time, again in the words of Prudentius, Christ's light that purifies the conscience, as it 'drives away the shadows of night'? Is the 'contemplation of the flame' the contemplation of God as 'the eternal fire' and of Christ as 'the true fire', who 'fills the righteous with light and burns the guilty'?[330] Or does Gregory here associate it more specifically with the saint? As Gregory tells it, the light of this candle-flame, potentially so rich in symbolic quality and in any case sanctified by its contact with the saint's tomb, drove out the heat of fever which is associated with darkness and night and probably, implicitly, also with sin. A metaphor has become reality:[331] the action of the physical light as symbol of the purificatory power of holiness precipitates the action of that which it stands for. If this is 'magic', modern psychotherapy has rediscovered it: the transforming effects on the psyche of mental images are increasingly recognized.[332] We shall return to this theme in the following essay, where it will be developed through an investigation of Gregory's reports of dreams and visions.

But it is the second part of his instructions 'ask the omnipotence of the saint to save him',that Gregory best understands for at the end of the story he says almost bluntly: 'these things were brought about by the saint's power'. 'Omnipotence'? and again: 'power (*virtus*)'? Should the sick man pray to God and to the saint separately? However often Gregory reiterates that God gives the saints their power to perform

---

328. As in *Glor. mart.* 15; *Virt. Mart.* 1.18 and 2.11.
329. Sanders 1965a: 164. See also: Maclean 1915: 55; Pax 1960: 108-9; Pax 1961: 1026; Daniélou 1969: 789; Lautman 1981.
330. Prudentius, *Perist.* 2.393-4.
331. Compare on the purifying flame, Bachelard 1961: 29.
332. Discussion and literature on waking dream therapy may be found in the following chapter, n. 68.

miracles,[333] a phrase like this seems to be one more indication that for him it was the saint whom he primarily thought of as dispensing compassion, able to do anything and everything. The form of the request to the saint is, as so often in Gregory's stories, a mixture of prayer, meditation and contact-magic. The transition between supplication and symbolic manipulation and that between the transformation of the heart through meditation and through the 'power' of the saint are both fluid. The notion that the symbol participates in the reality for which it stands and that symbolic action therefore cannot but result in concrete effects is such a self-evident part of Gregory's thinking that he is hardly or not aware of it. For him, it is simply the way things are.

Because we can take a critical distance from at least some of our mental phenomena as such, we know that the flame, lamps and light are archaic symbols for life that can influence perception.[334] Contemplatives and psychologists tell us that such symbols, through their direct, non-verbal effective impact, can set off psychic change: for instance, in the direction of enhanced vitality. The latter occurs only, however, when such symbols are directly experienced as living realities. This story shows that Gregory and at least a number of his contemporaries could experience them in this unreflecting way. But Gregory does not connect this light with 'life' or its enhancement. He identifies it with the saint's *virtus* that drives out sin and illness. Purification by the saint's power coincides with the light entering the sick man's eyes because metaphor and physical reality must correspond: in symbolic action, they coincide. Images and action based on them constrain physical as well as mental phenomena and events. Images cut through physical causes and dominate reality.

'HEAVENLY PURIFICATION': LIFE, LIGHT AND HOLY POWER

> O inexpressible remedy! O ineffable pigment! O praiseworthy antidote! O heavenly purification (*purgatorium coeleste*), so to speak, which is more effective than the skill of doctors, stronger than the sweetness of herbs, more potent than all ointments, and which cleans out (*mundat*) the belly like scammony, the lungs like hyssop, and even purifies (*purgat*) the head like pyrethrum. Indeed, it not only restores sick bodies but — something which is greater than all these things — it even removes and mitigates the very stains in men's consciences (*ipsas illas*

---

333. Such as *Virt. Mart.* 1.32; *tribuente Domino et iuvante patrono*; 4.12: *fides nostra retinet in multorum sanctorum virtutibus unum Dominum operari*. Of St Genesius, however, he lets someone speak of 'the power of his own sanctity (*propriae sanctitatis virtus*) (*Glor. mart.* 68). See p. 000.
334. See Herzog 1966: 73, 80; Van Assendelft 1976: 140; Sanders 1965a: 164; Bachelard 1949: 10-14, 1961:1 on flame as an 'operateur des images'. Compare Cumont 1949: 49-50.

conscientiarum maculas abstergit ac levigat)... Finally, we implore his power (*virtutem ejus deposcimus*) that, [in the same way] as he accomplishes such [miracles (*miracula*), mentioned earlier] from his tomb, he should deign to revive (*suscitare*) us, already dead to God on account of our sins, out of the tomb of this death, so that in that time of the resurrection of our flesh he may obtain forgiveness (*venia*) for us when he is led forward to receive his crown.[335]

Gregory is speaking about St Martin's *virtus*. Not only does it cleanse the body, thereby healing it,[336] but it also purifies the conscience, which thereby becomes eligible for the eternal life. It is difficult to understand how such a view of purification as a concerted, positive effort centring on forgiveness could ever have been relinquished in favour of an impersonal and fiery purgatory.[337] Gregory's independent spirit is evident in the fact that, as we saw earlier (p. 157), he simply disregards the available biblical and early Christian notions of purgatorial fire. Instead, he concentrates on the beneficent cleansing action of a holy power that is often imagined and experienced as light. Light had been an antique symbol of life; in Gregory's time it was a symbol of the true life: that in Heaven. Is there a significant relation between life and holy power through the light-quality they are both thought to possess? What does Gregory mean by 'reviving from the tomb of the death which is sinfulness'? How does this purification of conscience, which is evidently also a kind of 'resurrection', take place?

One way is to take the saint's life as a model for one's own, and so to become worthy of being saved; in this context Gregory calls saints 'doctors of eternal life'. They, in turn, had tried to follow (*sequi meditabantur*) the example of their predecessors according to the precept 'Ask and it will be given to you', asking and being abundantly given by God the qualities of righteousness.[338]

> The saints tried to receive (*percipere*) these things from the Divine Majesty: asking Him constantly to instill them into their hearts (*ut ipse insinuaret cordi*), to cause them to be done through their works (*perficeret in opere*) and spoken through their mouths (*loqueretur in ore*), so that their spirit would be more easily purified (*quo facilius purgata mens*) in thought, word and deed, and that they would have only holy thoughts, speak only righteous words and perform only honourable deeds. Because of this, since they subjected themselves in these things which are pleasing to God, they obtained the remittance of their sins, were saved from the contagion

---

335. *Virt. Mart.* 3.60.
336. As, for instance, explicitly in *Virt. Jul.* 11 and in *Virt. Mart.* 4. *prol.*: *infirmitates nostras purgaret*. Sometimes it 'purifies' even a field: *procellae ab agris hoc liquore purificatis saepe prohibitae sunt.* (*Virt. Mart.* 1.2).
337. As already in early seventh-century Gaul by Bishop Eligius of Noyon (Le Goff 1981: 139).
338. *Vit. patr.* 16. *prol.* (John 16:24). Similarly *Vit. patr.* 10. *prol.*

of filthy meanness and invited to enter the heavenly kingdom on account of their merits.

Here it is direct divine action that purifies and informs human consciousness. In his saints' lives, Gregory often speaks of the 'tabernacle' that they make for God or the Holy Spirit in their hearts.[339] Elsewhere, he makes it very clear that even saints cannot accomplish this by their own strength alone: they are chosen by God and their holiness is His work.[340]

In an epilogue to the second book of the *Miracles of St Martin*, after thanking 'the Lord's goodness' which, through the intercession (*suffragium*) of St Martin, has allowed him to finish it, Gregory describes how the saint, in turn, 'purifies' him:[341]

> ...praying that what the confessor [St Martin] often grants to the people, he would bestow on me, a sinner, more generously: that he would purge (*purget*) me of the errors, which he often notices and pays attention to, that he would give me back the light of truth (*lumen veritatis*) save me from falling into unfaithfulness, cleanse (*mundet*) my heart and spirit of the livid leprosy of lust, purge (*purget*) my thoughts of wicked desires, and that he would dissolve and destroy the whole mass of crimes weighing on me...

But, as he says in the prologue to the third book, the saint's power could act only in a truly contrite heart:[342]

> ...if the soul is humbled (*humilietur animus*) at his blessed tomb and a prayer is sent to heaven, if tears flow and true repentance (*compunctio*) follows, if sighs come forth from the depths of the heart and the wicked breast is beaten — then weeping turns into joy, guilt discovers forgiveness, and the grieving heart finds its remedy (*invenit ploratus laetitiam, culpa veniam, dolor pectoris pervenit ad medelam*). For very often the touching of the blessed tomb has commanded bleeding to stop, the blind to see, the crippled to rise, and even bitterness of heart (*pectoris amaritudo*)[343] to disappear completely...

In this extremely revealing, and hitherto neglected passage, Gregory describes from the inside what he reports from the outside as happening in the many, many miraculous cures he records. The 'humbling of the soul' and 'repentance'[344] are the necessary preconditions: 'grief of the heart' at one's sinfulness, past and present. For, as Gregory's stories abundantly show, illness is often regarded as a punishment for sin, one's

339. *Vit. patr.* 1. *prol.*; 2. *prol.*; 4. *prol.*; 7. *prol.*
340. *Vit. patr.* 10. *prol.: nisi fuerit, sicut saepe testati sumus, Dei adiutorio provocatus.*
341. *Virt. Mart.* 2.60.
342. *Virt. Mart.* 3.*prol.*
343. Compare *Virt. Mart.* 1.36.
344. Compare on Gregory's pastoral purpose, Schlick 1966: 281-2. Schlick 1963 was unfortunately not available to me. On public penitence in the first six centuries, see Berrouard 1974, and Vogel 1975.

own or sometimes someone else's.[345] It is obvious that the subsequent contact-magical act of touching the tomb is experienced not as a contradiction but as a self-evident mode of communication.

Contrition (*compunctio cordis* and related expressions), the quality of being crushed or wounded in spirit, can be for Gregory the pivot of a conversion to the spiritual life, as in the case of the nun who had a vision of Paradise.[346] Her decision to let herself be walled in as a recluse can be understood as an attempt at purification by self-punishment. In the case of another hermit, too, Gregory speaks of the man's desire 'to be converted (in this case, restored to the spiritual life) through the practice of penitence (*poenitendo converti desideravit*)'.[347] God brings back runaway monks by 'wounding their hearts'; they too 'did penitence (*poenitentia*) for their transgression'.[348] In the sixth century, the indelible, public penitence had fallen into disuse and Irish tariffed penitence had not yet been introduced. What did Gregory mean by the term 'penitence'?[349] A moment or short period of spontaneous private contrition or repentance as expressed by tears, prayers and abstinence seems to be the essence of it.[350] Was this experienced primarily as a compensation, a *satisfactio* for their sins (Gregory does not use this word, though it does occur in connection with 'penitence' in a letter he quotes),[351] or was perhaps the seeking of the personal experience of forgiveness the most significant element? It is the latter that Gregory seems to be suggesting.[352]

The general pattern of these cures which effect a spiritual as well as physical 'rebirth', may perhaps be formulated as something like this. First, distress at mental, emotional or physical deprivation or disturbance and the conscious breaking down over a short or longer period of time of all psychological 'defences' (contrition through prayer, tears, fasting),

345. Formulated as a general principle in *Virt. Mart.* 2.40: *infirmitates...quae perfert populus, indignatio Domini commovet.*
346. *Hist.* 6.29.
347. *Vit. patr.* 10. prol.: *si post ignorantiam poenitendo converti desideravit.* Also *Vit. patr.* 10.2.
348. *Vit. patr.* 1.3. Compare Vogel 1975: 6-8.
349. Compare Berrouard 1974, Vogel 1975, and Adnès 1984.
350. Compare *Hist.* 8.20; 10.1. Gregory lets two kings lying on the ground under their shields during a heavy storm also 'do penitence (*paenitentiam agebant*)' (*Hist.* 3.28); here, this can only mean repentance in the form of a short, spontaneous self-castigation.
351. *Hist.* 9.41; *Virt. Mart.* 3.56. *Virt. Mart.* 3.57.
352. Compare, however Gregory's relating without comment a priest's refusal to give 'penitence' to one he 'burned' to death for insulting him evidently an unforgiveable crime (*Vit. patr.* 8.11).

accompanied by the cultivation of complete confidence (*plenus fide*) in what was regarded as the purificatory, restorative, regenerative power of God or the saint. Then the precipitation, through some 'trigger', of a more or less sudden 'breakthrough' (sometimes preceded by a brief crisis), and the sudden cure, experienced as the inflow of 'holy' energy, the sensation of joy, peace and a 'new life'. I was not really surprised to find that in essence the same pattern has been observed in Lourdes in the seventeenth century as well as in more recent times.[353] The pattern of cures in Gregory's stories (in which, however, not all elements are always mentioned) fits that of his prologue, except that there he omits to mention the unshakeable confidence he stresses in the stories, probably because he takes it to be self-evident.

The purificatory aspect of contrition or 'penitence' has just been examined. There is one story in which Gregory explicitly mentions, besides 'penitence', something like retribution, and there he says that it is God who 'often crushes with his rod of correction the arrogance of a proud mind'.[354] After King Sigismund of Burgundy had killed his son by his first wife on the wicked advice of his second wife, he went, stricken with regret and grief (*compunctus corde; paenetens*), to the monastery of Agaune which he had founded and 'spent many days in weeping and fasting':[355]

> there, prostrated on the ground by the tombs of the happy legion of the blessed martyrs, he did penitence (*poenitentiam egit*), praying that the divine revenge (*ultio divina*) would pay him back (*retribueret*) for that which he had done in this life, so that he would be absolved at the Last Judgment if the wicked things he had done had been requited (*repensetur*) before he left this world: and he gave the abbey very many gifts in lands as well as in other goods, and established the daily psalmody (*psallentium quotidianum*) there. Afterwards he was captured by King Chlodomer and by his orders put to death with his sons; carried to the abbey, he was then buried there. That he was admitted to the company of the saints is proved by what happens: for if now those suffering from fever devoutly celebrate a mass in his honour (*in ejus honore missas devote celebrant*) and offer a gift to God for his repose (*ejusque pro requie Deo offerunt oblationem*), at once their fevers are extinguished (*restinctis*), their shaking is subdued (*compressis*) and they are restored to their former health.

This murderer managed to become regarded as a saint by personal 'penitence' and, one suspects strongly, especially by institutional means such as endowing the monastery, and establishing what was probably a perpetual chant there.[356] Having a mass said 'in his honour' may indicate

---

353. As described by de Viguerie 1983.
354. *Glor. mart.* 74.
355. *Hist.* 3.5. The following: *Glor. mart.* 74.
356. Compare Marius Aventicensis, *Chronica,* anno 515: *...monasterium Acauno*

that he has achieved status of saint,[357] but, as though it were at the same time still doubtful — and this is something which Gregory does not mention anywhere else in connection with other dead persons, saints or otherwise — gifts could be made 'for his repose'. The context seems to suggest that these are material gifts.[358]

Although Ambrose, Augustine and Gregory's contemporary Pope Gregory all asserted the efficacy of masses, prayers and alms for the dead,[359] this is the only trace, in Gregory of Tours' work, of anything resembling actions by the living to improve the condition of the dead. What is more, the whole story is couched in terms of a retribution which equals the weight of the crime and how to arrange this before the Judgment. Sigismund's later being callously and dishonourably put to death seems to be the 'revenge before death' that he asked for, perhaps making his sainthood possible. In similar stories, where the culprit did not have the prudence or the means to found a monastery, Gregory interprets a miserable death as no more than simply a just punishment.[360] No other story of Gregory's exhibits a similarly abstract calculation with regard to the economy of salvation. There is no hint here of purifying grace or forgiveness. Was it the only way Gregory, perhaps influenced by the Germanic law codes, could think of to explain the facts?

Many passages show that his attention is also fixed on the saint as personal intercessor in the court of the Last Judgment.[361] Gregory frequently alludes to dead saints and martyrs as already inhabiting Paradise, but he also occasionally uses the traditional phrase that they 'rest in the bosom of Abraham'.[362] Sinners (that is, everyone other than saints and martyrs) go directly at death to an 'infernal prison', for the rich imagined or even seen as flames, to await Judgment.[363] At the end of the

> *Sigimundo constructum est; anno 522: Segericus filius Sigimundi regis iussu patris sui iniuste occisus est; anno 523: Sigimundus...in habito monachale...in puteo est projectus.* See also Ueding 1935: 167-78 on Agaune, who says (168-9, 173) that the chant was probably established at the foundation of the monastery and not after the murder, which took place later.

357. Compare *Virt. Mart.* 1.12.
358. Or has Gregory misunderstood a practice, attested to in contemporary Italy, of offering the Eucharist? See Gregorius Magnus, *Dial.* 4.57.2: *offerre pro eo sacrificium...pro absolutione illius.* Compare Le Goff 1981: 125-6.
359. Le Goff 1981: 89-90, 113-14, 125-28.
360. As, for instance, *Virt. Mart.* 1.2; *Virt. Jul.* 13-20.
361. For instance, *Virt. Mart.* 1.23, 24, 40; *Glor. conf.* 99, 110; *Virt. Jul.* 13, 50, *Vit. patr.* 19.4; 20.2.
362. As in *Hist.* 10.13. The meaning of *In psal.* 14 is unclear: *Quod ipse* [Christus] *est mons in quo animae justorum requiescant.*
363. *Hist.* 10.13: *ita credimus et peccatoris in illo infernali carcere usque ad iudicium retineri...*; (*dives*), *qui flammis tartareis cruciabatur...* Compare Le Goff 1981: 88.

second book on the *Miracles of St Martin*[364], Gregory asks for the saint's power to purify him on earth,

> so that when, at Judgment, I shall be placed on the left side, he will deign to lead me out from the midst of the goats with his sacrosanct right hand and keep me behind his back while the sentence of the Judge is being awaited. And when the Judge has decided that I should be sent away to the infernal flames (*flammis infernalibus deputatus*), that he will cover me with the sacrosanct cloak, which covers him in his glory (*gloria*), and excuse me from punishment (*excuset a poena*) while the angels say to the King, as they once said about the revived monk:[365]
>
> 'This is the man for whom Martin pleads'. And let it happen, even though (*quia*) I do not merit to be clothed in that brightness (*claritas*) or to be freed from (*liberari*) the servants of Tartarus rushing upon me, that my sins should not weigh so heavily on me that I should be separated from the kingdom of the One to whom I have faithfully borne witness in the life of this world.

Punished by the servants of Tartarus and yet not separated from the Kingdom of Christ? At the end of his book on the *Glory of the martyrs*,[366] Gregory, as he quite often does, advises men to seek their patronage (*patrocinium*),

> ...so that, in that time of judicial investigation (literally: weighing; *examinationis tempus*) when eternal glory (*gloria*) surrounds them, we will either be excused or have to go through a light punishment because of their mediating forgiveness (*nos aut excuset mediatrix venia, aut levis poena pertranseat*), so that those who were redeemed by the price of their precious blood should not be condemned [to suffer] eternally for their sins (*nec damnet reos pro criminis actione in perpetuum, quos pretiosi sanguinis commercio reparavit*).

'Not eternally' can only mean in some sense 'temporary'. One is tempted to think of the 'light punishment' as something like a purgatory here, but the emphasis seems to be not on purification so much as on retribution: as in the contemporary Salic code of law, the latter can be commuted into the payment of a fine or compensation by others.

To review the evidence on purification: the martyrs seem, on only a slightly lower level, to duplicate the role of Christ, redeeming sinners' souls with their blood. In fact, for ordinary men Christ has obviously become the great, unapproachable King or Judge, and the mediator between men and the divine Majesty is now the saint, radiating the brightness of his heavenly *virtus*. He is the one who transmits 'forgiveness' and 'rebirth' to the contrite penitent in this life, and leads the latter to eternal life by his example and his intercession after he has

---

364. *Virt. Mart.* 2.60.
365. Severus, *Vit. Mart.* 7.6. Gregory's plea for Martin's help at this moment resembles that of Severus in *Ep.* 2.17-8.
366. *Glor. mart.* 106.

first 'purified' body and spirit by his holy power in the earthly life.

In Gregory's stories, this earthly life and man himself are experienced as being 'dark'; it is the true, heavenly, life that is imagined as light. A purification by the saint's power that leads to a new life, spiritually and physically, can coincide with the contemplation of a candle flame or with the perception of sudden, 'new light'. It looks as though life, light and holy power are so intimately related that they are often metaphors of each other: holy power, too, is a 'living metaphor'[367] — one that is not recognized as such — of creative vitality. Notwithstanding Gregory's preoccupation with a symbolism and 'power' that shades off into beneficial magic, his view of purification centres on individual, interior effort and on the compassionate forgiveness by the saint. Because of his unreflective view of reality as symbolically structured, he does not seem to have experienced a contradiction in combining these two attitudes in one act, such as contritely touching the tomb or meditating on a candle flame. This is because he was inclined to think of interior events in two ways: through visible, exterior ones, and through metaphors which he (unreflectingly) visualized as potent, sensory reality. For Gregory, therefore, interior events, exterior ones, metaphors and spiritual reality tend to coalesce. As E.R. Curtius, inspired by C.G. Jung, said about late antique literature already in 1948, it 'speaks the eternal language of dreams'.[368]

CONCLUSION: GREGORY'S CHIAROSCURO WORLD

Gregory's imagery and what he describes as perceptions of visible light are modelled, on the one hand, on the traditional experience and metaphorical language of illumination as these occur in the ancient mysteries and in Hellenistic light mysticism, and, on the other hand, on the traditions of spontaneous luminosity connected with the presence of the deity in the biblical tradition as well as in the antique pagan cults. Instead of man's divinization or mystical contemplation however, the context is awed respect for a saint's 'power' or purification and regeneration by it. The late antique tendency toward the erosion of the distinction between metaphorical and physical light is evident in Gregory's tendency to visualize metaphors as concrete reality and in his frequent reports of spontaneous luminosity.

Purification is, indirectly, more associated with light than with fire, which has only negative, destructive, and diabolic qualities. Fire, in fact,

---

367. This is, of course, Paul Ricoeur's phrase and the title of his book: *La metaphore vive* (Ricoeur 1975).
368. Curtius 1953: 105.

is treated as though it were a metaphor for violence. Only when the saint chastises by a 'divine fire' that drives out demons or leads to repentance is it possible to speak of a certain kind of purification by fire. Though Gregory uses image-elements that later turn up in the doctrine of purgatory, he interprets them as simple punishment. The story of the three young men whose purity and holiness made them impervious to the fire in the Chaldean furnace is Gregory's image-model for the relation of the holy to fire; not only holy persons, but also relics simply do not burn. This is the basic assumption underlying a number of fire-ordeals which he tells us about. Fire, in fact, is used to threaten people into obeying the church's precepts: casualties by lightning are interpreted as punishment by saints, and the perception of supernatural fire around the tomb of an avaricious woman is taken to indicate her punishment in hell. When we look at which crimes Gregory associates with infernal punishment, we get an indication of what he considered to be the most serious problems of his time: injury to or usurpation of church property (other property is not mentioned in this context), heresy, sedition against ecclesiastical superiors, probably also injury to church officials, and — prominently — any insult to the saint. Crimes other than those against the church are not linked with infernal punishment. It is clear that the church felt threatened, socially and economically. She had no weapons against superficially Christianized barbarian warriors other than threats of 'heavenly', or infernal, fire.

The saint, and especially his holy power, is at the centre of everything. He is thought of as dealing out most of the punishments. But it is also in terms of 'power' that regeneration is acted out in miraculous cures. Gregory is one of the first to identify spontaneous brightness or fiery light (which occur in the Bible as manifestations of all the three persons of the Trinity, and in monastic literature as prayer, heavenly life or love) as the holy power of a saint's relics. Such light is visible *virtus*. In cures, life, light and holy power may be 'living metaphors' of each other; each transforms psychical as well as physical reality.

Gregory suggests that symbolic acts such as making the sign of the Cross, touching the tomb, lighting candles and reciting sacred words, but also prayers, tears, fasting and even threats, are responsible for helping to bring holy power to the spot or to make it effective there. Symbolic thinking, however, was the essence of the late antique mentality. At the popular level, but not only there, the practice of magic was widespread. In order to be understood at all and in order to be accepted, the church had to adapt the existing forms of action and categories of thought and try to give them new content. Gregory tells us explicitly how to exert pressure on a saint, but regards this as the fulfilment of one of Christ's promises: 'Ask and it shall be given to you'. The relation with the saint is a practical working relationship, with obligations on both sides. There were certain inherited modes of action that seemed self-evident as modes of communication. In order for the system of saintly patronage as an institution to be effective in an otherwise insufficiently ordered society, it was necessary to be able to formulate and press requests publicly and to receive public 'answers'. When we view the situation in this manner, it becomes clear how agile and practical a diplomat Gregory really was. But he was, obviously, also sincere. His deep humility before the saint is truly spiritual.

An examination of his handling of metaphors shows that Gregory prefers thinking in visual units to thinking in abstract categories: his imagery tends to be treated as though it were a reality visible to the senses. This thinking in visual units (the latter can be real events but also images he has gleaned from reading or from the liturgy) is responsible for his lack of interest in concrete causal connections and in the surface cohesion of a story. In other words, it is responsible for what many have designated as his discontinuities as well as his lack of clarity or 'obscurity'. Beyond the surface ambiguities and contradictions, however, there turns out to be a dynamic, verbally inexpressible cohesion of images of which Gregory himself does not always seem to be fully aware. This is probably because he *experiences* the images almost more than he *uses them 'to think with'*: when called up, they seem to be present as potent spiritual realities rather than as 'things thought about'. This mode of thinking experience has been called 'naive' and 'archaic' and also described as waking dreams. It is in this sense only that Gregory may be called unreflective and 'naive' — but most certainly not simple. In Wheelwright's words: his experience of reality is so fluid, approximate, dynamic, tensive and presential that it can only be known and expressed indirectly.

Gregory's visual thinking also appears in his inclination to experience or describe a sensory event as though it were an interior one and, conversely, to become conscious of his imaginations as though they were sensory perceptions. He was more aware of and much more directly and emotionally receptive to visual images than the 'ordinary' western European adult today, in whom this receptivity usually goes on at a subconscious level. It is this, in a certain sense 'meditative' kind of receptivity that must have helped to make possible the psycho-physical cures that Gregory describes as miraculous. The transformational effect of immediately experienced or imagined symbols and images that Gregory describes is being rediscovered today in clinical psychotherapy. Gregory and his contemporaries regarded it, however, as the dynamic of an independent spiritual reality. In their 'dark' world this reality is, above all, the holy power of the saints, experienced in many different ways as a sudden flash of 'new light' that often brings 'new life'. 'Holy power' is a living metaphor of the essential dynamic of life: creative renewal.

Gregory's unclear, patchy presentation on the other hand, turns out to be connected with his inclination, alongside his literacy and his actively practical and diplomatic skill, towards an 'archaic' view of reality, structured by the not-quite-expressible 'dream' relations between immediately-experienced symbolic images rather than by the discursive logic of concepts. Sensory reality too seems to participate in the reality of that of which it is the metaphor or symbol. Upon closer inspection therefore — and reality is in the detail, after all — Gregory's *chiaroscuro* representation of events and his emphasis on miracles reveal a view of reality in which sensory perception, deliberate imagination and waking dreams often overlap or coalesce. His stories manifest a poetic perception however that, although it is largely unconscious and expressed in spiritual idiom, deserves to be recognized as a valid statement about human reality in any age.[369]

To return to our original question: Can Gregory's perception of the world's 'darkness', often lit up by the star-like luminosity of a saint, be in any way related to the society in which he lived, and if so, how? He must have arrived at this view, as I hope to have shown, through being brought up in a traditional pattern of thinking and feeling about darkness, fire and light that had been developing from pagan as well as Christian sources for centuries. As we have seen, it may be that: 'the world we perceive is a dream we learn to have from a script we have not written'.[370] Gregory, however, does seem to have made some — conscious? — choices: for instance, he simply skips the references to purifying fire that he must have seen in his sources (including the New Testament) and opts instead for something approaching purification by light. At the same time, we see him (consciously?) interpreting fiery as well as luminous phenomena in such a way as to underpin his ideas about saints and society. His 'metaphors' and perceptions of darkness, light and fire, then, are simply perceptual categories he learned as a child and he helped to

---

369. Modern philosophical inquiry has rediscovered and consciously used the mytho-poetic imagination as an extremely sophisticated tool for the description as well as the discovery of reality. See, especially, Ricoeur 1975. A survey of the recent uses of images in Vidal 1983. Viarre 1977 reports on the study of images in literary texts. See also Introduction n. 65.
370. Tomkins 1962: 13.

adapt and fit them into a social system. This adaptation should, in my opinion, not be mistaken for an origin or 'cause' of such a view. Why continue, while society changes fundamentally, to think of the world as 'dark'? It is obvious that sixth-century men had more reason to think so than first-century men. I suggest, however, that the relation between a world-view and society may be indirect, that it passes through the *ideals* that men — somehow — discover and long for. Gregory's ideal seems to be that of interior renewal. It is obvious that such an idea cannot merely arise out of or 'reflect' concrete social circumstances, though its form can be affected by them. It is something that is transmitted in a collective context and recreated in individual lives. For late antique men, God was Light, and 'new life' or Truth, was the contemplation of God as Light, projected into heaven but also occurring sometimes on earth as divine illumination. This is the most fundamental reason that their world seemed 'dark'. A factor contributing to this view, however, may be that men felt that the society in which they lived did not provide adequate opportunities to realize the spiritual ideal that they had in mind. Interior renewal was the essence of this ideal. But, in sixth-century Gaul, ideas tended to be apprehended and experienced in visible forms. The ideal could be seen, not only in nature and in light, but also in a fellow human being: the saint. Imaginations, dreams and visions of the saint in person are the subject of the following and last essay.

IV

DREAMS OF A VENERABLE PERSON
the power of an ideal

INTRODUCTION. ARMENTARIA: DREAM, WAKING VISION OR SENSORY REALITY?

...No one can doubt the past deeds of miraculous power (*virtutes*) therefore, when he sees the benefits that the present miracles (*signa*) confer: cripples are straightened, the blind are given back their eyesight, demons put to flight, and all other sorts of illnesses are cured by the saint's own healing. As for me, since the book about [St Martin's] life was written by men before my time, I will record, upon God's command, the present deeds of power as far as I am able to remember them. This I would not dare to do, had I not been instructed to do so twice or three times in a vision (*visum*). For I call on the almighty God as a witness that upon a certain occasion I saw in a dream (*somnium*), in the middle of the day, [a crowd of] many sick people, oppressed by various diseases, being healed in the church of our lord Martin; and my mother, who saw me looking at them, said to me, 'Why do you put off writing about what you see?...'.[1]

Gregory inherited a tradition which prescribed that a literary work should only be written upon request. Two of his most important models, Sulpicius Severus and Orosius, stated at the beginning of their works that they wrote only because they had been asked to do so, respectively, by a close friend and a revered teacher.[2] Gregory's allusion to a 'command by God (*Domino jubente*)' seems to be a new motif in the hagiographical tradition,[3] as is his bringing his mother Armentaria, who was then still alive, into the picture.[4] This is a touching tribute to his reverent affection

---

1. *Virt. Mart.* 1. *prol.*.
2. Severus, *Vit. Mart.*, *ded.* 1-6; Orosius, *Hist. adv. pag.* 1. *prol.*
3. Strunk 1970: 13-57 does not mention anything like it for Gregory's predecessors. On Gregory: 57-61.
4. On Armentaria: Stroheker 1970: 148. She came to visit him at Tours and was cured there after at least eight years had passed since the vision and after he had already written two books of miracles of St Martin (*Virt. Mart.* 2.60; 3.10). Gregory's reverent affection for her is evident in his mentioning her as *venerabilis mater* (*Virt. Mart.* 1.36); Fortunatus' poem to her (*Carm.* 10.5) may also have been written at Gregory's suggestion.

for her but may also mean that he is referring to an authentic experience and not merely restating a literary theme. But what *was* this experience? The description seems, even by Gregory's standards, unusually imprecise.

He says he will describe 'a command by God' but the only words spoken to him are by his mother. Upon his remonstrances that his language and style are inadequate to the task of writing about St Martin's miracles, she says that, on the contrary, his language will be better understood than that of orators by those for whom the stories are meant, and concludes: '... So don't hesitate, get on with [the writing]. It will be a crime if you are silent!' Gregory evidently expects his readers to recognize these words as a divine command. This fact can be understood when the dream is placed in the antique tradition of dreams in which a messenger of the gods or a revered ancestor or parent appears to give advice or to issue a command. The pagan authority on dreams, Macrobius, calls this kind of dream an *oraculum*,[5] a word which Gregory never uses. Instead, Gregory uses the terms *visum* and *somnium*, which Macrobius uses to indicate a nightmare and a vision of truth in allegorical form respectively. The interchangeable use of the terms *visum* and *somnium* for a veridical vision or dream (for which reason the term 'dream-vision' seems to be most appropriate) is found in the Vulgate translation of the New Testament, however, where the instructions are given by angels.[6] In the present case Gregory seems to be combining the tradition of the revered (parent) figure with that of the angel. In what follows, it will become evident that the kind of dream-vision in which something appears that we would today regard as an externalized part of the self[7] was rather frequent in his time. The venerable figure seen is often interpreted as being a dead saint, now living in heaven. Just as in this story, 'commands' from such a figure precipitate human decisions and the action following upon these. They seem to be crucial moments in which the initiation of change in human conduct is seen taking place. This is precious testimony and it is therefore worthwhile subjecting these dream-visions to a closer scrutiny.

Gregory's dream of his mother's 'command' presents us with other obscurities. Was this experience one of 'two or three' different dreams? Gregory says 'For...upon a certain occasion I saw in a dream in the middle of the day (*vidi ... per somnium media die*)', and says no more

---

5. Macrobius, *Comm.* 1.3 (Willis 1970: 10), as described in Lewis 1964: 63-4. Compare on this type of dream: Dodds 1951: 107-9; Nock 1972: 152-4; Dulaey 1973: 17-8: they were described as tall of stature and beautiful.
6. Budd 1971: Hanson 1980: 1407-9; Kelsey 1968: 80-101; Dinzelbacher 1981: 45-8.
7. Compare Douglas 1966: 83-4 who points to the same phenomenon in ancient Greece and present-day archaic cultures.

about the content of the other dreams. Does the immediately following phrase 'in the church of our lord Martin' refer to the place in which the dream was experienced or to the place in which the many simultaneous cures were seen taking place or, indeed, to both? If Gregory were experiencing a waking vision, mentioning the time of day, the place and the fact that his mother watched him having the vision, and then spoke to him (*et videbam eos, spectante matre mea, quae ait mihi*)[8] would make a coherent and rounded narrative. The words of his mother, who is physically present, taken in conjunction with the vision, would then have been understood by Gregory to be divinely inspired. The term *somnium*, however, which never indicates anything other than a dream during sleep, seems to make this interpretation impossible. Is Gregory then sleeping (holding a siesta) in the middle of the day (why should he mention this? his details are always significant) and dreaming of seeing a vision during which he is watched by his mother, who is herself also present in the dream? If this is what is meant, this double perspective — a vision within a dream-vision — would also be something new. Or are both mother and son seeing, in the dream, the crowd of people being healed? In that case, why should she be watching him instead of the cures, and why should she say he ought to write about what *he* sees? If, however, she were speaking as a dream-figure, she would fit into the oracular/angelic dream-tradition and this would more easily explain Gregory's interpreting her words as a divine command.[9] This latter view of the situation, in one way or another, then, would seem to be the most probable. But it has to be admitted, there is no explanation available that is completely satisfying.[10] However, unlike Severus' precision about his state of mind, when he had his dream of St Martin[11] (an account which Gregory was certainly familiar with), Gregory is not really interested in his own or others' manner of perception. The content of the dream, the message, blots out almost everything else. He is immersed in it.

Obviously, Gregory realized that what happened was — in one way or another — a visionary experience. Obviously too, what he saw and heard

8. Bordier 1860: 4 n. 2 reports, on the authority of Ruinart, that one ms. (Bec.)has: *et vidi matrem meam expectantem*.
9. Severus' friend Postumianus, while in Egypt, dreamed that Severus stood before him and invited him to board a ship, bound for Narbonne, then lying in the harbour. This is not designated as a divine command however (Severus, *Dial*. 1.1).
10. One ninth-century manuscript has 'in the middle of the night' instead of 'in the middle of the day': Cod. Paris. lat. 2204, according to Krusch 1885: 585 note Praef. n. The rest of the text may (also) have suffered mutilation at an early date.
11. Severus, *Ep*. 2.2.

in the dream-vision seemed to him more real than everyday sensory reality. In the preceding chapter, we saw that his tendency to think in metaphors as images of sensory-concrete events, sometimes coalescing with waking dreams, could strongly influence his perception of sensory reality. In this chapter I shall approach the matter from the opposite end: from the perceptions that he himself designates as visionary. If, as Bachelard has said: 'les rêves et les rêveries ne se modernisent pas aussi vite que nos actions. Nos rêveries sont des véritables habitudes psychiques fortement enracinées',[12] the dream-visions and apparitions of venerable or angelic figures that Gregory reports may be the persistence of an ancient dream in a Christian context.[13] At the same time, however, the precise content of this dream and its function for the individual and for society are likely to yield significant information about both of these in Gregory's time.

'From the perspective of phenomenology, images are the concretization of emotions',[14] a psychiatrist says. In Gregory's time, not only metaphorical images but dream-images too could sometimes appear as 'sensory reality'. Already in 1900 Bernouilli wrote: 'Wie gering aber für das damalige Empfinden der Unterschied von Traum und Wirklichkeit war, zeigt sich daran, dass derselbe unbekannte ehrwürdige Greis, der uns in zahlreichen Traumbildern vorkam, auch plötzlich unter die wirkliche Volksmenge getreten und sich als Sankt Martin zu erkennen gegeben haben soll'.[15] I hope to show in what follows that since this type of dream-experience was regarded as revealing an objectively existing spiritual reality, men were alert to it and wished to detect it also while awake. Unlike most modern western Europeans, they were inclined to be somewhat aware of the constant and involuntary 'imaginal' thought going on in all of us.[16] It probably interpenetrated more with their perception than it does with ours. In Gregory's stories we see this happening.

While the longer, usually ecstatic, dream-visions of early Christian men and women (having almost always 'the other world' as their subject

---

12. Bachelard 1961: 6. Compare Gaus 1975: 429-30.
13. Compare Eitrem 1947: 41: 'Das heidnische Orakeln setzte sich in christlichen Formen fort'. Le Goff 1977: 305 speaks of the saints as replacing an ancient élite of heroes and kings as *receivers* of dreams. Post 1986: 134-9 shows the persistence of what he calls the *advocatus*-iconography from the pagan into the Christian context.
14. Epstein 1981: 18.
15. Bernouilli 1900: 319 referring to *Virt. Mart.* 1.6.
16. Epstein 1981: 157-8. Compare Singer 1974: 171-200; Cartwright 1978: 66.

matter) have been individually and collectively studied,[17] the much more numerous short ones that are reported in Christian narrative sources as occurring under ordinary circumstances have not yet been systematically examined. I will consider Gregory's reports of such dream-visions, grouping them as follows, into four categories, according to their functions for the individual and/or for society: those instituting or legitimizing new cults, those involved in cures, those giving practical advice or aid, and those which warned or punished. The coinciding of these groups of dream-visions with those of the most frequent miracles, as Gregory records them, can hardly be accidental. It looks as though the dream-visions and apparitions are the visionary counterpart, the imaginative content, of these miracles. They make visible the emotional content of what must have been a pattern of need and its fulfilment in individuals and in society in this period. They also show exactly how individual and social stability was maintained and change initiated through 'identifying with a symbol',[18] in this case the image of an ideal human being.

A. DREAM-VISIONS INSTITUTING NEW CULTS

VIRGINS 'WHITER THAN SNOW': THE DESIRE FOR THE VISIBLE PRESENCE OF THE HOLY
Dream-visions in which commands were given to begin the cult of a deity at a certain place were well-known in antiquity.[19] In Gregory's stories of comparable dream-visions, the saint has taken the place of the deity. Conversion from above seems to have been episcopal policy.[20] However, also in many other stories about 'signs' of the saint's 'presence' — one of the four largest categories of miracles in his writings — Gregory shows us that in this decentralized, arbitrary and violent society the initiative could sometimes come from the people themselves. Recently, P. Brown has

17. As most recently by Dinzelbacher 1981 (who gives a survey of previous studies: 267-80), Quillet 1981 and Patch 1970. Ciccarese 1981 identifies the sources of the longer visions in Gregory's works. Levison 1921 and Aubrun 1980 discuss early medieval visions in their religious, social, and political context, Kamphausen 1975 dreams and visions in Carolingian poetry. Brelich 1967 and Meier 1967 review dreams in ancient Greece, Kelsey 1968 treats the dreams of early Christianity and Dulaey 1973 those of Augustine. Dodds 1951 and 1968, and Nock (1933) 1972 also have a great deal to say about dreams. On dreams and society: Caillois and von Grunebaum 1967.
18. Epstein 1981: 163.
19. As Hanson 1980: 1398.
20. For instance Graus 1965: 140-65 and Stancliffe 1979: 47-51.
21. Compare Newbold 1983: 77.

described what the saint's *praesentia* meant, namely, mercy, concord. Once established, 'the shrine became a fixed point where the solemn, necessary play of "clean power" — of *potentia* as it should be — could be played out in acts of healing, exorcism and rough justice'.[22] What role do visionary experiences play, and for whom, in the 'discovery' of new relics, the confirmation of their authenticity, the building of a cult-centre, and the resistance that all this may meet with?

Gregory explicitly recognizes the role of dream-visions in the formation of a new cult. He says: 'it is [not] improper (*absurdum*) to believe that the Lord often deigns to reveal through visions (*per visiones expertas...revelare*) the manner in which...saints are to be honoured...'.[23] Who are the recipients of these dream-visions? In the following story, we see the initiative coming from the country folk and encountering episcopal opposition.[24] When Gregory's great-grandfather, also named Gregory, was bishop of Langres in the first half of the sixth century, a number of country people (*rustici*) began to pray at a certain tomb in the cemetery of Dijon and 'to receive what they asked for'; other stories usually mention cures as the most frequent requests. One of the recipients of such a favour subsequently took a candle to the tomb, lit it and left it standing there — the traditional gesture of worship.[25] A small boy who tried to take it away was three times prevented from doing so by an extraordinarily large snake. When such things were reported to the bishop, he forbade the people to worship (*adorare*) there. At this point it should be said that he was following a good precedent: already in the late fourth century, as everyone knew from Sulpicius Severus' stories, St Martin had once put a stop to a cult around a deserted tomb because, in his clairvoyance, he saw that it belonged to a brigand and not to a saint.[26] Gregory's great-grandfather, like other bishops, may also, however, have feared that a new local cult centre would diminish episcopal influence in the countryside.[27] The tomb at Dijon was large, and therefore the bishop and the other city people all assumed that it must contain the body of a pagan notable — but there was, in the end, no way of knowing for sure. Or was there? This is where the vision came in. For, as Gregory tells it, the martyr Benignus, who had been put to death in Dijon in the third

22. Brown 1981: 92, 93, 105.
23. *Glor. conf.* 40. Instructions on honouring that coincide with those for a cure in *Glor. conf.* 17 and 35. See also *Glor. conf.* 5 and *Virt. Jul.* 28.
24. *Glor. mart.* 50.
25. See p. 158.
26. Severus, *Vit. Mart.* 11.
27. Compare Wood 1979: 75.

century and whose resting-place was then unknown, appeared (*se...revelat*) to the bishop. (Gregory does not say whether this was in a dream or at what time of the day or night.) The martyr said to him, 'What are you doing? Not only are you casting aspersions on me but even on those who honour me. Stop this, I beg you, and let a building be placed over me instead, as soon as you can!' Shaken by this vision (*visione concussus*), the bishop rushed to the martyr's tomb and tearfully implored forgiveness for his ignorance. The vision here brought a certainty and thereby effected a legitimation that could have been attained in no other way. Socially speaking, it also made the bishops' *volte-face* possible with the minimum loss of prestige: he had acted not under the pressure of the peasants but upon a supernatural command. And so everyone's needs could be satisfied.

When, a few years later, travellers from Italy brought with them the history of Benignus' martyrdom, the number of miracles at his tomb increased.[28] Elsewhere, when no written passion could be found, a martyr appeared in a dream-vision to two abbots to let them know how he was martyred.[29] This suggests increased popularity but also — significantly, as we shall see — a connection between being able to entertain mental pictures of a saint and the effectuation of miracles. During the construction of a large church over the tomb of Benignus, however, it was the labourers who had a visionary experience:

> a certain old woman was seen (*visum est*) by the builders to come out of the church [of Paschasia, nearby]. She was clothed in black, with hair white as a swan and she had a beautiful face. Speaking to them, she said,
> 'Greetings, my dearest friends! Carry on with your good work; let the machines be set up by which this building will be raised, and let the work be accomplished as quickly as it deserves, with such a foreman. For if only your eyes could see more sharply, you would perceive the holy Benignus leading you in the construction!'
> Having said this, she returned to the church out of which she had come and never showed herself to anyone (*nulli comparuit*) thereafter. The men of the time thought that the blessed Paschasia had appeared (*apparuisse*) there.

Here everyone is wide awake (Gregory does not say that they are having their midday siesta) and engaged in practical activity. Gregory's verbs 'was seen', 'showed herself' and 'appeared' indicate an apparition or an epiphany. Yet it seems as though the appeareance was not, at the moment of its occurrence, experienced as something extraordinary. The woman's words probably express and fulfil a need felt by the workers, that is, for

---

28. In another story, Gregory expicitly says that a saint receives less veneration when the history of his passion is not known (*Glor. mart.* 63).
29. Compare *Glor. mart.* 55, *Virt. Jul.* 29.

the 'bodily' presence of the saint helping them. Only later do they, cautiously, identify her as a saint.

The same need is more acutely evident and visibly fulfilled in the story which Gregory must have heard from his predecessor about the translation of St Martin's tomb in Tours about 100 years before his time.[30] After three days of unsuccessfully trying to lift St Martin's sarcophagus to bring it to the new church, the priests were on the point of despair. Then, 'an old man appeared (*apparuit*) to them, whose venerable hair shone with a brightness like snow, and who said he was an abbot'. Here, again, we have the figure of an aged and venerable person. He seems to embody what P. Dinzelbacher calls the *senectus*-ideal[31] of the early Middle Ages. (This ideal cannot be found in the longer visions: the latter — evidently — do not always reflect contemporary preoccupations.) Again, we see that luminous white hair is found especially venerable or perhaps even heavenly; it resembles the hair of the risen Christ in Apoc. 1:14: 'his head and his hair were white as white wool, white as snow'. The 'abbot' then said to the priests,

> 'Why are you so upset and what are you waiting for? Don't you see St Martin standing here ready to help you as soon as you put your hand under [the sarcophagus]?' Then, while crosses and burning candles were held up and everyone joined in singing psalms antiphonally, he threw his cloak off and put his hands under the sarcophagus together with the priests. At the first try of the old man it immediately came up with the greatest of ease and was carried with the help of God, to its new place in the church.

When, after the ceremonies, the bishop wished to invite the 'abbot' to the meal that followed, he could not be found — although no one had seen him leave the church.

In the following story,[32] signs of a saint's 'presence' and not granted prayers, seem to stand at the beginning of a new cult. Gregory's report breathes the air of discovery:

> In the...territory of Tours there was a little hill, completely covered with briars, brambles and wild vines so dense that one could hardly get through. Rumour had it that two consecrated virgins were buried there. After the faithful had very often seen a divinely lit light (*lumen accensum divinitus*) there on the nights before holy days, one of them who was bolder than the others and relied on his nerve, dared to go there on a dark night. There he saw a candle of marvellous whiteness burning with an immense brilliance. When he had looked at it for a long time with wonderment, he left, and told the others what he had seen.
>
> After this, two virgins showed themselves in a dream-vision (*se...per visum ostendunt*) to one of the inhabitants of the village. They said they were indeed

30. *Virt. Mart.* 1.6.
31. Dinzelbacher 1981: 236.
32. *Glor. conf.* 18.

buried there and that they could no longer endure the beating down of the rains without some kind of shelter; if this man knew what was good for him, he would be well advised to cut down the brush and build a roof over their tombs. When the man woke up (*expergefactus*), however, other thoughts came into his mind and he forgot what he had seen. The following night the virgins appeared (*apparuerunt*) again with menacing faces threatening him terribly that if he did not cover the place he would die that very year. Terror-stricken by the vision (*territus...visu*), the man took an axe, chopped the brush away and uncovered the tombs. On these he found large drops of candlewax emitting a lovely smell like incense. With oxen and a cart he gathered stones, and in the summer he built a chapel. When he had finished the work, he went to the blessed [Bishop] Eufronius, who then administered the church of Tours, to ask him to consecrate it.

But the bishop, who was already failing through old age, excused himself from going, saying, 'As you see, my son, I am getting old, and the winter is more severe than usual: it rains almost continuously, the winds blow furiously, the rivers are swollen, and the very roads are flooded and dissolved in mire; my age does not permit me to travel now under such conditions'.

Having heard this, the man left the presence of the bishop and went home deeply grieved. But when the bishop lay down that night to sleep, he saw the two virgins standing by him (*vidit...astare sibi*). The elder of the two said to him with a sad face, 'Why are we out of your favour, most blessed bishop? What harm have we done to the region entrusted to you by God? Why do you look down on us? Why do you refuse to come to bless the building that a faithful man has made for us? Come now, we beseech you in the name of the almighty God, whose servants we are!' Having said this, she let the tears stream down her cheeks.

When the bishop woke up, he called the rector of the church house and said, 'I have sinned by not going with that man. For I have just seen the two virgins reproaching me for this, and I am afraid to incur the wrath of God if I refuse to go there'.

Then he left hastily to begin his journey. As he travelled, the rains stopped and the storm died down. Having accomplished his journey and consecrated the chapel, he returned home without difficulty. And he often used to describe the faces and the figures of the virgins: one he said to be taller than the other, but not on account of greater merit, for they were both whiter than snow. He called the one Maura, the other Britta, saying that they themselves had told him their names.

Here again the initiative is with the people of the countryside and the bishop is at first opposed. After the indirect signs of the virgins' presence, a dream gives the actual command to begin the cult. As Gregory's peasants often do,[34] this one at first disregards the dream. The bishop, however, acts immediately upon his dream-vision. Obedience to commands in dreams may thus have been part of a Christian culture that the church imposed on the peasants from above: elsewhere Gregory describes a lack of know-how with regard to the treatment of saints, holy things and even demons, as 'rusticity (*rusticitas*)', but this can

---

33. Compare on this terminology Hanson 1980: 1410.
34. For instance *Glor. mart.* 47.

occasionally apply to non-peasants such as himself as well.[35] The second command to the peasant is a direct threat; the command to the bishop is formulated as a tearful request (perhaps because of his position?). The women, in any case, are perfectly capable of using coercion if they wish to do so, and in this they are no less than men. Their words may reflect the bishop's initial reservations: 'What harm have we done to the regions entrusted to you...?' To his flock, the bishop could explain his visit to the shrine after all as a divine command, and the dream-vision moreover supplied a description of the physical appearance (in which white luminosity was again prominent) and the names (up till then evidently unknown) of the virgins. Again, a difficult situation was resolved smoothly according to everyone's needs through a dream.

Gregory mentions other cases in which overgrown tombs are 'discovered' to be those of saints by means of dreams.[36] In some cases, like that described above, part of the motive for such a discovery may have been simply the people's desire for a chapel that was nearby. After 270 A.D. there was migration from the valleys into the less fertile hill-country and many of these new villages did not yet have a church of their own.[37] In addition, the desire for relics and their benefits probably made the villagers interested in deserted tombs. What was then needed was an incontrovertible 'proof' that these were inhabited by saints. Not only cures and dreams but also luminous and olfactory phenomena, which may be grouped with dreams as, in a sense, visionary experiences, provided this: certainty from somewhere outside human society about a question which society itself could not definitively answer.[38] Sometimes, however, the initiation of a cult of one so recently deceased could have political undertones and was probably experienced as an indirect criticism of the bishop then in office.[39] In Bourges for instance, when the tomb of its first bishop Ursinus was revealed in a dream to the abbot of one of the city churches[40] (whom Gregory explicitly mentions as being a relative of the former bishop), Bishop Probianus (*552-558*) at first refused to take the matter seriously.[41] Here simultaneous dreams in which

---

35. As in *Glor. mart.* 6: this was in fact, a recognizable and healthy (temporary) scepticism as to how an undistinguished traveller from the East could have been able to obtain a piece of cloth that had enveloped the true Cross, when he (Gregory) knew that no one was allowed to even come near it there.
36. *Glor. conf.* 17, 80; *Glor. mart.* 46, 47, 62.
37. Stancliffe 1979: 46.
38. Sometimes, however, the bishop could not be convinced: *Glor. conf.* 60.
39. As Brown 1977 in Brown 1982: 245.
40. On the subject of 'abbot of a church', see Pietri 1983a.
41. *Glor. conf.* 80. Compare *Glor. mart.* 48, in which martyrs who have been burned

Ursinus appeared to Bishop Germanus of Paris, who was then staying with Bishop Probianus, as well as again to Abbot Augustus, led to a solution. When they had found out about each other's dreams, the two men first went secretly the following night and dug in the place that the saint had indicated in the dream. There they found a tomb with a perfectly preserved body — an unmistakable indication of sainthood in those days.[42] When they showed Bishop Probianus the next day what they had found, the matter was settled. Later, when the sarcophagus was ceremonially being carried on cross-beams into the main church and the door turned out to be too narrow for these beams, while the sarcophagus was too heavy to lift without them, Bishop Germanus knew what to do:

> he raised his voice and said, 'Holy Bishop of God, if it is your wish to enter into this church, let us feel the alleviation of your help!'
> And at once the sarcophagus, which till then had only been able to be carried by a large number of people, became so light that a few hands could carry it without beams to its place.

If Gregory himself believed, and expected his readers to believe, that such things could actually happen again and again, we should take such statements seriously. It is one of the many indications that Gregory and his friends asked for and received inner experiences which they then interpreted as being caused by the activity of a saint. When a heavy sarcophagus suddenly seems lighter, something has happened inside the carriers. Gregory and his contemporaries perceived that 'something' as outside themselves: the saint, invisibly, helping them. In the course of this study it will become evident that the image of the saint speaking or acting could be the form in which intra-mental as well as social processes were apprehended. This, of course, still occurs in so-called archaic societies today.[43]

A story such as that about how a bishop of Javols managed to substitute the veneration of St Hilary of Poitiers[44] for that of a lake on Mt Helarus in the Gevaudan country indicates that the cult of Christian saints was probably very useful in the conversion of the countryside. The fact that new chapels were consecrated with (certified) relics of known saints also points in this direction.[45] Gregory tells us of one bishop who

> into ashes which have been thrown into the river appear to say that their ashes are on the spot at which they were burned; these were collected, placed under the altar of a new, large church and worked many miracles.

42. As also in *Glor. conf.* 35. In *Vit. patr.* 7.4 Gregory typically connects the uncorrupted state of the body with the uncorrupted state of the man's soul during his earthly life.
43. As Douglas 1966: 83-4.
44. Or Hilary of Gabali (Bordier 1860: 345): *Glor. conf.* 2.
45. *Hist.* 10.30. Compare Stancliffe 1979: 56.

took the trouble to obtain exactly the right relics for one of the chapels in his diocese.[46] In that instance, however, although his body had not yet been found, the cult for that particular martyr was already in existence. Bishop Ebregisil of Cologne[47] had built a church in Xanten for Mallosus, who had been martyred there, 'so that, if he should receive some revelation (*revelatio*) about the martyr, he could, with God's help, place the holy limbs in it'. In the apse of the new church he included the old chapel that had been dedicated to the saint. Meanwhile, 'he waited for the kindness of the Lord to order something to be revealed (*revelari*) about [the resting-place of] the martyr.' Some time later, a certain deacon of Metz was informed where the martyr lay buried 'by being led there in a vision (*per visum ductus*)'. When this man subsequently came to the bishop and 'remembered the seemingly certain indications (*quasi certa signa*) that he had seen in his vision (*per visum viderat*)', although he had never been in the place before, he told the bishop to dig in the middle of the old chapel, which was now the apse of the new church. At a depth of seven feet, the bishop smelled an overwhelmingly lovely perfume and cried, 'I believe that Christ is revealing his martyr to me when he envelops me with such sweetness!' In fact, they soon found a perfectly preserved corpse, which could only be that of the saint. The searching continued, however; Gregory says in conclusion that the body of another martyr was thought to be buried in the vicinity but that its place had not yet been revealed (*revelatum*). Here, the bishop took the initiative to consolidate an already existing cult. The only certain way to find and identify relics was through revelation — which could be a dream but also a beautiful smell — and one could evidently ask for this.

Finally, Gregory tells how a dream not only started a cult but also helped to effect what looks like a conversion.[48] One evening at sunset, pious travellers carrying relics of the martyr Saturninus asked hospitality of a poor man in the country around Brioude in Auvergne. When he had admitted them into his little house (perhaps built of wood and mud and with a roof of leaves or thatch)[49] they showed him what they were carrying. For safe-keeping, he suggested that they put the relics on top of a vase of grain in his store-room during their stay. After supper, they probably told him more about the martyr and about the benefits that could be gained through his relics. The next morning, the travellers left and continued their journey. That night,

46. *Glor. mart.* 62.
47. He may have told Gregory the following story when they met each other in Poitiers in 590 to check the revolt in the convent there (*Hist.* 10.15).
48. *Glor. mart.* 47.
49. As in *Glor. mart.* 10. Compare Lelong 1963: 112-3.

the man was admonished by a vision (*visum*) in which a certain old man said to him, 'Don't remain in this place, for it is sanctified by the relics of the martyr Saturninus'. The man, however, did not take the vision seriously (*parvipendens visionem*) and, in his boorishness (*ut habet rusticitas*), he forgot what he had been commanded to do. Soon, he lapsed into melancholy (*taedium*) and his slender means began slowly to dwindle; his wife too wasted away by another languor (*languor*). What more shall I say? Within a year he was reduced to such poverty that nothing remained to him to feed or clothe himself with, as human needs demand.

Having finally come to himself (*conversus ad se*), he said to his wife, 'I have sinned against God and his saints by not leaving this house as I have been commanded to do. And I know that the ills that we suffer have come on account of this. Let us now, however, obey the vision (*visio*) which we saw, and remove our house from this place, so that we may be saved'.

When he had broken down his cottage and taken it away, he built a chapel of wooden planks on the same spot, and poured forth prayers there every day, imploring the help of the martyr. Finally the illness (literally, wounding strokes: *plagi*) ceased; he went back to work and with such good results that in a short time he regained more than he had lost.

This vision, which is called *visum* as well as *visio*, occurred at night and was therefore probably a dream-vision. Who was the 'certain old man'? He did not speak of 'my' relics (in Gregory's version of the story at least) yet who could he be if not the saint himself? Or is the 'certain old man' whom we meet again and again in the visions Gregory describes, when not otherwise identified, simply the traditional pagan ancestor-figure now regarded as an angel? The command he gives is a very drastic one indeed: tear down your house and build a chapel for the saint in its place. In other words, destroy your old way of life and begin a new one. The concluding remark that he was better off in the end than before is typical Gregorian, practical psychology.

What, in fact, could have happened to this one poor nameless peasant (*quidam pauper*) who, from among the many such about whom we will never have similar information, was rescued from obscurity by Gregory's interest in his experience? There seem to be three crucial moments in the whole chronological sequence: first, the experience of the physical presence of the relics in his house for one night, second, the dream, and third, his ultimate insight into the connection of these two events with his by then deplorable physical and economic condition. This last entailed the decision to change his life. It seems likely that a nearby priest helped him arrive at this interpretation and this decision. Gregory's writings are full of stories about relics that, upon contact, heal or paralyze, revive from death or kill instantly: for Christians, they were objects filled with a terrifying power. As Gregory tells it, the words spoken by the old man in the dream the night after the travellers left indicate that the latter must also have told him about this quality; the place was now 'made holy' through the contact with the relics, and therefore no longer fit for ordinary human habitation. In another story, Gregory reports that a piece of the wood from St Martin's bed left lying around in the house of one of his (presumably Christian) servants caused the man and his whole family to fall ill; when, in accordance with a similar dream-command, they had given the wood to Gregory so that he could put it in an appropriate place, they regained their health.[50] In this case, however, the house is not 'sanctified'. The peasant's typical ignorance of how to feel and act towards holy objects and holy messages such as in dreams made him at first continue his life as though nothing had happened.

It is impossible to know, of course, whether or not his illness (and that of his wife) was in fact caused by a quite understandable internal conflict: they had, on the one hand, received what might be described as a new experience of the numinous brought about by the relics and the dream, and this brought with it also the vague realization that a change in old attitudes was called for; on the other hand, old habits die hard and common-sense objects most strongly that tearing down one's perfectly good house for some insubstantial idea is rather overdoing it and in any case quite impractical. It could also be, however, that these people simply came upon hard times and then, helped by the priest, found a 'cause' for these. In any event, Gregory suggests that their *taedium* and *languor*, which certainly sound like psychic rather than physical illnesses, were punishments by the saint[51] for their neglect of the command and for the dishonouring of his relics. However this may have been, the dream and its interpretation made sense of the situation and enabled the peasant to redirect his energy and so to do something about it. After all, he now had nothing more to lose.

In all the above cases, visionary experiences provided either an imperative to begin a new cult or else authoritative information that legitimized an already existing one, both of which expressed social needs or solved conflicts in a manner that could be satisfying to all parties involved. Put in another way, one could say that the image of the saint saying or doing something was the way in which at that time individual as well as social processes were apprehended. Gregory presents the peasants as the ones who usually took the initiative in starting a new cult, probably because this

50 *Virt. Mart.* 1.35. Sometimes saints appear to suggest improvements in their cult: *Glor. conf.* 5, 64.
51. Gregory reports that when Bishop Priscus and his house were 'struck by the *virtus*' of the just dead Bishop Nicetius, they were all 'trembling', 'pale', and 'stunned' (*tremens, decolor, stupidus*) (*Hist.* 4.36). Similarly *Virt. Jul.* 14.

results in better stories than all his dedications of new chapels with 'recognized' relics, which are, of course, the other side of the picture. His constant apologetic for the cult of saints and his recording of as many saints' miracles as he could also show that promoting the veneration of saints was conscious church policy — as long as these cults could be controlled by the bishop. The receptivity to dreams, on the other hand, is described as something the peasant still had to learn from priests and bishops. These dreams seem to continue, in Christian form, the ancient pagan dream tradition of venerable figures communicating commands.

The dream-visions described, then, helped found cults at specific places where a saint was experienced as especially accessible to human request, that is, the place where his physical remains were buried. There, visionary experiences could also occur which indicated that he was 'bodily' present helping his clients even in their physical work. All this seems to show that a deep need for the visible presence of the holy was being met. The scope of the saint's activity as a 'patron' in this decentralized society has been penetratingly described by P. Brown.[52] In what follows, I will try to show exactly how, in Gregory's stories, dreams could function in the cult of the saints.

B. THE SAINT IN VISIONARY EXPERIENCE DURING CURES

Cures are by far the largest category of miracles in Gregory's stories. It has been suggested that many of the reported illnesses were of nervous origin and that their incidence was almost certainly connected with the prevalent physical insecurity and frequent natural disasters such as famines and epidemics.[53] The dream-visions that Gregory records show how some of these cures took place.

First of all, he believes firmly that dream-visions can reveal the means by which the sick are to be cured.[54] As a child, he had himself twice had dream-visions (*visum noctis, visio*) in which a 'person (*persona*)' told him how his ailing father could be cured. The first time, the name of the Bible book Joshua (which Gregory thought he had at that time not yet heard) was to be inscribed on a sliver of wood which was to be placed under his father's pillow. The second time, the person told him to do what Tobith's son, upon the command of an angel (*angelus*), had done to heal his blind father:[55] let the heart and liver of a fish smoulder on hot coals and the smoke rise to 'fumigate' his father's eyes. It should be said at this point

---

52. Especially Brown 1981. See also Corbett 1981.
53. Oury 1983: 21; Rousselle 1976: 1104; Mollat 1978: 28-44.
54. *Glor. conf.* 40.
55. Tobith 6:6, 8:2-3.

that Gregory again thought he had not read (or heard about the contents of) the book and that, both times, his father was suffering from gout. In the morning, each time, Gregory told his mother what he had seen (*quae videram*) and she 'ordered the commands of the vision (*visionis praecepta*) to be carried out'. As soon as these 'remedies' were applied, his father recovered instantly (*statim, protinus*). Both remedies are pure magic. The first is an amulet using the power of the Biblical name that most resembles 'Jesus'. The second repeats an angelic prescription to drive out the demon causing blindness.[56] (Bearing in mind the instructions Gregory once gave to his brother-in-law to let the light of the candle-flame chase the darkness from his eyes and thereby cure his fever, is there, perhaps, also a contamination of meaning here (as elsewhere in Gregory's writings) between 'illness' in general and (spiritual) blindness, i.e. sinfulness?) In both cases, Gregory and his parents were hoping for or expecting a symbolic action to effect physical results. It was apparently not enough to simply find some such action or name in the Bible oneself: to be authoritative or perhaps even 'permitted', such a symbolic remedy had to be 'commanded' in a dream-vision, and this could be received even by a child. Nothing is said about any previous attempts at a cure with the Roman tradition of herbal home medicines;[57] perhaps they had been tried and had failed to bring improvement. The remedy-prescribing dream had also been an antique tradition at incubation centres, such as the temples of Asclepius.[58] In Gregory's case, the dream solved a problem not only by indicating a solution but, also at the same time, by furnishing the requisite authority for this solution. Gregory (is he conscious of continuing a pagan tradition?) carefully links both dreams to the Bible. Elsewhere, he mentions the fact that the martyrs Cosmas and Damian gave many people such instructions.[59] Two of the dreams occurring in Gregory's stories offer a somewhat different 'remedy': the provision of an, undoubtedly costly, cover for the open sarcophagus of a saint.[60] In both cases, instant recovery followed.

Elsewhere, Gregory lets us see that someone who was possibly the saint could appear in a dream-vision either to the patient himself or to one of his relatives, and say that the invalid should come to the saint's church to

56. On amulets with biblical and angel's names: Harmening 1979: 235-47 and d'Alverny 1962: 163-4. On fumigation and the magical use of Jesus' name: Aune 1980: 1545-9.
57. See Rousselle 1976.
58. See Meier 1949, 1967 and 1972.
59. *Glor. mart.* 97.
60. *Glor. conf.* 17, 35.

be healed there.⁶¹ As we shall see below, Gregory's stories show that people often stayed in the church, praying, even during the night, whether a vigil was being held or not. His friend Wulfilaicus even instructed a certain patient to sleep on a bed in the church during the night, after praying there the whole day.⁶² Other people make a point of sleeping as close to the church as possible.⁶³ This, of course, resembles the antique pagan practice of incubation, during which a god appeared in a dream to heal on the spot or to prescribe a remedy.⁶⁴ Although the term is not used and Gregory presents sleeping in the church as more or less accidental (even though he does mention elsewhere that churches are locked at night),⁶⁵ the whole situation as well as the dreams are very similar. As with the oracular dream, I think this is one of the many mental habits that, in Christian form, persisted from pagan Roman culture. Recent research has demonstrated that continuities also existed in the fourth century between pagan remedies used in Gaul and the 'miraculous' cures of St Martin.⁶⁶ It is clear, and understandable, that converted men and women took many of the old pagan forms into their new, Christian religion.

As for the experiential content of these Christianized forms, we can be sure only of Gregory's own view of it. His description of the moment of healing, which we examined in the previous chapter, centres on contrition and forgiveness.⁶⁷ He believes that symbolic action and requests addressed to an omnipotent God achieve results only when carried out with the proper, humble and reverent attitude. What happens in the pagan and Christian cures involving visionary experience bears a striking resemblance to the conscious therapeutic uses made of imagination in modern psychological therapy.⁶⁸ One of the more prominent practi-

61. For instance, *Virt. Mart.* 2.23, 30, 31, 41; 4.17; *Virt. Jul.* 22, 47; *Glor. conf.* 35, 94, 104; *Vit. patr.* 8.8, 19.4.
62. *Hist.* 8.16. In *Virt. Mart.* 2.4 Gregory reports that a priest's slave was sleeping *in a bed* near St Martin's tomb when he was cured during a dream. Compare *Glor. mart.* 5 and *Virt. Jul.* 9 and see p. 237.
63. As in *Glor. mart.* 99; *Virt. Jul.* 42.
64. On incubation in antiquity, see Meier 1949, 1966, 1972; Mensching 1957: 67; Kelsey 1973: 47-50; Siefert 1983; Cumont 1949: 86; Dodds 1968: 46. Dulaey 1973: 186-8 gives an affirmative answer to the question of the existence of Christian incubation in Africa at the time of Augustine; Le Goff 1977: 305 recognizes it in Gregory's stories.
65. *Hist.* 7.22.
66. Rousselle 1976.
67. See pp. 202-3.
68. On the uses of imagination in modern psychotherapy see for instance, Singer 1974, Leuner 1980b and Epstein 1981. On imagination in ancient healing: Meier 1949 and Siefert 1983.

tioners of such a therapy even says: 'Stimulation of the deeper levels of the unconscious is the art of psychotherapy, which really can be described only by the unscientific term "exorcism" '.[69] The transformational potentialities of mental images can also be seen in Gregory's stories.

'A FILTHY AND DEADLY SHADE': THE EXORCISM OF NEGATIVE EMOTIONS

There is one dream-vision reported by Gregory in which 'a certain man' (who, in the context, is almost certainly St Martin), suggested yet another kind of remedy.[70] This story shows more clearly than any other what was then thought to be the cause and the nature of illness and of the cure. At the same time, however, we see as it were the concretizations of opposing emotions appearing as 'persons': on the one hand, a figure presented as generating hate and abject fear, on the other, one experienced as inspiring love and radiant confidence. This is one of the last stories Gregory wrote, for it took place in 593 shortly before his death, when King Childebert made his first royal entry into Orléans. One of the court servants was at that time stricken by the 'three-day fever' (perhaps a kind of malaria),[71] as a result of which he spent every third day shaking with fever. When Gregory, who was present for the celebration, heard about the man's affliction, he gave him a potion made of wine or water mixed with dust from St Martin's tomb — something he evidently carried about with him, perhaps in a little capsule on a chain around his neck.[72]

> As the man was drinking it, the shaking was suppressed (*compressus*) and he recovered his health.
>
> The following night, however, when the day approached in which he had been accustomed to start shaking [with fever], he saw in a dream-vision (*visum*) a most hideous figure (*persona teterrima*) coming towards him, who said to him,
>
> 'Look here, the time for your shaking has come, so why are you pretending that it hasn't? Come on, do what you always do!'
>
> As he was saying this, a certain man approached with a shining face, hair white as snow, and an elegant appearance, who said to the servant, 'Don't shake now, but make the sign of the venerable Cross upon your forehead and you will be cured instantly'.
>
> The servant thereupon woke up (*in hac visione expergefactus*), and after he had fortified (*munitus*) himself with this sign as he had been commanded to do, he never again suffered from that illness.

Late antique pagan as well as Christian tradition ascribed many illnesses to demons, and so, evidently, did Gregory. This cure, then, is basically an

---

69. Kretschmer 1962 in Tart 1969: 228.
70. *Virt. Mart.* 4.37.
71. Rouche 1981: 322.
72. Compare *Glor. mart.* 10, *Hist.* 8.15, *Virt. Mart.* 3.60 and *Virt. Jul.* 34.

exorcism;[73] and the latter, as the terms *compressus* and *munitus* already show, is a question of one power overcoming another. Although sometimes disguised as Christ,[74] an angel of light or St Martin,[75] apparitions of evil power in his stories are often dark, hideous, fearsome and foul-smelling.[76] The radiant and venerable aristocrat represents good, Christian power which is full of love and confidence. The one is the image of emotions that destroy individuals and communities, the other of feelings that work towards their integration. The dream-vision seems to be the mode in which inner emotional events and processes are apprehended: they appear in it as persons or figures outside oneself. The luminous and venerable old man who here gives the instructions for the cure seems to function as what in modern psychology is designated as the image or symbol of the ideal 'higher' self.[77] Later, we shall meet him again and again, more and less clearly perceived, in the stories of miraculous cures. But first a closer look at the visionary manifestations and actions of his opponent, the demon, and at the manner in which this latter held sick individuals in his power should make clearer what, in Gregory's view, actually happened in a cure.

A not inconsiderable number of the ailments that Gregory describes are specified as having come about suddenly. In these cases, Gregory mentions or seems to assume the agency of the devil, a demon or some shade or ghost. In the cases of possession this is, of course, very clear. Elsewhere, the formulation is significant: 'he was struck with blindness by the influx of the Treacherous One (*caecitate insidiatore immittente percussus est*)' or 'by the influx (*incursum*) of the Treacherous One'.[78] This could be understood as a concomitant spiritual blindness to the Truth as well, as in the case of the Arian bishop Cirola's attempt at a false miracle.[79] Insanity, too, is attributed to 'a wickedness of diabolical

---

73. As Brown 1981: 106-13. Compare on demons and/or sin as cause of illness in Gregory's stories, Blume: 1970: 167-8. In early Christianity: Kelsey 1973: 88-9,94-5 and 196-7. On demons as source of all misfortune: Brown 1970 in Brown 1972: 131. On the extreme preoccupation with demons and evil spirits in the early Middle Ages and the resulting need for exorcism, see Angenendt 1982 in Cristianizzazione 1982b: 186-9.
74. *Vit. patr.* 10.2.
75. *Vit. patr.* 9.2.
76. *Vit. patr.* 17.3, and *Vit. patr.* 11.1. Compare Severus' *Vita Martini* 24.8 and Fontaine 1968: 850.
77. On the hero as a symbol of transformation see Jung 1952: 284-345. Kelsey 1968: 206 however mentions 'the wise old man' and 'the Self (or inner redeemer)' as separate archetypes.
78. *Virt. Mart.* 2.15; *Virt. Mart.* 3.16,28.
79. *Hist.* 2.3.

origin',[80] but also to 'lunatic demons', having the appearance of frogs:[81] in the latter case, however, the illness is also called 'epilepsy'. Sudden nervous illnesses of contraction and paralysis are also associated with a 'diabolical influx (*incursio diabolica*)' or an 'influx of diabolical cunning (*immissio...artis diabolicae*)'.[82] How this could be experienced as happening is shown in the story of a man to whom, when he got up one morning and walked through the door of his house, 'it seemed...as though someone hit him on the head'; he fell down as if dead, and when he later regained consciousness he could not speak.[83] Elsewhere, 'a most hideous shade' once dragged a woman around in her house so that she was unable to speak afterwards; since this shade (or ghost) also bothered the other occupants of the house, they finally moved away.[84] It was demons also who brought or caused bubonic plague in Trier.[85]

These sudden illnesses are often explicitly described as beginning with a moment of fear: sometimes because of being enveloped in a cloud of swirling dust, chaff or by a swarm of flies, or by the blowing of a sudden violent wind, or by the apparition of an ugly shade or demon. Gregory describes this experience with expressions such as 'stricken with fear (*pavore perculsus*)', 'extreme fear (*pavor pessimus*)' and 'senseless with fear (*conterrita a pavore*)'.[86] The obscurity of night, in which all sensations were sudden because one could not see them coming, was also fearsome (*nox horribilis*).[87] Sometimes Gregory describes a sudden fear (*per visum periculi*) while lying in bed (asleep?) at night as the onset or crisis of an illness, but sometimes 'a demonic shade (*daemonis umbra*)' is in some way perceived.[88] Two boys became ill after they had been 'intensely frightened (*exterriti valde*)' by the apparition of 'a band of demons' looking like 'a choir of singing women' in the church at night and had forgotten to protect themselves with the sign of the Cross.[89]

The story of a bishop who had a similar experience is very revealing.[90] When Bishop Eparchius of Clermont once entered the church at night to sing songs of thanksgiving, 'he found the church full of demons and their

80. *Hist.* 10.25; similarly *Virt. Mart.* 1.26; 2.53.
81. *Virt. Mart.* 2.18.
82. *Virt. Mart.* 3.14. See Kelsey 1973: 8-9 on demons as 'complexes' and 'archetypes'.
83. *Virt. Mart.* 4.40.
84. *Virt. Mart.* 3.37.
85. *Vit. patr.* 17.4.
86. Respectively *Virt. mart.* 4.22; 1.26; 2.11. Similarly, *terror* in *Virt. mart.* 2.26, 31.
87. *Virt. Mart.* 2.17.
88. *Virt. Mart.* 2.11, 26; *Glor. mart.* 6.
89. *Virt. Mart.* 2.45.
90. *Hist.* 2.21.

chief himself, in the form of a woman hung with jewels sitting on the bishop's seat'. Since this figure is later called 'the Enemy', an appellation that Gregory elsewhere reserves for the devil,[91] it seems evident that the latter is taken to be the director of demons. Eparchius, with his clerical know-how, managed to keep his wits about him and addressed the figure as follows,

> 'O accursed whore, is it not enough for you to infect everything with your various kinds of pollutions (*variis pollutionibus infecire*)? Must you even defile (*coinguinas*) the seat consecrated to God by the stinking touch of your sitting on it? Get out of the house of God, so that it won't be besmirched (*polluatur*) any further by you!'
>
> The woman replied, 'Since you call me a whore, I will ensnare you with the desire for women!' Having said this, she vanished like smoke. Nevertheless, the bishop was thereupon tempted by feelings of bodily concupiscence. Since he had fortified himself with the sign of the Cross, however, the Enemy was not able to harm him.

Prudentius castigates the use of jewelry for women and contemporary hymns intended to be sung before going to sleep also ask for protection against lascivious demons, sometimes mentioning the efficacy of the sign of the Cross against these demons.[92] Suzanne Wemple has connected the gradual institutionalization of clerical celibacy in the Gaul of this period with a concern for what she designates as 'ritual purity'. This could take the form of misogyny, evident in the progressive exclusion of women from all participation in official church roles. Eventually they were not even allowed to come near the altar or to touch the Eucharist: as in this story, their touch was equivalent to 'pollution'.[93] A. Angenendt, however, has connected what he also calls a concern for purification and ritual purity with the excessive preoccupation with evil power in the form of demons; he calls their exorcism and the introduction of 'good' power (by blessings, for instance) the basis of early medieval religion.[94] The visionary experience shows the imaginations connected with such a practice.

Another story shows that the devil could also send a shade or ghost to induce someone to commit suicide (*instigante diabolo*).[95] With this deed in mind, a man withdrew to a quiet place in his house and attached a rope to an overhead beam. As he did this, even while he was tying the knot, he

91. As in *Hist.* 8.15: *per invidiam inimici.* Compare Bartelink 1970.
92. On jewelry for women: Prudentius, *Hamart.* 264-72. Protection against demons during sleep: Prudentius, *Cathem.* 6.131-6 and *Anal. hyumn.* 51.28 n. 26; 51.19 n. 19.
93. Wemple 1981: 127-41. The council of Autun (between 573 and 603), c. 42 decrees that women were not to touch the Eucharist with their bare hands (Maassen 1893: 183).
94. Angenendt 1982 in Cristianizzazione 1982a: 186-94.
95. *Glor. mart.* 28.

nevertheless kept calling upon the apostle Paul and saying, 'Help me, holy Paul!'

> Then a filthy and deadly shade (*umbra squalida atque funesta*), whose face resembled that of the devil, appeared to him (*apparuit ei*) and urged him on, saying, 'Go on, do it! Don't take so long! Finish what you've started!'
>
> And the man, as he went on making preparations to end his life kept on saying, 'Most blessed Paul, be my helper!'
>
> When the knot was ready and the shade urged the man more forcefully than before to go ahead and put his neck in it, suddenly there was another shade present, who was similar to the first one and who said to the latter, 'Get out of here as fast as you can, you bungler! Don't you see the apostle Paul coming here? This man has been calling upon him and here he is'.
>
> Then the shades disappeared (*evanescentes*) and the man came to his senses (*ad sensum suum reversus*). He traced the Cross of the Lord's power (*crux virtutis dominicae*) on his heaving breast, and letting tears flow profusely over his bended knees, he repented (*poenitentiam...agebat*) of his attempt.

These horrid shades appeared to the man while he was not in his right mind; it is not clear whether this other state of mind was initially induced by these shades (or the devil) or not. The presence of the apostle is here not seen but its effect is felt: the man is freed from something that, given his simultaneous invocation of the apostle, he must have experienced as an involuntary urge. The phrase 'the Cross of the Lord's power'[96] indicates again that this was an exorcism, a therapy effected by the putting to flight of evil spirits by a good 'power'. Before, the man had felt himself to be in the power of the shade. Gregory's people are sometimes said to have valiance in battle (also designated by the term *virtus*),[97] but whenever they think they can rely on themselves alone to achieve what they want, they are disappointed.[98] As Gregory says again and again,[99] man can do nothing substantial without divine aid.

Nevertheless, man was most certainly not helpless. Gregory's stories show that the saint's 'power' that one needed could be more or less manipulated according to a definite set of rules, so as to achieve the desired results. In the visionary experience above, the apostle functions as an exorcist and is felt to be the initiator of the return to common-sense consciousness; he acts as a catalyst to the return of the healthy

96. See Harmening 1979: 237-8.
97. For instance, about the sons of Clovis: *cumque magna virtute pollerent et eis de exercitu rubor copiosus inesset* (*Hist.* 3.1) and *virtus proelii* (*Hist.* 4.9). Similarly, *Hist.* 4.44, 6.4, 7.36.
98. As in *Glor. mart.* 36.
99. As, for instance, in *Hist.* 1.15; *Vit. patr.* 10. *prol.*; *Vit. patr.* 7. *prol.*: *nullus sine Dei ope valebit efficere*; *Hist.* 5.30: *nihil homini qui in Deo spem posuerat adversare valentes*; *Virt. Mart.* 3.34: *nihil medicorum poterat ars valere, nisi cum dominicum adfuisset auxilium.* Compare Friedrich 1951: 19.

personality. But this has come about only after long and continuous calling upon the saint; in other words, after a long effort to identify with the healthy self, of which the saint may be a kind of unconscious and glorified image. When meditated upon, the mental image of the saint may, like that of the Cross traced on one's breast or forehead, have imparted a feeling of strength and confidence — in Gregory's terms, 'power'. In the visions, this imagination is experienced as independent reality, almost certainly because this was exactly what people wanted and believed to be possible. Identifying with or 'living the function of' the symbol results in psychological improvement.[100]

One last story shows how Gregory related this view of illness and health to the fact of divine governance of all events in the world and hence to the state of contemporary society:[101]

> Sisulf, a very poor man from the country around Le Mans, suffered some unknown kind of villainy (*nequitiae*) while he lay sleeping in his garden in the middle of the day. For, as he awoke from his sleep, his fingers were contracted into his palms and he could raise his debilitated hand only with great pain. Stupefied by this pain, he lapsed again into sleep (*sopor*) and saw in a dream-vision (*vidit in visum*) a man standing in front of him, clothed in black but with white hair. Turning to him, this man said,
> 'Why are you so agitated and tearful?'
> Sisulf replied, 'Behold, venerable lord: after I had been sleeping a bit, I woke up with pain and lost the use of my hand. But I don't know what crime I have committed'.
> Then — just as our Lord spoke to his disciples about the man born blind, not because he had sinned, nor his parents, but so that the work of God could be manifested in him[102] — the man said to Sisulf, 'Your affliction is a sign of (*indicat*) the punishment of the sinful people. Go now, therefore, through the villages and fortified places of the region until you reach the city and preach that every man should abstain from robbery, perjury and usury, and that, on the Lord's day, he do no work except attend the solemn mysteries [of mass]. For we [i.e. the saints] have prostrated ourselves before the Lord beseeching forgiveness for the people, and up till now there has been hope of obtaining it if improvement would come about among them. Because it is the indignation of the Lord that causes (*commovet*) the wars, illnesses and the many other evils which the people suffer. And so announce to them quickly that they should try to improve themselves, lest they perish cruelly in their crime. As for you, when you have carried out what I have commanded, hurry to my church at Tours; there I will visit you (*visitans*). For I shall obtain from the Lord that you will be healed'.
> Sisulf then asked him, 'Tell me I pray, sir, who are you and what is your name?'
> The man said, 'I am Martin, bishop of Tours'.
> Upon these words of the saint, the poor man awoke from his sleep (*surrexit a somno*) and, taking up his staff, he began the journey....

100. Compare Epstein 1981: 163, 174-5.
101. *Virt. Mart.* 2.40.
102. John 9:3.

Seven months later, he arrived at Tours and was cured after prostrating himself in the church of St Martin for three days. Gregory says that he heard the story from the man himself.

Sisulf's sudden illness, which could also have been connected with his own sin or that of his parents, was a punishment by the Lord for the state of society; the devil or a demon as intermediate agent is not mentioned, but thereby not necessarily excluded.[103] Gregory's use of the word 'villainy' in fact strongly suggests the intermediate agency of the devil or a demon. The saints, on the other hand, are the intermediaries who ask for and transmit forgiveness and healing. The dream-vision made sense of an inexplicable situation and allowed the patient to do something about it: first, to concentrate on something else, so that his own condition became relatively less important, and second, to go to St Martin's church with the confidence that he would be cured. The details of the dream-message, however, fit in so well with church policy and propaganda (especially the injunction about the observance of Sundays)[104] that one suspects some clerical influence, either upon Sisulf himself during his journey, or by Gregory, in the editing of the story. The man with white hair is addressed as 'venerable lord (*venerabilis dominus*)', and thus seems to have the appearance of someone who rules or has power over men: a member of the ruling class which exercised rights of patronage over the less fortunate. In this case, he identifies himself, upon request, as Martin. The heavenly patron, as Gregory often calls St Martin[105], not surprisingly resembles the earthly one.

Thus the devil, demons or shades, as dynamic images of destructive feelings, can be experienced as the agents that cause illness — even if this happens with the permission or at the command of the Lord as a punishment for sin. The model of the cure is an exorcism: the saint as the dynamic image of positive, constructive emotion drives the evil spirits away. A modern practitioner of the waking-dream therapy has stated:[106] 'Imagination is at once an organ of perception and a force that breathes life, or creativity, into the concrete world. Further, it fuels will.

---

103. For instance, in a case of a man 'deprived of his right mind by diabolic cunning (*diaboli arte*)' who was cured by St Martin but did not, as he had promised, return each year to thank him, 'the power over him was again, as I believe, given to the Enemy (*data ut credo iterum inimico in eum potestate*)' (*Virt. Mart.* 2.53).
104. Stancliffe 1979: 69. The council of Mâcon in 585 was especially concerned with the observance of Sundays: De Clercq 1936: 51 (*Conc. Matisc.* a.585, c.1 in Maassen 1893: 165).
105. As, for instance, in *Hist.* 1.48; *Virt. Mart.* 1.32, 38, 40; 2.6.
106. Epstein 1981: 149.

Imagination and will act interdependently'. In Gregory's stories, meditatively identifying in prayer with the living image of the saint for whom all is possible, releases the positive energy to recover. As we shall see, the image of release in fact becomes manifest in a number of visions connected with cures.

It seems to me that cures and other helpful miracles hinged on this notion that 'all was possible' as an intrinsic quality of what Gregory designates as '(holy) power'. But this unlimited potentiality was an aspect of something deeper. The essence of the healing process was then as it is now not 'power' as pure force, but love. Psychiatry today has recognized that it is only love that heals the emotions and thereby the psyche and the body.[107] Gregory calls this aspect of the saint's power 'compassion (*misericordia*)'.[108] But he can also describe it in a more specific manner, as we shall now see.

'HE SPOKE IN A TENDER AND LOVING MANNER': THE IDEAL OF THE SPIRITUAL BRIDEGROOM

Of all the descriptions of visionary experiences of the saint as a healer, the following is the most detailed and full of feeling.[109] It is also one of the few in which it is not the saint's 'power' but his loving-kindness that is explicitly described as the central quality. Considering all this, it is hardly surprising that the original report derives from a woman. That Gregory can present her feelings so warmly and delicately says something not only about his attitude towards women but also about his qualities as a writer.

> A certain woman named Fedamia, [whose limbs] were fettered by the humour of paralysis (*paralysis humore constricta*) and who had no part of her body without pain, was carried by her relatives to the blessed church of St Julian and put on display there so that she might receive alms from the generous.
>
> One Saturday night, she lay in the arcade adjoining the holy church while the faithful and devout people celebrated the most holy vigil. As she was lying on a couch and sleeping a little (*paululum obdormisset*), she was — in a vision (*per visum*) — shaken and reproached by a certain man, who asked her why she had not joined the others who were presenting God with a night vigil. She answered that she was so feeble in all her limbs that she was unable to walk. Then, while he as it were (*quasi*) supported her and talked to her, the man led her to the [saint's] tomb. While she, in her sleep (*in sopore*), prayed there, it seemed to her as though (*visum est ei quasi*) a heap of chains (*catenae*) fell from all her limbs onto the floor. Awakened by this sound (*a quo etiam sonitu expergefacta*), she felt (*sensit*) that all her limbs had been restored to the fullest health. Immediately she rose from her bed and, to

---

107. Kelsey 1973: 278-306, especially 301.
108. As in *Virt. Mart.* 3. *prol.*
109. *Virt. Jul.* 9.

the astonishment (*stupens*) of all present, she entered the church loudly proclaiming her thanks.

Certain people say, too, that she used to describe the appearance of the man who had talked to her: she said that he was tall of stature, clothed in white, extremely elegant and had a joyful face; that he had blond hair mixed with white and walked gracefully; that his voice was honourable and that he spoke in a tender and loving (*blandissimus*; literally: caressing) manner; and, finally, that the whiteness of his skin shone brighter than the brilliance of lilies — so that among the many thousands of men whom she had seen [during her life], there was not one like him. Therefore it did not seem improbable (*absurdus*) to many people that the blessed martyr [Julian] had appeared (*apparuisse*) to her. This woman was healed after eighteen years [of illness].

Though the external circumstances are very different, this dream vision has the same internal structure as the vision of the nun at Poitiers.[110] The essential elements are: first, the passionate desire to find life in its most essential, vital quality; second, a man who in an elegant and kind manner brings the woman to this 'inner centre'; and third, the experience of being loved as a beautiful woman and a bride by the ideal spiritual bridegroom. In the nun's vision, the elements appear in that order; for Fedamia, the second and third coincide. It seems to me that this is something like the essence of all bridal mysticism.

Radegunde, also at Poitiers, had a similar vision which is reported by her pupil Baudonivia,[111] who was one of the two people to whom it was told. The external situation is different again: Radegunde saw the vision (*visum*) a year before she died and it showed her 'the place that had been prepared for her' in heaven. Here, however, the bridegroom — identified as Christ himself — appears as 'a very wealthy man, most beautiful, and as it were of youthful age'. 'As he stroked her gently and spoke to her in a tender and loving manner (*suavi tactu blandoque conloquio*)', he chided her for her excessive self-chastisement in her yearning for him: '...for I am always with you. Know, you precious gem of mine, that you are the brightest jewel in my crown'. In a vision many years earlier, when Queen Radegunde had just fled from her husband to be able to begin the conventual life,[112] she had 'seen in a vision (*visum*) a ship in the shape of a man; on all his limbs men were sitting, and she herself was sitting on his knee. The man said to her, "Now you are sitting on my knee; later you shall sit in my heart (*in pectore meo sessionem habebis*)" '. In Radegunde's earlier vision, the aristocratic ideal is again evident, but the man has the appearance of eternal youth; this is striking when one remembers that Radegunde herself, by this time, must have been at least

110. *Hist.* 6.29.
111. Baudonivia, *Vit. Rad.* 20.
112. Baudonivia, *Vit. Rad.* 3.

sixty years old.[113] In all these visions, the loving tenderness of the men's conversation and their gentle touch seem to be very similar. For these women, evidently, this was the way to their 'inner centre'. The fact that such imaginings could be apprehended as objective spiritual reality in a veridical (dream-)vision has preserved these very intimate moments for posterity.

For Fedamia, experiencing the image of the saint in this manner as a living reality precipitated the loosening of the contortions in her limbs; her paralysis may have had a nervous origin.[114] It very much looks as though the identification with the *living image* of the ideal spiritual bridegroom somehow liberated a creative, vital energy that effected her recovery.

'CHAINED BY THE DEVIL': IMAGES OF IMMOBILIZATION AND RELEASE
During Fedamia's prayer at the tomb, 'it seemed to her as though a heap of chains fell from all her limbs onto the floor' and she was 'awakened by this sound'. These invisible chains (though it is not clear how they are related to the 'humour') are evidently regarded as the effective means by which she had been held in paralysis. If they can be heard falling, they cannot be merely metaphorical. They must be an invisible reality — a revealing glimpse of Gregory's view of that kind of illness. This makes the other stories in which his mention of 'chains' in connection with illness could be understood metaphorically now look rather different.

The following parallelism of images may be what Gregory, if not also Fedamia, had in mind. A woman suffering from afflicted hands came to the church of St Medardus to celebrate a vigil there 'with total faith'[115] and was

> confident that her hands, cramped by a humour (*humore ligatae*), could be loosened (*dissolvi*) by the power (*virtus*) of one who had, by the strength of his power (*potentia virtutis*) undone the chains (*catenae*) of unfortunate men [i.e. prisoners]. And it happened that, while mass was being celebrated [the following day] the dry bonds of her nerves were loosened (*resolutis nervorum arentibus ligaturis*).

Her hands were cramped by a 'humour' but, evidently at the same time, by 'dry bonds of nerves', which seems to be a contradiction. But Gregory

---

113. Aigrain 1924: 162-5: Radegunde died in 587 and saw this vision in the year before her death.
114. On the nervous origins of illness in connection with miraculous cures: Kelsey 1973: 243-81; Rouche 1981: 324, 327. Rousselle 1976: 1104 says that many illnesses in the fourth century were probably of a nervous kind and that the whole situation in which men lived was 'anxiogène'.
115. *Glor. conf.* 93; similarly, but without the parallel image, *Virt. Mart.* 2.3.

needs something to correspond to the prisoner's chains that the saint has so often undone: here the model of the cure is not exorcism but release from captivity. Perhaps, besides assuming in a matter-of-fact way that paralysis is *brought on* by a 'humour', Gregory imagines some kind of invisible bonds as actually doing the restricting, in this case holding the fingers in their cramp. Such a mental picture would also explain the simultaneous presence, in Fedamia's case, of the humour and the audible chains. The notion that something which looks like constriction could come about in another way, as well as the notion that bonds or chains can be spoken about as existing without a correspondent in concrete, if invisible, reality seems to be uncongenial to Gregory. Apart from his general tendency to envisage metaphors as objective spiritual realities, his reasoning is probably a very simple deduction: if something has visible effects, it must really exist, even though it can't be seen.[116] Gregory uses the same kind of phrase, however, for deafness and muteness: 'the bonds of his ears and his jaws were broken (*disruptis aurium et faucium ligaturis*)'.[117]

Elsewhere, he speaks of 'the chains of blindness (*caecitatis catenae*)';[118] but he does not pursue this image: the afflicted man, who had been advised in a dream-vision (*per visionem ... somnii*) to ask for the saint's help, was later 'illumined by the power of the saint (*virtute beati confessoris illuminatus est*)'.

'Illumination', the healing of blindness, goes back to a Biblical precedent. But so does the cure of paralysis.[119] Instead of referring back to Christ, however, Gregory (sometimes) sees a correspondence between the saint's releasing cripples from their immobilization and his freeing prisoners either during his life or after his death. This theme of captivity and liberation probably impressed Gregory and his readers because it was something that almost everyone, directly or indirectly, could know about. During the many civil wars, prisoners were taken from all social classes. Gregory often notes that the church or holy men used the resources they had or were given to ransom captives.[120] As we shall see

---

116. Compare *Virt. Mart.* 2.47. Severus, *Dial.* 3.10. Two centuries earlier, Severus reports that pearls were once seen glistening on St Martin's hands while he celebrated the Eucharist: as he moved, they were also heard softly colliding.
117. *Virt. Mart.* 1.7.
118. *Virt. Mart.* 4.20.
119. For instance, John 9 and Mk 2:3-4. A survey of Jesus' healing in Kelsey 1973: 69-103.
120. As in *Virt. Mart.* 4.46, *Hist.* 6.8 and 7.1. Conciliar legislation ordered all the faithful to pay the tithe which would be used by the church to ransom captives (*Conc. Matisc.* a.585, c. 5: Maassen 1893: 166-7).

below, the dead saint also liberates prisoners miraculously. Bishops, including Gregory himself, try to see to it that the secular authorities are sufficiently impressed by this miracle to respect the men's new freedom.[121] They did this also for slaves, whose cure releases them from 'the enchainment by the yoke of servitude'.[122] Not only Gregory's stories but also the canons of contemporary church councils give the impression that arbitrary imprisonment by men unchecked by superior authorities was in fact not uncommon in this period.[123] Recourse to the saint's supernatural aid may have been the only way to freedom.

The resemblance between the miraculous release of a prisoner immobilized by a block and chain and that of a helpless cripple is fairly obvious. Gregory used it because, as many of his stories show, he looked for meaning in congruence: if two phenomena or events in some way resembled each other, he wished to regard them as having the same meaning in the spiritual sphere. Christ healed a cripple but the real model of liberation was, of course, His salvation of man from sin.[124]

In the previous chapter, we saw that Gregory not infrequently associates a physical cure with the forgiveness of sins and/or the conversion to the spiritual life, and that he stresses the saint's intercession at the Last Judgment.[125] In one of his more panegyrical passages,[126] Gregory reveals that he saw a particular saint's cure as symbolic of three kinds of liberation: at Judgment, of the soul from sin, and, in the present, both of the body from illness and of the person from the servile condition:

> O what a wonderful deliverance (*redemptio*) by the blessed man! Whoever thus redeemed [anyone] with a thousand talents as this advocate, pleading for leniency in the face of our crimes (*nostrorum criminum suffragator*) released (*absolvit*), at one blow, in a single moment, without gold coins, a body from illness and a condition from its burdens?

Elsewhere, Gregory concludes a description of the miraculous liberation of a prisoner from his chains by hoping that the saint would 'absolve me from the fetters of my sins as he lifted from this [priest] the enormous weight of his chains!'[127] Liberation from enchainment is one of the

---

121. As, for instance, in *Hist.* 4.35; 6.8; 10.6; *Virt. Mart.* 1.11; 4.35; *Vit. patr.* 8.3, 9. Compare Brown 1981: 113 and Scheibelreiter 1983: 188-92.
122. As, for instance, in *Virt. Mart.* 2.30.
123. For instance, *Conc. Tur.* a. 567, c. 27 and *Conc. Matisc.* a. 585, c. 12, 14 (Maassen 1893: 135, 169-70).
124. Compared by Gregory to Zorobabel's liberation of the Jews from their Babylonian captivity in *Hist.* 1.15.
125. See pp. 205 ff.
126. *Virt. Mart.* 2.4.
127. *Virt. Mart.* 1.23.

traditionally Christian dynamic models structuring Gregory's view of miraculous cures.

Not surprisingly, the devil appears to be responsible, directly or indirectly, for various kinds of chains. Exactly what kind of chains are meant is not clear when Gregory reports that Abbot Sequanus of the region of Langres 'when he was alive, often liberated men from their enchainment by the devil (*a vinculo diabolici nexus absolvit*), just as, after his death, he freed at his tomb by his merits those oppressed by the chain (*catena*) of the slaves' prison'.[128] Judging from Fedamia's experience, the diabolic enchainment probably refers to some kind of paralytic illness. But, when provoked, saints sometimes could turn the tables and punish insult or perjury with rigidification or paralysis.[129] In one such case, a perjurer who had been turned as it were into a bronze statue by the martyr Marcellus of Châlons was 'granted absolution from his enchainment by the cunning of the devil (*absolvi diaboli arte vinctum*)'.[130] Is Gregory's thinking muddled here? Earlier, we saw that saints had no qualms about 'burning' people who had insulted them with lightning or fever;[131] rigidification or illness is likewise said to be caused by their power (*virtus*).[132] Or is, in this case, the saint letting the devil do it for him?

There is one story in which this is explicitly said to be the case.[133] A certain man 'was cheated of his reason by diabolic cunning' (i.e., he went mad) when he was suddenly enveloped by a cloud of dust and chaff (often seen by Gregory as an indication of diabolic agency)[134] while drunkenly riding on his horse. Because of his paranoiac frenzy, he was then bound with ropes and chains and kept in confinement. Later, however, he was healed by St Martin in Tours and promised to return each year with gifts for the saint. He eventually failed to carry out this promise, however, although he served God assiduously as a monk. Consequently, Gregory says, 'the power over him was, as I believe, again given to the Enemy', i.e. he probably lapsed back into alcoholism and in any case again into madness (*amentia*). After a second cure, 'because of his sins (*peccatis facientibus*)' he still could not abstain from alcohol and died as a wretchedly ill and miserable man. Here, Gregory needed a scapegoat to

128. *Glor. conf.* 86.
129. As, for instance, in *Hist.* 2.37; 5.36; 6.6, 36; *Glor. mart.* 20, 53; *Virt. Jul.* 39; *Vit. patr.* 8.9.
130. *Glor. mart.* 52.
131. See pp. 157 ff.
132. See n. 116.
133. *Virt. Mart.* 2.53.
134. See pp. 106 and 232.

explain why two of St Martin's cures were in the end ineffective, and saint's punishments, however inhuman, of those who insulted them were excellent propaganda for the otherwise defenceless church.[135] This unpitying story is something like a magical weapon built of words. Gregory needed such stories as these in order to be able to govern and even to stay alive in a society which, as his accounts show, respected nothing other than effective power.

Liberation from a (possibly diabolic) enchainment is another model of a cure. Like that of purification or exorcism, it derives from the Bible, but in a twofold way. It resembles or 're-enacts' not only Christ's cure of the cripple but also his act of releasing all men everywhere from the bondage of sin. At the same time, releasing from imprisonment or bondage was an image that could have powerful appeal for the less fortunate in society. Gregory nowhere explicitly makes all these connections; he probably did not stop to reflect on why he sometimes imagined chains. The isolation of another one of the dynamic models of his thinking and the tracing of its origins makes sense only for those, like us, who cannot otherwise clearly understand what he is doing.

'AS THOUGH SOMEONE': THE DOCTOR

As we have seen, a cure could begin with the patient himself or one of his friends or relatives having a dream in which the advice was given to go to the saint's tomb to be healed. This 'invitation' may be the visualization of a decision at the instant that it was being made: it expresses and at the same time confirms the confidence that a cure is possible. For relatives, who often had to arrange the journey and the transport, the dream-vision could function as a supernatural command.

This decision to abandon other attempts at healing and to put all one's trust in the curative power of a saint is the first crucial moment in the process of a cure. It initiates what one might designate as the 'build-up' of a cure: perhaps an arduous journey to the shrine, and then days, weeks, months or even years of praying, hoping and waiting in an attitude that Gregory described as 'full of faith (*fide plenus*)' or 'a mighty faith (*fides strenua*)'. The following story is a more elaborate description of this typical state of mind:[136]

> A certain Julian, who had deformed hands and feet, piously came from Spain to this doctor [*medicus*: i.e. St Martin], saying, 'For I believe without doubt (*indubitanter*), most holy bishop, that you are able to grant me the same cure which

---

135. Compare, for instance, *Vit. patr.* 8.11, *Hist.* 4.36; 7.29. See also n. 229.
136. *Virt. Mart.* 3.21; similarly *Virt. Mart.* 4.30.

you are accustomed to grant to others who trust (*sperans*) in you'. In this confident belief (*credulitas*) he persisted (*insistens*) in assiduous prayer, not doubting the compassion of the Lord, and [eventually] his hands and feet were straightened and he was restored to health.

The repeated emphasis on the absence of doubt seems significant. The latter, in itself, is no mean achievement. At the same time, however, there is an element of manipulation in this 'absence of doubt'. The saint is thereby compelled to do what is expected. This aspect of manipulative pressure becomes visible when Gregory tells of a woman who refused to arise from the floor before she had been completely healed, and of the grandmother who put her dead baby grandson in front of the altar 'with certain trust (*spes non incerta*)' but nevertheless said to St Martin 'as though she saw the saint with her visible eyes': '...if you do not [revive my grandson] we will no longer worship you, nor will we light the lamps or show you any kind of honour'.[137] Quoting Luke 11:8, Gregory elsewhere endorses persistent and even importunate asking as a legitimate way of obtaining what one wants — and what one has a right to have, for Christ had said that all that one asked in his name would be given.[138]

The second crucial moment in a cure, according to Gregory, is another moment in which an important change is initiated: the onset of the cure itself. We have already seen that this moment could occur during liturgy, while the saint's passion or miracles were being read aloud in church or at the moment that physical contact was made with his (derivative) relics.[139] It is described as a break in the continuity of consciousness, a sudden pulse coming from without which initiates the cure. P. Brown has suggested that this may sometimes have to do with an intense identification with the saint's overcoming death through his martyrdom, which brings on a similar victory in the patient over his illness.[140] Other imaginings also seem to have 'triggered' a cure. For it is at this decisive moment that visionary experiences of the saint are sometimes reported. The saint could then come as one giving instructions, as an exorcist or as a liberator from 'enchainment'. But he could also be thought of and experienced as a doctor who healed by more or less recognizable medical techniques.[141] This comes out in the following story.[142] A woman with a cramped hand, the palm of which was putrefying, came to St Martin's feast to be healed but was disappointed. That night she woke up and,

137. *Virt. Mart.* 3.39; 3.8.
138. *Glor. mart.* 13; Mk 11:24.
139. For cures during liturgy see chapter III n. 309.
140. Brown 1981: 80-5.
141. Rousselle 1976: 1104.
142. *Virt. Mart.* 2.56.

trying to overcome her distress at not having been cured, gave thanks to God for all her other blessings.

> As she was saying this with many tears, she fell asleep again. Then [suddenly] a man with hair white as a swan, clothed in purple, and holding a cross in his hand, stood before her and said, 'You will now be cured, in the name of Christ, our Redeemer'.
> And, taking her hand, he put his fingers between her fingers which were sticking into the palm and, lifting them a bit, straightened them. While she was seeing this in the dream-vision, she woke up (*Dum haec in visu videret evigilans*) and lifted her healed hand, from which the blood was still flowing, up high in the praise of God.[143]

There is one case in which a patient may have been awake during such an experience. Let us consider again the story examined earlier (p. 194) of the blind boy whose parents had given him to a band of beggars so as to receive alms because they were too poor to feed him.[144] The boy was lying immobile 'at the feet of the saint' after the vigil of Christmas when 'he felt as though someone (*sensit quasi...aliquis*) punctured his eyes with a sharp pointed instrument. As the blood issuing from his eyes ran down his cheeks, he turned his face upwards and saw a [lighted] candle shining above him...'. When he saw the candle, he must have been awake; before then and at the moment of the pain, he may have been awake but could equally well, after staying awake at night for so long, have been at least half asleep. Here, for obvious reasons, the 'someone' is felt, not seen.

In a few cases, Gregory himself interprets what is seen or experienced in terms of a specific kind of contact without, however, reporting that the person being healed actually felt it as such. In the following story, for example, he is conjecturing. After spending three years in St Martin's church, Theodemundus, who was deaf and mute and lived from alms, was at a certain moment 'warned (*commonitus*) by the divine goodness' and went to stand before the altar, raising his eyes and hands towards heaven.[145] While he was standing there, blood and pus started coming out of his mouth, 'so that it might be thought that someone was cutting [in] his throat with a surgical instrument (*ita ut putaretur quod aliquis ferramento guttur ejus incideret*)'. Thereafter he mentions 'bloody threads' hanging from the man's jaws and that the 'bonds' of his ears and throat were 'broken'. But the saint's 'surgery' is different from that performed with real instruments, however. Reporting a cure of blindness, Gregory says elsewhere:[146]

143. Similar stories are: *Virt. Mart.* 2.4, *Glor. mart.* 5 and *Virt. Mart.* 3.1.
144. *Virt. Mart.* 3.16.
145. *Virt. Mart.* 1.7.
146. *Virt. Mart.* 2.19.

> Prostrated before the bed [of the saint in the monastery of Candes, where the latter had died], [a blind man] spent the whole night in tears and prayers, immobile, moistening the ground with his tears and warming the venerable wood of the rail with his sighs. When dawn came, however, the cataracts on his eyes were opened and he deserved to see the light of day.
> What have doctors ever been able to do with their surgical instruments which resembles this? They cause more pain with their doings than cures when they stretch the eyelid and pierce the eye with their lancets, experiences which resemble more the torments of death than that they restore eyesight. And if the doctors are not careful, they condemn the poor patient to permanent blindness. For this man, however, the will (*voluntas*) of the blessed confessor was the surgical instrument, and (miraculous) power (*virtus*) alone the ointment.

Another extensive passage expressing the saint's power alone as the remedy for all ailments[147] also points to a spiritual rather than quasi-physical mode of healing: '...O heavenly purification, as it were, that is greater than the cleverness of doctors, the sweetness of herbs, the strength of all ointments!'. In the above story, the state of mind before the cure is correspondingly emphasized. Is Gregory not aware of what, to us, seem to be contradictions? It looks as though he simply wishes to imagine a palpable, concrete, potentially visible manner of healing. In physical cures then, at least, the *effect* of a saint's 'will' and his 'power' is described as in some way resembling that of visible instruments and remedies. For example, '...it cleans the stomach like scammony, the lungs like hyssop, the head like pyrethrum'.[148] How can one otherwise explain the frequent eruptions of blood and pus? Gregory did not have anything resembling our mental model of psychosomatic cures. Instead, he used a mental model of concrete, physical techniques. Although his description of contrition and the experience of inflowing forgiveness[152] shows that he was aware that the 'power' of the saint could heal the heart, he did not see a direct connection between this and a physical cure.

Summing up, dream-visions of the saint could be experienced at each of the two points of discontinuity in a cure: first, at the moment of the decision to abandon other remedies and trust only and completely in the saint's healing power; and second, at a similar sudden pulse of energy that precipitated recovery. Sometimes the latter moment is accompanied by the imagining of the saint as a doctor who touches the sufferer with a surgical instrument or in a professional kind of way. Sometimes, however, the touch itself is central.

---

147. *Virt. Mart.* 3.60. See pp. 200 ff.
148. *Virt. Mart.* 3.60.
149. *Virt. Mart.* 3. *prol.*

'A HEALING TOUCH': EXORCISM OR THE TRANSMISSION OF VITAL ENERGY?

A last, but by no means least important, model of cure which has precedents in the Bible and is very similar to that of exorcism is what I shall call 'the healing touch'.[150] When the touch of the saint is said to 'drive out' illness by his '(miraculous) power', one could say that what is taking place is simply an exorcism. In Gregory's stories cures are very often precipitated by contact with a holy object through which the *virtus* of the saint is thought to be transmitted. In his preface to the third book of St Martin's miracles, Gregory combines a number of elements. He begins by speaking of the saint as a 'doctor (*medicus*)' who 'drives out (*purgaret*)' illness. Then he says,

> For (*nam*) if one comes to his tomb and humbles one's soul...in true compunction (*compunctio*)...his sins will be forgiven and his heart will be healed (*dolor pectoris pervenit ad medelam*). For very frequently the touch (*tactus*) of the blessed tomb commands (*imperavit*) bleedings to stop, the blind to see, the crippled to rise and even bitterness of heart (*pectoris amaritudo*) to disappear completely.

Gregory piles image upon image here. What is the connection between St Martin's curing illnesses as a doctor, his healing the heart by granting 'forgiveness', and the touch of his tomb 'commanding' both physical and mental disturbances to disappear? Concerning the latter Gregory adds:

> For I call God as well as the hope that I placed in [the saint's] power (*virtus*) to witness that I believe I will not be cheated of his compassion (*misericordia*): because (*quia*) as often as a headache came upon me, or...I became hard of hearing, or... a pain appeared in any other part of my body, as soon as (*statim*) I held the painful place against (*attigi*) either the tomb or the cloth hanging over it, I was healed on the spot, wondering in silent astonishment (*mirans tacitus*) at the pain's immediate disappearance upon that touch (*tactus*).

'Driving out' illnesses through the 'touch' of his tomb, which then 'commands' all discomfort to disappear sounds like straightforward exorcism. The 'command' also seems to account for the suddenness of the cure. The intervening sentence, however, suggests something that all Gregory's stories with their description of long and tearful prayer also indicate: this cannot happen without the heart's also being cleansed of sin.[151] Gregory attributes the final cure to the direct effect of the saint's power and not to that of the cleansed heart, as we ourselves might be inclined to do. While the necessary condition of the heart is recognized, the purgative power which is at the same time the life- and health-

---

150. Compare *Hist.* 6.6: *tactus sacer*; *Virt. Mart.* 3.49; *Vit. patr.* 9.2: *manu imposita*; 10.2: *manus imposerat*. Compare Aune 1980 in Haase 1980: 1529; Meier 1949: 63.
151. Compare Schlick 1966.

restoring energy is experienced as coming from without. *Vitality or spiritual energy seems to have been thought of as (miraculous) 'power' and projected more or less completely onto the saint.* Brown has connected the act of identification with the saint with something like an identity crisis in the late antique world: 'the identity, placed at the nadir of uncertainty by the...deep sense of sin, cried out for some intimate thread of stability'.[152] In the visionary experiences surrounding cures, this saint could also be visualized as someone who was the ideal, spiritualized, human being, whose touch or smile changed one's life.

In one story, a perjurer who had been punished during the very act of his crime by losing the use of his tongue and voice, went to pray at a saint's tomb to be cured and, 'as he afterwards said, he felt as though someone (*sensit ... tanquam si aliquis*) touched his throat'.[153] Gregory adds:

> This was, I believe, the (miraculous) power (*virtus*) of the Lord's confessor. Thereafter he went to the priest who was present and asked him by making gestures to make the sign of the Cross over his throat. When the priest had done this, the man again prostrated himself in prayer. Very soon (*protinus*) [however] he rose because he had been given back the use of his voice, and with his own words related all that he had experienced.

Here again the touch of one who is presumably regarded as being the saint (at least by Gregory) is felt as the turning point, the onset of the cure, which this time took a little more time, and concentration, to be achieved. Gregory also describes several other cures in which a supplementary period of prayer and tears was required to 'complete' the healing process.[154] This once more shows that such prayerful concentration brings about the state of mind in which it was possible to discover a new vitality. The latter is imaginatively experienced as the 'power' of the saint.

There are three stories, however, in which not fear and power but love and gentleness seem to bring on the cure. Perhaps significantly, two of these concern women. Beside Fedamia's experience, which has already been examined, there is the case of the nun Apra:[155]

> As she lay with paralyzed hands and feet, imploring the help of the saint day and night, on a certain night she seemed to see an old man coming to her (*visum est ei...venisse ad se senem*), who [then] stroked (*attrectaret*) all her limbs with a gentle

---

152. Brown 1981: 57. Compare Misch 1955: 374 on Gregory's use of the credo at the beginning of the *Histories*: 'Diese Glaubensgewissheit ist an die Stelle des Selbstgefühls der Persönlichkeit getreten ...'.
153. *Glor. conf.* 29. A similar story is *Virt. Mart.* 3.23.
154. For instance *Virt. Mart.* 2.23.
155. *Virt. Mart.* 2.31.

touch (*molli tactu*). When she woke up in the morning, she felt that one hand and one foot had been healed, and, astonished, did not know who had done this...

Gregory, however, does know: he includes the story in his record of St Martin's miracles. In the last story, 'the blessed confessor [Martin] appeared (*apparuit*) to [Count Alpinus of Tours] in a dream-vision (*in visu nocte*), with a smiling face (*hilari vultu arridens*) and carrying his usual arms (*consueta arma*)'.[156] When the saint made the sign of the holy Cross over his diseased foot, 'the pain fled (*fugatus*) very quickly, and he arose healthy from his bed'. It does not seem wholly fortuitous that one of the three recorded visions of St Martin as a soldier (this had been his previous career) should have occurred to a count, whose office was as much a military as an administrative one.[157] One wonders, however, if the 'usual arms', interpreted as visible military equipment, is not a curious misunderstanding of a passage in Severus' Life of St Martin mentioning the saint's 'accustomed arms'[158] — there meaning the spiritual arms of prayer and fasting. Typically it is again a metaphor which is understood — apparently by everyone — to be concrete, sensory reality. In this story, the purgative power is transmitted objectively by the sign of the Cross. As with Fedamia, however, the smiling face must at the same time have dispelled any fear and radiated the warmth of unselfish spiritual love. The fact that this detail was remembered indicates that it must have made a deep impression on the count. Gregory's recording it may mean that he recognized its distinctive quality.

The touch of the saint, then, either through his person in a dream-vision or through his tomb when one is awake, could drive out mental and physical distress, but not before severe contrition had also cleansed one's heart of sin. Gregory shows that the healing touch is sometimes experienced only as an impulse of purgative power but that it may also sometimes transmit the vitalizing energy of spiritual love. The humble words of Abbot Aredius indicate with what tender immediacy the touch of the saint could be experienced even when one was, ostensibly, wide awake:[159]

> For the man of God himself stated that he felt as it were the hand (*sensisse se quasi...manum*) of the blessed Martin when, having made the sign of the cross over them, he stroked diseased limbs with a healing touch (*tactu salutari palparet*).

156. *Virt. Mart.* 1.24.
157. The other appearances of St Martin as a soldier are to an epileptic (*Virt. Mart.* 2.18) and when he frees prisoners (*Virt. Mart.* 4.26). Compare on the function of *comes*: Ewig 1976 in Atsma 1976a: 410-2.
158. Severus, *Vit. Mart.* 16.7: *familiaria in istius modi rebus arma, solo prostratus oravit* (by prayer, he cures a girl).
159. *Virt. Mart.* 4.6.

THE SMILING, WHITE-HAIRED MAN AS A SYMBOL: THE TRANSFORMING POWER OF A HUMAN IDEAL

Let us review the evidence thus far: at the onset of an illness or its crisis, a dark horrid figure is sometimes seen, perhaps a visualization of negative, destructive emotions. Once the illness has begun, there are two critical moments. The first is only mentioned by Gregory if a visionary experience accompanied it; it is that in which the patient, or one of his relatives or friends, is either instructed how to bring about the cure himself or is told to come (or bring the sufferer) to a saint's tomb to be healed there. Here the decision that one is going to recover is made. The initial confidence necessary to do this is as it were imparted by the venerable or supernatural figure, representing the ultimate authority of divine omnipotence. It is clear that the latter is in fact a crucial notion. Even when no dream-vision is reported at this point, divine omnipotence alone made possible the interior build-up of the unshakeable confidence that Gregory mentions so often as the state of mind necessary to 'merit' a cure. Without deciding the question of whether the cure is initiated from within or from without the human person, it is safe to say that the reparative process at least included a mobilization of all one's interior resources towards recovery.

The second critical moment is that in which, after a period of inner preparation, the onset of the cure is experienced as a sudden burst of vital energy which precipitates the liberation from a painful oppression or constriction. In dream-visions, this sudden impulse is experienced as the effect of the presence or of a command, gesture, act or touch by a venerable man whom Gregory, at least, usually understands to be the saint. For what actually happens at this moment Gregory has various models which are not mutually exclusive. The saint can appear as one who either exorcises an evil spirit, liberates from the 'chains' of disability, cleanses and practises surgery like a doctor, or transmits by his simple touch a cleansing and vitalizing energy. The latter is usually designated as (miraculous) 'power' but is sometimes also described as having the quality of gentle loving-kindness. In various places, Gregory indicates that at this same moment the consciously cultivated tearful contrition is suddenly transformed into a joyful certainty that one's sins are forgiven. Elsewhere, he sees cures as symbolizing the liberation from sin. Therefore, although Gregory uses forms and techniques that are reminiscent of magic and uses the term 'power', the essence of a cure seems to be the experience of a liberating forgiveness, and this can only proceed from a spiritual love. When dream-visions are reported, this experience of love, forgiveness and creative vitality is visualized as a smiling, white-haired, venerable man. As Fontaine has said,[160] the saint is the new type of ideal humanity, constantly recreated to find in him reasons for living and surviving.

Vigils, fasting, prolonged singing and prayer are likely to have increased the awareness of the imaginal kind of thinking that becomes visible in dreams but which, as modern research shows, probably goes on below the level of consciousness twenty-four hours a day.[161] In the dreams that Gregory reports, the imagination of the saint as physically, if invisibly, present and omnipotent seems to have initiated the process of recovery. It looks as though the saint in his various modalities was not only a consciously recognized human ideal but at the same time what modern psychology designates as an archetype or symbol of transformation.[162] Today, such images consciously used to effect psychic healing in the so-called 'waking dream' methods of psychotherapy.[163] In Gregory's time involuntary imaginal or dream-thinking seems to have intruded more into consciousness and perception than it does today, and this is probably intimately connected with the otherwise general tendency at that time to think and perceive in terms of images. Sudden changes and transformations — miraculous cures — are effectualized dream-logic.

C. VISIONS OF ADVICE AND AID

Other visionary experiences let us see how Gregory and at least some of his contemporaries appear to have visualized the dynamics of personal, social and political events. As might be expected, Gregory looks for the origins and the effective causes of these in the spiritual world, and the latter sometimes becomes visible in dreams. Except when we are explicitly told that the apparition is an angel, the figure that is seen is in most cases probably assumed to be a saint. We see him appearing at critical moments, often when some kind of an impasse has been reached: it is then his words or actions which provide the way out.[164] As we shall see below, for those with a clear conscience this is a very positive and helpful, perhaps even fulfilling, experience. However, those who have been misbehaving (who will be looked at in the next section) find the saint's appearance most unnerving or fear-inspiring, and sometimes even deadly.

160. Fontaine 1979: 936.
161. Singer 1974: 181-5; Kelsey 1968: 7; Cartwright 1978: 66.
162. See, for instance, the section on the symbol of the hero in Jung 1952: 284-345.
163. For instance, Singer 1974 and Epstein 1981.
164. Compare La Barre 1967 in Caillois 1967: 209: the cultural hero does the dream-work for his society.

Whatever the saint does is always necessary, but is thought to be beyond human means to achieve. Using the notion of spiritual causation in miracles and dream-visions to fill the gaps in one's technical or medical knowledge, one's institutions or diplomatic possibilities, or one's control over oneself or others is an important aspect of Gregory's manner of thinking. But sometimes, as for example with the fire in Paris (see p. 143), there are no 'gaps', and spiritual causation seems to be regarded as a separate, simultaneous and concurrent stream of reality. That this causation is the one which is in fact considered as decisive is shown by Gregory's statement about the priest Eufrasius' unsuccessful attempt to secure the office of bishop of Clermont: the reason he did not succeed is that he pursued it with the means of this world (i.e. gifts to the king) instead of 'through God'.[165] This seems to indicate that the sense of the constant presence of such a parallel stream of reality piloting visible events need not necessarily be produced by or dependent upon insufficiencies in rational knowledge.[166] Two centuries earlier Bishop Cyprian of Carthage and the emperor Constantine, consummate diplomats and eminently practical organizers, are known to have been sensitive to and to act upon dream-visions and intuitions.[167] In late Antiquity the latter were generally regarded as a parallel and even superior mode of knowledge co-existing with that acquired through observation and reasoning.[168] Gregory too, at a much less sophisticated and erudite level, combined astute diplomacy, alert observation and no-nonsense practicality with a particular kind of 'imaginative thinking'. I shall therefore try to describe not only the social functions of the dream-visions of saints, but also something of how Gregory perceived and thought about what he regarded as the other stream of reality as it worked in and through men.

165. *Hist.* 4.35.
166. See on causal thinking and the parallel belief in a *höhere Determination*, Mensching 1957: 8. But compare Evans-Pritchard on the working of witchcraft among the Azande: they 'undoubtedly perceive a difference between what we consider the workings of nature on the one hand and the working of magic and ghosts and witchcraft on the other hand ... The Zande actualizes these beliefs rather than intellectualizes them ... their ideas are imprisoned in action ... witchcraft is less an intellectual symbol than a response to situations of failure' (Evans-Pritchard 1937: 81, 82, 83).
167. Kelsey 1968: 123-6, 144-55. Compare von Harnack 1902.
168. Cumont 1949: 91, 346; Kelsey 1968: 71; Dodds 1968: 9; Nock (1933) 1972: 128; Stancliffe 1983: 193.

'A VENERABLE OLD MAN IN CLERICAL HABIT': AN IMAGE OF REASSURANCE AND STABILITY

It was in church that this heavenly reality was sensed to be almost palpable. Cures and other miracles showed the 'presence' of a saint at his shrine: the dreams and the visions of patients during their cure confirmed it. Gregory says, 'If only our eyes weren't obscured by the darkness of our many sins, we would certainly see you coming...'.[169] There is considerable evidence, too, that heavenly beings were thought not only to visit or sing — secretly — in churches at night,[170] but to participate in some way during the celebration of liturgy by men.[171] Abbot Venantius was particularly good at discerning this.[172] Once he heard a voice from a tomb participating in the Lord's prayer. Another time, in the same church, he also saw someone who was almost certainly St Martin. Because of his failing eyesight, he once entrusted the celebration of mass to a priest, but he himself stayed nearby. When the moment came that the Eucharist had to be blessed with the sign of the Cross, the abbot

> gazing attentively (or: in wonderment) (*intuitus*), ...seemed to see what looked like (*vidit quasi*) a ladder placed up to the window of the apse and what looked like (*quasi*) a venerable old man in clerical habit climbing down it and then blessing with his extended right hand the sacrifice offered on the altar.
>
> This happened in St Martin's church. I don't know why [the abbot] alone deserved to see it, however, and no one else. Anyway, he told his brother monks about it afterwards, and it is certain that it was the Lord who showed (*demonstrasse*) this to His faithful servant, and that it was He who deigned to reveal to him the secrets of heavenly mysteries (or the hidden things of heaven: *arcanorum secreta coelestium*).

The implication seems to be that heavenly beings are there even when not seen. Gregory tells us that Abbot Venantius thought of men as participating in the simultaneous praise of God taking place in heaven.

The story of a disconsolate mother shows that this merging of earthly and heavenly praise was possibly constant. Her only son died young of fever, some time after he had been admitted to the monastery of St Mauricius (St Moritz).[173] After she had buried him she could not get over her grief and came to weep and wail at his tomb every day.

> Finally, the blessed Mauricius appeared to her in a dream-vision (*apparens per visum noctis*) and said, 'Why do you keep lamenting the death of your son, woman? Aren't you ever going to stop?'

---

169. *Virt. Mart.* 3.16. Compare *Virt. Mart.* 2.40, 3.8 and *Glor. conf.* 94.
170. As in *Glor. conf.* 72 and *Glor. mart.* 33.
171. For instance, in *Glor. conf.* 47.
172. *Vit. patr.* 16.2. Compare Blaise 1954: 730-1.
173. *Glor. mart.* 75.

'All the days of life', she said, 'are not enough to contain my grief. As long as I live, I shall weep for my only child...'.

Then the saint said, 'Don't weep for him as though he were dead, but be comforted: know that he lives with us and that he enjoys eternal life in our company. And, so that you will really believe what I say, get up tomorrow morning in time for matins and you will hear his voice in the choir of the singing monks. And what is more, not only tomorrow, but all the days of your life you will hear his voice in the singing...'. [...]

[The next morning] she went to the church to find out whether the vision she had seen was true (*aliqua de visione quam viderat probatura*). Everything went according to the holy promise and she soon recognized that the things that had been divinely announced [to her] were being carried out (or fulfilled). For when the cantor had begun the responsorium and the group of monks the antiphon, the mother heard the voice of her child, and gave thanks to God. The other thing which had been promised through the martyr was also completely carried out, so that all the days of her life, whenever she came to the singing, she heard the voice of this child among the voices of the others singing the melodies.

Though the figure in the dream-vision (*visum noctis, visio*) is here explicitly identified as the martyr, he is treated as the instrument (*martyris ore*) through which a divine announcement is made (*divinitus nuntiata*) and later carried out or fulfilled (*impleta*). People *wanted* to hear heavenly voices. The dream-vision of the martyr here gave solace to a bereaved mother by pointing to the invisible presence and participation of the dead as heavenly beings in the life on earth. The knowledge and experience of this presence gave comfort, peace, joy. In an age when nothing human seemed certain or stable, it must also have generated a feeling of basic order and security.

The world certainly looked confusing and evil in this period, and men felt themselves powerless to do anything about it. The story of the hermit Patroclus' dream-vision shows that he needed divine help even in maintaining his self-chosen exile. After having retired to 'the deep solitudes of the forests', he once felt the desire to return to the life in the world (*saeculum*) 'growing in his heart', and prayed that God would let him do only that which was acceptable to Him.[174]

Then an angel of the Lord appeared to him in a dream-vision (*visum*) and said, 'If you wish to see the world (*mundus*), here is a pillar; if you climb on top of it you can look from there at everything that is going on'.

In front of him, in this vision (*visio*), there was in fact a pillar of wondrous height. When he had climbed up to the top, Patroclus saw murders, robberies, mass slaughter, adulteries, prostitution and all the wrongs (*prava*) that are done in the world. Coming down again, he said, 'I pray, O Lord, don't let me return to these perversities (*pravitates*) which, in my life dedicated to you, I had forgotten long ago'.

---

174 *Vit. patr.* 9.2.

The angel then said to him, 'Stop seeking the world, then, lest you perish with it. Go, instead, to the chapel in which you prayed to the Lord, and what you will find there will be a consolation to you in your exile'.

When he went into the chapel, he found an earthen roof-tile on which the sign of the Lord's cross was visible. He recognized it as a divine gift, and understood that it would be for him an invincible protection against all the enticements of worldly temptation.

Here the worldly life as seen from a great height, is not a tempting prospect — quite the contrary. Everything is wrong with it: the terms *prava* and *pravitates* denote misshapenness, perversity. What is more, it will perish. The visionary image of the world here cured the hermit's desire to return to it and gave him the strength to decide to stay in the wilderness, where people who wanted to be cured nevertheless came to see him. The finding of a divine gift after a dream-vision is an antique tradition;[175] in this case it is said to work like an amulet.

Gregory's efforts in writing about the events, saints' lives and miracles of his time show that, notwithstanding his disapproval of his society's many evils and notwithstanding the fact that he regarded spiritual reality as more powerful than its physical counterpart, he himself, at least for quite a long time,[176] was not completely pessimistic about human society. Other stories of his show, however, that he desired and expected the constant presence and aid of heavenly beings outside of liturgy as well.[177]

'SOMEONE WHO LOOKED LIKE A BISHOP': THE SOLUTION OF PRACTICAL PROBLEMS

Above, we saw that, on occasion, people asked for the (invisibly present) saint to help them carry his sarcophagus through a narrow church door and that, in other similar situations, a heavenly figure appeared who said that a saint was already helping with physical work.[178] If we are to believe Gregory, people were inclined to think that they could do nothing difficult or strenuous without supernatural aid; this is, in any case, what he personally believes. Supernatural aid in a dream-vision could help to renew a decision but it could also present the solution of a difficult technical problem. Whether the above kind of story was based on actual events or not is less important than the fact that Gregory *wants to believe* it and wants others to believe it. For him, the story is a model of how

---

175. Caillois 1967 in Caillois and von Grunebaum 1967: 34.
176. See p. 60.
177. That apparitions of 'angels' are still seen today is demonstrated by Moolenburgh 1983.
178. See p. 219.

human decisions and human ideas originate and take form: they are given, implanted, by a supernatural being. For instance, when a number of days had been spent in unsuccessful attempts to raise the columns for the church of the Holy Virgin because they were too large and heavy (six feet in circumference),[179]

> the Holy Virgin appeared to the [by then desperate] builder in a dream-vision (*apparuit ...per visum*) and said,
> 'Cheer up! I'm going to show you how these columns can be raised'.
> And after she had showed him how to adjust the machines, how to hang the blocks and pulleys and how to attach the ropes, she said,
> 'Take three schoolboys with you, so that you can carry this out with their help'.
> When the builder woke up and had done everything according to the instructions, he called three schoolboys and [with their help] set up the columns in no time. It was given to the people to see this astounding miracle (*miraculum admirandum*): that which many strong men had been unable to lift, being raised by three little boys without the effort of real work.

If it is true that, as his description of the ropes and pulleys seems to indicate, Gregory is acquainted with the mechanical principle involved, then his calling it nonetheless an 'astounding miracle' corroborates the view that belief in miracles need not hinge upon a lack of rational knowledge. Gregory, capable of perfectly adequate reasoning, has a *preference* for the sudden image, intuition, breakthrough. For him these somehow possess more reality value than anything arrived at by reason alone. He relates them to the transcendent supernatural reality which, according to church tradition, is the most enduring, stable and powerful in existence. In Gregory's mind and perhaps that of some of his contemporaries, the action patterns of this reality can become visible as sudden images: often of the ideal heavenly-human being, the holy man or woman.

This ideal, usually elderly, figure could also give timely advice or aid. Once a (church) 'abbot' and his 'companions' were lying sleeping around a furnace that was heating the chalk (for restoration purposes?) in the church in which Bishop Illidius lay buried. The door of this furnace started to crack and was about to fall apart,[180] when

> immediately someone who looked like a bishop stood by the priest [i.e. probably the 'abbot'] in a vision (*astitit...per visum quasi sacerdos*) and said, 'Get up quickly and wake up those who are sleeping so that the oven doesn't fall apart upon them...'.

Needless to say, all of them escaped in time and, after a prayer at the

---

179. *Glor. mart.* 8; *Glor. conf.* 61.
180. *Vit. patr.* 2.4. Similar in *Virt. Mart.* 1.20 and *Vit. patr.* 2.4. On 'abbots' of churches see Pietri 1983b.

saint's tomb, the priest (abbot) repaired the furnace so that, 'with the help of the bishop (*antistite opitulante*)' the heating of the chalk could be brought to a good end. This latter phrase (*antistite opitulante*) is one of very many similar ones scattered throughout Gregory's writings, referring either to a saint or to God.[181] In his view, evidently, even in ordinary, practical affairs, very little, if anything, could be brought to a good end without the constant support and assistance of the supernatural stream of reality.

'I AM MARTIN...YOUR LIBERATOR': THE RELEASE OF PRISONERS
It was no different in the administration of justice. Brown's statement about sorcery beliefs in the Later Empire, that they 'may be used like radio-active traces in an X-ray: where they assemble, we have a hint of pockets of uncertainty and competition...',[182] may be applicable *mutatis mutandis* to the quasi-magical use of saintly 'power' in Merovingian society. Wherever the church's interests or views meet resistance or competition and there is as yet no generally accepted institutional way of overcoming these, the saint's power is often used to work out a solution. However, unlike sorcery, which, being illegal, was usually carried out in secret,[183] the saint's 'power' is articulately and openly invoked: belief in the saint's power, when the latter could be convincingly enough demonstrated, is itself becoming an institution, functioning as a tool of social manipulation.

A number of Gregory's stories let us see that the administration of justice, already extremely complicated because of the existence side by side of different legal codes applicable to Franks and Gallo-Romans, could be very arbitrary, especially for the unarmed lower social strata of society. In the next section of this chapter, those cases will be examined which were solved by dreams and visions in which the saint appeared to intimidate or punish the authority in question. He could also appear, however, to the prisoner and somehow liberate him, just as Joseph of Arimathea was set free by an angel — an (apocryphal) incident Gregory mentions, as it were as a model in his brief sketch of biblical history.[184] Such dreams or visions provide incontrovertible proof that it was indeed the saint who made the chains break and drop off, something which

---

181. For instance *Hist.* 2.31: *praecurrente potentia Dei*; 10.29: *Christo cooperante*; *Gloria mart.* 44: *virtute beati martyris praeeunte*.
182. Brown 1970 in Brown 1972: 128.
183. On magic and religion, see Aune 1980 in Haase 1980: 1570-6.
184. *Hist.* 1.21. The story is based on the *Gesta Pilati* 11-5, in: von Tischendorf (ed.), *Evangelia apocrypha*, 2.Aufl., 367, 370 (Buchner 1967: 28 n. 1).

happened more often, in the absence of a visible agent, when a saint had been called upon.[185] The priest Wiliachar, for instance, who perhaps through no fault of his own, had incurred the anger of King Clothar, felt his iron chains fall apart 'like clay' three times when he invoked St Martin's aid, at the very instant that he pronounced the saint's 'most holy name (*nomen sacratissimum*)'.[186] The last time was at the court in the presence of the king and many witnesses. The king then, 'being an intelligent man, recognized that the power of St Martin was at work there (*videns virtutem sancti Martini ibidem operari*)' and restored the priest's liberty. This miracle was apparently necessary to convince the king to respect the church's right of sanctuary: someone who had sought the protection of the saint in his church, could not be imprisoned again. The emphasis with which Gregory says that the chains did not drop off before the holy name had been pronounced (in the prayer for aid), and that upon the pronouncing everything fell off at once, not only proves the saint's agency but looks very much like name magic,[187] here being practised in public. The distinction between prayer and magic cannot always be made.[188]

Several times, as Gregory reports it, a saint was actually seen by the prisoners, as he was freeing them.[189] In 591, Gregory, on his way to see King Childebert, heard the following story from someone in the district of Rheims.[190] With some other people, this man's servant had been put in a prison with a roof made of heavy wooden planks nailed down and weighted with large stones; the door was reinforced with iron and by a bolt with a lock.

> ...but the power (*virtus*) of the bishop, as the story-teller himself stated, removed the stones, threw the roof off, broke the chains, opened the beam that held the prisoners' feet together, and without opening the door brought the men outside by lifting them into the air, saying, 'I am Martin, soldier of Christ, your liberator (*absolutor*). Leave in peace, and don't be afraid'.

When Gregory later told the king about 'the miracle of this holy power (*virtutis hujus...miraculum*)', the latter told him that some of the liberated men had already been to see him and that he had waived their payment of the fine due to the state treasury. The angel who freed Joseph of Arimathea had lifted the walls — why not believe that St Martin lifted a roof? One suspects that these people were simply helped out by their

---

185. As, for instance, in *Hist.* 4.19; 5.8; 6.8; *Vit. patr.* 7.3.
186. *Virt. Mart.* 1.23.
187. Aune 1980 in Haase 1980: 1545-9.
188. Aune 1980 in Haase 1980: 1551-7.
189. *Hist.* 8.33. Compare *Hist.* 5.8.
190. *Virt. Mart.* 4.26.

friends; Gregory's detailed description shows that from the outside it may not have been too difficult to take the roof off. Perhaps there were those who knew how to use the current belief in saints' power to their own advantage. What the saint looked like is not said, except perhaps in his own words that he was a 'soldier'. Physical liberation from chains is here again associated with spiritual liberation from sin, this time explicitly by Christ; this means, in my opinion, that the words are Gregory's own interpretation, for edificatory purposes, of whatever it was that he was told.

On another occasion, in what may have been either a civil war or a popular uprising, stones and torches were thrown about by the crowd and someone killed a man with a sword.[191] A few days later, the dead man's brother struck down the murderer. The local authority (*iudex*) then had him locked up because he had 'dared to avenge the death of his brother at the whim of his own will, without awaiting [the decision of] the judge'. Other stories of Gregory's also show that blood revenge, though commuted into financial compensations in written Salic law, could still occur among those with Frankish-sounding names.[192] Since Gallo-Romans are known to have, upon occasion, borne Frankish names,[193] however, they could also have tended towards Frankish customs. Gregory does not say whether this man was a Frank or someone subject to Roman law. However this may have been, once in prison he began to 'invoke the names (*nominibus invocatis*) of many saints and to pray for their compassion' — again a curious mixture of what may be name-magic and prayer. But

> he turned to the holy man of God as though he were his own patron, saying, 'I have heard about you, holy Nicetius, that you are powerful in works of mercy and generous (*pius*) in liberating those who are put in chains and implore your help. I pray (*deprecor*) now that, because of that eminent kindness with which you so frequently shone in the liberation of other prisoners, you will deign to visit me'.
>
> Then, after he had slept a little, the blessed man appeared (*apparuit*) and said, 'Who are you, who invoke (*invocas*) the name Nicetius and whence do you know who he is, since you persist in beseeching him [to come] (*eum obsecrare non desinis*)?'
>
> When the man had told him from beginning to end how he came to perpetrate his crime, he added, 'Have pity on me, I beg you, if you are the man of God whom I invoke'.
>
> The holy man then said to him, 'Rise in the name of Christ and walk away free; for no-one will detain you'.
>
> Upon these words the man woke up and was astonished to find himself released: the chains had fallen apart and the beam was broken. At once and without fear he

191. *Vit. patr.* 8.7.
192. As *Hist.* 7.47; 9.19.
193. For instance, one of Gregory's great-uncles: Gundulfus (Stroheker 1970: 180).

went to [the saint's] tomb, no-one stopping him. Later, when the judge had waived the penalty for his criminal fault, the man was released and went home.

The qualities of power and generosity that the man attributes to the saint epitomize the mixed nature of this request for pity. It is an invocation of the saint's name and, at the same time, such a persistent appeal to repeat previous liberations and to come, that the saint, as his words show, is thereby forced to do so in spite of himself. The breaking of the fetters, too, appears to happen upon the pronouncement of the name of Christ.

Notwithstanding these clearly magical elements, the basic message is the superior quality of heavenly justice.[194] To maintain order in society, the earthly judge is obviously right to imprison someone breaking the law and committing arbitrary violence. A heavenly authority, however, can cut through legal quibbles to the real point: that the first murderer had a capital penalty waiting for him anyway, and that there were attenuating circumstances for the second, who in daily life was probably not a violent man. A dream-vision makes all this visible and explicit, for the man himself as well as for the judge, to whom the story must have been told. The report of the vision would not have been enough to convince the judge, however, without the broken chains. Is there perhaps a factual basis for these events in that the quality of the iron used at that time was actually inferior? At least as important is the fact that the man had sought sanctuary in the church of the saint. A saint who could appear and break chains would certainly be able to punish violation of the sanctuary of his church. As the church would have it, he was an authority with whom earthly judges did well to reckon.[195]

'A LUMINOUS MAN': PROPHECY

Some of Gregory's stories show that spiritual causation in natural calamities as well as in large-scale political and military events could be foretold and influenced, as well as carried out, by angels and saints. When Gregory's uncle Gallus was bishop of Clermont the bubonic plague raged in Provence and elsewhere in Gaul.[196] After the bishop had prayed night and day that he would not have to endure seeing his flock being slaughtered, 'an angel of the Lord appeared to him in a dream-vision (*visum noctis*) whose hair as well as whose robes were white as

---

194. See on this, Brown 1981: 93.
195. The saint sometimes 'liberated' men already hanging on the gallows, as in *Virt. Mart.* 3.53.
196. *Hist.* 4.5 and *Glor. mart.* 50. Similar stories are *Hist.* 2.13 (compare *Hist.* 2.1), *Hist.* 8.33 and *Hist.* 10.24.

snow', and who told him 'that his prayer had been heard'.[197] During his life the city would be spared; after eight years, however, the city would suffer: i.e., the bishop would be dead by then. Here a dream gave reassurance through prophecy. The bishop thereupon instituted 'rogations', days of collective penitence, in the middle of Lent, in which a procession on foot was made to the church of St Julian in Brioude, about 72 km away. This suggests that the latter saint may have been especially expected to provide protection. Then something strange happened in Clermont: '...the walls of houses and churches were suddenly seen to appear as marked with signs which the common people therefore called Thau'. This sign had, of course, once saved the houses of the righteous in Jerusalem from destruction.[198] And in fact, while other regions were devastated, the plague did not 'strike (*attigit*)' Clermont 'through the intercession (or interposition) of the holy Gallus' prayer (*intercedente oratione*)'. That this choice of words may indicate that the prayer is regarded as a 'shield' for the city in a virtually concrete sense is corroborated by Gregory's saying elsewhere that the plague was 'driven off (*depulsa est*) by the holy bishop Gallus' prayer'.[199]

Gregory's formulation, *in subita contemplatione...signari videbantur*, suggests that the 'signs' may have been a visionary phenomenon, although presumably everyone saw them. Ascribing the interpretation of the signs as 'Thau' to the common people, is one of Gregory's ways of suggesting an explanation without implicating himself.[200] It seems unlikely, however, that this group would be conversant enough with Biblical history to arrive at such an identification without clerical help. Whether visionary experience or not, it is not easy to explain these signs — a point to which I will return later.[201] Is it conceivable that a group affiliated with or consisting of the lower clergy, thinking of the Old Testament situation, decided to practise some sympathetic 'magic' by secretly marking the houses at night?[202]

There is another story about Clermont during the same plague, in which Gregory, in a somewhat more concrete formulation, says that the walls of houses and churches 'were suddenly seen to be signed and

---

197. Compare Judges 6:12 and Acts 10:31.
198. Ezek. 9:4.
199. *Glor. mart.* 50. Compare *Vit. patr.* 17.4. On pagan rites connected with the city walls as a defence against demons, illness and death, see Eliade 1952: 49.
200. Similar, for instance, is his reporting of a pagan omen in *Hist.* 6.45.
201. See pp. 288 ff.
202. Compare clerical magic in *Hist.* 5.5 and 9.37. On magical characters and the sign of the Cross: Harmening 1979: 237-8; runes: Salin 1959: 137-9.

marked (*in subita contemplatione...signarentur atque caraxarentur*)'. In it, we are told that Gregory's mother had a dream:[203]

> ...it appeared to her in a dream-vision as though (*apparuit in visu noctis quasi*) the wine which was kept in our cellars had been turned into blood. She lamented and cried,
>
> 'Woe is me! My house is designated for the plague (*signata plagae*)!'
>
> Then a certain man said to her, 'Do you know that the day after tomorrow, which is the first of November, the passion of the martyr Benignus will be celebrated?'
>
> 'I did know that', she said.
>
> 'Go', the man said, 'keep a vigil the whole night in his honour and let masses be said, and you will be rescued from the plague'.
>
> When she woke up from her sleep, she carried out what she had been commanded to do; and while the neighbouring houses were marked, ours remained untouched.

Gregory expects it to be understood that the vigil and the masses for the saint would support her request for his help in sparing her house, not only of the plague but also from the mysterious and frightening signs. The 'certain man', who is probably understood to be the martyr himself, 'commands' her what to do to allay anxiety: trust in the (in this case promised) help of a saint and make this plain to him and to others by certain recognized gestures of supplication. The latter at the same time function as a kind of individual propitiatory rite of 'rogation' to avert, in the wake of omens, an impending disaster. The difference with Bishop Gallus' dream-vision is significant: the latter prayed directly to God and was visited by an angel who told him that his request had been granted; Gregory's mother was told to ask a dead saint to save her, that is, to intercede for her with God. The latter listens only to the prayers of the righteous, Gregory says elsewhere.[204] Ordinary people therefore need a saint, on earth or in heaven, to transmit their requests to God.

Sometimes prayers for protection thus led to dream-knowledge of the divine plans for the future. Gregory relates a number of cases in which knowledge of the future was communicated in an unspecified manner, using expressions such as 'warned by God's foreknowledge', or else simply saying 'revealed by a vision', without giving further details.[205] Besides the visions of Salvius, of the nun of Poitiers and of Abbot Sunniulf,[206] Gregory tells of one other saint's vision of heaven. This one[207] was interpreted, however, as an announcement of his imminent decease:

203. *Glor. mart.* 50.
204. In *Virt. Jul. prol.*, for instance.
205. For instance, *Hist.* 2.1; 9.26; *Virt. Jul.* 6. See also *Hist.* 6.39.
206. *Hist.* 7.1; 6.29 and 4.33, respectively.
207. *Vit. patr.* 12.3.

he was carried through the air to 'the presence of the Lord' surrounded by angels, some of whom, reading from a book, dictated to Isaiah the words he was to prophesy while others sang praises. Near the end of his earthly life, Bishop Nicetius of Trier 'saw the apostle Paul and John the Baptist inviting him to come and enjoy eternal repose, showing me a crown decorated with heavenly pearls and saying, "Such splendours will you enjoy in the Kingdom of God"'.[208]

The same bishop had earlier had a dream (*visum noctis*) in which 'the Lord showed (*ostendere*) him' facts about the future Frankish kings:[209]

> ...he saw in a dream a large tower, so high that, seen from below, it seemed to reach heaven. It had many windows (*fenestrae*), and he saw the Lord standing on its highest point while his angels were stationed in the afore-mentioned look-outs (*speculae*) [the 'windows']. One of these angels held a large book in his hand and said, 'This king will live so long in the world and that king so long', and he named them all individually, those who were living at that time as well as those who were then yet to be born, and he announced how they would reign and how long they would live. After the name of each king [had been pronounced] the other angels replied 'Amen'.
>
> And what the saint had announced [i.e. predicted] about these men through this revelation (*revelatio*) was later fulfilled (*impletum est*).

This dream has an archetypal quality. The image of the tree, pole, mountain, tower or ladder that reaches from the earth to the sky appears in the mythologies of otherwise very diverse Asian, European and American archaic and traditional cultures; Eliade speaks of these images as ' "ouvertures" vers un monde trans-historique'.[210] Social and economic conditions as well as the specific cultural heritage influence the experienced form of this 'symbolisme du Centre' as he calls it: meaning the centre of the world or 'the heart of reality', the point of intersection and communication with the divine world or 'the sacred'.[211] The writings of the Church Fathers as well as early Christian liturgical texts also assimilated the Cross to a ladder, a column or a mountain as well as to a tree, the Tree of the World.[212] The many-windowed tower, however, with angels looking out of it and prophesying, and God standing on top of it,

---

208. *Vit. patr.* 17.6. Perhaps his dream of fishing in the sea (17.5) was also in a way prophetical.
209. *Vit. patr.* 17.5.
210. Eliade 1952: 229, 59-60.
211. Eliade 1952: 69, 50, 234.
212. Eliade 1952: 214-5. See also pp. 116 ff. The tower as an image may, however, be derived from a Celtic motif, as Pernoud 1957: 70 citing Dottin 1920. Severus, too, mentions a pagan tower with a crown on it: Severus, *Dial.* 3.8. There is a tower built on water which is a symbol of the church in one of the visions of the *Shepherd of Hermas* (Vision 1.1.3) in K. Lake (ed.), *The apostolic Fathers* vol. 2 (Loeb): 7-8 (mentioned in Patch 1970: 89-90).

seeing and ruling the world, also comes close to representing Gregory's view of the vertical axis, the stream of supernatural reality immanent in the life in this world.

Obviously, however, the possibility of deception in dreams is very real. Alongside a belief in veridical dreams, the Bible as well as antique culture contained a tradition warning against illusions.[213] The Parisian citizens' first reaction to the woman's dream about the impending city fire shows that also in Gregory's time belief in dreams was not uncritical:[214] '...many people laughed at her and said that she must have consulted the oracle of lots,[215] or that she had dreamed some kind of nonsense (*vana aliqua somniasset*) and that in any case the noonday demon made her say this ...'.[216] The woman replied that this was not so, '...on the contrary, I speak truth, for I saw in a dream (*vidi per somnium*)...'. Events, three days later, proved her right. In his classification of dreams, Macrobius had used the term *somnium* for a veridical dream that presented truth in allegorical form.[217] It seems clear, however, that Gregory regarded the woman's dream as a literal pre-vision of the future in the supernatural dimension. A strictly figurative prophetic message is the waking vision of Bishop Salvius, who saw a naked sword in the sky above King Chilperic's house and then foretold (*praedixit*), twenty days before the fact, that the latter's two sons would die.[218] The implication is that the bishop's holiness made him, as Gregory formulates it elsewhere, 'worthy' of seeing it and understanding its significance. Gregory himself, standing next to him, saw nothing. Besides one priest's dream of two doves symbolizing the arrival of two unexpected guests,[219] there are no other explicit indications that he regarded images perceived in dreams or visions, designated as such, as significant. Considering Gregory's waking scrutiny of visible phenomena for indications about the future however, it is likely that, aware of possible delusion, he did pay cautious attention to dream phenomena in his personal life. But this intimate process, if it took place, did not get written into his stories, which were intended for the edification of the faithful.

Verbal messages by supernatural figures were less ambiguous and carried more authority than silent symbolic forms, and in fact this is

213. Budd 1971; Harmening 1979: 95-117.
214. *Hist.* 8.33.
215. See Harmening 1979: 191-4.
216. As in Ps. 90:6. Compare *Virt. Mart.* 3.9: a *daemon meridianus* caused a contracted foot.
217. Macrobius, *Comm.* 1.3.10. See Lewis 1964: 63-4.
218. *Hist.* 5.50.
219. *Hist.* 3.15.

how the visionary prophecy that Gregory reports is more frequently experienced. In one story, Gregory ridicules prophecy by a contemporary woman that he was told about 'who had the spirit of prophecy (*habens spiritum phitonis*)', and attributes her powers to the devil, 'who was a liar from the beginning'[220] and then mentions a dream that he himself had shortly afterwards. When, after having celebrated a vigil (a fact which is probably meant to be significant), 'I was lying on my bed and sleeping, I saw an angel (*angelus*) flying through the air. As he flew over the holy church he shouted with a loud voice, "Alas! Alas! God has struck Chilperic and all his sons, and none of those who have come from his loins will ever remain to reign in his kingdom!"' At that time, Gregory adds, the king still had four sons. When 'these things were later carried out (*inpleta*), I knew for sure that what the soothsayers (*arioli*) promised was false'. Had he until then been having doubts about his dream?

'THE PLEADING OF THE BISHOP': HEAVENLY DIPLOMACY

Whereas the angel Gregory saw simply communicated a divine decision about a major political event, the one who appeared to Bishop Gallus informed him of the result, as it were, of heavenly diplomacy on the subject of a large-scale social catastrophe. The latter was also the subject of the other prophetic dreams that Gregory tells us about. In the middle of the fifth century, Bishop Aravatius (Servatius) of Tongeren, a man 'of utmost sanctity', tried to prevent the Huns' invasion of Gaul with vigils, fasts, tears and prayers.[221] 'However, he felt through the spirit that, on account of the sins of the people, this was not granted to him'. Thinking that the support of 'the patronage (*patrocinium*) of apostolic power (*virtus*) would help him obtain more easily those things for which he humbly supplicated the divine compassion', he went to Rome and spent many two- or three-day periods without food or drink in unceasing prayer at St Peter's tomb. The apostle was said to have finally appeared to him, saying, 'Why are you disturbing me, most holy man?' and informing him that God's decision was unalterable: but that the bishop would die quickly so that he might be spared seeing it. Like that of Bishop Gallus, this story shows that an apostle's influence as well as a saint's had its limitations: the deserved punishment of sins could weigh more heavily. In the story of another vision about this time, the dead St Stephen was seen pleading with the apostles Peter and Paul to spare the city of Metz because his relics were kept in a chapel there and he wanted

---

220. *Hist.* 5.14; Acts 16:16.
221. *Hist.* 2.5.

'the people to know that he had some influence with the Lord (*aliquid me posse cum Domino*)'.²²² But the 'Lord's sentence over [the city] had already been pronounced' and all he could obtain through the apostles was that his chapel might escape destruction.

Where two holy men failed, a woman got her way, perhaps because she pleaded for the safe return of only one person, her husband.²²³ This, however, happened to be Aetius, the Roman general in Gaul, who led the Roman-Gothic-Frankish coalition against the invading Huns, and he was likely to survive only if he won the battle. She, too, spent days and nights praying in the churches of Peter and Paul. One night, a drunken man fell asleep in a corner of St Peter's church and, unnoticed by the guardians, was locked in. Waking up in the middle of the night, he saw that all the lamps were lighted, realized that this must have a supernatural cause and, thoroughly frightened, tried to find a way out of the building. When he did not succeed, and lay cowering in a corner to wait until matins, he saw two figures greeting each other respectfully and inquiring about each other's health. The elder of the two (presumably Peter) then said,

> 'I can no longer endure the tears of Aetius' wife. She has been begging me continuously to bring her husband back (*reducere*) safely from Gaul. Although divine judgment had already prescribed otherwise, I have nevertheless obtained the enormous favour of his life. And so I'm off to get him back from there alive! If anyone should happen to have heard this, however, I adjure him to keep silent about it and not to presume to divulge God's secret, or he will disappear quickly from this world'.

At the crack of dawn the next morning the man, who could not keep the news to himself, told the lady everything anyway — and promptly died on the spot. This latter event, though unfortunate, was no doubt regarded as proof of the truth of his story. Here, importunity or pressure has been exercised successfully: Peter could no longer endure it. As we have seen, Gregory recommends such pressure to back up justifiable requests and supports this with biblical passages.²²⁴ It is also notable that Peter went in person to save Aetius. In the battle, the Hunnish leader Attila, 'seeing that his army was being decimated, fled from the scene'. Gregory continues: 'So (*nam*), no one will doubt that the Hun's army was put to flight through the pleading (*obtentus*) of the afore-mentioned bishop'. Apparently, God is taking care of the large-scale event while Peter himself protects an individual, Aetius. Dreams, then, show that the diplomacy as well as the physical protection of a patron in heaven was necessary for survival in the late Roman world.

222. *Hist.* 2.6.
223. *Hist.* 2.7.
224. See chapter II n. 147, 148.

THE HEAVENLY PATRON: THE IMAGE OF THE IDEAL GOVERNOR

Dream-visions, then, can be experiences of supernatural help, usually by a saint, in small and great events. They make visible what was regarded as a more powerful, concurrent stream of reality determining all natural and human events. A large number of these visionary experiences occur at moments when individual ingenuity or social or political institutions appear to be inadequate to handle the situation: during the liturgy, at moments of personal danger, when confronted with a technical problem, in the administration of justice, and in the face of natural or human calamities. In all cases, the aid or solution is experienced as supernaturally given, not as worked out by man himself. This resembles the situation in certain 'primitive' societies, in which new ideas or institutions are acceptable only if they are sanctioned by a supernatural dream.[225] The visionaries, and those supporting them, in the present case the church, are the innovators. This view of inner and outer events seems to betray an incomplete sense of self resulting in a very deep sense of human inadequacy and extensive dependence on the aid and support of a higher authority: the saint functioned in fact as the other half of one's personality.

The imputed approachability of the saints and what was regarded as their reciprocal obligations with men made the latter feel far from helpless, however. Their belief in the saint's effective patronage functioned as a social institution.[226] Dreams and imaginings of the ideal patron helped to maintain social stability, resolve disputes, offer protection, guarantee justice and innovate when and where necessary. This seems to confirm Brown's statement that 'what a society regards as holy...is a precipitate of that society's needs and structure'. It also seems to confirm E. Durkheim's statement about the ideal as 'a natural product of social life': 'society cannot create or recreate itself without at the same time creating an ideal'.[227] An examination of the saint's role in cures has shown that he functions in the same way for the individual. We have also seen, however, that this ideal is not *only* a 'precipitate' of social needs and structure or 'a natural product' of social life: it is a symbol of transformation transmitted through many centuries of social changes, adapted to, but not, in essence, created by the specific needs of the society in which it functions.

---

225. Devereux 1967 in Caillois and von Grunebaum 1967: 197.
226. Compare Douglas 1966: 89: 'It's misleading to think of ideas such as destiny, witchcraft, mana, magic as part of philosophies ... they are institutions'.
227. Brown 1973 in Brown 1982: 263 and Durkheim 1960: 603.

The dreams and visionary experiences described in the next section show, however, that in sixth-century Merovingian society, intimidation by a saint could be an important social instrument. Because the church had been forbidden to use armed violence, she was forced to find other ways to defend her interests.

D. VISIONARY WARNING AND PUNISHMENT

M. Douglas has said that

> ..a primitive world view looks out on a universe which is personal in several different senses. Physical forces are thought of as interwoven with the lives of persons. Things are not completely distinguished from persons and persons are not completely distinguished from their external environment. The universe responds to speech and mime. It discerns the social order and intervenes to uphold it.[228]

Gregory's view of how accidents, sudden illness, possession by evil spirits or death (as 'divine punishments') befall those who have perpetrated certain crimes resembles this kind of thinking. His stories make visible a belief in, as it were, the immanent divine justice that the unarmed church needed to establish in society in order to protect herself from arbitrary aggression and spoliation. When conciliar legislation had forbidden the clergy to defend their interests by violence (i.e., arms), the bishops had resorted to threats of excommunication and curses involving divine punishment (*anathema; maledictio*).[229] In what Gregory lets bishops say and also in the dream-visions, we see that this immanent divine justice is imagined as being carried out by the saint in person. In some dream-visions however, misbehaving priests and bishops who could not otherwise be brought under control were castigated or punished. Here, too, the vision compensates for a deficiency, in this instance in the ecclesiastical disciplinary machinery.

Considering the many stories about true contrition and Gregory's emphasis on the grace of forgiveness, it is at first sight surprising to find that some stories about punitive miracles and/or dream-visions are decidedly vindictive in tone. Closer examination shows, however, that such stories usually concern not ordinary misdeeds but those which are directed against one's own family or against the church.[230] Dependents of the saint (and *ipso facto* of the bishop) were also designated as his *familia*, however, and the imagining of immanent divine justice as personal action

---

228. Douglas 1966: 88.
229. *Conc. Aurel.* a.541, c.23 (Maassen 1893: 92); *Conc. Tur.* a.567, c.25 (Maassen 1893: 134). On this kind of thinking, see Douglas 1966: 85-8. Compare Gregory's thinking on this point in Reydellet 1977: 177-8.
230. See on this Blume 1970: 71.

by an angry saint must be a reflection of contemporary practices of vengeance via kinship relations. Visualized in this way, it would be something even illiterate, warlike Franks could understand.[231] This function of the saint's power can only point to the fact that, in this period, the church as an institution must have felt severely threatened by the society which, as Gregory's stories show, it tried to dominate in order not to be dominated by it. To do this, the church needed to show (for instance by reports of visions) that the superior, heavenly authority whose representative on earth it claimed to be, was in effective control of events.

The experience of such a vision however, as Gregory describes it, also produces a powerful emotion: fear. Its effect can be the inverse of a cure. It can temporarily incapacitate or even kill its recipient or the one to whom the threat is addressed. Not only the direct, affective experience of images but also that of what looks like the magical power of the spoken word, or curse, seem to be involved in some of these cases. Visions could be accepted as true or rejected as 'dream fantasies' but they could not be reasoned with: for the person concerned, they either possessed or did not possess the irrational compulsiveness of dreamlife. Alongside certain stories of non-visionary punitive miracles, visions of warning and punishment show that this dreamlife or dream-thinking must have been, at least for a number of people, a mode of consciousness that could be easily called up and which could decisively influence behaviour, if not also physical condition.

The context in which dream-visions of warning and punishment occurred becomes clearer if we begin by looking at a dream in which Gregory perceived[232] the inner dynamic of an existing, very problematical situation in which he found himself. His view of this situation reveals so much about his world-picture and his use of the dream also tells us so much about the latter as a social instrument and about his personality, that it is worth treating in some detail. When King Guntram began to investigate the murder of his brother King Chilperic in 584, the widowed Queen Fredegunde accused the chamberlain Eberulf. The king thereupon vowed that he would kill the man and all his offspring into the ninth generation, a statement indicating how the individual in this time was still immersed in his family.[233] When Eberulf heard this, he fled to his spiritual 'family': Gregory was the godfather of his son. Accordingly, Eberulf sought asylum and installed himself in the church of St Martin — even

---

231. Compare Riché 1976 in Plongeron and Pannet 1976: 88.
232. *Hist.* 7.22.
233. Schmid 1967: 233 and passim.

though, as Gregory says pointedly, he had often enriched himself at the expense of the latter's properties — and expected Gregory, as his son's godfather but also as mouthpiece of the saint, to defend him and his interests against the king. The latter, meanwhile, confiscated and redistributed the chamberlain's properties.

There was double trouble in another way too. Not only did Eberulf continue to live out in the church his apparently accustomed life-style of wine, women and song with a murder now and then thrown in for good measure, but the armed bands sent by the king to prevent his escape plundered St Martin's estates in the region as well as those of Eberulf. The latter accused the bishop of not protecting these and swore vengeance. One night, moreover, he discovered that the door of the sacristy through which his servants had been accustomed to enter the church at night (the other doors being locked) had been barred. The reason that Gregory gives for this is that his clergy (very likely including himself) had been offended by Eberulf's servants' looking disrespectfully at the holy paintings and ornaments in the church. Thereupon Eberulf burst into the vigil which Gregory was at that moment holding and in a violent, drunken way accused Gregory with many curses (*maledictiones*) of trying to keep him away from the fringe of (the cloth covering the tomb of) St Martin: this fringe was regarded as one of the most important ducts of holy power. Gregory was stupefied by this attack, thought Eberulf had gone mad (*insania*) and tried to mollify him with friendly words. When this did not have any effect and the man seemed to be 'driven by a demon', Gregory simply kept silent, finished the vigil and left, sorrowing that such violence should have occurred without any respect for the saint, right in front of his tomb. The latter statement is significant, as is also the one referring to Eberulf's injury to the saint by plundering his properties. Gregory is preparing the reader to expect vengeance by the saint for all these insults to his honour.

Then Gregory says that 'in these days' he had a dream 'which [he] told to Eberulf in the holy church in the following manner' — a formulation which may indicate that Gregory did not tell him the dream exactly as he experienced it. As will become obvious, Gregory's telling Eberulf the dream was almost certainly intended to convince him in an indirect manner of his own good intentions and to warn Eberulf to make the right supplicatory gestures towards the saint whose protection he had sought. At the same time, however, Gregory is using it to express his own opinion on the matter as well as to find out about Eberulf's intentions, a ploy which we will see him use again in a more dangerous situation with King Guntram. Gregory tells Eberulf:

> It seemed to me as though I were celebrating the sacred ceremony of mass in this

church. When the silken cloth had already been spread over the altar and the Eucharist, I suddenly saw King Guntram enter [the church]. He shouted very loudly,

'Get this enemy of our family out of here! Tear this murderer away from the sacred altar of God!'

When I heard this, I turned to you and said,

'Take hold of the altar cloth covering the sacred gifts [i.e. the Eucharist], you unhappy man, so that will not be thrown out of here!'

Then you took it in your hand, but loosely; you didn't really hold on to it. I, however, spread out my arms and stood chest to chest with the king and said,

'Don't take this man out of the holy church or your life will be in danger: the holy bishop [Martin] will strike you with his power (*virtus*)! Don't kill yourself with your own javelin! If you do this, you will lose the present life as well as the eternal!'

When the king would not listen to me, you let go of the [altar] covering and came to stand behind me. I was extremely annoyed with you [for doing this, and said so]. Then you went back to the altar and took hold of the covering but let it go again. While you were only loosely holding onto the covering and I was vigorously resisting the king, I woke up terrified. I didn't know what the dream might mean.

It looks as though Gregory here puts his own criticism of Eberulf's conduct into the mouth of King Guntram. When he had related the dream to Eberulf, the latter said that 'it accorded exactly with his thoughts': he had decided that if the king were to order him to be taken out of the church, he would hold onto the altar covering with one hand and with his other hand strike down with his sword first Gregory and then whoever else of the clergy he could find so as to avenge the injury he (thought he had) suffered at their hands. Gregory says he was again speechless with amazement and thought that the devil must be speaking through him, 'for he never showed the least fear (*timor*) of God'. Later, Gregory reports in an equally visual, dramatic manner how, while he was staying on an estate about thirty miles away, an assassin sent by King Guntram (Gregory lets this stand without comment), posing as a friend, killed Eberulf in the church. Gregory concludes that Eberulf 'did not deserve to be saved by [St Martin] because he had never known how to ask him for this in faith'. The assassin was speedily cut down by Eberulf's servants, who were thereupon killed by the furious dependents of the church: a crowd of registered poor (*matricularii*) and possessed persons 'avenging the violence done to the church... And so the vengeance of God (*Deo ultio*) came upon those who had defiled the blessed church with human blood'. The king, Gregory says, again without comment, took all the properties and possessions that had belonged to the assassin and distributed them among his followers. These left his widow completely destitute behind in the holy church. There is criticism implied here too. Gregory is not indifferent: he is letting the truth tell itself. The implication may be that she joined the group of the registered poor who were cared for by the church on a permanent basis.

The triad of injury, protection and vengeance is central in this story. The concepts that operate in earthly society operate in the heavenly society as well and both are visible in concrete events. What becomes clear here is that, in the *social* context, St Martin's power is thought of as an immanent and semi-automatic kind of divine justice or vengeance. The exertion of influence upon it is possible, though not certain, by the right attitude and the right mode of supplication. The semi-automatic holy power of this divine justice inheres especially in certain 'sacred' objects, such as the church building, the Eucharist and its covering, and the fringes of the covering of St Martin's tomb, but it is in fact always present, never far away. In dream-visions of warning and punishment this immanent divine justice appears as personalized in a saint.

'A FRIGHTENING PERSON': CRITICISM, WARNING AND INTIMIDATION

Gregory himself was twice admonished in a dream. Here is one of his first-hand reports.[234] Once, during a Christmas eve vigil, when he had retired to his room to sleep for a while,

> a certain man came towards me and said, 'Get up and go back to the church!'
>
> I woke up, made the sign of the Cross and went back to sleep. The man did not leave it at that and repeated his words. When I did not get up after the second warning and again fell asleep, he struck me on the cheek and said,
>
> 'What's this? You who ought to be admonishing others to keep the vigil are letting yourself be overcome by sleep?'
>
> Terrified by this, I [got up and] hurried back to the church.

This is a clear case of the personification of a bad conscience, appearing in what must have been a state of half-sleep. It took three warnings for Gregory to take notice; this occurs too in a few other dream-visions he tells us about and for the same reason.[235] In the following story, a command is given to a priest three times.[236] In the main church of Narbonne hung a painting that represented (*indicat*) our Lord as (*quasi*) crucified and wearing only a loincloth.

> This painting was looked at a great deal by the people. Then there appeared in a dream-vision (*visum*) to a certain priest called Basileus a frightening figure (*persona terribilis*) who said,

---

234. *Glor. mart.* 86. The other warning he received is related in *Virt. Mart.* 2.1.
235. *Virt. Mart.* 3.42; *Glor. conf.* 90. Compare Benz 1969: 175; Dulaey 1973: 149; Pernoud 1957: 65 states that the number three was extremely significant for the Celts. Salin 1959: 454 says that many Celtic and pre-Celtic artistic habits reappeared when Roman government and civilization declined in Gaul.
236. *Glor. mart.* 22.

'All of you are covered with various kinds of clothes and, together, keep looking at my nakedness. Hurry up, and cover me with a cloth!'

But the priest did not understand the vision (*visio*) and the next day did not remember having had it. The figure appeared (*apparuit*) to him again, and again it made no impression on him. On the third day after the second vision, however, [the man appeared again and] struck the priest with hard blows, saying, 'Didn't I tell you to cover me with a cloth so that I would not be seen naked? And you did nothing about it. Go now, and cover that painting in which I appear (*appareo*) crucified, or a swift death will overtake you!'

The priest, upset and very frightened, told the story to his bishop, who at once ordered a covering to be hung over the painting...

Here a priest, who would not be listened to if he spoke on his own authority, was able to express criticism by means of a dream which is typical for this period. A command, physical violence, and the threat of death all produce fear, which in turn finally gets things done. In the other visions, too, this pattern, in many variations, keeps recurring.[237] In this context, it is almost certainly significant that someone just then felt nakedness to be inappropriate for Christ as supreme, fear-inspiring authority.[238] Gregory mentions Christ, if at all, as the Lord of Creation; it is not clear whether the heavenly judge or king who appears in certain visions is the Father or the Son. When a compassionate healer appears, it is, as we saw above, the saint, not Christ. In the sixth-century sources that are extant, there is one exception to this imagining of Christ as a stern authority: Queen Radegunde, as nun, saw him in a vision as a rich, beautiful and loving youth. This image, however, may be connected with her personal and family history.[239] Many, many other stories too make it clear, through miracles or through punishments of those who fail to do so, that the church, its sacraments, its rules and its clergy are to be held in awe.[240] A certain Dado, for instance, possibly a country gentleman, had promised to give two chalices, acquired as booty in a military expedition, to a village church containing relics of St Nicetius of Lyon, if he returned home safely.[241] Once home, however, he gave only one and, instead of the

---

237. Dinzelbacher 1981: 148-9 and 167 notes that the early medieval longer visions have the quality of fear, power, distance and tend to be in terms of reward and punishment.
238. Compare, by way of contrast, Severus' report of St Martin recognizing the devil in an apparition in imperial garb, saying he was Christ: Severus, *Vit. Mart.* 24.4-8.
239. Baudonivia, *Vit. Rad.* 20.
240. For instance, *Hist.* 4.36 (slander of a dead bishop is punished by sudden death); *Hist.* 4.39 (the same punishment for slandering a living bishop); *Virt. Mart.* 1.29: *vindex est enim Deus velociter servorum suorum*; *Virt. Jul.* 17 (sudden death for taking church property).
241. *Vit. patr.* 8.11.

other, gave 'a Sarmatian cloth to cover the altar of the Lord and the gifts (*oblationes:* the Eucharist) on it'. However,

> the blessed man [Nicetius] appeared to this man in a dream (*apparuit...per somnium*) and said,
>> 'Why are you so slow in carrying out your promise and why are you being dishonest? Go and give the church the other chalice as you promised, or you and your house will perish! As for the covering, it is too loose in texture to be placed on the gifts of the altar: it does not sufficiently cover the mystery of the body and the blood of the Lord'.
>
> The man, frightened out of his wits, at once carried out his promise.

Again a vision and a threat of death to his whole house was necessary to enforce respect. Gifts in return for a cure were an antique pagan tradition; they do not occur in the Bible.[242] We see here that a country church could be dependent on gifts even for its liturgical apparatus, and that such equipment was apparently not always easy to come by.

Relics, too, were essential for a church, almost certainly to ensure the presence and aid of the saints concerned. An 'abbot' in the region of Bourges bought some relics of St Vincent from someone who must have presented himself as a travelling salesman.[243] 'It was revealed (*revelatum*)' to him, however, and also 'shown in a dream-vision (*per visum manifestum*)' to the archpriest living close to the monastery, that these relics had been stolen from the church of another village and should be returned. On another occasion[244], someone else had a similar idea. He stole 'silk cloths woven with gold and decorated with gems' from the church of the martyr Felix in Narbonne, planning to sell them with great gain 'in other regions'. On his way, he met a man who told him he had many friends in various regions and also a large and quiet house in which this 'great treasure' could be safely deposited to be sold whenever he wanted to do so. The thief was then led back to the city he had just come from but did not recognize the way 'because God had closed his eyes'. Only after he had, on the advice of the unknown man, deposited his goods in the church of the martyr did he recognize it for what it was - but by then his companion had disappeared: 'whence it cannot be doubted that the blessed martyr himself had appeared (*apparuisse*) to him'. Over against this charming story, however, stand many ills and evils inflicted by other saints whose churches or properties were robbed.[245] In pagan Roman society, taking responsibility for these ills

242. In Matth. 10:8 Jesus says that all cures are free. Meier 1949: 65 reports that in the pagan tradition patients fell ill again if they did not offer a gift in time.
243. *Glor. mart.* 89.
244. *Glor. mart.* 91.
245. As, for instance, *Hist.* 3.12, 16: 4/16. 38:7.10, 21, 35; 8.12; 9.30; *Virt. Jul.* 13, 14, 15, 16, 17.

would have been understood as an admission to the practice of destructive magic[246], but the Merovingian clergy conceived of such events as autonomous, immanent divine justice. Fear of such 'punishment' was evidently necessary to protect church property: visions worked in the same direction. One of Gregory's servants and his family were afflicted with an illness until, warned in a dream (*visum noctis*) by 'a frightening figure (*persona terribilis*)', he let a relic of St Martin which had been left lying about the house be given a more appropriate place.[247] These visionary warnings, reinforced by illness, achieved their purpose. More often, the saint simply punished the wrong-doer. In the following section, we shall see how this punishment could also be executed through or in a vision.

In one case, a vision was the means by which a member of a bishop's clergy could express criticism of his superior's behaviour,[248] something which may then have been almost impossible in any other way. In court, members of the lower clergy were not allowed to testify against their bishop.[249] When, after the death of Bishop Nicetius of Lyon (573), his successor Priscus and his wife 'did many evil things (*contra rationem*)' — such as persecuting and killing his predecessor's friends — 'the saint appeared to someone [an abbot] in a dream (*somnium*) and said, "Go and tell Priscus to stop his evil works and begin doing good ones. And also say to the priest Martin, 'Because you consented to these deeds, you will be chastised. If you aren't willing to mend your ways, you will die'."' The dreamer told this story the next morning to a deacon and asked him, as a friend of the bishop's, to transmit the message to him as well as to the priest. The deacon however, probably out of fear, procrastinated. That night the saint appeared to him in his sleep, asked why he had not gone to say what the abbot had told him, and pummelled his throat with his fists. The next morning, the deacon, with a painful and swollen neck, went and told the men all that he had heard, but they called his story 'dream phantasies (*fantasia somniorum*)' and were not impressed. The priest later died, thus fulfilling the words of the dream. Gregory had already mentioned earlier that the bishop and his whole house had become ill and thereafter remained pale, weak and stunned (*stupidus*), 'so that no one doubted that they had been struck (*percussus*) by the power (*virtus*) of the

---

246. Compare Brown 1970 in Brown 1972: 129-30: 'in popular belief the line between [saints and sorcerers] was very thin: St Ambrose, to name only one saint, was associated with twelve deaths — more deaths than stand to the credit of any Late Roman *maleficus*'.
247. *Virt. Mart.* 1.35. Compare *Glor. mart.* 47.
248. *Hist.* 4.36.
249. Compare *Hist.* 5.49.

holy man'. This is again a formulation with a clearly magical ring. The swollen neck 'proved' the sincerity of the dream-teller and, even though the content of the dream was not taken seriously, perhaps saved him from imprisonment or worse.

In another case, the same treatment could have another function. A priest who had protested, when Bishop Nicetius' will had been read out loud in public, that the latter had left nothing to the church in which he was buried, was made to eat his words.[250] The night after the public reading, the dead bishop appeared (*apparuit*) to him, wearing a 'shimmering robe' and accompanied by two other bishops, to whom he accused the priest of uttering blasphemies against him,

> '... not realizing that I left the most precious thing I have to the church: the dust of my body'.
> The others said, 'He has done ill to slander a servant of God'.
> Then the saint turned to the priest and began to pound his throat with his fists, saying, 'Sinner worthy of being ground underfoot! Stop speaking so foolishly!'

The next morning the priest's throat was so painful that he could hardly swallow; he kept his bed in agony for forty days. Then, when he had 'invoked the name of the confessor' he was given back his health and never dared utter such words again. Nicetius' epithet for the priest could hardly be more vindictive; his, apparently customary, hard-handed manner of warning gets the point across. After relating a further incident, Gregory concludes: 'So much for deeds of revenge (*ultiones*)'.

'*A THREATENING FACE*': CURSES AND INSTANT VENGEANCE

Divine or saintly 'vengeance' specifically designated as such is a prominent theme in Gregory's writings, for the reasons already mentioned. There are as many or more cases in which this term does not occur but the meaning is the same.[251] Gregory also uses variations on the term 'the judgment of God (*iudicium Dei*)' or 'the vengeance of God (*Deo ultio*)' in this context;[252] it is something individuals can invoke. Before the battle with his rebellious son Chramn, for instance, Gregory lets King Clothar say,[253] 'Look down from heaven, Lord, and judge my cause[254] for I suffer injuries undeservedly from my son; ...and impose the judgment (*iudicium*) that you once gave between

---

250. *Vit. patr.* 8.5.
251. For instance, *Virt. Jul.* 45: *insipientes corrigat*; 21: *multa in praevaricatoribus ostendit*.
252. For instance, *Hist.* 6.31: *iudicium Dei*; *Virt. Mart.* 1.2: *iudicio Dei prosequente*; *Hist.* 4.14: *Dei ultio*; *Hist.* 4.39: *divina ultio*; *Hist.* 8.31: *Deus ultor*.
253. *Hist.* 4.21.
254. Compare Ps. 80:15; 43:1.

Absalom and his father David'. Here the battle becomes an ordeal[255] as well as a revenge. Somewhat differently, the pretender Gundowald, on realizing that he had been betrayed by one whom he had trusted,[256]

> raised his hands and eyes to heaven and said, 'Eternal judge and true revenge (*ultio*) of the innocent, O God, from whom all justice proceeds, in whom no falsity or craftiness can exist, to you I commend my cause, praying that you will immediately wreak revenge upon those (*ut sis velociter ultor super eos*) who gave me, innocent, into the hands of my enemies'.

The traitor was later executed upon the order of King Guntram, whom Gregory usually regards as being on the side of God and who gave half of Gundowald's treasure 'to the poor and to the churches'.[257] Variations on a formulation such as 'the divine majesty was the avenger of innocent blood' are to be found scattered throughout Gregory's works.[258]

But God is the special avenger of the clergy, as for instance in: 'The vengeance of God (*ultio divina*), which always protects his servants from the mouths of rabid dogs, was at hand'.[259] Bishop Praetextatus, who had displeased the maleficent Queen Fredegunde for political reasons, was struck down by her men as he knelt in the church.[260] When the queen later hypocritically came to him as he lay dying on his bed and asked if he wanted her to send some experienced doctors to treat his wounds, he refused and said, '... you will be cursed in the world (*maledictus in saeculo*) and God will be the avenger (*erit ultor*) of my blood on your person'. This combination of curse[261] and divine revenge (was the latter thought to carry out the former?) is an unarmed bishop's only weapon in a treacherous and violent society: it shows again the impossibility of any clear-cut distinction between magic and religion.

Many stories describe the tremendous 'power' inhering in and acting through contact with saints' relics. Alongside their positive and constructive qualities they can also do harm: perjurers are rigidified or thrown over backwards in a kind of fit, horses refuse to move, sarcophagi become too heavy to lift, and when not properly handled, relics can cause illness.[262] Even the most well-meaning person could inadvertently make a *faux pas* in

---

255. As in *Hist.* 7.32 and *Hist.* 10.3.
256. *Hist.* 7.38.
257. *Hist.* 7.40.
258. As in *Hist.* 7.3. Further, for instance, *Hist.* 7.29: *Adfuit autem Dei ultio de praesenti super eos qui beatum atrium humano sanguine polluerunt.*
259. *Hist.* 8.12.
260. *Hist.* 8.31.
261. On the magic of spoken words, see Harmening 1979: 221. On magical prayer, including curses: Aune 1980 in Haase 1980: 1551-5. Compare, on the power of words, also Van der Leeuw 1956: 14.
262. *Glor. mart.* 54, *Virt. Mart.* 1.35 and *Hist.* 5.8, respectively.

the required 'etiquette', and Gregory connects purely formal mistakes with inevitable and to our minds disproportionately harsh consequences, as the following stories show. One motivation for this harsh treatment must have been the enforcement of absolute and total reverence. A further reason for it was the compulsively analogical manner of thinking and doing things that is evident in Gregory's stories. An act or event either tends to conform to earlier models, or as it were, to constrain another event of the same or inverse type to happen. The images or forms themselves appear to possess a potency due to their resemblance to, and thus participation in, a model: they can also, through their form alone, trigger a new occurrence of the same sort of event. In my view, the many invocations of saints in which it is somehow emphasized that they 'always' aid those calling upon them also fall into this category. They have some of the qualities of sympathetic magic. If the attitude of supplication is right, the effect seems to be expected to follow 'automatically' from the pronouncement of the formula and the name of the saint.

Likewise, as Gregory interprets it, a physical slight to relics sometimes entailed 'necessary' consequences, as it were, that had nothing to do with their victim's intentions. Bishop Sidonius' sister and wife had a church (*templum*) built for the martyr Anatolian.[263] During the construction (evidently in a cemetery) however, they unknowingly let other saint's bones which they had found in the ground, be buried together in a heap.

> That this was not acceptable to God or to the martyr appeared (*apparuit*) to someone in a dream-vision (*visum*). He saw the blessed Anatolian, [standing next to] other saints, loudly complaining and saying,
> 'Woe is me, for on my account many of my brothers have been injured! Indeed, I say it also because those who have begun [this work] will not be able to finish it'. And so it happened.

The beautifully decorated church later caved in. In another story the saintly bishop Quintianus enlarged the church of a beatified former bishop in Rhodez, and in doing so moved the saint's relics.[264] He, too, was told that this was not 'acceptable': 'appearing in a dream-vision (*visum*) to the bishop, the saint said, "Because you dared to move my bones, which were resting in peace, I will remove you from this city, and you will be an exile in another region...".' Here again, one act brings on another of the same type. Gregory then goes on to relate how the bishop was forced to flee from the city by a different causal chain: because he was suspected of Frankish sympathies by the then Visigothic rulers. In Clermont, whose bishop he

253. *Glor. mart.* 64.
254. *Vit. patr.* 4.1.

eventually became, he later managed to manoeuvre the count of the city, who had arrested and imprisoned one of his relatives, into a corner by means of a curse.[265] The old man had himself carried to the count's house; there

> he shook the dust off his shoes against it[266] and said,
> 'Cursed be this house, cursed be also its inhabitants for eternity, let it be deserted and uninhabited!'
> The people standing around all said 'Amen'. Then the bishop added,
> 'I ask you, Lord, that no-one of this house which did not listen to its bishop, ever be raised to the episcopal office!'

Again a 'congruent' punishment, and again too the combination of a curse and a prayer for harm. Very soon after this, one person after another in the house developed an acute fever. After three days the count, fearing the worst, asked for forgiveness at the feet of the bishop. This was granted; the bishop then gave him 'blessed water' to sprinkle against the walls of his house; when this had been done, everyone recovered. The curse about the exclusion from the episcopal office later also came true.[267]

The list of the deaths which Gregory interprets as divine or saintly punishments for offences is long.[268] Three of these were announced or in some way brought about by dream-visions. In the eighth year of his episcopate, Pappolus of Langres, who according to Gregory was a decidedly bad bishop, had a dream:[269]

> On a certain night as he lay sleeping, the blessed Tetricus [one of his predecessors and a distant relative of Gregory's] appeared (*apparuit*) to him with a threatening face (*vultu minaci*) and said, 'What are you doing here, Pappolus? Why are you defiling (*polluis*) my seat? Why are you plundering my church? Why are you dispersing the sheep entrusted to me? Get out of here, give up the bishop's office and take yourself as far away as you can from this region!' As he said this, he struck Pappolus' chest with a heavy blow from a switch (or rod) that he held in his hand.
> Pappolus awoke from this, and while he was thinking about what it could mean, he felt a sharp stitch in his chest and was tortured by extreme pain.

From then on he could neither eat nor drink and expired, spitting blood, on the third day.[270] For Gregory, this dream was not a projection of one individual's bad conscience onto the person who had been wronged, but the saint pronouncing a thinly veiled curse and inflicting a fatal blow.

265. *Vit. patr.* 4.3.
266. Matth. 10:14-5.
267. *Hist.* 4.35.
268. Sudden deaths as punishment in, for instance: *Hist.* 2.23; 4.18; 5.17; 8.12, 40; *Glor. mart.* 24, 47, 78; *Virt. Jul.* 13, 15; *Virt. Mart.* 1.17, 30, 31; *Glor. conf.* 62, 66, 78, 92; *Vit. patr.* 8.11.
269. *Hist.* 5.5.
270. Compare Kelsey 1973: 247-9.

Doubtless, the implication is that the many other deaths which occurred as punishments or vengeance by the saint could have come about in like manner. This dream-vision proves that it is indeed the saint who is acting. The message is, of course: 'Let other bishops beware!' A story such as this was probably one of the few ways of enforcing discipline among this privileged group.

In other dream-visions we see the wronged party formulating in another way what in essence and in effect remains a curse: they invite the miscreant to come instantly to the heavenly court for judgment.[271] If we are to believe Gregory, another dream brought on the instant death of the person to whom it was addressed. It is, however, the final scene in a longer story[272] about a situation that evidently occurred more often and was potentially threatening to each and every bishop: the take-over by lower clergy of the church revenues and of administrative power. The victim this time was the eminent and saintly bishop Sidonius Apollinaris of Clermont, and Gregory says, typically, 'But the divine compassion did not for long wish to endure this injury unavenged (*inulta*)'. The night before the morning that the two priests had planned to drag the bishop out of the church and presumably kill him, one of them died suddenly when his intestines came out during a bowel movement. Gregory explains this by an analogy:

> So it is absolutely certain that the crime of this man was no less than that of Arius, whose bowels likewise came out of his lower parts into the latrine. Because it can be no less than heresy to accept that in the church a bishop, to whose care the sheep have been entrusted, should not be obeyed and that one to whom neither God nor men have entrusted anything should seize the power [of this office] (*potestas*).

Though the other priest was still alive, the bishop was immediately restored to his power. Later, on his deathbed in the church, while everyone bewailed the imminent loss of their shepherd, Sidonius murmured something about his brother Aprunculus being their next bishop. Gregory explains this prophecy by the 'inflowing of the Holy Spirit'. The people, however, 'did not understand and thought he was speaking in delirium (*in extasi*)', because at that time Aprunculus was bishop of Langres. However, suspected of Frankish sympathies by the Arian authorities there, Aprunculus fled soon thereafter to Clermont and indeed became bishop there.

In the meantime, with Sidonius out of the way, the other priest again took over the church revenues and the episcopal administration and let himself be carried around the city as though he were already bishop.

> ...On the Sunday after the death of the holy man [Sidonius], he had a meal prepared and ordered all the citizens to be invited to the church house. [When all were there,]

---

271. As in *Hist.* 3.36.
272. *Hist.* 2.23.

he insulted the notables by being the first to lie down on his couch.

Then the cup-bearer handed him a cup and said, 'My lord, I saw a dream (*vidi somnium*) which, if you will permit me to do so, I will make known: I was dreaming last night when I suddenly saw (*videbam hac nocte dominica et ecce*) a large house, and in this house a throne was set, upon which someone more powerful than all the others and like a judge was sitting, surrounded by many priests in white robes as well as a countless multitude of all kinds of people. As I was looking at this, trembling (*trepidus*), I saw in the distance Sidonius standing among them, absorbed in a litigation with that priest who was so dear to you and who died a few years ago. When the latter had been convicted, the king ordered him to be thrust into the deepest and narrowest dungeon. Once that man was taken away, [Sidonius] brought forward a further complaint against you, saying that you had been an accomplice in the crime for which the other had just been condemned. And then, when the judge carefully began to look for someone whom he could send to you [with this message], I started to hide myself among the others and stand behind them, thinking by myself that I might be sent since [Sidonius] knew me. As I was silently turning this over in my mind, [suddenly] the people around me were all gone. Being now the only one left in the hall, I was called by the judge and came nearer. Seeing his power (*virtus*) and magnificence, I was stunned (*hebes effectus*) and began to totter on my legs out of fear.

But he said, 'Don't be afraid, lad, but go and tell that priest: "Come to answer for yourself in your case, because Sidonius has requested you to be summoned". So don't make any delay in going there, because the king commanded me to say these things with a great sanction, saying, "If you say nothing, you will die a miserable death!"'

When [the cup-bearer] had said this, the priest was terrified, let the cup fall from his hand and died immediately; he was carried as a dead man from where he fell and was buried, to inhabit hell with his companion.

Such a judgment upon contumacious clergy did the Lord manifest in this world that one died the death of Arius and the other was dashed headlong to the ground from the height of his pride, like Simon Magus upon the prayer of the apostle. Doubtless these men, who did wicked things together against their holy bishop, now also inhabit hell together.

This dream makes visible how divine justice and government are carried on simultaneously with that on earth and fill the lacunes in the latter. The emphasis on authority is conspicuous: that of the notables (which the priest disregarded), that of the judge-king (Christ?) which 'stunned' the cup-bearer almost to the point of collapse, and that implicit in the threat of death. The summons is in fact a command: 'Drop dead this minute' — which, according to Gregory's report, the terrified priest did. He was killed by fear.[273] The literal repetition of the 'powerful and magnificent' king's words must have maximized their intensity and immediacy: such words could kill.

We have seen also, however, that the right words could instantly heal

---

273. Compare Kelsey 1973: 251-2 on how terror or despair can kill.

and bring on divine aid. Words must have been experienced not as neutral vehicles for independently existing meanings but as somehow intimately linked with the reality they pointed to. The different deaths of the two priests indicated, through their participation by analogy in earlier deaths, the nature of their crimes: heresy and pride. We have seen that, in and outside of visions, mental images could be experienced as independent realities producing visible and even drastic effects. The words of the butler must have created just such an image. Not only that, but his repetition of the judge-king's words must have been experienced as though the latter himself were speaking: like 'the word of the Lord, which he put in the mouth of the holy Sidonius', according to which, as Gregory tells it, Aprunculus eventually became bishop of Clermont. Finally, words seem to bring on their effect by a kind of inherent compulsion: they themselves make reality conform (or react) to the image to which they refer. In Gregory's time, the obvious model of this kind of thinking was, of course, the liturgical formulae connected with the transformation of the bread and wine into the body and blood of the Lord.[274] All this seems to indicate, in my opinion, that for Gregory and a number of his contemporaries, mental images and concepts possessed a more powerful reality than physical phenomena and events, which tended to conform to or be reflections of the former.

The preoccupation of sixth-century church legislation in Gaul with questions of church property is reflected in the very large number of Gregory's stories in which injury to such properties is punished by (sudden) illness or death not long thereafter.[275] This kind of, often very vindictive, propaganda becomes understandable when we remember that the church had no other weapon to protect itself.[276] We never hear of secular judges punishing those guilty of aggression against the church or its functionaries; on the contrary, it is sometimes officials of the count or king who carry out what Gregory sees as the violation of ecclesiastical rights and properties.[277] The frequency of punitive 'miracles' in this sector clearly indicates that there is a fundamental conflict here about the nature and role of the secular state versus that of the church.

King Chilperic's bitter remark that it is the bishops and not the king who exercise the real power in the kingdom[278] leads us to the heart of the matter.

274. Angenendt 1982 has pointed to the extensive influence of liturgy on the life of the church in this period.
275. See n. 240.
276. See n. 135.
277. *Hist.* 3.16; *Virt. Jul.* 14, 17. In *Virt. Mart.* 1.29 a king himself seizes church property.
278. *Hist.* 6.46.

According to Gregory,[279] King Clothar had burned the tax lists and permanently waived all taxes for the diocese of Tours, and his successor Charibert had later sworn not to change the situation. When King Childebert's officials in Gregory's time came with lists to exact taxes nonetheless, Gregory reminded them of this situation and warned them of the possible consequences of acting against King Charibert's oath. The tax roll they showed him must have been kept and brought forward by some enemy of the city, he says; he calls upon God to 'judge (*judicavit*)', i.e. wreak vengeance upon, that person. The very same day, the son of the man who had produced the roll fell ill and he died two days later. The king later sent a letter that the citizens of Tours were to be exempted from taxes out of respect for St Martin.

Gregory's strength and diplomacy rested squarely on the 'power (*virtus*)' imputed to the patron saint of Tours and of the whole Frankish kingdom.[280] When, on an earlier occasion,[281] he had got nowhere in his attempts to procure from King Guntram amnesty for two men who had sought asylum in the church of St Martin, he used his last resort, saying 'Let your Majesty listen to me, O King. Behold, I have been sent to you as an envoy by my lord. What can I say to the one who has sent me if you are not willing to give me an answer?' The king, who must have regarded himself as everyone's highest lord, sat up with astonishment (*obstupefactus*) and asked, 'And who is then this lord of yours who sent you?' Upon which Gregory answered, smiling, 'The blessed Martin sent me' — and got his way. As we saw earlier, when Roccolenus tried to threaten Gregory into handing over Duke Guntram out of the sanctuary of St Martin's church,[282] Gregory replied that if Roccolenus tried to enforce this, St Martin would make both him and the king who had ordered it feel the consequences. How great St Martin's power was thought to be is shown by what Gregory lets one of his predecessors in the see of Tours, Bishop Injuriosus, say to King Clothar in order to induce him to waive the taxes (one-third of the income of all the churches) for the city:[283] 'If you want to take God's properties (*res Dei*), the Lord will speedily relieve you of your kingdom.

---

279. *Hist.* 9.30.
280. *Hist.* 2.37: Clovis goes to the church of St Martin before the battle with the Visigoths, makes gifts to it after the victory and receives his consulship there (*Hist.* 2.38). On St Martin as patron of the Merovingian kingdom, see Ewig 1961 in Atsma 1976: 376-84.
281. *Hist.* 8.6.
282. *Hist.* 5.4.
283. *Hist.* 4.2. Compare *Hist.* 5.34. Conciliar legislators had also called those who seized church property the 'murderers of the poor' (*Conc. Aurel.* a.549, c.13; Maassen 1893: 104).

For it is unjust (*iniquus*) that the poor, whom you should feed from your stores, should fill your stores with their gifts'.

The strength of Gregory's position, however, also required the saint's *presence* at the shrine. Once,[284] one Christmas morning after the vigil in the cathedral, when Gregory was on his way to St Martin's church with a large crowd of people, a possessed man cried out that St Martin had left for Rome and was no longer able to do anything for the people of Tours. Everyone, including Gregory, was horrified (*etiam nos ipsi pavore concutimur*): he 'entered the church weeping loudly', he says. 'There all prostrated themselves, praying to deserve the presence (*praesentia*) of the saint'. Had some personal enemy of the bishop perhaps put the possessed man up to this? It was a dramatic situation. While mass was being celebrated, a certain Bonulf with a crooked foot was suddenly seized by violent pains and crying out, and everyone (as Gregory says) 'was standing around [him] in tears, waiting for the arrival of the saint'. After the ceremony, the 'contracted nerves of the man's foot' suddenly softened, some blood came out, and, suddenly, his foot was healed. Gregory must have been delirious with joy. He gave thanks to the Lord 'with his eyes full of tears' and said to the people: 'Let all fear depart from your hearts, for the blessed confessor lives here with us (*nobiscum habitat*)! And don't believe the devil...'.

Gregory's stories show that the church, using the idea of the superiority of government and justice of God to that of the Merovingians as a justification and the threat of divine or saintly power as the means, tried to exempt its properties from all secular interference and to set itself up as in fact a kind of 'state within a state'. The fact that the Merovingian kings also had a minimal conception of government and thus left a great deal to be done must have been largely responsible for this policy. The church could rightly claim to protect the rights of those who had no kin or other means of protecting themselves and their interests. Reflecting contemporary society, the church thus acted like what Brown has called 'an artificial kinship group' and, as we saw Gregory doing, used the 'power' of the saints, its 'patrons'.[285]

In several cases, Gregory reports that those engaged in plundering a church or injuring its property were stricken on the spot with illness or death.[286] In one of these cases, there is a unique vision.[287] The Count of Bourges sent some of his soldiers to exact a fine from the men living on a

---

284. *Virt. Mart.* 2.25. Similarly: *Virt. Mart.* 3.50.
285. Brown 1981: 31.
286. *Hist.* 3.16; 8.12; *Virt. Jul.* 5, 17; *Virt. Mart.* 1.30.
287. *Hist.* 7.42. Compare a dream in this context in *Virt. Jul.* 13.

property belonging to St Martin which lay in his territory. This was because they had not participated, as they should have done, in a military expedition. The steward of the estate tried to prevent this and said,

> 'These are the holy Martin's men. Don't injure them in any way because they are not accustomed to going on expeditions in such cases'.

But the leader said, 'Your Martin whom you always irrelevantly (*inaniter*) bring forward in these things means nothing to us. You and these men will pay the fine because you have neglected [to carry out] the command of the king'.

Saying this, he strode into the hall of the house. At once he fell to the ground, struck by pain, and began to suffer greatly. Turning to the steward, he said with a feeble voice,

> 'Please be so kind as to make the sign of the Cross over me and to invoke the name of the blessed Martin, for now I know that his power (*virtus*) is great.[288] When I entered the hall of the house I saw an old man holding in his hand a tree whose branches suddenly spread so as to fill the whole room. One of these branches came up against me with such a blow that I was shaken and fell'.

Making a gesture to his men, he then asked them to carry him out of the hall. Outside, he began to invoke the name of St Martin with great concentration (*attentius*). Through this he felt better and was cured.

This man visualized the saint's power as shooting through the house like branches from a tree. As far as I have been able to discover, this is an original contribution to tree-symbolism: the tree as a spreading umbrella of power. Instant emotional-physical reactions to the suggestion of coming into contact with numinous power are found throughout Gregory's works: the cure and the stroke are the opposite ends of a whole range of possibilities.[289]

Two final dreams on this theme, both about King Chilperic (who was by then dead), are nothing if not high politics.[290] King Guntram, Chilperic's only surviving brother and usually described by Gregory as favourable to the church, was nevertheless a year later talking to Gregory about sending the latter's friend Bishop Theodore of Marseille into exile again because he suspected him of having arranged Chilperic's murder. The king finished by saying '... I shall not be counted as a man if I am not able to avenge him before the year is over!' Gregory, however, replied,

> 'What killed Chilperic if not his own wickedness and your prayers? For he played a lot of very mean tricks on you, and it is these that are responsible for his death. This, I might as well tell you, I saw very clearly in a dream-vision (*per visionem somnii inspexi*): I saw him accepting tonsure and thereafter being as it were (*quasi*) ordained as bishop; then he was carried around, preceded by burning lamps and candles, on a

---

288. Compare Ex. 18:11; Ps. 147:5.
289. Punishment by being beaten with a switch or a stick was a contemporary practice: as in the council of Narbonne in 589, canon 14 (Mansi 9: 1017), cited in Fournier 1979: 46.
290. *Hist.* 8.5.

bishop's chair which was bare except for a sprinkling of ashes on it'.

When I had finished this story, the king said,

'I too saw another dream-vision (*vidi ... visionem*) which announced his death. For three bishops led him into my sight, bound by chains; one of these bishops was Tetricus [of Langres], another was Agroecula [of Châlons] and the third was Nicetius of Lyon. Two of these said, "Unfasten him, we pray, and permit him to go after he has been chastised". But Bishop Tetricus was against this and said bitterly, "That will not happen: he is going to be consumed by fire for his crimes!"

And while they hotly debated, as it were, among themselves about this for a long time, I saw in the distance a cauldron with boiling water above a fire. Then, while I wept, they seized Chilperic, broke his bones and threw him into the cauldron. At once, he was so completely dissolved and liquefied among the vapours of the boiling water that not the least trace of him remained'.

When the king had finished saying this, we were both astonished (*admirantibus nobis*) and [then] got up, for the meal was over.

Gregory expects his own dream to speak for itself: the bareness of the bishop's chair and the ashes on it indicate that Chilperic is an anti-bishop, a bishop of the devil's anti-church, and hence that his murder is a fully justified divine punishment. Here a dream is used to express fundamental criticism without incurring any responsibility for it. An instance of very daring diplomacy indeed is Gregory's mention of Guntram's own prayers as having helped to kill his brother. The attention, in any case, is directed away from the actual physical event to its spiritual causes, which alone are regarded as important. The king, surprisingly, tells his earlier dream in which three dead bishops act as executioners to the then still living king. In Frankish law, a cauldron of boiling water was used in an ordeal, not as a punishment.[291] A sacrificial death in a sacred cauldron is a Celtic motif, however.[292] It is impossible to know whether King Guntram (or Gregory) was acquainted with this.

The fact that in this royal dream dead bishops appear as deciding the fate of a king and putting it into effect seems to confirm King Chilperic's bitter statement. Gregory, in his other stories, too, will have us believe that dead bishops, represented of course by living ones, were unobtrusively ruling the realm. To combat this kind of power, one had to beat the bishops at their own game, as Chilperic ostensibly did in Gregory's dream. It certainly would have been enlightening if, as Brown suggests, this king had left us *his* history of the Merovingian church.[293] By relating his dream about Chilperic, Gregory saved his friend from being exiled. Here, a dream is

291. See p. 99.
292. Salin 1959: 8. See also Pernoud 1957: 80. Eliade 1967 in Caillois and von Grunebaum 1967: 319 reports that Siberian shamans experience being cut up in pieces and put to boil in a cauldron as part of their initiatory dream.
293. Brown 1977 in Brown 1982: 244.

used as a diplomatic means of communicating criticism of royal behaviour, something which would have been extremely risky in any other way. It gave the king insight into where the 'real' guilt for the murder was to be sought and so solved an otherwise complicated problem. The intriguing thing about Gregory is that he seems to be absolutely sincere and truthful, in this case about his dream, but at the same time fully conscious of the manipulatory aspect of his story. Even dreams experienced by two individuals independently (about someone's being assimilated to the devil and about his punishment by three dead bishops) could function as intimidations and help justice to take its course.

DEAD BISHOPS AS RULERS OF THE KINGDOM?: THE PERSONALIZATION OF IMMANENT DIVINE JUSTICE

Gregory combined a heavy personal dependence upon divine aid with a superlative agility in interpreting and manipulating its manifestations in human lives so as to conform to and promote his idea of God's — and in practice also the church's — government. His reports of monitory and punitive visions, as the complement and support of the many personal disasters interpreted as punitive miracles, show that the church in his time tried to rule by fear of divine power, which was generally seen as being embodied in the saint as the ideal bishop.[294] As an 'artificial kinship group' with heavenly 'patrons' (often dead bishops) who offered protection and exacted vengeance, the church's 'government' followed the pattern of contemporary society, but, so to speak, one level 'higher': the 'power' imputed to heavenly patrons far surpassed that of earthly ones, and living bishops acted as their mouth-pieces and representatives. This personalized imagining of immanent divine justice, experienced as objective visible reality in the dream-visions and acted out in society, was the church's recipe for survival in an inadequately organized, arbitrary and violent society.

CONCLUSION. GREGORY: THE DREAM-ELEMENT IN PERCEPTION, TRANSFORMATION AND SOCIETY

Dream-visions, as Gregory describes them, reveal the other, usually invisible, stream of reality which he regards as determining all natural and human events. This reality, through miracles or visions, can intervene to fill gaps in men's knowledge or remedy inadequacies in social institutions, but it is also something with which one must keep on good terms even when

---

294. Compare Reydellet 1977: 201-2.

everything else is in order. Without its support, all human effort, however expert, is in vain. In Gregory himself, at least, this resulted in a constant alertness for sensorily apprehensible signs of the spiritual element in objects and events: he looked through visible phenomena at divine activity in men and in the world. Visionary experience, the content of which was in general agreement with Christian tradition or church policy and whose recipients were devout Christian believers, could be accepted as supernatural revelation, especially if there was also some later confirmation of its message. The venerable figure who appears in most of these dream-visions and, except when specifically designated as an angel, is there usually understood to be a saint, looks like a Christian adaptation of the persisting antique dream-tradition in which a god or a revered ancestor appears with advice or warning.

We have seen, however, that Gregory reports dream-like perceptions as also occurring simultaneously to a number of individuals who are all wide awake. His descriptions, even of concrete sensory events or objects, can have a dream quality: 'une épaisseur onirique, une brume d'imprécision'.[295] Like his report of the vision involving his mother, Gregory's description of the buildings in Clermont at the time of the plague[296] which were 'suddenly seen to appear as marked with signs (*in subita contemplatione ... signari videbantur*) which the common people called "Thau"' is characteristic of the imprecision or obscurity which we have been trying to penetrate. Is it his faulty grammar that is responsible for the double qualification (hedge?) 'seen to appear'? (In the other version[297] of this event he simply says 'were suddenly seen to be signed and marked'.) What does he mean by 'suddenly seen'? Why not call them 'prodigies that appeared', as he does with similar mysterious and indelible signs which appeared overnight 'scratched by I don't know whom' on household utensils over a wide region in 587?[298] Does he vaguely suspect — and perhaps without completely disapproving — clerical magic at the back of it?[299] It looks as though Gregory was not sure and, as more often, thinking too many things at once.

In fact, he could never be sure of the quality of the reality that confronted him. Roses, for instance, could have been picked in June in Monegunde's little garden in Tours, but they could also 'appear' on their bushes in January and even 'appear' freshly cut in the middle of a

295. Bachelard 1961: 22.
296. *Hist.* 4.5.
297. *Glor. mart.* 50.
298. *Hist.* 9.5.
299. Compare Hist. 5.5 and 9.37.

November night on a martyr's tomb.³⁰⁰ When he heard of a stolen chicken turning into stone during the cooking he was not surprised because he had held olives in his hand that had been miraculously turned into stone.³⁰¹ He must have drunk wine that was grown and pressed on church properties and stored in its cellars, but he once also drank wine that was created overnight by saintly power.³⁰² Some people saw saints and angels 'appear' in church during the day as well as at night; Gregory explicitly says that he thinks of St Martin as bodily, if invisibly, present when a cure takes place.³⁰³ When Gregory was admonished by what must have been a heavenly messenger in a dream to get up and join the vigil, he had first made the sign of the Cross at the figure.³⁰⁴ For the devil could be in a swirling cloud of dust or in a fly buzzing in a cup.³⁰⁵ Sensory reality was a very relative thing. It was often shot through with spiritual messages and qualities, if indeed it was not actually created out of nothing on the spot.

Moreover, the most decisive and most real events were almost always invisible: just sometimes, a fortunate person could see them in a dream or a vision. For Gregory, spiritual reality and dream-reality tended to coincide.³⁰⁶ The analogical, visually-spatially discontinuous, dynamic of imaginal or dream-thinking³⁰⁷ is the dynamic he ascribes to divine or saintly 'power', and he thought about the latter in terms of visible events. His inclination to think in images instead of in abstract concepts encouraged a blurring of the distinction between dream, thought and perception. Bachelard has said: 'Pour l'homme primitif, la pensée est une rêverie centralisée'.³⁰⁸ Instead of a linear, discursive progression in time, there is a simultaneous presence of all elements spatially organized around a central image as a picture which can be seen³⁰⁹ at a glance. Early medieval

---

300. *Hist.* 6.44; *Virt. Jul.* 46b.
301. *Glor. conf.* 109; *Glor. mart.* 96.
302. *Virt. Jul.* 35.
303. *Glor. mart.* 33; *Glor. conf.* 72; *Vit. patr.* 16.2.
304. *Glor. mart.* 86.
305. *Virt. Mart.* 3.20; *Glor. mart.* 106.
306. Kelsey 1968: 11 says: 'Depth psychology calls this reality the unconscious; the early Christian community called it the spiritual world; and these two different terms may well refer to the same reality, as the Catholic theologian Victor White has suggested in *God and the Unconscious*' (Cleveland 1961).
307. Epstein 1981: 155; Singer 1974: 177-8. Compare on discursive and dream-thinking: Jung 1952: 9-51.
308. Bachelard 1949: 50.
309. See n. 307 and compare Müller 1957: 422 on 'primitive' logic moving along optical processes; Haeckel 1960: 1270 on mythical image-thinking: 'myths are not thought but seen'; and Nock 1972:182 on the late antique concept of philosophical truth as a 'seeing': *epopteia*.

church paintings betray exactly this manner of looking at spiritual reality.[310] Because it is presented not as a continuation of space from the viewer into the picture but as an autonomous, objective reality whose perspective is within itself, it requires from the viewer a mental act of deplacement, of entering into the picture. This is the kind of deplacement, of entering into images as living realities, which takes place in meditation as it is described by monastic writers in Gregory's time as well as by psychologists today.[311] Meditation as it is observed today produces a kind of perception that is characterized by tending to see all boundaries as fluid, important objects as radiating luminosity from within, as it were, a falling-away of the third dimension, and a breakdown of the subject-object distinction[312] — precisely the qualities that characterize Gregory's perception and thinking as we can distill it from his writings. Alongside his keen ability to observe, his practical common sense and his psychological insight, he preferred and cultivated a meditative attitude which was intimately connected and tended to coalesce with his thinking in terms of images, and with his paying attention to sudden intrusions into consciousness of imaginal or dream-thinking.

The dream-visions and apparitions which Gregory reports make visible what the people concerned imagined and saw at moments when some decisive change took place in themselves. They show two crucial things. First, change is experienced as being sudden, a discontinuity in mental processes, an injection from without. Second, change is experienced as having been set in motion by an ideal or an anti-ideal in image-form: the initiation of change is apprehended in the form of images and in the dream mode of thought. Some changes were, apparently, unsolicited; many others were diligently asked for. Gregory does not think of individual human beings, even as saints, as initiating change. God acts through them, and only in apparently new ways, for His principles and purposes are amply known through the Bible and the saints' lives. This — in essence — is the 'script' from which Gregory and his contemporaries learned to have their 'dream' of themselves and of the world.

I interpret the fact that the most frequent kinds of miracles coincide with the situations in which dream-visions or apparitions were experienced as an indication that it was these situations which were most in need of support or innovation. To review these: dream-visions make known the 'presence' of a saint's body in a certain spot and command that

---

310. Cazenave 1981. Dinzelbacher 1981: 12-6 also noted the similarities between early medieval visions and early medieval art.
311. For instance von Severus and Solignac 1980: 909-11.
312. Deikman 1966 in Tart 1979: 199-228.

arrangements be made for a cult there; the dream-vision itself, since it is regarded as a supernatural revelation, is thus the legitimation of this new cult. In a decentralizing society, such dream-visions probably expressed a deep need for the visible presence of a heavenly intercessor and protector as local 'patron' who would heal, give protection and provide justice. The command in the dream functioned to mobilize social activity towards its fulfilment. A second kind of visionary experience was that connected with cures: it could communicate a command to come to the saint's shrine to be cured there or be a healing act at the moment of recovery. Whereas a dark, horrid figure could be seen as the agent of the illness, the appearance of a luminous, smiling and venerable man — as a spiritual bridegroom, liberator, doctor or repository of vital energy — initiated recovery. The experience, after an intensive preparation through prayer, of the living image of someone who was regarded as the ideal spiritual human being could effect a sudden transformation, a spiritual as well as a physical regeneration. Modern psychology has recognized the venerable old man as a symbol bringing about psychical transformation: images, as concretizations of emotions, fuel the will and thus initiate change, action. This is evident, too, in a third kind of dream-vision or apparition in which men experience the reassurance or aid of the saint in a dangerous, uncertain or problematical situation. Here the imagined supernatural authority and power of the saint as the ideal patron serves to strengthen group solidarity but also to formulate and legitimize new solutions and procedures that compensate for inadequacies in the organization of the contemporary society.[313] Personal, social and technical innovation can thus be initiated through the appearance of an ideal human being in dreams: the saint seems to function as something like the other half of the personality. What we see in Gregory's stories is that men needed an ideal to make them co-operate and innovate in society:[314] what is more, they needed to experience this ideal as a person who could sometimes be 'seen' and who produced visible effects. Their dreaming of their ideal human being helped them to translate some of their (piecemeal) imaginings of how human society should be governed into practical reality.

Finally, parallel with the many punitive miracles which the unarmed church needed to claim in order to protect herself and her dependents from arbitrary agression and spoliation, there are monitory and punitive dream-

---

313 Compare Hallowell 1967 in Caillois and von Grunebaum 1967: 260 on dreams as necessary to maintain the socio-cultural system of the Ojibwa people.
314. Compare Evans-Pritchard 1965: 98, quoting Pareto (1917): 'It is by aspiration to the ideal that human societies subsist and progress' and (115) '[these] are constructs of the heart rather than of the mind'.

visions which intimidate or actually kill their recipients. When the dream is intended for a third party and is so communicated, it functions as criticism or as a curse — for which the person telling the dream cannot, however, be held responsible. Such dreams make visible the belief in the 'power' of the saint, often a dead bishop, to enforce justice and avenge wrongs: a belief which seems to make comprehensible in a visual manner what would otherwise be an abstract kind of divine, immanent justice. The way in which this semi-automatic justice or 'power' is addressed often resembles magical manipulation. This is, in my opinion, because symbolic thinking was in that period so ingrained and so self-evident that men were not aware of it. At the same time, men like Gregory were constantly aware of supernatural 'power', divine or diabolic, all around them. The way to speak to and understand it was in and through symbols.[315] Hence Gregory could combine real spirituality with symbolic 'manipulation'. The belief in immanent divine justice through dead saints and bishops, visualized and hence authenticated in dreams as revelations of supernatural reality, functioned as a social and political instrument in the hands of living bishops. Gregory, although he sincerely believed in the truth of such dreams, fully realized this.

The imagined and dreamed image of the saint, then, is a transmitted and constantly recreated ideal and a symbol supporting and renewing social reality as well as the interior man. The two are, of course, intimately related.[316] Gregory is scarcely or not at all conscious of his images as his own mental phenomena. They often 'think' him more than he thinks them. G.S. Kirk has said: 'The more practised at remembering dreams an individual or society is — and that will depend on an awareness of the importance of dreams — the more likely he or it will be affected by dream modes of thought during waking life'.[317] It is difficult to distinguish, even conceptually, between the modes of conscious and less conscious or unconscious imagination.[318] The philosopher-psychologist William James

---

315. Compare Langer (1942) 1980: 151: 'The practical efficiency attributed to sacra is a dream-metaphor for the might of human ideation'.
316. Meslin 1974: 623-4.
317. Kirk 1970: 272.
318. On conscious and unconscious symbols, see Meslin 1975 in Ménard 1975: 29. Singer 1974: 172-3, quoting Krippke and Sonnenschein 1973, notes the 'complexity of covert information processing along the kinds of directed thought or cognitive activity that we normally view as part of consciousness. There may even be fluctuations in the degree of awareness of such processes ...' and speaks of 'parallel processing' (183). Compare Cartwright 1978: 66, quoting Foulkes and Scott 1973,: 'Hallucinatory experiences are part of normal mental activity throughout the 24-hour cycle. The bases of dreams, the imagistic thought-style,

already formulated this in 1902:[319]

> ...our normal waking consciousness, rational consciousness as we call it, is but one special type of consciousness, whilst all about it, parted from it by the filmiest of screens, there lie potential forms of consciousness entirely different...; they...are discontinuous with ordinary consciousness. Yet they may determine attitudes...

He saw men's spiritual ideals as originating in a non-rational, non-discursive mode of consciousness:[320]

> The further limits of our being plunge, it seems to me, into an altogether other dimension of existence from the sensible and merely 'understandable' world. Name it the mystical region, or the supernatural region, whichever you choose. So far as our ideal impulses originate in this region (and most of them do originate in it, for we find them possessing us in a way for which we cannot articulately account), we belong to it in a more intimate sense than that in which we belong to the visible world, for we belong in the most intimate sense wherever our ideals belong. Yet the unseen region in question is not merely ideal, for it produces effects in this world. When we commune with it, work is actually done upon our finite personality, for we are turned into new men, and consequences in the way of conduct follow in the natural world upon our regenerative change. But that which produces effects within another reality must be termed a reality itself, so I feel as if we had no philosophic excuse for calling the unseen or mystical world unreal.

Gregory is inclined to regard visible, sensory reality as an epiphany of the divine, and the divine as 'such stuff as dreams are made of'. Divine truth was dream-truth. Gregory wants to be aware of it as much as he possibly can. The preponderance of the dream-element in his thinking and perception is the essence of his imprecision.

       and the non-reality-bound content are available, just under the surface, while we are actively attending to the external world of information'.
319. James 1958: 298.
320. James 1958: 388-9.

GENERAL CONCLUSION
views from a many-windowed tower

Gregory of Tours was a capable administrator, a clever diplomat and a courageous, saintly bishop. He was also a born story-teller. Modern readers, however, have almost always experienced his writings as a jumbled, if often delightful, mosaic: a very loosely — if at all — connected whole of visual impressions of concrete, sensory reality. Some have seen this lack of a larger internal coherence as a 'reflection' of the decentralized society in which he found himself. At the same time, they have been puzzled by what seemed to be an elusive kind of imprecision in Gregory's descriptions of individual events. Almost always, they have attributed this imprecision to something like 'muddled thinking'. No one seems to have seriously considered the question of how such demonstrable intelligence and determination could have been content with what looks like confusion.

The starting-point for the studies in this book was the assumption that for Gregory, there must have been other, for us not immediately evident, patterns of coherence. To find these patterns, Gregory's thinking on four subjects or themes was investigated as it occurred scattered through his writings: his treatment of extraordinary natural phenomena or prodigies, his view of ordinary natural phenomena and miracles involving these, his use of light imagery and descriptions of light phenomena, and his many reports of dreams and visions in which saints appeared. Not only the thought-patterns themselves were sought but also any ways in which they could be related to contemporary social reality.

An examination of the *Histories* shows that Gregory begins by noting and interpreting extraordinary natural phenomena in a Christianized version of the Roman manner as prodigies or signs of divine displeasure announcing some imminent, albeit temporary, punishment. He tries, moreover, to see some symbolical resemblance between the form of the phenomenon, especially in the sky, and the event that it 'prefigures'. In the prefaces to the first books he says, accordingly, that no one should take the present wars and misfortunes to indicate that the end of the world is near because the same more or less balanced mixture of good and evil occurred in the historical books of the Old Testament in the time of the prophets. Later, after continual and extreme calamities, and perhaps after having come up against wandering impostors who claimed to be apostles or even Christ himself, Gregory must have reconsidered his view. In the latter part of the *Histories* he explicitly says that all the signs as well as the misfortunes indicate that 'the last times' have now begun. In the preface to the first book, he had defended his 'mixed and muddled', strictly chronological arrangement of events not only by pointing to a similar arrangement in the Old Testament but also with the argument that this made the counting of the years since the beginning of the world easier. His lack of interest in what we think of as historical causation and development and in the coherence of events in a larger context and longer period of time is connected with the fact that, for him, historical or 'horizontal' time was primarily duration, a succession of discontinuous events. His interpretation of prodigies shows that he tended to conceive of a 'vertical', divine causality that patterned otherwise unrelated events in a similar, symbolical way. Gregory's time is also 'vertical': simultaneous events are related to each other and to events hundreds of years earlier (especially those in the Bible) through their sharing a symbolical form that is given them from 'above' by God. Historical, factual reality is discontinuous; divine, symbolical, reality as a consistent and unchanging pattern is coherence. For Gregory, this general truth is so self-evident that he does not put it into words.

His treatment of water and plant life as ordinary phenomena and as they are involved in miracles shows more precisely how, for him, natural and human change takes place: not through the influence of immediate, earthly antecedents but through flashes of divine power. The latter operates according to certain well-known patterns in the form of image-models of spiritual truth such as the Virgin Birth, Moses' bringing forth a spring from bare rock and the sprouting of seeds. Natural and human reality do not evolve: they pulse, leap, erupt. For Gregory the phenomena of the natural world were materialized metaphors or symbols of spiritual truths, and these can function (for instance as ordeals) in society. His stories of visible events too seem to be, in some barely conscious way, metaphors of spiritual truths, and the latter, for him, tend to be the same as truths of interior experience. Instead of abstract concepts, he uses images of visible events to think with. Such images are related to each other in ways that discursive thought or logic cannot grasp. Gregory's habit of analogical association, proceeding by sudden 'leaps' across a void, determines his view of reality as essentially miraculous. The wonders of divinely-caused rebirth and regeneration which he sees in natural phenomena are, for him, models of the rebirth and resurrection of man into Paradise. Moreover, in comparison with what he sees as the ubiquitously evident transience of the works of men — and what he means by this is probably also what we would call the contemporary mutation of later antique civilisation — these visible works of God are, by contrast, permanent. The miracle of renewal or, even, spontaneous new creation, in nature and in men takes place according to what Gregory regards as timeless models of divine activity (like our models of causation and development) which, in his view, structure reality. His thinking in images rather than in concepts is probably connected with the late antique drift towards irrational knowledge, but may also have been influenced by the then largely oral culture around him.

An investigation of what he does with light and fire, as imagery and as phenomena, reveals his experience of something like a continuum between mental imagery and sensory reality. Physical phenomena are not only metaphors or symbols of spiritual truths: they tend to participate directly in the reality they indicate. The Eucharist as a sensory object that is at the same time the spiritual body of Christ, and, as such, works effects may have been an unconscious model here. His descriptions show that when Gregory uses metaphors of light or fire, he tends to imagine them as visible phenomena with which he is, to a certain extent, emotionally involved. Hence he cannot reflect on his own thinking. Conversely, when he speaks of natural light or fire, they tend to have qualities and effects of a spiritual kind. When the preoccupation with light and dark in the liturgy of the period is taken into account, it is hardly surprising that he not infrequently reports perceptions of supernatural light or fiery light phenomena in connection with the holy. This, however, is also an ancient tradition in the Hellenistic as well as the Jewish world. New with Gregory is that both light imagery and perceptions of supernatural light are concentrated around the saints and their miraculous power, an indication that these are the central facts in his life. Whereas natural fire not infrequently has a diabolic quality, holy power can also punish or purge as 'divine fire'; more often, however, it purifies and heals as light. Gregory does not speak of a purifying fire after death: the cleansing of body and soul by a saint on earth has the same function. Since Antiquity, light had tended to be identified with life, earthly or divine. Since the first century B.C., the true life, that in God, had tended to be identified with contemplation, which was at the same time an inflowing, of ineffable light. The resultant experience of this world as 'dark' is then, in the sixth century, an inherited tradition, but it is continued probably also because men felt there to be insufficient opportunities to realize this contemplative spiritual ideal in the society around them. What Gregory says about the saint's holy power — recognizable by its light-quality — makes it look as though this power is itself, for him, a 'living metaphor' for the essential dynamic of true life: creative renewal.

How mental images, experienced as dreams and regarded as spiritual reality, can initiate change in individuals and in society is evident in Gregory's stories about dreams, visions and apparitions. In these too, the figure of the saint dominates the scene. Dream-visions of the saint express unconscious wishes and tend to occur in four kinds of situations: when there is a need for the institution or the legitimation of a new cult, before or during miraculous cures, when advice or aid are necessary, and when justice demands warning or punishment. Since the most frequent miracles fall into these same categories, it looks as though the dreams make visible what people imagined as happening in these cases. The figure of a venerable, often light-giving, presence looks like a new human ideal. As Gregory tells it, the 'power' of this ideal person transforms, protects and liberates individuals, stabilizes and innovates in society and — as a kind of personalization of immanent divine justice — acts as a compensation for arbitrary, inadequate Merovingian government. We see very concretely how an imagined ideal can maintain and recreate individuals and society. What we also see is that, for Gregory, sensory experience, conscious imagination and involuntary iconic or dream modes of thought tend to overlap and merge. Since Gregory regarded a certain type of dream-reality as spiritual reality, he was always looking for it and expecting it. Thus he paid far more attention than we do to the imaginal or iconic thought that continues day and night, also in present-day Europeans, alongside discursive thinking and active attention to sensory reality. The dream-element in his perception and thinking made Gregory able to see 'miracles', also in sensory reality. But it also made him incapable of reflecting very much on his own thinking. It is the essence of his imprecision.

The experienced functioning of psychic reality seems to be Gregory's model for the dynamic structure of the visible world: another indication that for him the self and the visible world form a continuum. His stories of visible events can, to a large degree, be read as also being descriptions of interior events apprehended and made conscious in visible forms. His imaginative thinking as such and its model of reality do not seem to be intrinsically less valid or more 'mythical' than our thinking in terms of abstract concepts and mechanistic or organic models. Literacy, social, practical intelligence and adult wisdom were compatible with it.

In his stories we see that, somewhat adjusted, traditional ideal images (representations rooted in the as yet non-verbalized contents of consciousness) kept individuals and society going, recreated and renewed them. These images and symbols had to be adapted to be able to function in existing thought-patterns and institutions. This adaptation should not be mistaken for a mere 'reflection' of an individual or the society in his or its practical needs and state at that moment. It is on this point that, notwithstanding my great admiration for his imaginative insights in late antique religious experience, I differ with P. Brown.[1] As I hope to have shown, it was a personal spiritual ideal that had been developing for centuries through many social changes that was translated and fitted into a sixth-century social system according to its needs and possibilities. The ideal of inner regeneration and its derivative, that of the spiritual person, the saint, cannot be demonstrated to derive, in essence, from the society that surrounds them, although they can acquire social functions. They may be, in M. Eliade's words, 'transtemporal'[2] ideals that are transmitted, adapted and recreated in individual and social life. More: as vehicle-images of unconscious wishes, they point to a future state of man and society and help to realize these.

Alongside their constructive and repressive social functions, Gregory's tales of saint's miracles and visions could be, for those who listened to them meditatively, models of true reality as being psychic creativity. To regard them as illusion, suggestion or magic is to miss the point that they transmit an ideal in more or less visible form. This ideal can inhere in the dynamic form of the event but it can also appear as a vision of a venerable, caring man. In both forms, the ideal speaks to the emotions, gives new energy, initiates action and change. It is through imagination that the ideal is visualized and actualized.

What emerges from this investigation is a world-view and a manner of thinking that indeed exhibits striking similarities with those of recent and present-day 'primitive' societies as they have been described by Lévy-Bruhl and his school. Although Gregory is demonstrably capable of rational and conceptual thinking, his whole manner of apprehending and interpreting himself and his environment is through images which, as Lévy-Bruhl described it,[3] he sees as 'participating' in all reality, and in which he himself tends to 'participate' affectively. Gregory's thinking is not primarily a rational, dialectical kind of thinking in images, exhibiting some of the same basic structures as the society around him, as Lévi-Strauss has described 'la pensée sauvage'.[4] Gregory's analogical,

---

1. As also on essentially the same, but more theologically formulated, points, J. Fontaine in Fontaine 1982. Post 1986 shows that there is much more continuity than Brown is willing to admit between pagan and Christian motifs in the context of the cult of the saints.
2. Eliade 1952: 222.
3. Lévy-Bruhl 1963: xxxii-vi.
4. Lévi-Strauss 1962: 349-57. Although Lévi-Strauss is describing the thought of totemistic societies, he says explicitly (quoting A. van Gennep, *L'état actuel du problème totémique* (Paris, 1920): 345-46) that the

metaphorical and, especially, dream-like manner of thinking is perhaps best described as a kind of 'seeing'[5] in which the boundaries between observer and observed are fluid, indistinct. Alongside this kind of thinking, Gregory continued to observe and act in empirical, practical ways and to be able to draw shrewd conclusions from the facts that came to his knowledge. For him, however, reasoning was not the way to arrive at the real truth about life.

Mytho-poetic imagination is once again becoming respectable, not only as a consciously used and extremely sophisticated philosophical tool for discovering and describing human reality but as an instrument of personal development. For Gregory, the mysterious, imaged dynamics of the creative imagination were those of spiritual reality. One of his images for the relation of this reality to human history is that of the many-windowed tower in Bishop Nicetius of Trier's dream. God stands on top of it and in the 'look-outs' of the windows stand angels, one of whom reads aloud from a large book the names, dates and qualities of future Frankish kings. Not only does this dream-image show where Gregory located the driving force in human history, but it also seems to portray something of his own many-levelled perception along the axis uniting heaven and earth.

The 'lack of structure' and 'imprecision' that Gregory has so long been accused of do not directly 'reflect' either any real confusion on his own part or that of the decentralized, fluid society in which he found himself. Gregory had — in his own way — a very structured and precise idea of how human society should be organized and governed. He also had some clear ideas, based on traditional images, about his ideals and about the structure of reality. The failure of many twentieth-century historians to recognize the reality-value of his manner of thinking, including their condescending designation of it as 'naive' or 'simple', may be a reflection of the excessively verbal and rational orientation which has until recently been a dominant trait of Western culture.[6]

    thought-systems he describes also occur in non-totemistic societies (Lévi-Strauss 1962: 214).
5. Müller 1957: 422.
6. Compare Gerritsen 1978: 15: 'Wie Middeleeuwers voor naïef houdt, kijkt alleen maar in een spiegel'. (Whoever regards medieval men as naive, is merely looking in a mirror.)

BIBLIOGRAPHY

PRIMARY SOURCES

ALCUINUS. Commentariorum in Apocalypsin libri quinque. In: Migne, J.P. (ed.) 1851. *Patrologia latina* 100: 1085-1156. Paris.

AMBROSIUS. Hexaemeron libri sex. In: Migne, J.P. (ed.) 1845. *Patrologia latina* 14: 123-274. Paris.

AMBROSIUS. De mysteriis liber unus. In: Migne, J.P. (ed.) 1845. *Patrologia latina* 16: 389-410. Paris.

AUGUSTINE. *City of God.* Dods, M. (transl.) 1950. New York.

AUGUSTINUS, AURELIUS. *De civitate Dei libri 22.* Dombart, B. and A. Kalb (eds.), 1955a and b. Turnhout. Corpus christianorum, ser. lat. 47, 48. 2 vols.

AVITUS VIENNENSIS. Homilia in rogationibus. Peiper, R. (ed.). 1883. *Alcimi Ecdicii Aviti Viennensis episcopi, Opera*: 108-12. Berlin. Monumenta Germaniae Historica, Auctores antiquissimi 6.2.

BALON, J. 1965. *Traité de droit Salique.* Étude d'exégèse et de sociologie juridique. Namur. Ius medii aevi 3 (1-2).

BAUDONIVIA. *Vita sanctae Radegundis.* In: Krusch 1888: 377-95.

Bible, The Holy. Revised standard version. 1952. New York.

BIEZEN, J. VAN and J.W. SCHULTE NORDHOLT 1967. *Hymnen,* een bloemlezing met muziek uit de vroeg-christelijke en middeleeuwse gezangen van de Latijnse en Griekse kerk. Tournai.

BLUME, C. and M. DREVES (eds.) 1907 and 1908. *Analecta hymnica Medii Aevi.* Volumes 50 and 51. Leipzig.

BORDIER, H.L. (ed. and transl.) 1857, 1860, 1862, and 1864. *Les livres des miracles et autres opuscules de Georges Florent Grégoire,* évêque de Tours. 4 vols. Paris.

BRAUN, R. 1964. See: Quodvultdeus.

BUCHNER, R. 1967a and b. See: Gregorius Turonensis.

CASSIANUS, JOHANNES. Collationes. In: Migne, J.P. (ed.) 1858. *Patrologia latina* 49:477-1328. Paris.

CASSIODORUS, *Variarum libri 12.* Fridh, A.J. (ed.) 1973. Turnhout. Corpus christianorum, series latina 96: v-499.

CHRONICA Gallica a. 452 et 511. Mommsen, Th. (ed.) 1892. *Chronica minora saeculi* IV-VII.1: 615-65. Berlin. Monumenta Germaniae Historica, Auctores antiquissimi 9.

CLERCQ, C. DE (ed.) 1963. *Concilia Galliae.* Turnhout. Corpus Christianorum, series Latina 148a.

CONSTANTINUS LUGDUNENSIS. *Vita Germani.* Borius, R. (ed. and transl.). Paris. Sources chrétiennes 112.

DALTON, O. (ed. and transl.) 1927. Gregory of Tours, *The history of the Franks.* 2 vols. Oxford.

ECKHARDT, K. (ed.) 1962. *Pactus legis Salicae.* Hannover. Monumenta Germaniae Historica, Legum sectio I. Leges nationum Germanicarum 4.1.

EUCHERIUS. Formularum spiritualis intelligentiae ad Uranium liber unus. Migne, J.P. (ed.) 1859. *Patrologia latina* 50: 727-72.

EUSEBIUS PAMPHILUS. De vita Constantini imperatoris libri quattuor. In: Migne, J.P. (ed.) 1857 *Patrologia graeca* 20: 910-1233. Paris.

FONTAINE, J. (ed. and transl.) 1967, 1968, 1969. See: Severus, Sulpicius, *Vita Sancti Martini.*

FORTUNATUS, VENANTIUS. *Opera poetica.* Leo, F. (ed.) 1881. Berlin. Monumenta Germaniae Historica, Auctores antiquissimi 4, pars prior.

FORTUNATUS, VENANTIUS. *Opera pedestria.* Krusch, B. (ed.) 1885. Berlin. Monumenta Germaniae Historica, Auctores antiquissimi 4, pars posterior.

GIESEBRECHT, W. (transl.) 1851. Gregorius von Tours, *Zehn Bücher Fränkische Geschichte.* 2 vols. Berlin. Geschichtsschreiber der deutschen Vorzeit, 6. Jahrhundert: 4, 5.

GREGORIUS MAGNUS. *Dialogi.* de Vogué, A. (ed.) and Antin, P. (transl.) 1978, 1979, 1980. 3 vols. Paris. Sources chrétiennes 251, 260, 265.

GREGORIUS MAGNUS. Moralium libri sive Expositio in librum b. Job. In: Migne, J.P. (ed.) 1849. *Patrologia latina* 75: 509-1162.

GREGORIUS TURONENSIS. De cursu stellarum ratio qualiter ad officium implendum debeat observari. (*De cursu stell.*) Krusch, B. (ed.) 1885. Arndt, W. and B. Krusch (eds.) *Gregorii Turonensis opera*: 854-72. Hannover. Monumenta Germaniae Historica, Scriptores rerum Merovingicarum 1.2.

GREGORIUS TURONENSIS. In gloria martyrum (*Glor. mart.*), De virtutibus sancti Juliani (*Virt. Jul.*), De virtutibus sancti Martini (*Virt.*

Mart.), In gloria confessorum (*Glor. conf.*) and Vitae patrum (*Vit. patr.*). Krusch, B. (ed.) 1885. In: Arndt, W. and B. Krusch (eds.), *Gregorii Turonensis opera*: 451-820. Hannover. Monumenta Germaniae Historica, Scriptores rerum Merovingicarum 1.2.

GREGORIUS TURONENSIS. *Historiarum libri decem. (Hist.)* Buchner, R. (ed. and transl.) 1967a and 1967b. 2 vols. Darmstadt. Ausgewählte Quellen zur deutschen Geschichte des Mittelalters. Freiherr vom Stein-Gedächtnisausgabe 2, 3.

GREGORIUS TURONENSIS. In psalterii tractatum commentarius. *(In psal.)* Krusch, B. (ed.) 1885. In: Arndt, W. and B. Krusch (ed.) *Gregorii Turonensis opera*: 873-7. Hannover. Monumenta Germaniae Historica, Scriptores rerum Merovingicarum 1.2.

HIERONYMUS. Translatio Chronicorum Eusebii Pamphili. In: Migne, J.P. (ed.) 1866. *Patrologia latina* 27: 9-507. Paris.

HILARIUS PICTAVIENSIS. Tractatus mysteriorum. Feder, A. (ed.) 1916. *Hilarius Pictaviensis Opera*: 1-38. Wien. Corpus scriptorum ecclesiasticorum latinorum 65.

HILARIUS PICTAVIENSIS, Tractatus super Psalmos. In: Migne, J.P. (ed.) 1844. *Patrologia latina* 9: 231-889. Paris.

ISIDORUS Hispalensis. *Etymologiarum sive originum libri 20.* Lindsay, W.M. (ed.) 1957. 2 vols. Oxford.

KRUSCH, B. (ed.) 1885. See: Gregorius Turonensis.

KRUSCH, B. (ed.) 1888, *Vitae sanctorum generis regii.* Hannover. Monumenta Germaniae Historica, Scriptores rerum Merovingicarum 2.

KRUSCH, B. (ed.) 1896. *Passiones vitaeque sanctorum aevi Merovingici.* Hannover. Monumenta Germaniae Historica, Scriptores rerum Merovingicarum 3.

KRUSCH, B. AND W. LEVISON (eds.) 1951. *Gregorii episcopi Turonensis Libri Historiarum decem.* Editio altera. Hannover. Monumenta Germaniae Historica, Scriptores rerum Merovingicarum 1.1.

LACTANTIUS, Lucius Caelius Firmianus. Carmen de ave phoenice. In: Brandt, S. and G. Laubmann (eds.) 1893: *Lactantii Opera omnia* 2, 1: 135-47. Wien. Corpus scriptorum ecclesiasticorum latinorum 27.

LACTANTIUS, Lucius. Divinae Institutiones. In: Brandt, S. and G. Laubmann (eds.) 1890. *Lactantii Opera omnia* 1. Wien. Corpus scriptorum ecclesiasticorum latinorum 19.

LATOUCHE, R. (transl.) 1963a. Grégoire de Tours, *Histoire des Francs*. Paris. Les classiques de l'histoire de France au Moyen Age 27.

MAASSEN, F. (ed.) 1893. *Concilia aevi Merovingici*. Hannover. Monumenta Germaniae Historica. Concilia 1.

MACROBIUS, Ambrosius Theodosius. *Commentarii in somnium Scipionis*. Willis, J. (ed.) 1970. Leipzig. Bibliotheca Graecorum et Romanorum Teubneriana.

MARIUS Aventicensis. Chronica. Mommsen, T. (ed.). 1894. *Chronica minora saeculi IV-VII*. 2: 225-40. Berlin. Monumenta Germaniae Historica, Auctores antiquissimi 11.

OMONT, H. 1882. 'Les sept merveilles du monde au Moyen Age'. *Bibliothèque de l'école des chartes* 43: 40-59, 431-2.

OROSIUS, *Historiarum adversum paganos libri septem*. Zangemeister, C. (ed.) 1889. Leipzig. Corpus scriptorum ecclesiasticorum latinorum 5.

PAULINUS Petricordiensis, De vita sancti Martini libri sex. Migne, J.P. (ed.) 1861. *Patrologia latina* 61: 1007-74. Paris.

PLINIUS, Naturalis historia. Rackham, H. (ed. and transl.) 1979. *Pliny's Natural history* vol. 1. London. Loeb Classical Library 330.

PROSPER (Aquitani) Tiro, Epitoma Chronicon. In: Mommsen, Th. (ed.) 1892. *Chronica Minora saeculi IV-VII*. 1: 341-485. Berlin. Monumenta Germaniae Historica, Auctores antiquissimi 9.

PROSPER Aquitani. Expositio psalmorum. In: Migne, J.P. (ed.) 1861. *Patrologia latina*. 51: 277-426. Paris.

PROSPER Aquitani. Liber sententiarum. Gastaldo, M. (ed.) 1972. Corpus christianorum ser. lat. 68A: 215-365. Turnhout.

PRUDENTIUS. Apotheosis. Thomson, H.J. (ed. and transl.) 1949. *Prudentius*: 116-99. London. Loeb Classical Library 387.

PRUDENTIUS. Liber cathemerinon. Thomson, H.J. (ed. and transl.) 1949. *Prudentius*: 6-115. London. Loeb Classical Library 387.

PRUDENTIUS. Hamartigenia. Thomson, H.J. (ed. and transl.) 1949. *Prudentius*: 200-73. London. Loeb Classical Library 387.

PRUDENTIUS. Peristephanon liber. Thomson, H.J. (ed. and transl.) 1953. *Prudentius*: 98-345. London. Loeb Classical Library 398.

QUODVULTDEUS, *Liber promissionum et praedictorum Dei*. Braun, R. (ed. and transl.) 2 vols. 1964a and b. Paris. Sources chrétiennes 101, 102.

SCHULTE NORDHOLT, J.W. 1964. *Hymnen en liederen.* Hilversum-Antwerpen.
SEVERUS, SULPICIUS. Chronica. Halm, C. (ed.) 1866. *Sulpicii Severi Libri qui supersunt*, 1-105. Wien. Corpus scriptorum ecclesiasticorum latinorum 1.
SEVERUS, SULPICIUS. Dialogi. Halm, C. (ed.) 1866. *Sulpicii Severi libri qui supersunt*: 152-216. Wien. Corpus scriptorum ecclesiasticorum latinorum 1.
SEVERUS, SULPICIUS. Epistolae 3. Halm, C. (ed.) 1866. *Sulpicii Severi Libri qui supersunt*: 106-51. Wien. Corpus scriptorum ecclesiasticorum latinorum 1.
SEVERUS, SULPICIUS. *Vita Sancti Martini.* Fontaine, J. (ed. and transl.) 1967. Commentaire 1968, 1969. 3 vols. Paris. Sources chrétiennes 133, 134, 135.

THOMSON, H.J. (ed. and transl.) 1949. See Prudentius.
THORPE, L. (transl.) 1974. *Gregory of Tours, The history of the Franks.* Harmondsworth.

VERGILIUS. Aeneis. Ribbeck, O. (ed.) 1895. *P. Vergili Maronis Opera* 2,3. Leipzig.
VERGILIUS. Eclogae. Ribbeck, O. (ed.) 1894. *P. Vergili Maronis Opera* 1: 1-58. Leipzig.
VERGILIUS. Georgica. Ribbeck, O. (ed.) 1894. *P. Vergili Maronis Opera* 1: 61-208. Leipzig.
VIRGIL. See: Vergilius.
VITA sancti Caesarii episcopi Arelatensis libri 2. In: Krusch 1896: 433-501.
VITA sancti Nicetii episcopi Lugdunensis. In: Krusch 1896: 518-24.
VITA Hilarii Arelatensis. In: Migne, J.P. (ed.) 1859. *Patrologia latina* 50: 1219-46. Paris.

ZEUMER, K. (ed.) 1886. *Formulae Merovingici et Karolingici aevi.* Ordines iudiciorum Dei: 604-29. Hannover. Monumenta Germaniae Historica. Leges sect. 5.

SECONDARY SOURCES

AALEN, S. 1951. *Die Begriffe 'Licht' und 'Finsternis' im Alten Testament, im Spätjudentum und im Rabbinismus.* In: Skrifter utgitt av Norske Videnskaps-Akademi i Oslo, IIe Historisk-Filosofisk Klasse 1: 1-351. Oslo.

AALEN, S. 1960. 'Licht und Finsternis'. In: *Die Religion in Geschichte und Gegenwart*. Third edition. 4: 357-9. Tübingen.

AALEN, S. 1976. 'Glory, honour. Doxa. Time'. In: *The new international dictionary of New Testament theology* 2: 44-52. Grand Rapids.

AALST, P. VAN DER. 1962. 'Leven of licht?' *Het Christelijk Oosten en hereniging* 14: 83-128.

ADNÈS, P. 1976. 'Larmes'. *Dictionnaire de spiritualité* 11: 287-303. Paris.

ADNÈS, P. 1984. 'Pénitence: durant les trois premiers siècles; aux 4e et 5e siècles; vers une nouvelle forme de pénitence'. *Dictionnaire de spiritualité* 12: 943-70. Paris.

AIGRAIN, R. 1924. *Sainte Radegonde*. Paris.

AIGRAIN, R. 1953. *L'hagiographie*. Ses sources, ses méthodes, son histoire. [Poitiers].

d'ALVERNY, M.-T. 1962. 'Survivance de la magie antique'. In: Wilpert, P. (ed.), *Antike und Orient im Mittelalter*: 154-78. Berlin. Miscellanea mediaevalia 1.

AMPÈRE, M.J.-J. 1839. *Histoire littéraire de la France avant le douzième siècle* II. Paris.

ANDERSON, C.S. 1982. *Divine governance, miracles and laws of nature in the early Middle Ages:* 'De mirabilis sacrae Scripturae'. University of California, Los Angeles. *Dissertation Abstracts International* 43.4 (October 1982): 1249-A.

ANGENENDT, A. 1982. 'Die Liturgie und die Organisation des kirchlichen Lebens auf dem Lande'. In: *Cristianizzazione* 1982a: 169-226.

ANTIN, P. 1963. 'Notes sur le style de St Grégoire de Tours et ses emprunts (?) à Philostrate'. *Latomus* 22: 273-84.

ANTIN, P. 1967. 'Emplois de la Bible chez Grégoire de Tours et Mgr Pie'. *Latomus* 26: 778-82.

ARIÈS, Ph. 1976. 'Culture orale et culture écrit'. In: Plongeron and Pannet 1976: 227-40.

ASSAGIOLI, R. 1965. *Psychosynthesis*. New York.

ASSENDELFT, M.M. VAN. 1976. *Sol ecce surgit igneus*. A commentary on the morning and evening hymns of Prudentius. Groningen.

ATSMA, H. (ed.) 1976 and 1979. *E. Ewig, Spätantikes und Fränkisches Gallien*. Gesammelte Schriften (1952-1973), 1 and 2. München. Beihefte der Francia 3.1 and 2.

AUBRUN, M. 1980. 'Caractères et portée religieuse et sociale des "Visiones" en Occident du VIe au XIe siècle', *Cahiers de civilisation médiévale* 23: 109-30.

AUERBACH, E. 1938. 'Figura'. *Archivum Romanicum* 22: 436-89.

AUERBACH, E. 1946. *Mimesis.* Dargestellte Wirklichkeit in der abendländischen Literatur. Bern.
AUERBACH, E. 1957. *Mimesis.* The representation of reality in western literature. Trask, W. (transl.) Garden City.
AUERBACH, E. 1958. *Literatursprache und Publikum in der lateinischen Spätantike und im Mittelalter.* Bern.
AUERBACH, E. 1964. *Typologische Motive in der mittelalterlichen Literatur.* Second edition. Krefeld.
AUNE, D.E. 1980. 'Magic in early Christianity'. In: Haase 1980: 1507-57.

BAAL, J. VAN. 1960. *De magie als godsdienstig verschijnsel.* Inaugurele rede. Amsterdam.
BACHELARD, G. 1949. *La psychanalyse du feu.* Paris. NRF Collection psychologie 7.
BACHELARD, G. 1960. *La poétique de la rêverie.* Paris.
BACHELARD, G. 1961. *La flamme d'une chandelle.* Paris.
BACHELARD, G. 1973. *Le droit de rêver.* Paris.
BAKER, D. (ed.) 1979. *The church in town and countryside.* Oxford.
BANNIARD, M. 1978. 'L'aménagement de l'histoire chez Grégoire de Tours. A propos de l'invasion de 451'. *Romanobarbarica* 3: 5-38.
BARTELINK, G.J.M. 1970. 'De abstracte aanduidingen voor de duivel bij Gregorius van Tours'. *Hermeneus* 41: 139-42. Also published as: 'Les dénominations du diable chez Grégoire de Tours'. *Revue des études latines* 48 (1970) [1971]: 411-32.
BASTIDE, R. 1967. 'Sociologie du rêve'. In: Caillois and von Grunebaum 1967: 177-88.
BAUMANN, H. 1959. 'Mythos in ethnologischer Sicht'. *Studium generale* 12: 1-17, 583-97.
BEIRNAERT, L. 1950. 'La dimension mythique dans le sacramentalisme chrétien'. In: *Eranos-Jahrbuch* 17: 255-85. Zürich.
BELL, D.N. 1978. 'The vision of the world and the archetypes of the Latin spirituality of the Middle Ages'. *Archives d'histoire doctrinale et littéraire du Moyen Age* 51 (1977) [1978]: 7-31. Paris.
BENZ, E. 1969. *Die Vision.* Erfahrungsformen und Bilderwelt. Stuttgart.
BERGER, K. 1980. 'Hellenistisch-heidnische Prodigien und die Vorzeichen in der jüdischen und christlichen Apokalyptik'. In: Haase 1980: 1428-69.
BERNOUILLI, C.A. 1900. *Die Heiligen der Merowinger.* Tübingen.
BERROUARD, M.-F. 1974. 'La pénitence publique durant les six premiers siècles. Histoire et sociologie'. *La Maison-Dieu* 118: 92-130.
BEUMANN, H. 'Gregor von Tours und der *sermo rusticus*'. In: Pepgen, K. and St. Skalweit (eds.) 1964, *Spiegel der Geschichte.* Festgabe für

Max Braubach: 69-98. Münster in Westfalen. Reprinted in: Beumann, H. (ed.) 1972. *Wissenschaft vom Mittelalter.* Ausgewählte Aufsätze: 41-70. Köln-Wien.

BIANCHI, D. 1961. 'Da Gregorio di Tours a Paolo Diacono'. *Aevum* 35: 150-66.

La BIBBIA nell' alto medioevo 1 and 2. 1963 a and b. Spoleto. Settimane di studio del Centro Italiano di Studi sull'alto Medioevo 10.

BIETENHARD, H. 1975. 'Fire: pyr.'. In: *The new international dictionary of New Testament theology* 1: 653-7. Grand Rapids.

BIEZAIS, H. (ed.) 1979. *Religious symbols and their functions.* Stockholm. Scripta Instituti Donneriani Aboensis 10.

BLAISE, A. 1954. *Dictionnaire latin-français des auteurs chrétiens.* Turnhout.

BLOCH, R. 1963. *Les prodiges dans l'antiquité classique.* Paris. Mythes et religions.

BLÖCKER, M. 'Wetterzauber. Zu einem Glaubenskomplex des frühen Mittelalters'. *Francia* 9: 117-31.

BLOMGREN, S. 1936. 'Ad Gregorium adnotationes'. *Eranos* 34: 25-40.

BLUME, I. 1970. *Das Menschenbild Gregors von Tours in den 'Historiarum Libri decem'.* Erlangen.

BODKIN, M. 1963. *Archetypal patterns in poetry.* London.

BÖCHER, O. 1978. 'Water, lake, sea, well, river'. in: *The new international dictionary nof New Testament theology* 3: 982-91. Grand Rapids.

BOESCH GAJANO, S. 1977. 'Il santo nella visione storiografica di Gregorio di Tours'. In: *Gregorio di Tours* 1977: 27-92.

BOGLIONI, P. 1974. 'Miracle et nature chez Grégoire le Grand'. In: *Épopées, légendes et miracles.* Cahiers d'études médiévales 1: 11-102. Montreal.

BOGLIONI, P. (ed.) 1979. *La culture populaire au Moyen Age.* Montreal.

BOLTON, W.F. 1959. 'The supra-historical sense in the Dialogues of Gregory I'. *Aevum* 33: 206-13.

BONNET, M. 1890. *Le latin de Grégoire de Tours.* Paris.

BREDE KRISTENSEN, W. 1949. *Het leven uit de dood.* Second edition. Haarlem.

BRELICH, A. 1967. 'Le rôle des rêves dans la conception religieuse du monde en Grèce'. In: Caillois and von Grunebaum 1967: 281-89.

BRINCKEN, A. VON DEN. 1957. *Studien zur lateinischen Weltchronistik bis in das Zeitalter Ottos von Freising.* Düsseldorf.

BROEK, R. VAN DEN. 1971. *The Myth of the phoenix according to classical and early Christian traditions.* Leiden.

BROWN, P. 1970. 'Sorcery, demons and the rise of Christianity: from late Antiquity into the Middle Ages'. In: *Witchcraft confessions and accusations*: 17-45. Association of social anthropologists monographs 9. Reprinted in: Brown, P. (ed.) 1972. *Religion and society in the age of St Augustine:* 119-46. London.

BROWN, P. 1971. *The world of late Antiquity*. From Marcus Aurelius to Muhammad. London.

BROWN, P. 1973. 'A dark Age crisis: aspects of the Iconoclastic controversy'. *English Historical Review* 88: 1-34. Reprinted in Brown 1982: 251-301.

BROWN, P. 1977. 'Relics and social status in the age of Gregory of Tours'. The Stenton lecture 1976. University of Reading. Reprinted in: Brown, 1982. 222-50.

BROWN, P. 1981. *The cult of the saints*. Its rise and function in Latin Christianity. Chicago-London. The Haskell lectures on history of religions, new series 2.

BROWN, P. 1982. *Society and the holy in late Antiquity*. London.

BRUNHÖLZL F. 1975. *Geschichte der lateinischen Literatur des Mittelalters* I. München.

BUDD, P.J. 1971. 'Dream'. In: *The new international dictionary of New Testament theology* 1: 511-3. Grand Rapids.

BÜCHNER, V.F. 1913. *Merovingica*. Amsterdam.

BULTMANN, R. 1940. 'Zur Geschichte der Lichtsymbolik im Altertum'. *Orientalistische Literaturzeitung* 43: 150-75. Reprinted in: Dinkler, E. (ed.), 1967. *R. Bultmann, Exegetica.* Aufsätze zur Erforschung des Neuen Testaments: 323-55. Tübingen.

BUNDY, M.W. 1927. 'The theory of imagination in classical and mediaeval thought'. *University of Illinois studies in language and literature* 12.2-3: 7-285. Urbana.

CAILLOIS, R. 1967. 'Prestiges et problèmes du rêve'. In: Caillois and von Grunebaum 1967: 24-6.

CAILLOIS, R. and G.E. von Grunebaum (eds.) 1967. *Le rêve et les sociétés humaines*. Paris.

CAMELOT, P.-T. 1976. 'Lumière: étude patristique'. In: *Dictionnaire de spiritualité* 9: 1149-58. Paris.

CAMERON, A. 1975. 'The Byzantine sources of Gregory of Tours'. *Journal of theological studies* 26: 421-6.

CAQUOT, A. and M. LEIBOVICI (eds.) 1968. *La divination*. Paris.

CARTWRIGHT, R.D. 1978. *A primer on sleep and dreaming*. Reading (Mass.).

CAZENAVE, A. 1981. 'A propos de l'iconographie et du langage à l'époque romane'. In: Kluxen 1981b: 547-56.

CHADWICK, O. 1949. 'Gregory of Tours and Gregory the Great'. *Journal of theological studies* 50: 38-49.
CHADWICK, O. 1968. *John Cassian*. Second edition. Cambridge.
CHATILLON, F. 1977. 'L'illusoire mimésis et les aléas d'une translation'. *Revue du Moyen Age Latin* 24 (1968) [1977]: 91-7.
CHENU, M.D. 1968. *Nature, man and society in the twelfth century.* Essays on new theological perspectives in the Latin West. Taylor, J. and L.K. Little (transl.). Chicago-London 1968.
Le CHIESE nei regni dell' Europa occidentale e i loro rapporti con Roma sino all' 800, 1 and 2. 1960 a and b. Spoleto. Settimane di studio del Centro Italiano di Studi sull'alto medioevo 7.
CHYDENIUS, J. 1975. 'La théorie du symbolisme médiéval'. *Poétique* 6.23: 322-41.
CICCARESE, M.P. 1981. 'Alle origini della letteratura delle visioni: il contributo di Gregorio di Tours'. *Studi Storico Religiosi* 5: 251-66.
CLARKE, H.B. and M. BRENNAN (eds.) 1981. *Columbanus and Merovingian monasticism.* Oxford. BAR series 114.
CLASEN, S. 1970. 'Das Heiligkeitsideal im Wandel der Zeiten'. *Wissenschaft und Weisheit* 33: 46-64, 132-64.
CLERCQ, C. DE 1936. *La législation religieuse franque de Clovis à Charlemagne.* Étude sur les actes de conciles et les capitulaires, les statuts diocésains et les règles monastiques (507-814). Louvain-Paris. Université de Louvain, Receuil de travaux publiées par les membres des Conférences d'Histoire et de Philologie, 2e série: 38.
CLOSS, A. 1960. 'Feuer: Religionsgeschichte'. In: *Lexikon für Theologie und Kirche*, second edition 4: 106-7. Freiburg.
CLOSS, A. 1961. 'Licht: religionsgeschichtlich'. In: *Lexikon für Theologie und Kirche*, second edition 6: 1022-3. Freiburg.
COLLINS, R. 1981. 'Observations on the form, language and public of the prose biographies of Venantius Fortunatus in the hagiography of Merovingian Gaul'. In: Clarke and Brennan 1981: 105-31.
CORBETT, J.H. 1981. 'The saint as patron in the work of Gregory of Tours'. *Journal of medieval history* 7: 1-13.
COURCELLE, P. 1951. 'Philostrate et Grégoire de Tours'. In: *Mélanges J. de Ghellinck* 1: 311-9. Gembloux. Museum Lessianum, sect. historique 13.
CRISTIANIZZAZIONE ed organizzazione ecclesiastica delle campagne nell' alto medioevo: espansione e resistenze, 1 and 2. 1982 a and b. Spoleto. Settimane di studio del Centro Italiano di Studi sull'alto medioevo 28.
CUMONT, F. 1949. *Lux perpetua*. Paris.

CURTIUS, E.R. 1953. *European literature and the Latin Middle Ages.* Trask, W.R. (transl.). New York. Bollingen series 36.

DAGENS, C. 1977. *Saint Grégoire le Grand.* Culture et expérience chrétiennes. Paris. Études Augustiniennes.

DAM, R. VAN 1985. *Leadership and community in late antique Gaul.* Berkeley - Los Angeles -London.

DANIÉLOU, J. 1958. *Bible et liturgie.* Paris.

DANIÉLOU, J. 1963. 'La typologie biblique traditionelle dans la liturgie du Moyen Age'. In: *La Bibbia* 1963a: 141-61.

DANIÉLOU, J. 1969. 'Feuersäule (Lichtsäule, Wolkensäule)'. In: *Reallexikon für Antike und Christentum* 7: 186-90. Stuttgart.

DARLAPP, A. 1960. 'Magie'. In: *Lexikon für Theologie und Kirche* 6: 1274-6. Second edition. Freiburg.

DAVY, M.-M. and others 1976. *Le thème de la lumière dans le Judaisme, le Christianisme et l'Islam.* Paris.

DAWID, M. 1958. *Weltwunder der Antike.* Baukunst und Plastik. Frankfurt am Main.

DEIKMAN, A.J. 1966. 'Deautomatization and the mystic experience'. *Psychiatry* 29: 324-38. Reprinted in: Tart 1969: 23-44.

DELEHAYE, H. 1906. *Les légendes hagiographiques.* Second edition. Bruxelles.

DELEHAYE, H. 1925. 'Les recueils antiques de miracles des saints'. *Analecta Bollandiana* 43: 71-85, 305-25.

DEMM, E. 1975. 'Zur Rolle des Wunders in der Heiligkeitskonzeption des Mittelalters'. *Archiv für Kulturgeschichte* 57: 300-44.

DEVEREUX, G. 1967. 'Rêves pathogènes dans les sociétés non occidentales'. In: Caillois and von Grunebaum 1967: 189-204.

DILL, S. 1926. *Roman society in Gaul in the Merovingian age.* London. (Reprint 1966).

DINZELBACHER, P. 1981. *Vision und Visionsliteratur im Mittelalter.* Stuttgart. Monographien zur Geschichte des Mittelalters 23.

DODDS, E.R. 1951. *The Greeks and the irrational.* Berkeley.

DODDS, E.R. 1968. *Pagan and Christian in an age of anxiety.* Cambridge.

DÖLGER, F.J. 1920. *Sol salutis.* Gebet und Gesang im christlichen Altertum. Münster in Westfalen. Literaturgeschichtliche Forschungen 4-5.

DÖRRIE, H. 1975. 'Philosophie und Mysterium. Zur Legitimation des Sprechens und Verstehens auf zwei Ebenen durch Platon'. In: Fromm, H., W. Harms and U. Ruberg (eds.), *Verbum et signum.* Beiträge zur Bedeutungsforschung. Studien zu Semantik und Sinntradition im Mittelalter 2: 9-24. München.

DOUGLAS, M. 1966. *Purity and danger.* An analysis of concepts of pollution and taboo. London.
DULAEY, M. 1973. *Le rêve dans la vie et pensée de St Augustine.* Paris. Études Augustiniennes.
DU PLESSIS, M. 1968. 'L'aveux d'ignorance de Grégoire de Tours'. *Revue des langues romanes* 78: 53-69.
DURKHEIM, E. 1960. *Les formes élémentaires de la vie religieuse.* Le système totémique en Australie. Fourth edition. Paris.

EBERT, A. 1874. *Geschichte der christlich-lateinischen Literatur* 1. Leipzig.
EDSMAN, C.-M. 1940. *Le baptême de feu.* Uppsala.
EDSMAN, C.-M. 1949. *Ignis divinus.* Le feu comme moyen de rajeunissement et d'immortalité: contes, légendes, mythes, rites. Lund. Skrifter utgivna av Vetenskaps-societeten 1.
EISING, H. 1960. 'Feuer: In der Heiligen Schrift'. *Lexikon für Theologie und Kirche* 4: 107-8. Second edition. Freiburg.
EITREM, S. 1947. *Orakel und Mysterien am Ausgang der Antike.* Zürich.
ÉLIADE, M. 1952. *Images et symboles.* Essai sur le symbolisme magico-religieux. Paris.
ÉLIADE, M. 1957. *Mythes, rêves et mystères.* Paris.
ÉLIADE, M. 1958a. 'Significations de la "lumière intérieure"'. In: *Eranos-Jahrbuch* (1957) 26: 189-242. Zürich.
ÉLIADE, M. 1958b. *Patterns in comparative religion.* Sheed, R. (transl.). New York.
ÉLIADE, M. 1959. *Naissances mystiques.* Essai sur quelques types d'initiation. Paris.
ÉLIADE, M. 1967. 'Rêves et visions initiatiques chez les chamans sibériens'. In: Caillois and von Grunebaum 1967: 315-24.
ENGEMANN, J. 1975. 'Zur Verbreitung magischer Übelabwehr in der nicht-christlichen und christlichen Spätantike'. *Jahrbuch für Antike und Christentum* 18: 22-48.
EPSTEIN, G. 1981. *Waking dream therapy.* New York-London.
EVANS-PRITCHARD, E.E. 1965. *Theories of primitive religion.* Oxford.
EVANS-PRITCHARD, E.E. 1968. *Witchcraft, oracles and magic among the Azande.* Oxford.
EWIG, E. 1961. 'Le culte de St Martin à l'époque franque'. *Revue d'histoire de l'église de France* 47: 1-18. Reprinted in: Atsma 1976: 355-70.
EWIG, E. 1976. 'Das Fortleben römischer Institutionen in Gallien und Germanien'. In: Atsma 1976a: 409-34.

EWIG, E. 1979. 'Die Verehrung orientalischer Heiligen im spätromischen Gallien und im Merovingerreich'. In: Atsma 1979: 393-410.

FEBVRE, L. 1941. 'La sensibilité et l'histoire'. *Annales d'histoire sociale* 3: 5-20.
FICHTNER, G. 1982. 'Christus als Arzt. Ursprünge und Wirkungen eines Motivs'. *Frühmittelalterliche Studien* 16: 1-18.
FINKENRATH, G. 1978. 'Mysterion'. In: *The new international dictionary of New Testament theology* 3: 501-6. Grand Rapids.
FISCHER, B. 1961. 'Liturgie: abendländische Liturgien'. In: *Lexikon für Theologie und Kirche* 6: 1091-5. Second edition. Freiburg.
FONTAINE, J. 1963. 'Une clé littéraire de la Vita Martini de Sulpice Sévère: la typologie prophétique'. In: *Mélanges offerts à Mlle. Christine Mohrmann*: 84-95. Utrecht.
FONTAINE, J. 1976. 'Hagiographie et politique de Sulpice Sévère à Venance Fortunat'. In: Riché, P. (ed.), 'Actes du Colloque de Nanterre 1974'. *Revue d'histoire de l'église de France* 62 (1975) [1976]: 113-40.
FONTAINE, J. 1979. 'Thèmes et méthodes de recherche hagiographique en 1979'. *Studi medievali* ser. 3. 20: 933-45.
FONTAINE, J. 1982. 'Le culte des saints et ses implications sociales'. *Analecta Bollandiana* 100: 17-41.
FOURNIER, P.-F. 1979. *Magie et sorcellerie*. Essai historique. Moulins.
FRANCISSEN, F.P.M. 1977. 'Numen inest in loco'. *Hermeneus* 49: 247-75.
FRIEDRICH, B. 1951. *Studien zu Gregor von Tours*. Inaugural-Dissertation Universität Heidelberg. Heidelberg.

GÄRTNER, B. 1978. 'Epiphaneia'. In: *The new international dictionary of New Testament theology* 3: 317-20. Grand Rapids.
GAIFFIER, B. DE 1970. 'Hagiographie et historiographie. Quelques aspects du problème'. In: *La storiografia* 1970a: 139-66.
GAMS, P.B. 1873. *Series episcoporum ecclesiae catholicae a beato Petro apostolo*. Regensburg.
GANDILLAC, M. DE 1981. Langage et connaissance religieuse dans le christianisme du Moyen Age latin'. In: Kluxen 1981a: 193-210.
GANSHOF, F.L. 1966. *Een historicus uit de zesde eeuw*. Gregorius van Tours. Brussel. Mededelingen van de Koninklijke Vlaamse Academie voor Wetenschappen, Letteren en Schone Kunsten van België, Klasse der Letteren 28.5.
GANZENMÜLLER, W. 1916. 'Die empfindsame Naturbetrachtung im Mittelalter'. *Archiv für Kulturgeschichte* 12: 195-228.

GARROD, H.W. 1919. 'Virgil and Gregory of Tours'. *Classical Review* 33: 28.
GAUS, H. 1975. 'Verwachtingen en problematiek van de mentaliteitsgeschiedenis'. *Belgisch Tijdschrift voor Nieuwste Geschiedenis* 6: 403-30.
GAUTIER DALCHÉ, P. 1982. 'La représentation de l'espace dans les "Libri Miraculorum" de Grégoire de Tours'. *Le Moyen Age* 88 (ser. 4: 38): 397-420.
GEARY, P.J. 1979. 'La coercition des saints dans la pratique religieuse médiévale'. In: Boglioni 1979: 147-61.
GEERTZ, H. AND K. THOMAS 1975. 'An anthropology of religion and magic, two views'. *The Journal of interdisciplinary history* 6: 71-110.
GERRITSEN, W.P. 1978. *De clepsydra*, een tunnel naar de antipoden, en de natuur in een middeleeuwse proeftuin. Een beschouwing over wereldbeeld en natuur in de middeleeuwen. Utrecht.
GILLIARD, J. 1979. 'The senators of sixth-century Gaul'. *Speculum* 54: 685-97.
GILSON, E. 1960. *The Christian philosophy of Saint Augustine*. Lynch, L.E.M. (transl.). New York.
GIORDANO, O. 1978-9. 'Sociologia e patologia del miracolo in Gregorio di Tours'. *Helikon* 18-19: 161-209.
GOFFART, W. 1982. 'Foreigners in the "Histories" of Gregory of Tours'. *Florilegium* 4: 80-99.
GOFFART, W. 1985. 'The conversions of Avitus of Clermont, and similar passages in Gregory of Tours'. In: Neusner, J. and E.S. Frerichs (eds.), '*To see ourselves as others see us*'. Christians, Jews and 'others' in late Antiquity. Chico, Calif.
GOGAUD, L. 1953. 'Cierges'. In: *Dictionnaire de spiritualité* 2: 897-8. Paris.
GOLDMANN, Z. 1975. 'Das Symbol der Lilie. Ursprung und Bedeutung'. *Archiv für Kulturgeschichte* 57: 247-99.
GOODENOUGH, E.R. 1969. *By light, light*. The mystic Gospel of Hellenistic Judaism. Amsterdam.
GOODMAN, F.D., J.H. HENNEY AND E. PRESSEL 1974. *Trance, healing and hallucination*. Three field studies in religious experience. New York-London.
GRANT, R.M. 1952. *Miracle and natural law in Graeco-Roman and early Christian thought*. Amsterdam.
GRAUS, F. 1965. *Volk, Herrscher und Heiliger im Reich der Merowinger*. Praha.
GREGORIO DI TOURS 1977. Convegni del Centro di Studi sulla spiritualità medievale 12 (1971). Todi.

GRIFFE, E. 1951. 'Aux origines de la liturgie gallicane'. *Bulletin de littérature ecclésiastique* 52: 17-43.
GRIFFE, E. 1975. 'A travers les paroisses rurales de la Gaule au sixième siècle'. *Bulletin de littérature ecclésiastique* 76: 3-26.
GRISEWOOD, H. 1952. 'St Gregory of Tours'. *The Month,* New series 7: 332-47.
GRUNDMANN, H. 1965. *Geschichtsschreibung im Mittelalter.* Göttingen.
GÜNTER, H. 1949. *Psychologie der Legende.* Studien zu einer wissenschaftlichen Heiligengeschichte. Freiburg.
GURJEWITSCH, A.J. 1978. *Das Weltbild des mittelalterlichen Menschen.* Lossack, S. (transl.). München.
GY, P.-M. 1976. 'Liturgie: liturgie occidentales'. *Dictionnaire de spiritualité* 9: 899-912. Paris.

HAASE, W. (ed.) 1980. *Aufstieg und Niedergang der römischen Welt* 2.23.2. Berlin.
HADOT, P. 1981. 'Antike Methodik der geistigen Übungen im Frühchristentum'. *Humanistische Bildung* 4: 31-62.
HAECKEL, J. 1960. 'Mythos: religionsgeschichtlich'. In: *Die Religion in Geschichte und Gegenwart* 4: 1268-74. Tübingen.
HAGIOGRAPHIES, CULTURES ET SOCIÉTÉS IV-XII siècles 1981. Paris. Actes du colloque Nanterre-Paris 1979.
HAHN, H.C. 1975. 'Darkness, night: nyx, skotos'. In: *The new international dictionary of New Testament theology* 1: 420-5. Grand Rapids.
HAHN, H.C. 1976. 'Light, shine, lamp: lampo, lychnos, phaino, phos.'. In: *The new international dictionary of New Testament theology* 2: 484-8, 490-5. Grand Rapids.
HAHN, H.C. 1971. 'Zeit, Ewigkeit'. In: *Theologisches Begriffslexikon zum Neuen Testament* 2(2): 1457-78. Wuppertal.
HALLOWELL, I. 1967. 'Le rôle des rêves dans la culture Ojibwa'. In: Caillois and von Grunebaum 1967: 257-81.
HALPHEN, L. 1925. 'Grégoire de Tours, historien de Clovis'. In: *Mélanges d'histoire du Moyen Age offerts à M.F. Lot*: 235-44. Paris.
HAMMAN, A. 1980. 'La prière chrétienne et la prière paienne, formes et différences'. In: Haase 1980: 1190-1247.
HANSON, J.S. 1980. 'Dreams and visions in the Graeco-Roman world and early Christianity'. In: Haase 1980: 1395-1427.
HARMENING, D. 1979. *Superstitio.* Überlieferungs- und theoriegeschichtliche Untersuchungen zur kirchlich-theologischen Aberglaubensliteratur des Mittelalters. Berlin.

HARNACK, A. VON 1902. 'Cyprian als Enthusiast'. *Zeitschrift für die neutestamentliche Wissenschaft* 3: 177-91.

HARTMANN, K. 1979. 'Denken, Wort und Bild'. In: Brunner, H., R. Kannicht and K. Schwager (eds. 1979), *Wort und Bild*: 13-28. München.

HAWKES, T. 1972. *Metaphor.* London.

HÉBERT, M. 1916. 'Documents fournis à la préhistoire par St Grégoire de Tours'. *Revue des études anciennes* 18: 123-41. Reprinted 1967. Amsterdam.

HEDWIG, K. 1980. *Sphaera lucis.* Studien zur Intelligibilität des Seienden im Kontext der mittelalterlichen Lichtspekulation. Münster. Beiträge zur Geschichte der Philosophie und Theologie des Mittelalters N.F. 18.

HEINZELMANN, M. 1973. 'Neue Aspekte der biographischen und hagiographischen Literatur in der lateinischen Welt (1.-6. Jahrhundert)'. *Francia* 1: 27-44.

HEINZELMANN, M. 1979. 'Une source de base de la littérature hagiographique latine: le receuil de miracles'. In: *Hagiographies* 1979: 235-59.

HELGELAND, J. 1980. 'Time and space: Christian and Roman'. In: Haase 1980: 1285-1305.

HELLMANN, S. 1911. 'Gregor von Tours'. *Historische Zeitschrift* 107: 1-43. Reprinted in: Beumann, H. (ed.) 1961. *Hellmann, S. Ausgewählte Abhandlungen*: 57-99. Darmstadt.

HERRMANN-MASCARD, N. 1975. *Les reliques des saints.* Formation coutumière d'un droit. Paris. Société d'histoire de Droit, Collection d'histoire institutionelle et sociale 6.

HERZOG, R. 1966. *Die allegorische Dichtkunst des Prudentius.* München. Zetemata. Monographien zur klassischen Altertumswissenschaft 42.

HIGOUNET, Ch. 1960. 'Le problème économique: l'Eglise et la vie rurale pendant le très haut Moyen Age'. In: *Le chiese* 1960b: 775-803.

HISTOIRE DES MIRACLES 1983. Actes de la Sixième Rencontre d'Histoire Religieuse à Fontevraud 1982. Angers. Publications du Centre de Recherches d'Histoire Religieuse et d'Histoire des Idées 6.

HOFIUS, O. 1971. 'Wunder'. *Theologisches Begriffslexikon zum Neuen Testament* 2(2): 1443-52. Wuppertal.

HOLTE, R. 1979. 'Gottessymbol und soziale Struktur'. In: Biezais 1979: 1-14.

HOPFNER, Th. 1935. 'Die orientalisch-hellenistischen Mysterien'. In: *Paulys Real-Encyclopädie der classischen Altertumswissenschaft.* New edition 16: 1315-50. Stuttgart.

HUGENHOLTZ, F.W.N., W. DEN BOER AND TH. J. G. LOCHER

1960. *Gestalten der geschiedenis in de Oudheid, Middeleeuwen en de Nieuwe Tijd.* Den Haag.

HUXLEY, A. 1959. *The doors of perception* and *Heaven and hell.* Harmondsworth.

ILLMER, D. 1981. 'Sprache und Wissenschaft im Übergang von der Spätantike zum frühen Mittelalter'. In: Kluxen 1981b: 547-56.

IRSIGLER, F. 1969. *Untersuchungen zur Geschichte des frühfränkischen Adels.* Bonn. Rheinisches Archiv 70.

IVANKA, E. VON 1959. 'Dunkelheit, mystische'. In: *Reallexikon für Antike und Christentum* 4: 350-8. Stuttgart.

JAMES, E.O. 1966. *The tree of life.* An archeological study. Leiden. Studies in the history of religions 11.

JAMES, W. 1958. *The varieties of religious experience.* New York.

JONG, M. DE 1986. *Kind en klooster in de vroege middeleeuwen.* Amsterdam.

JUNG, C.G. 1944. *Psychologie und Alchemie.* Zürich. Jung, C.G. (ed.), Abhandlungen 5.

JUNG, C.G. 1952. *Symbole der Wandlung.* Analyse des Vorspiels zu einer Schizophrenie. Fourth edition. Zürich.

JUNG, C.G. 1964. *Man and his symbols.* London.

JUNG, C.G. 1971. *Synchronizität als ein Prinzip akausaler Zusammmenhänge.* Olten.

JUNGBLUT, J.B. 1977. 'Recherches sur le "rythme oratoire" dans les "Historiarum libri"'. In: *Gregorio di Tours 1977:* 325-64.

KAMPHAUSEN, H.J. 1975. *Traum und Vision in der lateinischen Poesie der Karolingerzeit.* Bern-Frankfurt am Main. Lateinische Sprache und Literatur des Mittelalters 4.

KEE, H.C. 1983. *Miracle in the early Christian world.* A study in socio-historical method. London.

KELSEY, M.T. 1968. *Dreams, the dark speech of the spirit.* A Christian interpretation. New York.

KELSEY, M.T. 1973. *Healing and Christianity in ancient thought and modern times.* London.

KIRK, G.S. 1970. *Myth.* Its meaning and functions in ancient and other cultures. Cambridge.

KLUXEN, W. et al. (eds.) 1979 a and b. *Sprache und Erkenntnis im Mittelalter* 1 and 2. Akten des 6. internationalen Kongresses für mittelalterliche Philosophie 1977. Berlin-New York. Miscellanea mediaevalia 13.1 and 2.

KOEBNER, R. 1915. *Venantius Fortunatus.* Leipzig. Goetz, W. (ed.) Beiträge zur Kulturgeschichte des Mittelalters und der Renaissance 22.
KOESTLER, A. 1972. *The roots of coincidence.* London.
KÖPKE, R. 1852. 'Gregor von Tours'. *Allgemeine Monatschrift für Wissenschaft und Literatur* 1852: 775-800. Reprinted in: Kiessling, F.G. (ed.) 1872. *R. Köpke, Kleine Schriften zur Geschichte, Politik und Literatur*: 289-321. Berlin.
KÖTTING, B. 1982. 'Wohlgeruch der Heiligkeit'. In: *Jenseitsvorstellungen in Antike und Christentum.* Gedenkschrift für A. Stuiber: 168-75. Münster. Jahrbuch für Antike und Christentum, Ergänzungsband 9.
KOLENKOW, A.B. 1980. 'Relationships between miracle and prophecy in the Greco-Roman world and early Christianity'. In: Haase 1980: 1470-1506.
KRETSCHMER, W. 1962. 'Meditative techniques in psychotherapy'. *Psychologia* 5: 76-83. Reprinted in Tart 1969: 219-28.
KRUSCH, B. 1931. 'Die Unzuverlässigkeit der Geschichtsschreibung Gregors von Tours'. *Mitteilungen des Österreichischen Instituts für Geschichtsforschung* 45: 486-90.
KRUSCH, B. 1932 and 1933. 'Die handschriftlichen Grundlagen der "Historia Francorum" Gregors von Tours'. *Historische Vierteljahrsschrift* 27: 673-757; 28: 1-21.
KRUSCH, B. 1934. 'Kulturbilder aus dem Frankenreiche zur Zeit Gregors von Tours (ob. 594). Ein Beitrag zur Geschichte des Aberglaubens'. *Sitzungsberichte der Preussischen Akademie der Wissenschaften* 1934: 785-800.
KURTH, G. 1893. *Histoire poétique des Mérovingiens.* Paris.
KURTH, G. 1919a and b. *Études Franques.* 2 vols. Paris-Bruxelles.
KURTH, G. 1919. 'De l'autorité de Grégoire de Tours'. In: Kurth 1919b: 117-206.
KURTH, G. 1919. 'Grégoire de Tours et les études classiques au sixième siècle'. In: Kurth 1919a: 1-29.

LA BARRE, W. 1967. 'Le rêve, le charisme et le héros culturel'. In: Caillois and von Grunebaum 1967: 205-12.
LADNER, G.B. 1973. 'Gregory the Great and Gregory VII: a comparison of their concepts of renewal'. *Viator* 4: 1-31.
LADNER, G.B. 1979. 'Medieval and modern understanding of symbolism: a comparison'. *Speculum* 54: 223-56.
LANCZKOWSKI, G. 1960. 'Formen der Magie'. In: *Lexikon für Theologie und Kirche* 6: 1276-7. Second edition. Freiburg.

LANGER, S.K. 1953. *Feeling and form*. A theory of art developed from 'Philosophy in a new key'. London.
LANGER, S.K. 1980. *Philosophy in a new key*. A study in the symbolism of reason, rite, art. Third edition. Cambridge, Mass.
LANNE, E. 1976. 'Liturgie eucharistique en Orient et en Occident (1er-4e siècles)'. *Dictionnaire de spiritualité* 9: 884-99. Paris.
LANOWSKI, J. 1965. 'Weltwunder'. In: *Lexikon für Theologie und Kirche* 10: 1020-30. Second edition. Freiburg.
LATOUCHE, R. 1943. 'Grégoire de Tours et les premiers historiens de France'. *Lettres d'humanité* 2: 81-101.
LATOUCHE, R. 1962. 'De la Gaule romaine à la Gaule franque: aspects sociaux et économiques de l'évolution'. In: *Il passagio* 1962a: 379-409.
LATOUCHE, R. 1963b. 'Quelques réflexions sur la psychologie de Grégoire de Tours'. *Le Moyen Age* 69: 7-15.
LAUTMAN, F. 1981. 'Cierges et culte des saints: un compromis'. *Ethnologie française* 11: 239-42.
LE BRAS, G. 1960. 'Sociologie de l'église dans le haut Moyen Age'. In: *Le chiese* 1960b: 595-611.
LE CLERCQ, J. 1953. 'Contemplation et vie contemplative du VI au XIIe siècle'. *Dictionnaire de spiritualité* 2.2: 1929-48. Paris.
LE CLERCQ, J. 1963. 'L'écriture sainte dans l'hagiographie monastique du haut Moyen Age'. In: *La Bibbia* 1963a: 103-28.
LECOUTEUX, Cl. 1982. 'Paganisme, Christianisme et merveilleux'. *Annales* 37: 700-16.
LEEUW, G. VAN DER. 1961. *Einführung in die Phänomenologie der Religion*. Second edition. Darmstadt.
LE GOFF, J. 1967. 'Culture cléricale et traditions folkloriques dans la civilisation mérovingienne'. *Annales* 22: 780-91.
LE GOFF, J. 1977. 'Les rêves dans la culture et la psychologie collective de l'Occident médiéval'. In: Le Goff, J. 1977. *Pour un autre Moyen Age*. Temps, travail et culture en Occident: 18 essais: 299-306. Paris.
LE GOFF, J. 1981. *La naissance du Purgatoire*. Paris.
LEHMANN, P. 1963. 'Der Einfluss der Bibel auf die frühmittelalterliche Geschichtsschreibung'. In: *La Bibbia* 1963a: 129-40.
LEIPOLDT, J. 1957. *Von Epidaurus bis Lourdes*. Bilder aus der Geschichte volkstümlicher Frömmigkeit. Hamburg-Bergstedt.
LEITMAIER, L. 1960. 'Gottesurteil'. In: *Lexikon für Theologie und Kirche* 4: 1130-2. Second edition. Freiburg.
LELONG, Ch. 1963. *La vie quotidienne en Gaule à l'époque mérovingienne*. Paris.
LEONARDI, C. 1982. 'L'esperienza spirituale nel Medioevo'. *Studi Medievali*, third series 23.1: 449-59.

LEUNER, H. (ed.) 1980a. *Katathymes Bilderleben.* Ergebnisse in Theorie und Praxis. Bern-Stuttgart.

LEUNER, H. 1980b. 'Grundlinien des Katathymen Bilderlebens aus neuerer Sicht'. In: Leuner 1980a: 9-56.

LEVISON, W. 1921. 'Die Politik in den Jenseitsvisionen des frühen Mittelalters'. In: *Festgabe Friedrich von Bezold*: 81-100. Bonn-Leipzig.

LÉVI-STRAUSS, C. 1962. *La pensée sauvage.* Paris.

LÉVY-BRUHL, L. 1922a. *Les fonctions mentales dans les sociétés inférieures.* Sixth edition. Paris.

LÉVY-BRUHL, L. 1922b. *La mentalité primitive.* Paris.

LÉVY-BRUHL, L. 1963. *Le surnaturel et la nature dans la mentalité primitive.* New edition. Paris.

LEWIS, A.R. 1976. 'The dukes in the "Regnum Francorum", A.D. 550-751'. *Speculum* 51: 381-410.

LEWIS, C.D. 1961. *The poetic image.* London.

LEWIS, C.S. 1964. *The discarded image.* Cambridge.

LILJA, S. 1972. *The treatment of odours in the poetry of Antiquity.* Helsinki. Commentationes Humanorum Litterarum 49. Societas Scientiarum Fennica.

LIMET, H. and J. RIES (eds.) 1980. *L'expérience de la prière dans les grandes religions.* Actes du Colloque de Liège et Louvain-la-Neuve 1978. Louvain-la-Neuve. Homo religiosus 5.

LIMET, H. and J. RIES (eds.)1983. *Le mythe et son langage.* Actes du Colloque de Liège et Louvain-la-Neuve 1981. Louvain-la-Neuve. Homo religiosus 9.

LÖBELL, J.W. 1869. *Gregor von Tours und seine Zeit.* Second revised edition. Leipzig.

LÖFSTEDT, B. 1978. 'Zu Gregorius Turonensis "Hist. Franc. 2.31"'. *Acta classica* 21: 159.

LÖWE, H. 1951. Besprechung: Gregorii Episcopi Turonensis libri Historiarum X. Ed. alteram curaverunt B. Krusch und W. Levison'. *Historische Zeitschrift* 177: 340-3.

LOF, L.J. VAN DER. 1974. 'Grégoire de Tours et la magie blanche'. *Numen* 21: 228-37.

LOHMEYER, E. 1919. *Vom göttlichen Wohlgeruch.* Heidelberg. Sitzungsberichte der Heidelberger Akademie der Wissenschaften, Philosophisch-Historischen Klasse.

LOTTER, F. 1971. 'Legenden als Geschichtsquellen'. *Deutsches Archiv* 27: 195-200.

LUDWIG, A.M. 1966. 'Altered states of consciousness'. In: Tart 1969: 9-22.

MALCOLM, N. 1967. *Dreaming.* London.
MANGENOT, E. 1932. 'Baptême par le feu'. In: *Dictionnaire de théologie catholique* 2.1: 355-60. Paris.
MANITIUS, M. 1896. 'Zur Frankengeschichte Gregors von Tours'. *Neues Archiv* 21: 549-57.
MANITIUS, M. 1911. *Geschichte der lateinische Literatur des Mittelalters* 1. Reprint 1959. München.
MANSELLI, R. 1976. 'Simbolismo e magia nell' alto medioevo'. In: *Simboli* 1976a: 293-329.
MANSUY, M. 1975. 'Symbole et transcendance'. In: Ménard 1975a: 49-62.
MARIGNAN, A. 1890. *Le culte des saints sous les Mérovingiens.* Paris. Etudes sur la civilisation française 2.
MARKUS, R.A. 1978. 'The cult of icons in sixth-century Gaul'. *Journal of theological studies* 29: 151-7.
MARROU, H.I. 1938. *Saint Augustine et la fin du monde antique.* Paris.
MASTRELLI, C.A. 1976. 'Riflessi linguistici della simbologia nell' alto medioevo'. In: *Simboli* 1976b: 789-811.
MATHISEN, R.W. 1984. 'The family of Georgius Florentius Gregorius and the bishops of Tours'. *Medievalia et Humanistica* N.S. 12: 83-95.
MATTHIEU, D. 1976. 'Lumière: étude biblique'. In: *Dictionnaire de spiritualité* 9: 1142-9. Paris.
MAY, G. 1978. *Schöpfung aus dem Nichts.* Die Entstehung der Lehre von der 'creatio ex nihilo'. Berlin. Arbeiten zur Kirchengeschichte 48.
MAY, R. 1961. *Symbolism in religion and literature.* New York.
McCOMISKEY, T. 1976. 'Light, shine, lamp: emphanizo'. In: *The new international dictionary of New Testament theology* 2: 488-90. Grand Rapids.
MEIER, C.A. 1949. *Antike Inkubation und moderne Psychotherapie.* Zürich.
MEIER, C.A. 1967. 'Le rêve et l'incubation dans l'ancienne Grèce'. In: Caillois and von Grunebaum 1967: 290-305.
MEIER, C.A. 1972. *Die Bedeutung des Traumes.* Olten-Freiburg im Breisgau. Lehrbuch der Komplexen Psychologie C.G. Jungs 2.
MÉNARD, J.-E. (ed.) 1975a. *Le symbole.* Strasbourg.
MÉNARD, J.-E. 1975b. 'Symboles et gnose'. In: Ménard 1975a: 33-48.
MENSCHING, G. 1957a. *Das Wunder im Glauben und Aberglauben der Völker.* Leiden.
MENSCHING, G. 1957b. 'Die Lichtsymbolik in der Religionsgeschichte'. *Studium generale* 10: 422-32.
MENSCHING, G. 1971. *Topos und Typos.* Motiven und Strukturen

religiösen Lebens. Bonn. Untersuchungen zur allgemeinen Religionsgeschichte N.F. 8.

MESLIN, M. 1973. *Pour une science des religions*. Paris.

MESLIN, M. 1974. 'Pour une théorie du symbolisme religieux'. In: *Mélanges d'histoire des religions offerts à Henri-Charles Puech*: 617-24. Paris.

MESLIN, M. 1975. 'De l'herméneutique des symboles religieux'. In: Ménard 1975a: 24-32.

MEUNIER, R.A. 1946. *Grégoire de Tours et l'histoire morale du centre-ouest de la France*. Poitiers. Publications de l'université de Poitiers. Série des Sciences de l'Homme 9.

MICHEL, A. 1924. 'Feu du Jugement. Feu du Purgatoire'. In: *Dictionnaire de théologie catholique* 5.2: 2239-61. Paris.

MICHEL, A. 1931. 'Ordalies'. In: *Dictionnaire de théologie catholique* 11.1: 1139-52. Paris.

MIKOLETZKY, H.L. 1970. 'Über Geschichte und Biographie im frühen und hohen Mittelalter'. *Mitteilungen des Instituts für Österreichische Geschichtsforschung* 78: 13-26.

MISCH, G. 1955. *Geschichte der Autobiographie im Mittelalter* 2.2. Frankfurt am Main.

MOHRMANN, Chr. 1947. 'Transformations linquistiques et évolution sociale et spirituelle'. *Vigiliae christianae* 1: 186-90. Reprinted in: Mohrmann, Chr. 1965. *Études sur le latin des chrétiens* 3. Roma. Storia e letteratura 103.

MOHRMANN, Chr. 1961. 'Locus refrigerii'. In: *Études sur le latin des chrétiens* 2: Latin chrétien et médiéval: 81-91. Roma. Storia e letteratura 87.

MOHRMANN, Chr. 1968. 'Sakralsprache und Umgangssprache'. *Archiv für Liturgiewissenschaft* 10: 344-54. Reprinted in: Mohrmann, Chr. 1977. *Etudes sur le latin des Chrétiens* 4: 161-74. Roma. Storia e letteratura 143.

MOL, H. 1976. *Identity and the sacred*. A sketch for a new social-scientific theory of religion. Oxford.

MOLINIER, A. 1901. *Les sources de l'histoire de France* 1. Paris.

MOLLAT, M. 1978. *Les pauvres au Moyen Age*. Étude sociale. Paris.

MONOD, G. 1872. *Études critiques sur les sources de l'histoire mérovingienne* 1. Paris.

MOOLENBURGH, H.C. 1983. *Engelen als beschermers en helpers der mensheid*. Deventer.

MOULE, C.F.D. (ed.) 1966a. *Miracles*. London.

MOULE, C.F.D. 1966b. 'The vocabulary of miracle'. In: Moule 1966a: 235-38.

MÜLLER, W. 1957. 'Optische Sprachen und Religionswissenschaft'. *Studium generale* 10: 415-22.
MULLER, H.F. 1945. *L'époque mérovingienne.* New York.
MUNDLE, W. 1978. 'Apokalypto; deloo'. In: *The new international dictionary of New Testament theology* 3: 310-17. Grand Rapids.
MUNSON, Th.N. 1975. *Religious consciousness and experience.* Den Haag.

NEWBOLD, R.F. 1983. 'Patterns of communication and movement in Ammianus and Gregory of Tours'. In: Croke, B. and A.M. Emmett (eds.) 1983. *History and historians in late Antiquity*: 66-81. Sydney.
NIE, G. DE 1986. 'Een ontzagwekkende man. Beelden van de heilige in visioen en maatschappij in zesde-eeuws Gallië'. In: Stuip, R.E.V. en C. Vellekoop (eds.), *Visioenen.* Utrecht. Bijdragen tot de Mediëvistiek 6.
NOCK, A.D. 1952. 'Hellenistic mysteries and Christian sacraments'. *Mnemosyne* ser. 4.5: 177-213.
NOCK, A.D. 1972. *Conversion.* The old and the new in religion from Alexander the Great to Augustine of Hippo. Reprint. London-Oxford.

OBERMAN, H.A. 1986. *Die Reformation von Wittenberg nach Genf.* Göttingen.
OEING-HANHOFF, L. 1961. 'Licht: philosophisch'. In: *Lexikon für Theologie und Kirche* 6: 1023-5. Freiburg. Second edition.
OHLY, F. 1976. 'Halbbiblische und ausserbiblische Typologie'. In: *Simboli* 1976a: 429-73.
OHLY, F. 1977. 'Vom geistigen Sinn des Wortes im Mittelalter'. In: Ohly, F. 1977. *Schriften zur mittelalterlichen Bedeutungsforschung*: 1-31. Darmstadt.
OLDONI, M. 1972. 'Gregorio di Tours e i "Libri Historiarum": letture e fonti, metodi e ragioni'. In: *Studi medievali* ser. 3.13.2: 563-700.
OLPHE-GALLIARD, M. 1953. 'La contemplation dans la littérature chrétienne latine: Saint Augustin et Cassien'. In: *Dictionnaire de Spiritualité* 2.2: 1911-29. Paris.
ORBÁN, A.P. 1970. *Les dénominations du monde chez les premiers auteurs chrétiens.* Nijmegen.
OTTO, R. 1936. *Das Heilige.* Über das Irrationale in der Idee des Göttlichen und sein Verhältnis zum Rationalen. München.
OURY, G.-M. 1983. 'Le miracle dans Grégoire de Tours'. In: *Histoire des miracles* 1983: 11-28.

PATCH, H.R. 1970. *The other world*, according to descriptions in medieval literature. New York.

PATRUCCO, M.F. 1981-2. 'Il quotidiano e le strutture: note sulla vita familiare nell'alto medioevo'. *Romanobarbarica* 6: 129-58.

PAX, E. 1960. 'Feuer: in der Liturgie'. In: *Lexikon für Theologie und Kirche* 4: 108-9. Second edition. Freiburg.

PAX, E. 1961. 'Licht: In der Liturgie'. In: *Lexikon für Theologie und Kirche* 6: 1026-7. Second edition. Freiburg.

PERNOUD, R. 1957. *Les Gaulois.* Paris.

PETERS, E. 1978. *The magician, the witch and the law.* Philadelphia.

PETERSEN, J.M. 1983. 'Dead or alive? The holy man as healer in East and West in the late sixth century'. *Journal of medieval history* 9: 91-8.

PETIT, P. 1973. 'Emerveillement, prière et esprit chez Saint Basile le Grand'. *Collectanea Cisterciensia* 35: 81-107.

PICARD, J.-M. 1981. 'The marvellous in Irish and continental Saints' lives of the Merovingian period'. In: Clarke and Brennan: 91-103.

PIETRI, L. 1977. 'Le pèlerinage martinien de Tours à l'époque de l'évèque Grégoire'. In: *Gregorio di Tours* 1977: 95-139.

PIETRI, L. 1983a. *La ville de Tours de IV au VIe siècle*: naissance d'une cité chrétienne. Roma.

PIETRI, L. 1983b. 'Les abbés de basilique dans la Gaule du VIe siècle'. *Revue d'histoire de l'église de France* 69: 5-28.

PLONGERON, B. AND R. PANNET (eds.) 1976. *Le christianisme populaire.* Paris.

PORTMANN, A. 1950. 'Mythisches in der Naturforschung'. In: *Eranos-Jahrbuch* 17 (1949): 475-514.

POST, P.G.J. 1986. 'Heiligen tussen hemel en aarde. Kanttekeningen bij de reconstructie van opkomst, bloei, en functie van de laat-antiek christelijke heiligencultus door Peter Brown'. *Jaarboek voor liturgie-onderzoek* 2 (1986): 119-62.

PRIGENT, P. 1975. 'Symbole et Nouveau Testament'. In: Ménard 1975a: 101-15.

PULVER, M. 1944. 'Die Licht-Erfahrung im Johannes-Evangelium, im Corpus Hermeticum, in der Gnosis und in der Ostkirche'. In: *Eranos-Jahrbuch* 10 (1943): 253-296.

QUILLET, J. 1981. 'Le songe'. In: Hasenohr, G. and J. Longère (eds.) 1981. *Culture et travail intellectuel dans l'Occident médiéval*: 81-93. Paris.

RADDING, C.M. 1978. 'Evolution of medieval mentalities: a cognitive-structural approach'. *The American historical review* 83: 577-97.

RADDING, C.M. 1979. 'Superstition to science: nature, fortune and the

passing of the medieval ordeal'. *The American historical review* 84: 945-69.
RALL, H. 1937. *Zeitgeschichtliche Züge im Vergangenheitsbild mittelalterlicher, namentlich mittellateinischer Schriftsteller.* Berlin. Historische Studien 322. Reprint 1965.
REES, T. 1930. 'Nature (Christian)'. In: *Encyclopaedia of religion and ethics* 9: 210-17. New York.
RENO, S.J. 1978. *The sacred tree as an early Christian literary symbol*: a phenomenological study. Saarbrücken. Rupp, A. (ed.) Forschungen zur Anthropologie und Religionsgeschichte 4.
REYDELLET, M. 1977. 'Pensée et pratique politiques chez Grégoire de Tours'. In: *Gregorio di Tours* 1977: 171-206.
RICHÉ, P. 1962. *Éducation et culture dans l'occident barbare.* VI-VIIIe siècles. Paris. Patristica Sorbonensia 4.
RICHÉ, P. 1976. 'Croyances et pratiques populaires pendant le Haut Moyen Age'. In: Plongeron and Pannet 1976: 79-104.
RICOEUR, P. 1975a. *La métaphore vive.* Paris.
RICOEUR, P. 1975b. 'Parole et symbole'. In: Ménard 1975: 142-61.
RIES, J. 1983. 'Les recherches sur le mythe. Essai de synthèse et perspectives'. In: Limet and Ries 1983: 443-55.
RITZKE-RUTHERFORD, J. 1979. *Light and darkness in Anglo-Saxon thought and writing.* Frankfurt am Main. Sprache und Literatur. Regensburger Arbeiten zur Anglistik und Amerikanistik 17.
ROBERTS, J.T. 1980. 'Gregory of Tours and the monk of St Gall: the paratactic style of medieval latin'. *Latomus* 39: 173-90.
ROPERT [sic] 1976. 'Mentalité religieuse et regression culturelle dans la Gaule franque, du Ve-VIIIe siècle'. *Les cahiers de Tunésie* 24: 45-68.
ROSS, J.P. 1966. 'Some notes on miracle in the Old Testament'. In: Moule 1966a: 45-60.
ROUCHE, M. 1981. 'Miracles, maladies et psychologie de la foi à l'époque carolingienne en Francie'. In: *Hagiographies* 1981: 319-37.
ROUSSELLE, A. 1976. 'Du sanctuaire au thaumaturge: la guérison en Gaule au IVe siècle'. *Annales* 31: 1085-1107.
ROUSSET, P. 1959. 'Recherches sur l'émotivité à l'époque romane'. *Cahiers de civilisation médiévale* 2: 53-67.
ROUSSET, P. 1956. 'Le sens du merveilleux à l'époque féodale'. *Le Moyen Age* 62: 25-37.
RUDOLPH. K. 1977. *Die Gnosis.* Wesen und Geschichte einer spätantiken Religion. Göttingen.
RYCROFT, C. 1979. *The innocence of dreams.* London.

SALIN, E. 1959 and 1973. *La civilisation mérovingienne d'après les sépultures, les textes et le laboratoire.* Volumes 4 and 2. Paris.
SALLERON, L. 1983. 'Le miracle. Des Évangiles à Lourdes'. In: *Histoire des miracles* 1983: 179-91.
SANDERS, G. 1965a and b. *Licht en duisternis in de christelijke grafschriften.* Bijdrage tot de studie der Latijnse metrische epigrafie van de vroegchristelijke tijd. Brussel. Verhandelingen van de Koninklijke Vlaamse Academie voor Wetenschappen, Letteren en Schone Kunsten van België, Klasse der Letteren: 27.56, volume 1 and 2.
SAS, L.F. 1955. 'Language and society in Merovingian Gaul'. *Kentucky foreign language quarterly* 2: 189-94.
SCHEIBELREITER, G. 1983. *Der Bischof in merowingischer Zeit.* Wien-Köln.
SCHLICK, J. 1966. 'Composition et chronologie des "De virtutibus sancti Martini" de Grégoire de Tours'. In: *Studia patristica* 7.1: 278-86. Berlin. Deutsche Akademie der Wissenschaften zu Berlin, Texte und Untersuchungen zur Geschichte der altchristlichen Literatur 92.
SCHMID, K. 1967. 'Über das Verhältnis von Person und Gemeinschaft im früheren Mittelalter'. *Frühmittelalterliche Studien* 1: 225-49. Berlin.
SCHMIDT, L. 1906. 'Zu Gregor von Tours'. *Neues Archiv* 31: 240.
SCHMITT, P. 1945. 'Archetypisches bei Augustin und Goethe'. In: *Eranos-Jahrbuch* 12: 95-115.
SCHNACKENBURG, R. 1961. 'Licht: in der Schrift'. In: *Lexikon für Theologie und Kirche* 6: 1025-6. Second edition. Freiburg.
SCHREINER, K. 1966. 'Zum Wahrheitsverständnis im Heiligen- und Reliquienwesen des Mittelalters'. *Saeculum* 17: 131-69.
SCHULZ, H.J. 1961. 'Liturgie: orientalische Liturgien'. In: *Lexikon für Theologie und Kirche* 6: 1086-7. Second edition. Freiburg.
SEEBASS, H. 1976. 'Holy: hagios'. In: *The new international dictionary of New Testament theology* 2: 224-9. Grand Rapids.
SEVERUS, E. VON and A. SOLIGNAC. 1980. 'Méditation: de l'Écriture aux auteurs médiévaux'. In: *Dictionnaire de spiritualité* 10: 906-14. Paris.
SIBUM, L. 1962. 'Licht van de wereld'. *Het christelijk Oosten en hereniging* 14: 7-50.
SIEFERT, H. 1983. 'Inkubation, Imagination und Kommunikation im antiken Asklepiuskult'. In: Leuner 1980: 324-45.
SILBER, M. 1971. *The Gallic royalty of the Merovingians in its relationship to the 'Orbis terrarum Romanus' during the 5th and 6th centuries A.D.* Bern. Geist und Werk der Zeiten 25.

SILVESTRE, H. 1950. 'Grégoire de Tours avait-il lu Boèce?' *Latomus* 9: 437.
SIMBOLI e simbologia nell' alto medioevo 1 and 2. 1976a and b. Spoleto. Settimane di studio del Centro Italiano si Studi sull'alto Medioevo 23.
SIMONETTI, M. 1980. 'Qualche osservazione sul rapporto fra politica e religione in Gregorio di Tours'. In: *La storiografia ecclesiastica*: 27-43.
SINGER, J.L. 1974. *Imagery and daydream methods in psychotherapy and behavior modification.* New York-San Francisco.
SLÖK, J. 1960. 'Mythos, begrifflich und religionspsychologisch'. In: *Die Religion in Geschichte und Gegenwart* 4: 1263-8. Tübingen. Third edition.
SMALLEY, B. 1964. *The study of the Bible in the Middle Ages.* Reprint. Notre Dame, Ind.
SOLLE, S. 1975. 'Fire: kauma'. In: *The New international dictionary of New Testament theology* 1: 652-3. Grand Rapids.
SPRANDEL, R. 1972. *Mentalitäten und Systeme.* Neue Zugänge zur mittelalterlichen Geschichte. Stuttgart.
SPRANDEL, R. 1979. 'Vorwissenschaftliches Naturverstehen und Entstehung von Naturwissenschaften'. *Sudhoffs Archiv* 63: 313-25.
't SPIJKER, I. VAN 1984. 'Hagiografie en mentaliteitsgeschiedenis'. *Aanzet* (tijdschrift van geschiedenisstudenten [Utrecht]) 2: 27-34.
STANCLIFFE, C.E. 1979. 'From town to country: the Christianization of the Touraine 370-600'. In: Baker 1979: 43-59.
STANCLIFFE, C.E. 1983. *St Martin and his hagiographer.* History and miracle in Sulpicius Severus. Oxford. Oxford Historical Monographs.
STEINEN, W. VON DEN 1931. 'Heilige als Hagiographen'. *Historische Zeitschrift* 143: 229-56.
STOCKMEIER, P. 1980. 'Christlicher Glaube und antike Religiosität'. In: Haase 1980: 871-909.
LA STORIOGRAFIA ECCLESIASTICA nella tarda Antichità 1980. Atti del Convegno tenuto in Erice 1978. Messina.
STROHEKER, K.F. 1942. 'Die Senatoren bei Gregor von Tours'. *Klio* 34: 293-305. Reprinted in: Stroheker, K. 1965. *Germanentum und Spätantike*: 192-206. Zürich-Stuttgart.
STROHEKER, K.F. 1970. *Der senatorische Adel im spätantiken Gallien.* Darmstadt.
STRUBBE, E.I. and L. VOET. 1960. *De chronologie van de Middeleeuwen en de moderne tijden in de Nederlanden.* Antwerpen.
STRUBEL, A. 1975. '"Allegoria in factis" et "Allegoria in verbis"'. *Poétique* 6.23: 342-57.
STRUNK, G. 1970. *Kunst und Glaube in der lateinischen Heiligenlegende.*

Zu ihrem Selbstverständnis in den Prologen. München. Medium Aevum 12.

SVILAR, M. (ed.) 1983. *'Und es ward Licht'*. Zur Kulturgeschichte des Lichts. Bern und Frankfurt am Main. Universität Bern, Kulturhistorische Vorlesungen 1981/82.

TARDIEU, M. 1975. 'Psukhaios spinther. Histoire d'une métaphore dans la tradition platonicienne jusqu'à Eckhart'. *Revue des études augustiniennes* 21: 225-55.

TART, C.T. (ed.) 1969. *Altered states of consciousness*. A book of readings. New York-London.

TAUBER, E.S. and M.R. GREEN 1959. *Prelogical experience*. An inquiry into dreams and other creative processes. New York.

TAYLOR, H.O. 1957. *The classical heritage of the Middle Ages*. Fourth Edition. New York.

TAYLOR, H.O. 1959a and b. *The medieval mind*. 2 vols. Cambridge, Mass.

THOMAS, K. 1971. *Religion and the decline of magic*. Studies in popular beliefs in sixteenth and seventeenth century England. Second impression. London.

THOMPSON, J.W. 1942. *A history of historical writing* 1. New York.

THÜRLEMANN, F. 1974. *Der historischen Diskurs bei Gregor von Tours*. Topoi und Wirklichkeit. Bern-Frankfurt am Main. Geist und Werk der Zeiten 39.

TOMKINS, S.S. 1962 and 1963. *Affect, imagery and consciousness* 1 and 2. New York.

TORCHIO, A.M. 1982. 'L'osservazione della natura nell'alto Medioevo. Il contributo dei benedettini'. *La scuola cattolica* 110: 254-71.

UEDING, L. 1935. *Geschichte der Klostergründungen der frühen Merowingerzeit*. Berlin. Historische Studien 261.

UYTFANGHE, M. van 1976. 'La Bible dans les vies de saints Mérovingiennes. Quelques pistes de recherche'. *Revue d'histoire de l'église de France* 66. 62: 103-11.

UYTFANGHE, M. van 1981. 'La controverse biblique et patristique autour du miracle, et ses répercussions sur l'hagiographie dans l'Antiquité tardive et le haut Moyen Age latin'. In: *Hagiographies* 1981: 203-33.

UYTFANGHE, M. van 1984. 'Histoire du latin, protohistoire des langues romanes et histoire de la communication'. *Francia* 11: 579-613.

UYTFANGHE, M. van 1985. 'L'hagiographie et son public à l'époque mérovingienne'. *Studia patristica* 16: 54-62.

VAILLAT, C. 1932. *Le culte des sources dans la Gaule antique.* Paris.
VAUCHEZ. A. 1975. *La spiritualité du Moyen Age occidental.* Paris. L'historien 19.
VAUGHAN, R. 1986. 'Het verleden in de Middeleeuwen'. In: Teunis, H.B. and L. van Tongerloo (eds.) 1986, *Middeleeuwen tussen Erasmus en heden.* Bundel aangeboden aan Prof.dr.F.W.N. Hugenholtz. Amsterdam-Diemen. 11-23.
VEIT, W. 1963. 'Toposforschung. Ein Forschungsbericht'. *Vierteljahrsschrift für Literaturwissenschaft und Geistesgeschichte* 37: 120-63.
VERMEER, G.F.M. 1965. *Observations sur le vocabulaire du pèlerinage chez Égerie et chez Antonin de Plaisance.* Nijmegen-Utrecht. Latinitas Christianorum Primaeva 19.
VETERE, B. 1979. *Strutture e modelli culturali nella società merovingica.* Gregorio di Tours: una testimonianza. Galatina. Università di Lecce, Facultà di Letterature e Filosofia, Istituto di Storia medioevale. Saggi e ricerce 3.
VEUTHEY, L. 1971. 'Illumination'. In: *Dictionnaire de Spiritualité* 7: 1330-46. Paris.
VIARRE, S. 1977. 'L'étude des images dans les textes littéraires: problèmes de méthode'. *Lettres d'Humanité* 36: 368-76.
VIDAL, J. 1983. 'Aspects d'une mythique'. In: Limet and Ries 1983: 35-61.
VIGUERIE, J. DE 1983. 'Les caractères permanents du miracle'. In: *Histoire des miracles*: 193-200.
VOGEL, C. 1975. 'Boete en excommunicatie in de jonge kerk en de kerk van de hoge [vroege] Middeleeuwen. Een historische beschouwing'. *Concilium* 11.7: 5-15.
VOGÜÉ, A. DE 1976. 'Grégoire le Grand, lecteur de Grégoire de Tours?' *Analecta Bollandiana* 94: 225-33.
VOLLMANN, B.K. 1983. 'Gregor IV (Gregor von Tours)'. In: *Reallexikon für Antike und Christentum* 12: 895-930.
VOLLRATH, H. 1981. 'Das Mittelalter in der Typik oraler Gesellschaften'. *Historische Zeitschrift* 233: 585-94.
VOSS, B.R. 1970. 'Berührungen von Hagiographie und Historiographie in der Spätantike'. *Frühmittelalterliche Studien* 4: 53-69.

WALLACE-HADRILL, J.M. 1951. 'The work of Gregory of Tours in the light of modern research'. In: *Transactions of the Royal Historical Society*, 5th series, 1: 25-45. Reprinted in: Wallace-Hadrill J.M. 1962. *The long-haired kings*, and other studies in Frankish history: 49-70. London.

WALLACE-HADRILL, J.M. 1968, 'Gregory of Tours and Bede: their views on the personal qualities of kings'. *Frühmittelalterliche Studien* 2: 31-44.

WALLIS, W.D. 1918. 'Prodigies and portents'. In: *Encyclopedia of religion and ethics* 10: 362-76. Edinburgh-New York.

WALTER, E.H. 1966. 'Hagiographisches in Gregor's Frankengeschichte'. *Archiv für Kulturgeschichte* 48: 291-310.

WASZINK, J.H. 1943. 'Varia critica et exegetica'. *Mnemosyne* 11: 68-77.

WATTENBACH, W. and W. LEVISON 1952. *Deutschlands Geschichtsquellen im Mittelalter.* Frühzeit und Karolinger. 1. Weimar.

WEIDEMANN, M. 1982a and b. *Kulturgeschichte der Merowingerzeit* nach den Werken Gregors von Tours. Mainz. Römisch-Germanische Zentralmuseum, Monographien 3.1 and 2.

WEIMANN, K. 1900. *Die sittliche Begriffe in Gregors von Tours 'Historia Francorum'.* Duisburg. Phil. Diss. Leipzig.

WEMPLE, S.F. 1981. *Women in Frankish society.* Marriage and the cloister 500 to 900. Philadelphia.

WHEELWRIGHT, P. 1959. *The burning fountain.* Bloomington.

WHEELWRIGHT, P. 1971. *Metaphor and reality.* Bloomington-London.

WIENS, D.H. 1980. 'Mystery concepts in primitive Christianity and in its environment'. In: Haase 1980: 1507-57.

WINTER, J.M. VAN 'Kochen und Essen im Mittelalter'. In: Herrmann, B. (ed.), *Mensch und Umwelt im Mittelalter.* Stuttgart. 88-100.

WOOD, I. 1979. 'Early Merovingian devotion in town and country'. In: Baker 1979: 61-76.

WOOD, I. 1983. 'The ecclesiastical politics of Merovingian Clermont'. In: Wormald, P. with D. Bullough and R. Collins (eds.) 1983. *Ideal and reality in Frankish and Anglo-Saxon society*: 34-57. Oxford.

ZELZER, K. 1977. 'Zur Frage des Autors der Miracula B. Andreae Apostoli und zur Sprache des Gregor von Tours'. *Gräzer Beiträge* 6: 217-41.

ZUMTHOR, P. 1954. *Histoire littéraire de la France médiévale.* VI-XIVe siècles. Paris.

SAMENVATTING

Gregorius van Tours was een bekwaam bestuurder, een behendig diplomaat, en een vrome maar ook moedige bisschop. Hij was eveneens een geboren verteller van verhalen. Voor moderne lezers lijken zijn werken echter innerlijke samenhang te missen, te bestaan uit min of meer losse visuele impressies van zintuiglijk tastbare werkelijkheid; ze lijken ook van warrig denken, verregaand bijgeloof en een soort onbewustheid van zichzelf ('naïveteit') te getuigen. Moeten zijn schijnbaar onvermogen om in generaliserende begrippen te denken, de hiaten in — en vooral tussen — zijn verhalen en een zekere onduidelijkheid of onbepaaldheid die alles doortrekt samen als een 'weerspiegeling' worden gezien van de onveilige, onoverzichtelijke en half-barbaarse Merovingische maatschappij die hij probeerde te beschrijven? Of zijn zijn waarneming en denken zo anders gestructureerd dan de onze dat wij daardoor zijn bedoelingen niet herkennen?

Om deze vragen te beantwoorden werd een onderzoek gedaan naar zijn behandeling van vier onderwerpen: buitengewone natuurverschijnselen of zgn. voortekenen, gewone natuurverschijnselen en wonderen in dit verband, licht en waarnemingen van onaardse lichtverschijnselen, en dromen en visioenen waarin heiligen verschijnen.

Gregorius' gedachten over deze onderwerpen laten ons iets zien van zijn visie op God, de mens en de wereld. De voorwoorden tot de eerste 'boeken' van de *Geschiedenissen* en zijn behandeling van buitengewone natuurverschijnselen daarin tonen dat hij, toen hij begon te schrijven, bereid was om in de oorlogen en andere rampen van zijn tijd dezelfde vermenging van goed en kwaad te zien als in de tijd van de Oudtestamentische profeten. Vreemde verschijnselen in de lucht of in de natuur interpreteerde hij echter, in een verchristelijkte vorm van een oud Romeins gebruik, als voortekenen die Goddelijke toorn en zijn uitwerking aankondigen: ophanden zijnde straffen zoals de dood van een koning, een epidemie of een andere ramp. In de laatste 'boeken' van de *Geschiedenissen* blijkt Gregorius zijn standpunt te hebben herzien en gaat hij alle gebeurtenissen, inclusief de 'valse profeten' die toen in Gallië rondzwierven, zien als 'tekenen' van 'de laatste tijden' vóór het einde van de wereld. Dit zijn intern samenhangende visies op zijn eigen tijd.

Is zijn presentatie van gebeurtenissen in hun chronologische volgorde — om het aantal jaren te tellen vanaf de Schepping — verder alleen maar een 'verward mengelmoes' zoals hij zelf zegt? Zijn woorden tonen aan dat hij in staat was om zich een andere ordening voor te stellen. De wijze waarop hij de voortekenen met de gebeurtenissen die zij zouden aankondigen al dan niet expliciet in verband brengt, maar ook zijn manier om menselijke gebeurtenissen aan elkaar te relateren (al doet hij dit niet zo dikwijls), laten zien dat hij denkt en redeneert d.m.v. analogieën. De vorm van een verschijnsel of een gebeurtenis geeft de, door God gegeven, betekenis aan, weerspiegelt deze. Verschijnselen en gebeurtenissen die op elkaar lijken zijn met elkaar verbonden door het feit dat God door hen dezelfde boodschap naar de mensen stuurt. Deze verbanden kunnen door de tijd heen lopen maar ze kunnen ook in dezelfde tijdsspanne plaatsvinden, m.a.w. synchronisch zijn. De manier waarop Gregorius buitengewone natuurverschijnselen als voortekenen interpreteert maakt duidelijk dat hij verwacht dat menselijke en natuurgebeurtenissen in een bepaalde tijd overeenstemmende patronen zullen laten zien, die naar een specifieke manier van Goddelijk bezig-zijn met de mensen wijzen. De samenhang tussen de gebeurtenissen bestaat voor Gregorius uit symbolische patronen en niet uit intrahistorische causaliteit of ontwikkeling. Causaliteit en samenhang zijn niet 'horizontaal' maar 'verticaal'.

Wat Gregorius doet met water en plantaardig leven als natuurverschijnselen en als onderdeel van wonderen laat zien dat de tegenpool verval/dood — nieuwe schepping/eeuwig leven een grote rol speelt in zijn denken. Pijnlijk bewust van de vergankelijkheid van alle aardse dingen waaronder ook het werk van mensenhanden en -hoofden, zoekt hij en beschrijft hij voor zijn tijdgenoten niet alleen figuurlijke aanduidingen van de Goddelijke belofte van de wedergeboorte tot het eeuwig leven in zichtbare natuurverschijnselen: in de wonderen laat hij ook het steeds weer terugkerende, schoksgewijze dynamisme van vernieuwing en nieuwe schepping zien. In Gregorius' waarneming hebben deze dynamismen de neiging om zich te gedragen volgens bestaande, bekende patronen in beeld-modellen zoals b.v. de Maagdelijke Geboorte, Moses' doen ontstaan van een bron uit een kale rots en het ontkiemen van zaad. Hij ziet deze beeldpatronen als het ware 'automatisch' werkzaam: zij structureren zijn werkelijkheid. Misschien doordat hij geen intrahistorische ontwikkeling zoekt, verwacht Gregorius geen verbetering van betekenis in de menselijke samenleving op aarde. Het zijn de hemel en het Paradijs, de laatste voorgesteld als een nooit verwelkende, altijdbloeiende tuin waarvan men soms op aarde al een vleugje op kan vangen, waarnaar vooral gestreefd moet worden. De natuur — op zich al een wonder — maar ook andere zichtbare wonderen zijn de Goddelijke boodschap van vernieuwing aan de mensen, een boodschap die alleen duidelijk wordt wanneer men haar in eerbiedige verwondering ontvangt. Door de manier waarop Gregorius hen beschrijft worden zichtbare verschijnselen en gebeurtenissen tot onbewuste metaforen van innerlijke belevingen. Zijn spontaan-gevormde 'clusters' van traditionele beeldvoorstellingen zijn vaak meer indirect dan direct aangeduid. Gregorius kan wel degelijk in algemene begrippen denken: zijn algemene begrippen zijn echter in beeldvorm en niet los te maken van voorstellingen van zichtbare gebeurtenissen.

Gregorius en zijn tijdgenoten blijken de wereld als 'donker' te hebben ervaren. Zijn behandeling van licht en lumineuze verschijnselen duiden op zoiets als een ethisch dualisme in termen van de tegenstelling lichtdonker. De duivel, demonen en zonde worden beschreven in verband met zichtbare duisternis. Verzengend vuur wordt soms ook beschreven alsof het een manifestatie van de duivel is. Wanneer iemand echter wordt 'verbrand' door 'goddelijk vuur' (d.w.z. door koorts of ontsteking), kan het een straf of een louteringsmiddel van een heilige zijn. In tegenstelling tot enkele eerdere Christelijke auteurs beschouwt Gregorius verzengend vuur, ook na de dood, niet als louteringsmiddel en alleen als straf. De rechtvaardigen en het heilige kan het niet aantasten. Het is licht dat loutert wanneer het de duisternis van onwetendheid, zonde en demonische bezetenheid verdrijft. Het licht wordt voorgesteld en zelfs waargenomen vooral in verband met de heiligen en hun wondermacht, die voor Gregorius onafscheidelijk is verbonden met hun heiligheid. Heilige wondermacht is het centrale gegeven in zijn bestaan; vrijwel alles draait erom en vrijwel alles wordt erdoor verklaard. Het is misschien een niet als zodanig herkende metafoor voor de vitale vernieuwing die is geassocieerd met de hemel. Het *ware* leven — al eeuwenlang synoniem met licht — begint pas in de hemel, voorgesteld als onophoudelijk, weergaloos licht; daarbij vergeleken is het aardse licht 'donker'. Deze zienswijze heeft dus meer te maken met een traditioneel, contemplatief ideaal dan met de concrete maatschappelijke werkelijkheid van dat moment. Desalniettemin zal het mede het gevoel zijn geweest dat het onmogelijk was om dit ideaal in de maatschappij te verwezenlijken dat er voor zorgde dat de wereld als 'donker' gezien bleef worden.

Dat voor Gregorius metafoor en zichtbare werkelijkheid in elkaar overlopen, blijkt uit die passages in zijn werk waarbij hij gebruik maakt van wat wij als beeldspraak zouden beschouwen. Hij had de neiging om de beelden waarin hij over ideeën en gebeurtenissen dacht als werkelijk aanwezige, meestal onzichtbare, spirituele werkelijkheid te zien. Beelden en hun verhoudingen tot elkaar zijn altijd minder duidelijk dan begrippen; beelddenken is ook niet in staat tot zelfbespiegeling. Tegelijkertijd hoopte en verwachtte hij steeds dat deze spirituele werkelijkheid zich op ieder moment in het zichtbare zou manifesteren. De lumineuze verschijnselen die hij en zijn tijdgenoten soms waarnamen op plaatsen waar men de aanwezigheid van een heilige of zijn wondermacht vermoedde zijn misschien veroorzaakt door het afglijden van dit meer bewuste beelddenken in een onwillekeurige, wakende droom.

Het laatste onderzoek — naar dromen en visioenen waarin de heilige verschijnt — toont aan dat Gregorius waarschijnlijk vaak wakend droomde terwijl hij actief bezig was met practische zaken. Wanneer we hem mogen geloven speelden verbeelding, wakende dromen en dromen gedurende slaap een wezenlijke rol in de Merovingische maatschappij van zijn tijd: zij laten onbewuste wensen in beeldvorm zien. Dromen initieerden en legitimeerden de verering van een nieuwe heilige; in de genezingswonderen maakten zij de rol van de verbeelding in het moment van plotselinge genezing zichtbaar en hielpen daardoor anderen om een dergelijk proces te herhalen; zij brachten stabiliteit, bescherming en vernieuwing in een onvoldoende geordende maatschappij; en tenslotte ondersteunden zij de voor de kerk zo noodzakelijke voorstelling van de effectieve realiteit van de Goddelijke rechtvaardigheid. De droom en het visioen maakten dus het ideaal, de imaginaire structuur waarop de kerk haar invloed en bestuur baseerde, zichtbaar en ondersteunen dit, maar ze hielpen dit ideaal ook persoonlijke en maatschappelijke werkelijkheid worden. Tegelijkertijd laten ze zien hoe verandering plaatsvindt in individuen: in beide gevallen is de heilige, als de ideale mens, een symbool dat verandering teweeg brengt. De belangrijke rol van de droomwaarneming in het maatschappelijk leven en het gelijkstellen ervan met de waarneming van spirituele werkelijkheid leidden waarschijnlijk tot het aandacht hebben voor het doorgaande droomdenken terwijl men wakker is.

Gregorius' opvatting over de Goddelijke almacht en zijn verwachting dat veranderingen in de werkelijkheid op een plotselinge, onvoorstelbare manier zouden plaatsvinden zijn, samen met zijn beelddenken dat in droomdenken over neigt te gaan, verantwoordelijk voor zijn schijnbaar onvermogen om abstraherend te denken, zijn 'hiaten', zijn onbepaaldheid of onduidelijkheid en zijn gebrek aan reflectie of 'naïveteit'. Deze manier van denken kan samenhangen met het feit dat het maatschappelijke leven zich in Gregorius' tijd vooral mondeling en door gebaren afspeelde; slechts een kleine groep, waaronder echter ook juist Gregorius, kon lezen en schrijven. Gregorius' beelden zijn echter grotendeels afkomstig uit oude tot zeer oude tradities. Waar zij aangepast zijn aan de behoeften en mogelijkheden van de individuele en maatschappelijke werkelijkheid, is het echter niet zonder meer als een 'weerspiegeling' daarvan. Integendeel. Als visualisaties van *sui generis* idealen — innerlijke vernieuwing en de geestelijke mens — vonden ze hun oorsprong niet in de maatschappij van dat moment. Ze wezen naar de toekomst en hielpen om deze te verwezenlijken.

Gregorius' visie op de dynamiek van de menselijke en materiële werkelijkheid als gestructureerd zijnde door beeld-modellen lijkt sprekend op de werkelijkheidsbeleving van zgn. 'primitieve' samenlevingen zoals die beschreven werden door L. Lévy-Bruhl. Er zijn echter ook aanknopingspunten met het mytho-poëtische denken dat in de moderne filosofie, godsdienstfenomenologie en psychologie als hermeneutisch en als therapeutisch instrument wordt gehanteerd. Het 'gebrek aan structuur' en de 'onduidelijkheid' die Gregorius zo lang zijn verweten, zijn, in tegenstelling tot de gangbare mening over dit onderwerp, geen directe 'weerspiegeling' van verward denken of van zijn gedecentraliseerde maatschappelijke omgeving. Zijn verhalen laten zien dat hij, op zijn eigen manier, een zeer gestructureerd en precies idee had hoe de maatschappij eruit zou moeten zien. Ook had hij een aantal duidelijke opvattingen, gebaseerd op traditionele beelden, over de structuur van de werkelijkheid. Het feit dat vele twintigste-eeuwse historici de werkelijkheidswaarde van Gregorius' denken beduidend hebben onderschat, ook door het 'eenvoudig' of 'naïef' te noemen, weerspiegelt waarschijnlijk de tot voor kort overmatige verbale en rationele gerichtheid van de moderne Westerse cultuur.

INDICES

I. Names of persons, places, modern authors (**bold**) and ancient authors (*italics*), mentioned in the text

Abraham, 65, 68, 205.
Adam, 9, 58, 65.
Aegidius, bishop of Reims, 6.
Aetius, Roman general, 266.
Agaune, monastery of, 91, 204.
Agricola and Vitalis, martyrs, 104.
Alaric, Visigothic king, 63.
Albi, 40.
Alpinus, count of Tours, 249.
Amarandus, saint, 180.
Ambrose, bishop of Milan, 137, 205.
Ampère, M.J.-J., 1, 10, 11.
Anatolian, martyr, 278.
Andrew, apostle, 28, 126.
Angenendt, A., 233.
Angers, 40, 47.
Antichrist, 45, 52, 53, 58, 59, 63, 68, 90.
Antin, P., 20.
Aprunculus, bishop of Clermont, 280.
Aredius, abbot, 83, 85, 86, 102, 165, 249.
Arius, Arians, 32, 57, 63, 98, 148, 156, 231, 280-1.
Armenia, 139.
Armentaria, mother of Gregory of Tours, 4, 142, 213-5, 228, 262.
Asclepius, 195, 228.
Attila, leader of the Huns, 266.
Auerbach, E., 1, 9, 12, 17, 18, 19, 22, 26.
Augustine, bishop of Hippo, 21, 61, 65, 75, 90, 110, 113, 137-8, 147, 153, 177, 205.
Avitus, bishop of Clermont, 5, 124.
Avitus, bishop of Vienne, 32, 140.

Bachelard, G., 131, 192, 216, 289.
Banniard, M., 21.
Baudillius, martyr at Nîmes, 117.
Baudinus, bishop of Tours, 94.
Baudonivia, 127.
Bazas, 40.
Benedict of Nursia, 185.

Benignus, martyr at Dijon, 218-9.
Bernouilli, C.A., 216.
Berny-Rivière, 38.
Beumann, H., 20.
Bianchi, D., 13, 20.
Blume, I., 13.
Boesch Gajano, S., 12, 13, 18.
Bonnet, M., 15, 20, 123.
Bordeaux, 37, 40, 49.
Bourges, 37, 222-3.
Bracchio, abbot, 188, 190, 262-3.
Brown, P., 76, 217, 227, 244, 248, 257, 267, 286.
Brunhilde, queen, 6, 42, 46.
Brunhölzl, F., 13, 20.

Caesarius, bishop of Arles, 167, 169.
Caluppanus, hermit, 83.
Candes, monastery of, 246.
Cassian, John, abbot, 109, 135.
Cassiodorus, 73.
Cautinus, bishop of Clermont, 5.
Châlon-sur-Saône, 5, 6.
Charibert, king, 35, 105, 283.
Chartres, 37, 49, 62, 64.
Chelles, 45.
Childebert I, king, 35, 46, 105, 134.
Childebert II, king, 57, 99, 230, 258, 283.
Chilperic, king, 6, 34, 35, 36, 37, 38, 40, 42, 43, 44, 45, 46, 63, 64, 67, 99, 140, 264, 269, 282, 285-6.
Chinon, 37.
Chlodomer, king, 204.
Clothar I, king, 34, 35, 39, 105, 258, 283.
Clothar II, king, 46.
Chramn, son of King Clothar I, 35, 105, 267.
Chramnesindus, 12.
Christ, 43, 45, 50, 58, 59, 61, 65, 67, 73, 77, 78, 79, 80, 84, 86, 91, 101, 109, 114,

116, 125, 129, 130, 132, 136, 144-5, 148, 165, 168, 171-2, 175, 190, 195-6, 199, 220, 224, 231, 238-9, 240, 241, 243, *272-3*, (281);
  false Christ: 53-5, 67-8.
Clement, martyr, 85.
Clermont [-Ferrand], 3, 5, 27, 28, 32, 34, 38, 39, 43, 104, 261-2, 288;
  church of Clermont: 125.
Clotilde, queen, 105.
Clovis, king, 3, 9, 29, 35, 44, 46, 63, 65, 66, 126, 134, 183.
Clovis, son of King Chilperic, 63.
Coblenz, 94.
Constantine, emperor, 183-4, 252.
Constantinople, 46.
Cosmas and Damian, martyrs, 228.
Courcelle, P., 20.
Curtius, E.R., 18, 20, 207.
Cyprian, bishop of Carthage, 252.

Devil, Satan: see Index of subjects.
Dijon, 218.
Dill, S., 2, 3, 8, 15, 16, 23.
Dinzelbacher, P., 220.
Diocletian, emperor, 63.
Douglas, M., 268.
Du Plessis, M., 19.
Durkheim, E., 267.

Ebert, A., 10, 15.
Eberulf, chamberlain of King Chilperic, 269-72.
Ebregisil, bishop of Cologne, 125, 224.
Eulalia, martyr at Merida, 122.
Eleusis, mysteries of, 110.
Eliade, M., 76, 90, 263.
Embrun, 80.
Eparchius, bishop of Clermont, 232-3.
Epidauros, sanctuary of, 194-5.
Epstein, G., 216, 236.
Etna, Mount, 71, 146, 147.
Eucherius, bishop of Lyon, 75, 82, 89, 110.
Euphronius, bishop of Tours, 6, 103, 221-2.
Euric, Visigothic king, 32.
Eusebius, bishop of Caesarea, 30, 58, 59, 60, 98, 140, 142.
Eve, 155.

Fedamia, 237-40, 248, 249.
Felix, martyr at Narbonne, 274.
Ferreolus, bishop of Limoges, 87.
Florentius, father of Gregory of Tours, 227-8.
Fortunatus, Venantius, 6, 102, 110, 111, 113, 114, 115, 116, 123, 126, 134, 152, 157, 161, 167, 169, 177, 183, 185.
Fredegunde, queen, 36, 37, 40, 41, 46, 101, 269, 277.
Friardus, hermit, 125.
Friedrich, B., 17, 18, 20.

Gallus, bishop of Clermont, 5, 33, 260-2, 265.
Ganshof, F.L., 11, 18.
Gautier Dalché, P., 21, 22.
Genesius, martyr, 96, 117.
Geneva, 27.
Germanus, bishop of Paris, 35, 65, 185, 223.
Giesebrecht, W., 10.
Greece, 161-2.
Gregory, bishop of Langres, 123, 218-9.
Gregory, bishop of Tours,
  life: 2-8;
  health: 5;
  education: 5-6;
  style: 75, 214;
  own observation of prodigies: 34-5, 40-2, 48;
  own observation/perception of nature miracles: 86, 94, 99-100, 103-4, 112, 124, 127;
  own perceptions of luminosity: 178, 189-91;
  witness to a cure or miracle: 202, 227-8, 230, 247, (261-2), 265, (275), 284;
  as author: passim.
Gregory I, pope, 16, 73, 76, 88, 89, 107, 112, 114, 124, 132, 134, 138, 147-8, 153, 161, 172, 185, 205.
Grenoble, 71, 75, 146, 147.
Grundmann, H., 11.
Günter, H., 72.
Gundowald, pretender, 46, 47, 277.
Guntram, king, 38, 46, 47, 51, 57, 63, 91, 105, 143, 269-72, 277, 283, 285-7.
Guntram Boso, duke, 99, 101, 283.

Halphen, L., 16.
Helen, empress, 93.
Hellmann, S., 16.
Herod, king, 45.
Hilary, bishop of Arles, 5.
Hilary, bishop of Poitiers, 183, 184.
Hilary, bishop of Poitiers, 5, 75, 89, 115, 223.
Hugenholtz, F.W.N., 11.
Huneric, Vandal king, 32.

Illidius, bishop of Clermont, 5, 256-7.
Injuriosus, bishop of Tours, 283-4.
Irenaeus, bishop of Lyon, 170.
Isaiah, prophet, 263.
Isidore, bishop of Seville, 17, 153, 157.

James, W., 292-3.
Jerome, 30, 58, 60, 97, 140.
Jerusalem, 45;
   the Temple: 58, 59, 65, 72, 177;
   (the heavenly Jerusalem?): 197.
Joannes, Breton hermit, 118-9.
John the Baptist, 157, 263.
John, pope, 148.
Jordan, river, 82, 95.
Joseph of Arimathea, 257, 258.
Julian, martyr, 5, 86, 87, 112, 121, 126, 145, 159-60, 166, 185-6, 237-9, 261.
Jung, C.G., 129, 207.
Jungblut, J.-B., 21.
Justin, brother-in-law of Gregory of Tours, 198, 228.

Kirk, G.S., 292.
Köpke, R., 10, 14, 15.
Kretschmer, W., 230.
Krusch, B., 16, 18.
Kurth, G., 15, 21.

Lactantius, 31, 56, 80.
Lake of Geneva, 91.
Langer, S., 176.
Latouche, R., 18.
Laurentius, martyr, 152.
Le Goff, J., 148, 151.
Lehmann, F., 20.
Lévi-Strauss, C., 23.
Levison, W., 11, 18.
Lévy-Bruhl, L., 23, 131.

Limoges, 145, 165-6.
Livy, 140.
Löbell, J.L., 11, 14.
Löwe, H., 18.
Loire, 38, 99, 162.
Lourdes, sanctuary of, 204.

Macrobius, 214, 264.
Mallosus, martyr at Cologne, 125.
Mamertus, bishop of Vienne, 33, 115, 140.
Manitius, M., 15, 19, 20, 84.
Marcellus, martyr at Châlons, 242.
Marius, bishop of Avenches, 31.
Marsat, chapel at, 178, 180.
Marseille, 51, 53.
Martin, bishop of Tours, 4, 5, 6, 7, 9, 29, 41, 44, 64, 65, 67, 83, 93, 94, 95, 99, 100-1, 104, 105, 106, 134, 135, 136, 137, 141, 142, 143, 146, 155, 162, 165, 166, 167, 170-171, 172, 186, 187, 188, 189, 190, 191, 193, 194, 195, 196, 198, 201, 202, 206, 213, 215, 216, 218, 220, 229, 230, 231, 235-6, 241, 242-4, 245, 247-9, 253, 258, 270-2, 275, 283, 284, 285, 289.
Martius, abbot at Clermont, 118-9, 170, 171.
Maura and Britta, virgins, 220-1.
Mauricius, saint (and monastery of), 253-4.
Maximus, bishop of Trier, 170.
Meier, C.A., 86.
Merovech, son of King Chilperic, 42.
Meslin, M., 26, 82.
Mikoletzky, H.L., 12.
Miro, king in Galicia, 119.
Misch, G., 11, 13.
Molinier, A., 15.
Monod, G., 10, 15, 18.
Moses, 83, 188, 190.
Mummolus, general of King Sigebert, 63.

Narbonne, 40;
   cathedral of Narbonne: 272-3.
Nero, 45.
Nicetius, bishop of Lyon, 6, 159, 167, 259-60, 273-4, 275-6, 286.
Nicetius, bishop of Trier, 263.
Nineveh, 33, 140.
Noah, 72.

Oldoni, M., 18, 20.
Origen, 150.
Orléans, 37, 140, 230.
Orosius, 24, 30, 31, 37, 56, 58, 59, 60, 140, 213.
Osiris, mysteries of, 110.

Pappolus, bishop of Langres, 279-80.
Paradise, 78, 116, 119-21, 123-8, 132; earthly Paradise: 79-80.
Paris, 39, 42, 63, 142, 143, 252.
Paschasia, saint, 219-20.
Patroclus, hermit, 254-5.
Paul, apostle, 137, 190, 193, 234, 263, 265.
Paulinus of Nola, 170.
Paulinus of Nola, 5, 147.
Paulinus of Périgueux, 5.
Pelagia, mother of abbot Aredius, 41.
Pelagius, pope, 52.
Persia, 139, 150.
Peter, apostle, 95, 194, 265-6.
Peter, brother of Gregory of Tours, 5.
Pietri, L., 3.
Plato, 177.
Pliny, 73.
Plotinus, 177, 185.
Poitiers, 38, 63, 78, 100-1, 121, 167, 183; convent of Poitiers: 126; nun at convent of Poitiers: 238-9.
Polycarp, martyr, 151.
Praetextatus, bishop of Rouen, 142, 277.
Priscus, bishop of Lyon, 275-6.
Probianus, bishop of Bourges, 222-3.
Prosper (Tiro) of Aquitaine, 30, 74, 75, 89.
Prudentius, 5, 20, 75, 79, 84, 89, 90, 98, 102, 138, 152, 161, 163, 169, 171, 172, 196, 199, 233.

Quintianus, bishop of Clermont, 167, 278-9.
Quirinus of Siscia, bishop, martyr, 98.
Quodvultdeus, 21, 75, 89-91, 151, 152.

Radegunde, queen, 6, 78, 126-7, 167, 238-9, 273.
Red Sea, 90.
Rigunth, daughter of Chilperic and Fredegunde, 43, 44.
Roberts, J.T., 19.

Roccolenus, military leader of King Chilperic, 99-101, 283.
Rome, 30, 33, 52, 92, 265.

Salvius, bishop of Albi, 38, 42, 43, 46, 79, 123-4, 125, 126, 133, 163, 197, 264.
Samson, son of Chilperic and Fredegunde, 42.
Saturninus, martyr, 224-6.
Schlick, J., 135.
Sedulius, 5.
Sequanus, abbot near Langres, 242.
Servatius, bishop of Tongeren, 265.
Severus, priest at Béziers, 117, 121-2.
Severus, Sulpicius, 30, 45, 59, 60, 63, 161, 169, 185, 186, 213, 215, 218, 249.
Sicily, 146.
Sidonius Apollinaris, bishop of Clermont, 280-1.
Sigebert, king, 6, 29, 34, 35, 36, 39, 46, 48, 63, 64, 65, 66, 99.
Sigismund, king of Burgundy, 204, 205.
Smalley, B., 13.
Sodom, 32, 143, 150.
Soissons, 39, 40.
Solemnis, saint, 179.
Spain, 40, 43, 51, 80, 86, 119, 125, 243-4.
Stephen, martyr, 182, 265-6.
Sunniulf, abbot, 150.
Symmachus, 148.

Tauredunum, 27, 31, 34.
Tertullian, 79.
Tetricus, bishop of Langres, 5, 279-80, 286.
Theodegisel, Visigothic king, 82.
Theoderic, king of Italy, 148.
Theodore, bishop of Marseille, 51, 285-6.
Theudebald, king, 33, 34, 42.
Theudebert I, king, 7, 33, 34, 36, 65, 105.
Theudebert, son of King Chilperic, 63, 64, 65, 99.
Theuderic, son of King Chilperic, 40, 41.
Thompson, J.W., 16, 17.
Thürlemann, F., 11, 12, 13, 20, 21.
Tiber, 52, 92.
Tomkins, S., 26.
Tours, 3, 4, 5, 6, 7, 8, 29, 37, 40, 41, 48, 50, 51, 55, 63, 64, 99-101, 112, 140, 145, 220, and passim;

council of Tours in 567: 77, 118.
Trojanus, bishop of Saintes, 186, 187.

Ultrogotha, queen, 134, 135, 136.
Ursinus, bishop of Bourges, 222.

Venantius, abbot, 253.
Victor of Marseille, martyr, 158, 159.
Victorius, 58.
Vienne, 32, 33, 115, 140, 141.
Vincent, martyr, 143, 274.
Virgil, 5, 6, 84, 185.
Virgin, the holy, 112-5, 122, 127, 142, 154, 178, 256.

Wallace-Hadrill, J.M., 11.
Walter, E.H., 20, 21.
Wattenbach, W., 11.
Wemple, S., 233.
Wheelwright, Ph., 194, 205.
Wiliachar, priest, 140, 258.
Wulfilaicus, 165-6, 229.

Zelzer, K., 18.
Zoroaster, 139, 146.
Zumthor, P., 12.

II. Subjects in the text

abstractions, thinking in terms of, 2, 22, 75, 108, 109, 130, 152, 175-6, *192*, *209-10*.
affective participation, see: astonishment.
ambiguity, see: imprecision.
analogous forms, see: correspondence.
apparition, see: appear, dream-vision.
appear (*apparere, ostendere, ostensus esse, se revelare*), 29, 41, 42, *43*, 48, *69, 83*, 86, 87, 107, 109, 188, 189, 190, 219, 220-1, 224, 238, 253, 262, 263, 273, 274, 288-9, 293;
see also: dream-vision.
archetypes, 76, 89, 92, 110, 129, 263.
asceticism, 79, 123-5, 129.
astonishment, awe, affective participation, 51, 63, *81-2, 88*, 95, 109, 113, *127, 129, 131*, 136, 174, 182, 192, 207, *209*, 220, 229, 237, 247, 259, 283, 286.
auspicium, 47.
awe, see: astonishment.

baptism, symbol of, 80, 87, 89, 90, 137.
bishops, situation of, 3, 5, 6-8, 149, 217, 218-9, 221-2, 224, 227, 236, 241, 268, 275, 279-84, 285-7.

causality, causative thinking, 28, 29, 33, 38, 51, 55, 56, 64, *68-9*, 107, 143, *209*, 278.
causation, divine, 11, 17, 21, 29, 38, 48, 51, *56, 62-3*, 69, 139.

celestial bodies (as metaphors),
moon, 171;
stars, 135, 137, 155, 168, 169, 170, 171, 172, 173, 175, 195, 210;
sun, 170-2, 175, 195;
as prodigies, 27-69.
coherence, 2, 10, *11, 12*, 13, 23, 25, 209.
comet, 28, 31, 34, 35, 38, 39, 47-8.
'command', 100, 111-2, 117, 140, 142, 145, 213-5, 217, 221-2, 225, 226, 227, 228, 230, 235, 243, 247, 250, 281.
compassion, 51, 154, 198, *237-9*, 247-9, 265, 273.
confidence, trust that a miracle will be granted, 136, *144*, 156, 166, *204*, 239, *243-4*, 250, 278.
conscious interpretation, stylistic effects, 9, 14, 16, 20-1, 22, 32, 34, 42, 56, 110, 269-71, 286.
contact (sanctification, healing), *93*, 96, 97, 104, 244, 245, *246-9*, 250.
contemplation, see: meditation.
contrition, see: repentance.
correspondence, congruence, analogous forms, 28-9, *34, 35, 36, 38*, 42, 52, *56-7*, 62, 64, *69*, 114, 140, 146, 164, 176, 240, 241, *278*, 279.
creatio ex nihilo, 81-2, 83, 108, 113, 127, 129.
creative power (divine), 109, 111, 117, 128, 130, 289.

credulity, Gregory's, 1, 3, 8, 12, 15, 16, 17, 21, 22, 23.
cures (miraculous), 6, 8, 86, 87, 99, 106, 117, 127, 134-6, 164, 179, *193-200*, 204, *208*, *209*, 213, 218, 222, *227-51*, 285, 291;
pattern of cures: *203-4*, 243-6, 250-1.
curse (*maledictio*), 44, 117, 159, 183, 268, 269, 270, 277, 279-80.

darkness (physical and metaphorical), 25, 28, 30, 31, 32, 45, 50, 133-9, 149, *155*, *161-5*, 171, 172, 178, 182, 196, 197, 198, 207, *210-1*, 220, 253.
demons, 79, 92, 93, 94, 102, 103, 104, 106, 158, 162, 163, 171, 182, 196, *230-7*, 264, 270.
Devil, Satan, the Enemy, etc., 50, 53, 64, 84, 85, 89, 91, 92, 93, 94, 95, 103, 104, 105, 106, 107, 141, 153, 156, 160, 163, *231-4*, 236, 242-3, 285-7, 289, 291, 292.
discontinuity, 1, 9-14, 17-8, 20, 21, 22-3, 28, 31, 32, 33, 38, 40, 50, *56-7*, *68-9*, 107, *113-5*, 128, *131*, *209*, 246, 289, 290.
disease (general), 4, 5, 28, 31, 32, 34, 35, 37, 38, 39, 40, 42, 43, 49, 51, 52, 53, 54, 55, 56, 232.
disease (symptoms, cures), *38*, 39-40, 49, 51, 196, *230-7*, 291.
dream-vision, vision, apparition, 2, 4, 23, 25, 38, 42, 43, 78, 133, 143, 147-8, 150, 156, 176-7, 178, 179, 180-1, *182-92*, 193, (194), 196, 207, 213-93;
terminology: 214-5;
simultaneous dream-visions: 222-3;
scepticism about dream-visions: 264, 269, 275-6.

eclipse, 28, 30, 31, 32, 38, 40, 50, 53.
empiricism, pragmatism (Gregory's), 8, 21, 33-4, 38, 40, 42, 47, 51, *56*, *99*, 122, 252, 290.
end of the world, 11, 31, 50, 51, *52*, *53*, *54*, *55*, 57, *58*, *59-60*, 62, 65, *66-8*.
epiphany, see: appear.

fear, 16, 28, 32, 36, 37, 48, 54, 88, 100, 101, 102, 106, 108, 134, 174, 183, 186-7, 208, 221, *232*, 259-60, 266, *268-87*.

fertilization (through divine action), 72, 77, 108, 130.
figurative or typological thinking, *12*, 13, 17, 29, *41*, 42, 48, *56-7*, 64, 71, 74, 75, 76, 85, 98, 100, 107, 108-11, 128, 192, 264.
fire (physical and metaphorical), 25, 33, 35, 37-41, 45, 48-9, 51, 53, 55, 57, *138-61*, 185-90, 208, 242.
forgiveness, see: repentance.
fragrance, 80, 87, 94, 121, 124-7, 198, 222, 224.

gems, 78, 122-3, 238, 274.
good and evil, 31, *57*, 58, 60, 68, 88, 89-90, 104.

heaven (abode of God and celestial beings), 46, 48, 54 (?), 98, 119, 125, 132, 133, (150), *197-8*, 201, 207, 214, 237, 262-3.
hell, 146-51, 153, 160, 208.
history, 1, 2, *9-22*, 26, 46, 57, *59-60*, *61-2*, 64, 66, 68, *69*.
human ingenuity, 71, 73, 81, *84-5*, 88.

ideal, 8, 25, 211, 213-93 (esp. *250-1*, *293*).
illumination (metaphor), 176-83, 184, (190), *192*, 193, 194, 195-6, 207, 211, 240.
image-models (of the structure, dynamic of reality), 82, 87, 91, 121, *122-3*, 128, 146, 147, 151, 154, 157, 161, 182, 193, 194, 198, 207, 208, 241-2, 246, 250-1, 255-6, 278.
imagery, see: images.
images, imagery, 2, 15, 26, 88, 108, 110, *114*, *115*, 116, *122-3*, *128*, *130-1*, *135*, 141, 147, 162, 167, *175-6*, *180-2*, 183, 192, 199, 200, *209*, 216, *219*, 235, 237, 239, 240, 244, 252, 256, 264, *267*, *282*, 289-90, 292.
imaginal thinking, primary thought processes, 2, 9, 22, 26, 136, 144, 174, *175-6*, *192*, *207*, *209*, 216, 251, 256, 290, 292-3.
immanence, divine, see: spiritual dimension of reality.
imprecision, ambiguity, 1, 2, 8, 9, *10*, 11-4, *15*, *16*, *17*, *19*, 22, 26, 38, 54-5, *59-60*,

69, 93, 110, 134, 160, 173, 175, *192*, *194*, 200, *209-10*, 214-5, 242, 243, *288-93*.
incubation, 229.
initiation of (individual and social) change, 214, 217, *243*, *244*, 250, *267*, 290, 291.
intellectual honesty (Gregory's), 35, 42, 48.
interior-exterior events, phenomena, 72-3, 82, 89, 101, 102, *107*, 125, *129-31*, 138, 139, 169, *172-3*, 176, 177, 182, 199, *207*, *209*, 223, 226, 231, 235, 239, 290.

justice, divine, 102, 241, 260, 268-87 (esp. *272*, *284*, *287*), 292.
juxtaposition (of facts, events), 33, 34, 37, 38, 40, 60, 100, 101.

light (physical and metaphorical), 23, 25, 27-8, 30, 31, 34, 37, 40-1, 47, 49-50, 53, 78, 123, 133-9, 220, 222, 266;
light lamps in honour of a saint: 161-211.
liturgy,
to avert plague: 262;
cures during liturgy: 195 n. 309, 237-9, 244;
for the dead: 153, 204-5;
vision during: 253-4.
luminous phenomena, 23, 25, 125, 134-9, *176-92*, 290.

magical practices (pagan and christian), 4, 36, 50, 53, 83, *86*, *92*, 96, 101, 160, (173), 198-9, 200, 203, 207, *208*, 228, 243, 244, 250, 255, 257-8, 259-61, 265, 269, 275-8, 288, 292.
meditation, meditative attitude, contemplation, 109, 198-9, 200, 207, *209*, *235*, 290.
melodies, singing, 80, 85, 93, 112, 113, 182-3, 220, 232, *254*.
mental habit, 55, 129;
see also: image-models.
metaphors, 15, 25, 82, 84, 86, 98, 101, 102, 125, 127, 129, 130-1, 133-211 (esp. *165-76*, *193-200* and *209-10*), 228, 231, 239-40, 249.
models of explanation, see: image-models.

moon (as metaphor), see: celestial bodies.
'mystery', 75, *81*, 90, 109, 110, 112, *113*, 116, 119-20, 125, 128, 129, 177-8, 190, 207.

naivety, unreflectiveness (Gregory's), 1, 9, 10, 14, *16-7*, 18, 19, *20*, 21, 22, 23, 26, *176*, 207, *209*.
nature, 21, 23, 25, 29, 33, *34*, 37, 55, 56, 69, 71-132, 142, 145, 191-2;
inherited view of nature: 73-6;
dynamics: 84-5, 117-8;
concept of nature: 111-5, 128;
delight in nature: 118-20.
new, 181, 182, 204, 207, 210, 290;
see also: regeneration.

observation, see: empiricism.
omnipotence, divine, 147, 181, 237, *250*.
'ordeals', thinking in terms of, 96, *97-8*, 99, 101, 155-6, 161, 208, 277.

pagan attitudes, practices, 4, 8, 21, 24, 30, 33, 37, 43, *44*, 45, 47, 56, 179, 183, 201, 207, 214, 215-6, 218, 223, 225, 227, 228, *229*, 252, 255, 262, 274-5, 288.
paradigms, see: image-models.
patron(age), 7, 181, 209, 236, 259, 265, 284, 287.
'penitence', see: repentance.
periodization, 'times', 1, 2, 9-14, 29-30, 52, *53*, *54*, 55, *58-62*, *65*, *67-8*.
phoenix, 79, 116, 151.
poetry (ornament, reminiscences of), 15, *19*, 20, 23, 77, 78, 84, 118, 121, 126-7, 128, *131*, 152, 175, 194, 210.
portent, prodigy, 23, 24-5, 27-69, 75, 85, 118, 121, 140, 184, 185, 288.
power (holy), miracle, 3, 4, 12, 13, 16, 21, 22, 25, 28, 50, 64, 71, 72-4, 76, 80, 81-2, 83, 84, *85-6*, 87, *94* (virtus), 96 (virtus), *100* (virtus), 101, 105 (virtus), *107*, *112* (virtus), 129, 131, 134-5, 141, 144, 145 (potentia), 146 (potentia), 151 (miraculum), 154 (virtus), 158-9, *170*, 173-4, 177, 178 (virtus), 180 (virtus), 181 (miraculum), 183, 185 (virtus), 187 (miraculum), 187-92 (virtus), 191 (miraculum), 193-200 (virtus), 198-200 (virtus, omnipotentia antestitis), *207* (as

'living metaphor'), *208* (*virtus*), *210*, 213 (*virtus, signum*), 217, 219, 225, 231, 234, *237*, 242, *246*, *247-9*, *256* (*miraculum*), 257-8 (*virtus, miraculum*), 270, 271, 272, *277-8*, *283*, 287, *289*, *292*, and passim;
  false miracles: 53, 55;
  see also: stunning effect of holy power.
power (physical, social, political, economic), 4, 7, 25, 143-4, 148, 222, *234*, 236, 280, 281.
pragmatism, see: empiricism.
prayer, 92, 94-5, 97, 99, 101, 103, 105-6, 113-4, 135-6, 144, 149, 151, 156, 166, 187, 258, 261;
  see also: tears, prayers and fasts.
pressure upon a saint, reciprocity, 95, *166*, 208-9, *234*, *244*, 259-60, *265-7*.
primitive oral culture, mentality, 23, 131, 140, 223, 252, 267, *268*, 289.
prophecy, 28, 38, 41, 44-5, 49, 50, 52, 53-5, 59, 61, 67, 68, 69.
prophets, false, 50, 52, 53, 54, 55, 56, 67, 68.
protection, 81, 88, 165, 183, 261-2, 266.
psychotherapeutic view of imagination, modern, 26, 129, 209, 216-7, 229-30, 231, 235, 236-7, 251, 290, *291*.
punishment (by God or a saint), 7, 11, 32, 33, 35-6, 37, 38, 45, 51, 52, 55, 64, *69*, 85, 104, 140, 143, 145-6, 147, 150, 153, 161, 163, 167, 204, 206, 208, 235-6, 242, 274-5, 279-82, 286, 287.
purgatory (fire), 147, 150, *151-61*, 201, 206 (?), 208.
purification, 25, 149-50, 246, 247;
  by fire: *151-61*, 208;
  by fire, light: 210;
  by holy power, sometimes as light: *193-207*.

reciprocal relationship with a saint, see: pressure upon a saint.
regeneration, rebirth, renewal, 25, 72, 75, 77, 78, 79, 80, 86, 87, 88, 90-1, 107-11, 117, 128, 129, 131-2, 194-6, 200-1, 203-4, 206, 208, *211*, 292-3.
relics, *85-7*, *91-2*, *93*, *94*, 103, *104*, 106, 142, 144, 154, 165-6, 183, 185-6, 188-90, 192, 208, 218, 222, 223, *224-6*, 227, 230, 274-5, 277-8.
renewal, see: regeneration.
repentance, contrition, forgiveness, 'penitence', 7, 96, 105, 132, 135, 159, 201, *202-3*, 206, *207*, 229, 236, *241*, 246, *247*, 249, 250.
revelation (*se revelare*), see: appear.

sacrality, sacred, 93, 94, 119, 145, 225-6.
saints, cult of the, 3, 4, 5, 7, 8, *94-6*, 101, 124, 125, 142, 144, 165, 167, 172-3, 178, 192, 210-1, 214, 216, 217-27, 223-4, 227, 228, 262, 266, 268, 269-72, *273*, 287, 288, 290-1, and passim;
  as intercessors at the Last Judgment: *205-7*;
  example of holy power: *198-200*;
  light lamps in honour of saints: 179-81.
sanctity, 50, 96, 98, *100*, *141*, *170*, 221, 264, 265.
Satan, see: Devil.
sensory experience and phenomena, see: visuality, empiricism.
show, be shown (*ostendere, ostensus esse*), see: appear.
'sign', 28, 30, 31, 34, *36*, 38, 40, 41, 42, 43, 45, 46, 47, 48, 49, 50, 52, *53*, *54*, *55*, 56, 61, 67, 185, 217.
singing, see: melodies.
slaughter, mass, 3, 27-8, 29, 31, 32, 34, 35, 37, 43, 45-6, 47, 48, 49, 55, 63, 68.
society, interrelations of mental phenomena with, 1, 2, 4, 8, 10-1, 12, 14, 17, 22, 23-4, 25-6, 73, 76, 88-91, 99-102, 104-6, 107, 108, 131-2, *133*, 138-9, 145-6, 155-6, 159, 160, 166-7, 181, *208-9*, *210-1*, 217, 219, 223, 226, 227, 235-6, 241, 243, 251-2, *257*, 258-60, 263, *267*, 268-9, 272, *282-4*, 287, *291-2*.
spiritual dimension of reality, 25, *38*, *43*, 51, *56-7*, 84, 86-7, *114*, 115, 117, 127, 142-4, 157-9, 160, 161, 162, *217-27* (esp. *219-20*, *223*, *227*), *234*, 251, *252*, 253, 254, 255, 257, 260, 263-4, 267, *287-93*;
  nothing is achieved without God's aid: *181-2*;
  idem, predestination: 202.

spring (symbolism of), 77-88.
star (as metaphor), see: celestial bodies.
stunning effect of holy power, *225-6*, 275-6, 281, 285.
stylistic effects, see: conscious interpretation.
suddenness, 28, 33, 36, 41, 62, 69, 85, 94, 99, 102, 103, 104, 106, *107*, *113-4*, 140, 148, 177, 182, 192, 195, 231, 244, 247, 250, 261, 288.
sun (as metaphor), see: celestial bodies.
symbol, symbolic thinking, 9, *22*, 25, 41, 43, 56, *69*, *75*, 79, 83, 86, 87, 88-9, *90*, 101, 111, 116, 127, 156, 162, 167, 174, 180, *200*, 207, *208*, 210, 217, 228, 229, 241, 264, *292*.

taxation, 37, 101, 159-60, 283-4.
tears, prayers and fasts, 33, 37, 51, 93, 94-5, 134-6, *140-1*, 165, 202-3, 204, 221, 235, 237, 246, *247*, 258, 265, 284; see also: prayer, repentance.
'times', see: periodization.
transformation (sudden), image-models of, 25, 26, 71-132 (esp. *111-505*, *122*, *128*, *130-1*), 251, *267*, 291;

see also: image-models.
transience, *71-2*, *78-9*, 87, 111, 121, *124*, 128.
tree (symbolism), 80, 110, 116-9, 285.
Truth, 134-5, 162, 163, 165, 168, 171, 182, 192, 202, *211*, 252, *256*, 271, 293.
typological thinking, see: figurative thinking.

vengeance, 148, 204-5, 206, 268-9, 270, 271-2, *276-7*, 280, 283, 285.
violence, savageness (physical and metaphorical), 3, 4, 7, 28, 38, 52, 57, 86, 94, 100, 102, 103, 141, 153, 159, 160, 208, 230-7, 270-3, 275, 277, 287.
vision, see: dream-vision.
visuality, 1, 2, 9, 12, 16, 17, *18*, 21, 22, 43, *175-6*, 192, 193, 207, *209*, 211, 246, 249, 288-9.

woman, 233, 237-8, 248-9, 253-4, 264, 265.
words, (power of), 72, 88, *108-9*, *130*, 135, *168*, 170-2, 175, 187, 189, 190, *282*.
world, worldly life, 46, 50, *60-1*, *74*, 79, *89*, 101, 107, 133, 167, 172, 197, 207, 210, *254-5*.

III. Passages in Gregory's works cited in the text

Historiae
Praefatio prima:57, 60, 68, 128.
Book I. Praef.:8, 9, 30, 52, 57, 60, 62, 68, 77; 1:111; 2:45; 4:71, 88; 5:139; 7:45; 10:90, 184, 189; 15:154, 234; 20:31; 21:257; 28:151; 29:170; 35:97; 37:141, 170; 39:171, 195; 44:155, 163; 46:100; 47:78, 123, 168; 48:236.
Book 2. Praef.:26, 30, 59, 60, 61, 68, 162; 1:155-6, 262; 3:32, 95, 104, 181, 231; 5:265; 6:265-6; 7:267; 16:125; 18:32; 19:32; 20:32, 35; 21:35, 232-3; 23:279, 280-1; 26:35; 31:126, 191, 257; 34:32, 115, 140; 37:44, 120, 183-4, 242, 283; 40:105-6; 43:35; 51:35.
Book 3. Praef.:62-3; 1:234; 5:204; 6:105-6; 12:271; 15:264; 16:282, 284; 28:97, 105; 36:33, 101, 280; 37:33.
Book 4. 2:283-4; 5:260, 288; 6:44; 9:33, 42, 118; 14:276; 16:105; 19:258; 20:140; 21:34, 276-7; 30:99; 31:27-8, 39; 33:119, 150; 34:103; 35:241, 252, 279; 36:167, 273, 275-6; 40:139; 47:63-4; 48:66; 49:64; 50:34, 64-6, 105-6; 51:39, 48, 105-6.
Book 5. Praef.:65-8, 105-6, 128; 1:100; 4:99, 283; 5:4, 279; 8:277; 14:44, 265; 17:37, 80; 18:42, 184; 23:41, 42; 29:275; 32:140; 33:37, 43, 48, 118, 140; 34:37, 43, 101; 41:38, 39, 43; 49:44, 105-6; 50:38, 43, 264.
Book 6. 6:247; 14:39, 45, 118; 25:185; 29:78, 79, 122-3, 203, 238-9; 31:276; 34:41; 35:41; 43:80; 44:43, 47, 121, 288-9; 45:43, 62; 46:45, 282.
Book 7. 1:46, 61, 79, 123-4, 133, 163, 197-8; 11:47, 118, 119; 12:154-5; 20:46; 22:229, 269-72; 29:44; 35:158; 38:277; 40:277; 42:284-5; 45:47; 47:259.

Book 8. 5:285-7; 6:283; 8:47, 118; 10:95; 11:46; 12:277; 14:94; 15:165-6; 16:145-6, 229; 17:48; 23:49; 24:48; 25:49; 29:46; 30:143; 31:142, 277; 32:142; 33:142-3, 185, 258, 264; 34:163; 36:102; 42:46, 49, 118, 144; 44:46.

Book 9. 3:46; 5:49, 118, 288; 6:49, 52, 61, 62, 68, 160; 9:102; 17:51; 19:102; 21:51; 30:283; 38:46; 39:111, 167; 41:203; 44:51, 118, 121.

Book 10. 1:52, 62, 92; 13:110, 113, 205; 18:46; 21:163; 23:52, 53, 185; 25:53, 62, 231-2; 29:83, 109; 30:51, 55, 62, 145, 223; 31:55, 67-8.

In gloria martyrum

Prol.:109, 128, 130, 168; 5:176-7, 81, 93; 6:93, 95, 222, 232; 8:178, 256; 9:154; 10:113, 122, 142; 12:164; 13:95, 244; 15:157-8; 18:154; 21:163; 22:272-3; 23:80, 125-6; 24:81; 25:82; 27:98; 28:114, 233-4; 29:103; 30:126, 154; 33:95, 289; 36:84, 111, 234; 37:163; 39:148; 41:152; 43:104; 46:117; 47:148, 224-6; 49:178; 50:4, 218-20, 260, 261-2, 288; 51:155; 52:242; 54:277; 55:219; 56:180-1; 57:149; 62:125, 224; 64:278; 67:117; 68:96; 69:97; 73:117, 122; 74:153, 204-5; 75:91, 253-4; 76:158-9; 77:117; 79:156; 80:98, 180; 83:103, 142, 185; 85:4, 186; 86:272, 289; 87:82; 88:163; 89:274; 90:122; 91:120, 274; 95:122, 141, 153; 96:94, 289; 97:228; 99:229; 105:149; 106:206, 289.

De virtutibus sancti Juliani

Prol.:154, 166, 262; 6:145; 9:173-4, 237-9, 13:145; 14:4; 15:4, 145; 16:4; 17:159-60; 18:161; 20:173; 25:86; 27:145; 34:185-6; 35:112, 113, 191, 289; 41:87, 126; 42:229; 45:29, 276; 46a:4; 46b:121, 238-9.

De virtutibus sancti Martini

Book 1. Prol.:4-5, 88, 213-6; 2:92, 93, 95, 106, 141, 163, 205; 3:170-1, 195; 6:169, 220; 7:240, 245; 9:94, 103, 104; 10:191-2; 11:98, 130; 12:134-5; 22:159; 23:205, 241, 258; 24:249; 26:232; 32:95, 200; 34:104; 35:226, 275, 277; 37:40; 40:86.

Book 2. 1:40, 115; 2:198-200; 3:81, 195; 4:241; 5:64; 6:64; 7:64, 67; 11:232; 12:40; 13:86, 195; 15:193, 231; 17:157, 162, 232; 18:196, 232; 19:75, 164, 245-6; 23:228-9, 248; 25:284; 26:232; 29:81, 193-4; 30:241; 31:248-9; 32:82; 37:99; 40:115, 202-3, 235-6; 45:232; 47:240; 51:40; 53:242-3; 56:244-5; 60:202, 206.

Book 3. Prol.:202, 237, 246-8; 6:165; 8:95, 244; 10:4; 14:232; 16:106, 194, 232, 245, 253; 20:106, 289; 21:243-4; 27:232; 28:231; 37:232; 39:95, 159, 244; 42:155, 272; 43:40; 52:40; 60:4, 200-1, 246.

Book 4. 6:249; 7:119; 9:40; 12:95; 17:106; 18:106; 20:240; 22:106, 232; 26:258-9; 31:83; 37:230-1; 40:232; 46:240; 47:40.

In gloria confessorum

2:223; 3:4, 142; 7:117, 153; 13:163-4; 14:141, 156; 17:222, 228; 18:103, 126, 169, 179, 220-2; 20:189-91; 21:179; 23:118, 120; 24:40; 29:248; 31:93, 94; 32:168; 35:228; 38:187; 39:188-9; 40:4, 218, 227-8; 41:124; 47:253; 50:117, 121; 51:122; 54:141; 55:141; 58:186-7; 61:256; 68:80; 70:95; 71:173-4; 72:182-3, 253, 289; 80:222; 84:4; 85:173; 86:242; 93:239; 98:111, 113; 102:41, 186; 104:126; 109:115, 289; 110:170.

Vitae patrum

Book 1. Prol.:123, 202; 3:203.
Book 2. Prol.:30, 75, 109, 130, 168, 172; 4:256-7.
Book 4. 1:167, 278-9; 3:279; 4:103.
Book 5. 3:156.
Book 6. 6:33; 7:124.
Book 7. Prol.:123; 2:4; 3:123, 173, 186; 8:124.
Book 8. 5:276; 7:259-60; 11:159, 273-4.
Book 9. Prol.:130; 2:104, 231, 254-5; 3:174.
Book 10. Prol.:202, 203; 2:231; 3:118; 4:79, 125.
Book 11. Prol.:79; 1:160, 231; 2:83; 3:79.
Book 12. Prol.:119; 3:41, 120, 188, 262.
Book 14. 1:151, 156, 170; 2:118-9, 120, 163; 3:171.
Book 16. Prol.:95, 201-2; 2:115, 253, 289.

Book 17. Prol.:102; 3:104, 160, 231; 4:93, 171, 232; 5:89, 263; 6:263.
Book 18. Prol.:103, 163, 171-2.
Book 19. Prol.:119; 1:120.
Book 20. 3:109.

De cursu stellarum ratio
9:71-2, 124, 128, 147; 10:41, 56, 76-7; 11:41, 108-9, 113; 12:41, 79, 116; 13:146-7; 14:146-7; 34:28, 34, 39.

In psalterii tractatum commentarius
1:116; 11:168; 12:151, 165; 20:148; 23:91; 26:165; 35:77, 165; 41:80; 42:165; 66:165; 73:111; 82:84; 88:91.

IV. Bible passages cited in the text

Old Testament
Genesis. 1:16-7/171; 2:9-10/116; 12:6-7/116; 7:23/88; 24:15ff/83.
Exodus. 11:8/285; 14:19, 21/90; 17:6/83, 91; 24:15-8/197; 24:17/184; 34:29-30/190.
Numbers. 20:11/83.
Joshua. 3:16/95.
Job. 7:12/93; 30:30/157; 37:14, 16/74.
Psalms. 1:2-3/116; 19:1/74; 33:15/166; 43:1/276; 80:15/276; 88:9/91; 90:6/264; 108:17/78; 127:1/181; 136:13/90; 147:5/285.
Proverbs. 26:27/35-6.
Ecclesiastes. 1:2/46, 79.
Isaiah. 55:10-11/108.
Jeremiah. 2:13/78.
Ezekiel. 8:6/52; 9:6/52; 11:1ff, 17ff/52; 9:4/261.
Daniel. 2:31-45/59; 3:13ff/154; 7/93.
Joel. 1:4/45; 2:30-1/45; 3:1-2/45.
Jonah. 3:5-10/140.
Habakkuk. 3:17/55.

Apocrypha
Tobit. 6:6/227-8; 8:2-3/227-8.
Wisdom of Solomon. 1:5/82; 114/98.

New Testament
Matthew. 3:16/122; 5:14/168-9, 171-2; 5:45/79; 8:32/93; 9:2/194-5; 10:8/274; 10:14-5/279; 10:29/79; 13:24ff/74; 14:30/95; 19:26/81; 20:3/90; 24:3/50, 61; 24:5-7/54; 24:5-8, 24/53; 24:15/58; 24:24/50, 54; 24:27/48, 50; 24:29/50; 24:30/50; 24:36/58.
Mark. 2:3-4/240; 4:26/108; 4:27/109; 4:28/108; 11:13-4, 20/117; 11:24/95, 136, 274; 13:6-8, 22/53, 54; 13:12/66; 16:5/172.
Luke. 11:8/95, 244; 17:24/48, 145; 21:8/54; 21:10-1/53, 54; 21:25/54.
John. 1:1/168; 1:3/109, 168; 1:5/177-8; 1:9/168, 171, 172; 2:1-10/112; 3:20/161; 4:13-4/78; 8:12/165; 9/240; 9:3/235; 12:24/111; 14:6/165; 20:22/172.
Acts. 2:3/184, 190; 2:3-4/187; 2:19/67; 2:37/78; 6:3/194; 9:3/137, 190, 193; 14:15, 17/74; 16:16/274.
Romans. 1:20/74; 6:3/80, 110; 6:4/110; 8:19-21/103.
1 Corinthians. 10:1, 2/74, 90; 10:4/83; 10:6, 11/74; 15:36/108, 111; 15:43/108.
2 Corinthians. 6:14/161, 163.
Galatians. 5:15/66.
Ephesians. 2:1/103; 2:2/79, 102; 4:29/72; 6:12/79, 102; 6:16/156.
Revelation. 1:14/220; 1:15/197; 6:12/28, 31; 8:3-4/151-2; 8:7/37, 39; 11:19/37; 12:1/197; 13:1/93; 14:2/197; 16:3-4/49; 21:1, 4/79; 21:10-23/197; 22:1-2/116.

Curriculum vitae

The author of this book was born on 8 January 1938 in Delft, the Netherlands. She emigrated with her parents to England in 1948 and to the United States in 1950; graduated from the Dwight Morrow High School in Englewood, New Jersey in 1954; received the Bachelor of Arts degree *cum laude* with Honors in History and the Helen Taft Manning Prize in History from Bryn Mawr College in Bryn Mawr, Pennsylvania in 1958; the Master of Arts degree in History from Radcliffe College, Harvard University, in Cambridge, Massachusetts in 1959; and received the Drs. degree *cum laude* in medieval history at the University of Utrecht in 1963. Since 1962 she has been employed as a lecturer in the Deparment of Medieval History at the Institute for History of the University of Utrecht. Alongside articles on Gregory of Tours, she has published an English translation of a classic French work on the Carolingian Empire as well as articles on the subject of regional history. Since 1982 she is editor-in-chief of 'Tussen Rijn en Lek', a modest quarterly concerned with the history of the Kromme Rijn region in which she lives.